Principles of Econometrics

Principles of Econometrics

Edited by **Courtney Hoover**

Willford Press
New York

Published by Willford Press,
118-35 Queens Blvd., Suite 400,
Forest Hills, NY 11375, USA
www.willfordpress.com

Principles of Econometrics
Edited by Courtney Hoover

International Standard Book Number: 978-1-68285-036-7 (Hardback)

Printed in China.

Contents

Preface

Econometrics is a branch of economics that aims to analyze financial and economic data sets by using various statistical, mathematical and computational tools. The aim of this book is to present researches and case-studies by experts from various parts of the world that have transformed this discipline and aided its advancement. The topics elucidated in the text are game theory, numerical and computational modeling, applications of econometrics in industrial engineering, etc. It provides a comprehensive insight into the field of econometrics. It aims to expand the research in this field and contribute towards its progress.

This book unites the global concepts and researches in an organized manner for a comprehensive understanding of the subject. It is a ripe text for all researchers, students, scientists or anyone else who is interested in acquiring a better knowledge of this dynamic field.

I extend my sincere thanks to the contributors for such eloquent research chapters. Finally, I thank my family for being a source of support and help.

Editor

Response surface and artificial neural network prediction model and optimization for surface roughness in machining

Ashok Kumar Sahoo*, Arun Kumar Rout and Dipti Kanta Das

School of Mechanical Engineering, KIIT University, Bhubaneswar-24, Odisha, India

CHRONICLE

Keywords:
Response surface model
ANN
Optimization
Factorial design
Machining

ABSTRACT

The present paper deals with the development of prediction model using response surface methodology and artificial neural network and optimizes the process parameter using 3D surface plot. The experiment has been conducted using coated carbide insert in machining AISI 1040 steel under dry environment. The coefficient of determination value for RSM model is found to be high (R^2 = 0.99 close to unity). It indicates the goodness of fit for the model and high significance of the model. The percentage of error for RSM model is found to be only from -2.63 to 2.47. The maximum error between ANN model and experimental lies between -1.27 and 0.02 %, which is significantly less than the RSM model. Hence, both the proposed RSM and ANN prediction model sufficiently predict the surface roughness, accurately. However, ANN prediction model seems to be better compared with RSM model. From the 3D surface plots, the optimal parametric combination for the lowest surface roughness is d1-f1-v3 i.e. depth of cut of 0.1 mm, feed of 0.04 mm/rev and cutting speed of 260 m/min respectively.

1. Introduction

Machining is a chip removal process in which less utility and less value raw materials are converted into high utility and valued products with definite dimensions, forms and finish, which satisfies some function. Solid-state manufacturing processes can be broadly classified in to metal forming and metal machining. During metal forming, the volume is conserved and shape is achieved through deforming the material plastically in processes like forging, rolling, drawing etc. However, these mostly serve as primary or basic operations for typical products. In around eighty percent of components produced through metal forming, machining is essentially required to achieve dimensional accuracy, form accuracy and good surface finish to achieve the functional requirements.

Keeping an eye to achieve higher productivity and good surface finish, research in the field of cutting tool materials have been taken place in recent years. The ease with which a work material can be machined is referred to as Machinability. It directly influences the effectiveness, efficiency and overall economy of the machining process. Surface quality has received serious attention for many years. It has

* Corresponding author.

formed an important design feature in demanding situations arising of fatigue loads, precision fits, corrosion resistance and aesthetic requirements. The surface quality is affected by the process parameters, machine tool condition, cutting tool geometry and condition and the machining operations. Therefore, research in the field of surface quality in machining is highly essential for functional requirements of the products. The surface roughness prediction model and optimization of process parameters is especially important for achieving better surface quality in machining. Therefore, the present paper deals with these aspects in details.

2. Review of literature

Gökkaya and Nalbant (2007a) observed that lower surface roughness was induced using a CVD multi layer coated tool outermost with TiN compared to uncoated, coated with AlTiN and coated with TiAlN using the PVD technique during dry turning of AISI 1015 steel. Tıgıt et al. (2009) compared the wear behavior of multilayer-coated carbide tools (TiCN+TiC+Al_2O_3+TiN) with different coating thickness of 7.5µm and 10.5µm to uncoated carbide tool. Multilayer TiN coated carbide tool with 10.5µm thickness performed better than uncoated carbide insert with respect to surface quality and cutting forces in machining spheroidal graphite cast iron in all cutting speeds. This indicated economical machining with respect to cutting energy and power consumptions.

Gillibrand et al. (1996) studied the economic benefit of finish turning with coated carbide and uncoated carbide cutting tool. It was observed that the machining cost using coated carbide is 30% less than uncoated carbide during finish turning of medium carbon steel. The surface roughness was low using TiN coated carbide tools and an improvement in tool life between 250 and 300% compared to uncoated carbide tools are achieved. Noordin et al. (2001) compared the performance of coated and uncoated carbide inserts during finish turning of AISI1010 steel. The tool of (CVD TiCN/TiC and PVD with TiN) performed better than CVD with (TiCN/TiC/Al_2O_3) and uncoated carbide insert as lower forces and surface roughness obtained and chips with minimum thickness produced that contributed to low chip strain and low residual stresses on the workpiece surface.

Che Haron et al. (2007) reported that the surface roughness for uncoated carbide tools was in the range of 0.36-4.05 µm and 0.30-1.51µm for coated carbide insert (CVD TiN/ Al_2O_3/TiCN) respectively during turning AISI D2 (22 HRC) steel. The lowest surface roughness value for both types of carbide tools were observed at cutting speed of 250 m/min and feed rate of 0.05 mm/rev. Gökkaya and Nalbant (2007b) investigated the effects of different insert radii, depths of cut and feed rates on the surface quality of the work pieces during machining of AISI 1030 steel without coolant by CVD multilayer coated carbide [TiC/Al_2O_3/TiN (outermost is TiN)] insert. It was observed that increase of insert radius decreases the surface roughness and increasing cutting speed and depth of cut increases the surface roughness.

Nalbant et al. (2007) found that, greater insert radius; low feed rate and low depth of cut could be recommended to obtain better surface roughness in turning AISI 1030 steel with TiN coated carbide insert. The experiment was performed utilizing Taguchi L_9 orthogonal array. Noordin et al. (2004) described the performance of a multilayer coated WC tool (TiCN/Al_2O_3/TiN) of CNMG120408-FN and TNMG120408-FN type during turning AISI 1045 steel (187 BHN) based on central composite design and response surface methodology (RSM). The feed was the most significant factor for surface roughness and the tangential force.

Risbood et al. (2003) found that, using neural network, surface finish could be predicted within a reasonable degree of accuracy in turning with TiN coated tools. Suresh et al., (2002) developed a surface roughness prediction model for machining mild steel using RSM with TiN-coated WC cutting tools. It was found that, the surface roughness was decreased with an increase in cutting speed and increased as feed elevated. An increase in depth of cut and nose radius increased the surface roughness. The optimal machining condition was obtained by genetic algorithm (GA) approach.

Dabnun et al. (2005) developed response model (surface roughness) utilizing factorial DOE and response surface methodology during machinability studies of glass ceramic using uncoated carbide inserts under dry cutting conditions. Feed rate was the main influencing factor on the roughness, followed by the cutting speed and depth of cut. Feng (2001) applied fractional factorial design approach to study the influence of turning parameters on surface roughness using multilayer coated carbide inserts (TiCN/Al_2O_3/TiN). Feed, nose radius, work material and speeds, the tool point angle were found to be the influencing parameters on surface roughness.

Most dominant interactions were found between work materials, point angle and speeds. The depth of cut was found to insignificant for surface roughness. Nalbant et al. (2007) developed predictive neural network model and found better predictions than various regression models for surface roughness in machining AISI 1030 steel using coated carbide tool (TiC/ Al_2O_3/TiN). Feed rate and insert nose radius were main influencing factors on the surface roughness. Depth of cut was not more informative than the other two. Sahoo and Sahoo (2011) developed RSM model for surface roughness and optimize the process parameter in machining D2 steel using TiN coated carbide insert. The developed RSM model sufficiently predicts the surface roughness in turning D2 steel.

Sahoo et al. (2013) presents the development of flank wear model in turning hardened EN 24 steel with PVD TiN coated mixed ceramic insert under dry environment. The paper also investigates the effect of process parameter on flank wear (VBc). The experiments have been conducted using three level full factorial design techniques. The machinability model has been developed in terms of cutting speed (v), feed (f) and machining time (t) as input variable using response surface methodology. The adequacy of model has been checked using correlation coefficients.

Quiza et al. (2008) performed experiment on hard machining of D2 steel (60 HRC) using ceramic cutting tools. Neural network model was found to be better predictions of tool wear than regression model. Park (2002) observed that PCBN cutting insert performed better in cutting force and surface roughness than ceramic tool in turning hardened steel. Feed rate was found to be significant on surface roughness while the effect of the cutting speed and depth of cut was negligible. The optimal cutting conditions for the best surface quality were selected by using Taguchi orthogonal array concept.

Ozel et al. (2007) found that neural network model was suitable to predict tool wear and surface roughness patterns for a range of cutting conditions in finish hard turning of AISI D2 steels (60 HRC) using ceramic wiper (multi-radii) design inserts. Lalwani et al. (2008) studied the effect of cutting parameters on cutting forces and surface roughness in finish hard turning using coated ceramic tool applying RSM and sequential approach using face centered CCD. A linear model fitted well to the variation of cutting forces and a non-linear quadratic model found suitable for the variation of surface roughness with significant contribution of feed rate. Depth of cut was significant to the feed force. For the thrust force and cutting force, feed rate and depth of cut contributed more.

Horng et al. (2008) developed RSM model using CCD in the hard turning using uncoated Al_2O_3/TiC mixed ceramics tool for flank wear and surface roughness. Flank wear was influenced principally by the cutting speed and the interaction effect of feed rate with nose radius of tool. The cutting speed and the tool corner radius affected surface roughness significantly. Sahin and Motorcu (2008) indicated that the feed rate was found out to be dominant factor on the surface roughness, but it decreased with decreasing cutting speed, feed rate, and depth of cut in turning AISI 1050 hardened steels by CBN cutting tool. The RSM predicted and experimental surface roughness values were found to be very close. Sahoo and Mohanty (2013) obtained the optimal values of cutting speed, feed and depth of cut to minimize cutting force and chip reduction coefficient during orthogonal turning using Taguchi quality loss function. The effectiveness of the proposed methodology is illustrated through an experimental investigation in turning mild steel workpiece using high speed steel tool. Sahoo (2014) studied the performance of multilayer coated carbide insert in the machining of hardened AISI D2 steel (53 HRC) using Taguchi design of experiment. Based on Taguchi S/N ratio and ANOVA, feed is the most influencing parameter for surface roughness followed by cutting speed whereas depth of cut has least significant from the experiments. In regression model, the value of R^2 being 0.98 indicates that 98 % of the total variations are explained by the model. It indicates that the developed model can be effectively used to predict the surface roughness on the machining of D2 steel with 95% confidence intervals. Pal and Chakraborty (2005) developed a back propagation neural network model for the prediction of surface roughness in turning operation of mild steel workpiece using high speed steel as the cutting tool. The performance of the trained neural network was tested with experimental data, and found to be in good agreement. Tsao and Hocheng (2008) predicted and evaluated thrust force and surface roughness in drilling of composite material using Taguchi method and the artificial neural network. A correlation was established between the feed rate, spindle speed and drill diameter. The correlations were obtained by multi-variable regression analysis and radial basis function network (RBFN) and compared with the experimental results. The results indicated the RBFN is more effective than multi-variable regression analysis.

Davim et al. (2008) developed surface roughness prediction models using artificial neural network (ANN) during turning of free machining steel and reported that the cutting speed and feed rate had significant effects in reducing the surface roughness, while the depth of cut has the least effect. Sharma et al. (2008) constructed neural network models for cutting forces and surface roughness for different cutting parameters such as approach angle, speed, feed and depth of cut. Surface roughness (*R*a) was positively influenced with feed and a negative trend was observed with approaching angle, speed and depth of cut. The neural network model for *R*a predicted with moderate accuracy. Cutting force (*F*c) increased with the increase in approach angle, feed and depth of cut where as it decreased with speed. Passive force (*F*p) increased with increase in depth of cut, speed and feed where as it decreased with increase in approaching angle. Feed force (*Ff*) increased with all variables, i.e. approaching angle, speed, feed and depth of cut. The neural network model for cutting force (*F*c) predicted with high accuracy and for cutting force *F*p predicted with moderate accuracy.

Ozel and Karpat (2005) predicted surface roughness and tool flank wear over the machining time through neural network modeling for variety of cutting conditions in finish turning of hardened AISI H-13 steel. It was observed that surface roughness reduced with the decrease in the feed rate, but the tool wear development was slightly faster. Also, it was observed that on increasing cutting speed, there was a significant increase in tool wear development but better surface finish was obtained. Bagci and Isik (2006) developed artificial neural network (ANN) and response surface (RS) model to predict the surface roughness on the turned part surfaces of unidirectional glassfibre reinforced plastics (GFRP), using cermet tools. They observed good agreement between the predictive model results and the experimental measurements.

Karayel (2009) presented a feed forward multilayered neural network for the prediction and control of surface roughness values for different turning conditions of st 50.2 steel, using a CNC lathe. It was observed that the feed rate was the dominant parameter for surface roughness and it increased rapidly with the increase in feed rate. The cutting speed had a critical value for which the best surface quality can be achieved. The effect of depth of cut on surface roughness was not regular and had a variable character. ANN produced an accurate relationship between cutting parameters and surface roughness. Sehgal and Meenu (2013) observed that the artificial neural network (ANN) model predicts with higher accuracy than response surface methodology (RSM) in context to surface roughness in end milling of Ductile Iron grade 80-55-06. TANSIG training transfer function along with PURELIN output transfer function is observed to be the most appropriate training transfer function.

Research in the field of surface quality in machining is highly essential for functional requirements of the products. Thus, the objective of the present work has been set to have a study to evaluate the performance of coated carbide tools under varying parameter of machining. The predictive model using response surface methodology (RSM) has been developed for surface roughness in machining AISI

1040 steel under dry environment. Next, the optimal parametric combination of process parameter has been obtained from 3D surface plot using RSM.

3. Experimental details

Over the last few years, coated carbide tools have been widely used; became popular and it is preferred to uncoated carbide tools in machining steels. For experimental investigations, commercially available PVD TiAlN coated carbide insert designated as CNMG 120408 EN-M52 was used and performed under dry environment. The 80^0 diamond-shaped insert is one of the popular inserts used with negative side cutting edge angle. AISI 1040 steel rods of 25 mm diameter and 75 mm length were turned on a high rigid lathe (HMT, NH-22, India). The cutting insert has the following specification: coating thickness 2-5 μm, grain size 1μm, hardness 1560HV and nose radius of 0.8 mm. The insert is mounted on a tool holder designated by ISO PCLNR2525M12 with cutting geometry as follows: clearance angle (αo) = 6^0, negative rake angle (γo) = -6^0, negative cutting edge inclination angle (λ) = -6^0 and major cutting edge angle or approach angle = 95^0, point angle = 80^0 and nose radius (r) = 0.8mm. The test specimen AISI 1040 is widely used for bolts for machines, plows, and carriages; cylinder head stubs, U-bolts, concrete reinforcing rods, and springs.

Table 1
Process parameters and their levels

Parameters	Notation	Unit	Levels of parameters		
			Level 1	Level 2	Level 3
Cutting speed	v	m/min	60	160	260
Feed	f	mm/rev	0.04	0.08	0.12
Depth of cut	d	mm	0.1	0.3	0.5

Table 2
Experimental observations

Run	Setting value			Average
	v	f	d	Ra (μm)
1	60	0.04	0.1	1.40
2	60	0.04	0.3	1.57
3	60	0.04	0.5	1.75
4	60	0.08	0.1	1.80
5	60	0.08	0.3	1.98
6	60	0.08	0.5	2.10
7	60	0.12	0.1	2.30
8	60	0.12	0.3	2.35
9	60	0.12	0.5	2.42
10	160	0.04	0.1	1.44
11	160	0.04	0.3	1.61
12	160	0.04	0.5	1.65
13	160	0.08	0.1	1.85
14	160	0.08	0.3	1.89
15	160	0.08	0.5	1.92
16	160	0.12	0.1	2.23
17	160	0.12	0.3	2.28
18	160	0.12	0.5	2.33
19	260	0.04	0.1	1.46
20	260	0.04	0.3	1.52
21	260	0.04	0.5	1.55
22	260	0.08	0.1	1.73
23	260	0.08	0.3	1.78
24	260	0.08	0.5	1.81
25	260	0.12	0.1	2.05
26	260	0.12	0.3	2.18
27	260	0.12	0.5	2.10

The arithmetic surface roughness average (Ra) of workpiece material is considered as the performance measuring criteria. The process parameters and their levels are shown in Table 1 (cutting speed in the range of 60-260 m/min, feed of 0.04-0.12 mm/rev and depth of cut of 0.1-0.5 mm respectively). The measurements of surface roughness were performed by a surface roughness tester (Taylor Hobson, Surtronic 25) with 0.8 mm sampling length and 4mm traversing length respectively. The measurements were repeated three times at different locations and average value was reported. The average surface roughness (Ra) was used to evaluate the surface roughness of machined surface. Experimental design by full factorial design (FFD) with three factors and three levels involves 27 numbers of experiments. The experimental results have been shown in Table 2.

4. Results and discussions

4.1. Prediction model (RSM and ANN)

Taking surface roughness as output and process parameters (cutting speed, feed and depth of cut) as input, the prediction model using response surface methodology (RSM) has been developed at 95% confidence level. Response surface methodology is a collection of mathematical and statistical techniques that are useful for the modeling and analysis of problems in which output or response is influenced by several input variables and the objective is to find the correlation between the response and the variables investigated (Montgomery, 1997). Using least square fitting, the model is developed. The experiments are conducted based on full factorial design, which gives a comparatively accurate prediction of surface roughness average. The first step of RSM is to find a suitable approximation for the true functional relationship between surface roughness and set of independent variables utilized. In the linear model, the surface roughness is well modeled by linear function. However, in the second order model like response surface methodology, there is a curvature in the system. The second order response surface representing the surface roughness (Ra, μm) can be expressed as a function of three process parameters such as v, f and d. It has been expressed applying regression analysis using least square method. The following second order equation for quality characteristics is obtained.

$$Ra = 0.8498 + 0.0018\, v + 9.1458\, f + 1.4222\, d - 0.0000\, v^2 + 16.3194\, f^2 - 0.5972\, d^2 - 0.0115\, vf - 0.0023\, vd - 3.9583\, fd$$

$$(R^2 = 99.2\ \%,\ R^2\ (adj) = 98.8\ \%) \tag{1}$$

This analysis is carried out for a level of significance of 5%, i.e., for a level of confidence of 95%. For model adequacy checking, the residual plots are examined for a regression model with designed experiment. The normal probability plot should not show violations of the normality assumption. In the ANOVA (Table 3) of response surface model, analyzing of variance shows that the terms having the values of probability less than 0.05 are significant. Using uncoded units, models are developed. From the RSM model, it is evident that the regression is significant. In addition, regression, linear, square and interaction terms from the RSM model are significant because P value is less than 0.05.

Table 3
Results of ANOVA for Ra 2nd order model.

Source	DF	Seq SS	Adj SS	Adj MS	F	P value	Remarks
Regression	9	2.5011	2.5011	0.2779	243.51	0.000	Significant
Linear	3	2.4256	0.0807	0.0269	23.59	0.000	Significant
Square	3	0.0131	0.0131	0.0043	3.83	0.029	Significant
Interaction	3	0.0624	0.0624	0.0208	18.24	0.000	Significant
Residual Error	17	0.0194	0.0194	0.0011			
Total	26	2.5205					

The main effect of feed was found to be the most significant factor. Each level of the factors affects the response differently. From ANOVA Table 4, main effect plot (Fig. 1) and interaction plot (Fig.2), it is evident that, feed is the significant factor affecting surface roughness followed by cutting speed and depth of cut. From interaction plot, all the interaction terms are significant. Also from the Eq. (1), it is seen that the RSM model has high determination coefficient (R^2 = 0.99 close to unity). It describes 99% of the variability in the response. It indicates the goodness of fit for the model and high significance of the model. In addition, the adjusted R^2 value is very close to the predicted R^2. Therefore, the predicted R^2 is in reasonable agreement with the adjusted R^2. It is evident that the unnecessary terms are not added in the model. This analysis showed that the prediction model sufficiently explains the relationship between surface roughness and the independent variables.

Table 4
ANOVA for Ra

Source	DF	SS	MS	F	P value	Remarks
v	2	0.1289	0.0644	15.75	0.000	Significant
f	2	2.2021	1.101	269.03	0.000	Significant
d	2	0.1077	0.0538	13.16	0.000	Significant
Error	20	0.0818	0.004			
Total	26	2.5205				

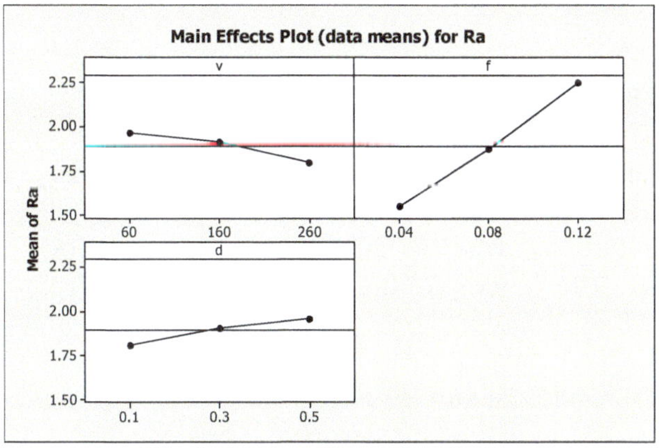

Fig.1. Main effect plot for Ra

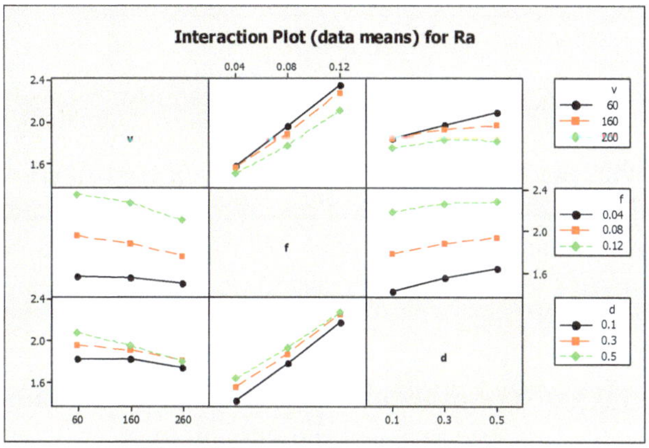

Fig. 2. Interaction plot for Ra

The data closely follows the straight line, which is observed from the Anderson-Darling tests (Fig. 3). Since the P value is greater than 0.05 (at 95 % confidence level), it signifies that the data follows a normal distribution and the model developed by Eq. (1) is suitable and quite adequate. The normal probability plot (Fig. 4) gives the information about the residuals, which is close to the straight line. It indicates that the errors are distributed normally and proposed model is significant.

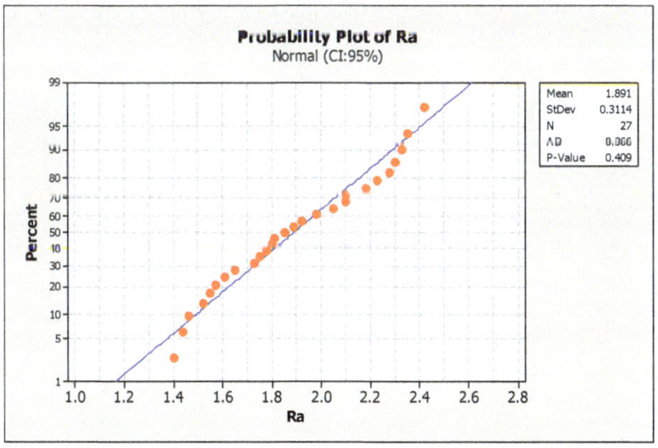

Fig. 3. Anderson Darling test of normality for Ra

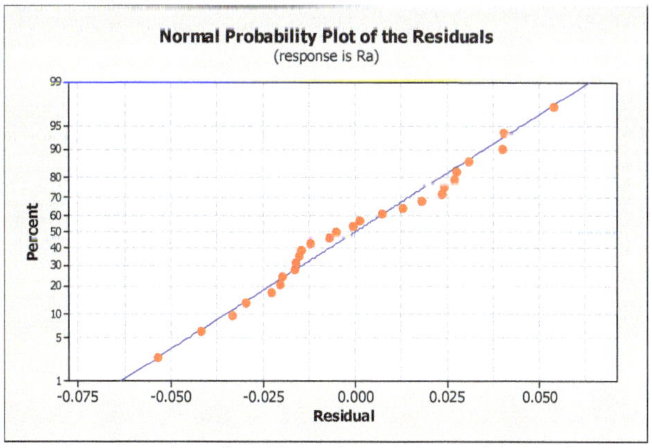

Fig. 4. Normal probability plot of the residuals for Ra

The graph of residuals vs. fitted values is shown in Fig. 5. No unusual structure is apparent except one point that is much larger or smaller than the others are. As its standardized residual is within the range of -3 to 3, the model proposed is significant. The graph of residual vs. order of data (Fig. 6) shows the residual for the run order of experiment. This implies that the residuals are random in nature and do not exhibit any pattern with run order. In addition, figure of residual vs. order of data revealed that there is no noticeable pattern or unusual structure present in the data.

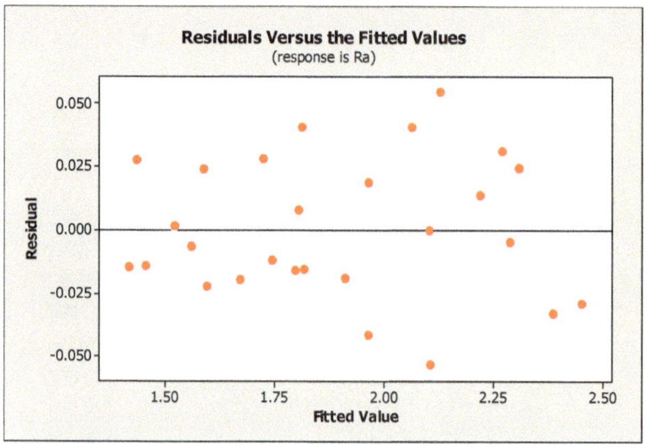

Fig. 5. Residuals vs. fitted value for Ra

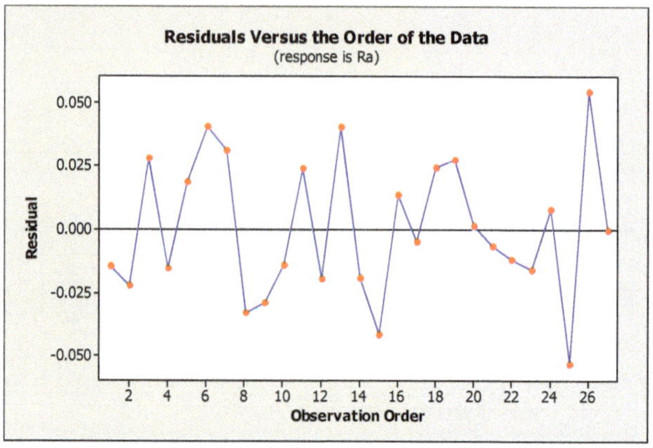

Fig. 6. Residuals vs. order of the data for Ra

Another predictive model based on ANN (Artificial neural network) is employed, and the experimental results are compared with it and also with RSM model. The neural network is constructed using the experimental database. About 80% of data are used for training, whereas 20% of data are used for testing of the model. The selected and optimized parameters for training of the ANN model have been presented in Table 5.

A comparison of experimental results with RSM and ANN results for surface roughness is presented in Table 6. It is observed that the maximum error between ANN model and experimental lies between -1.27 to 0.02 %, which is significantly less than the RSM model. However, this error can be further reduced if the number of test patterns will be increased. Hence, the developed ANN model can be effectively utilized for prediction of surface roughness in machining. The percentage of error for RSM model is found to be only -2.63 to 2.47. Hence, both the proposed RSM and ANN prediction model sufficiently predicts the surface roughness accurately. However, ANN prediction model is found to be better compared to RSM model.

Table 5
Input parameters selected for training

Input Parameters for Training	Values
Error tolerance	0.001
Learning rate (ß)	0.2
Momentum parameter(α)	0.01
Noise factor (NF)	0.001
Number of epochs	10,00,000
Slope parameter (£)	0.6
Number of hidden layer neuron (H)	7
Number of input layer neuron (I)	3
Number of output layer neuron (O)	1

Table 6
Comparisons of experimental vs. RSM and ANN for surface roughness

Run	Average Ra (μm) (Experimental)	Predicted (RSM)	Residuals (RSM)	% of error (RSM)	Predicted (ANN)	Residuals (ANN)	% of error (ANN)
1	1.40	1.41	-0.015	-1.07	1.41	-0.01	-0.71
2	1.57	1.593	-0.023	-1.46	1.59	-0.02	-1.27
3	1.75	1.722	0.028	1.6	1.72	0.03	0.01
4	1.80	1.816	-0.016	-0.88	1.80	0.00	0.00
5	1.98	1.962	0.018	0.9	1.97	0.010	0.005
6	2.10	2.06	0.04	1.9	2.07	0.03	0.01
7	2.30	2.269	0.031	1.34	2.25	0.05	0.02
8	2.35	2.383	-0.033	-1.4	2.39	-0.04	-0.01
9	2.42	2.45	-0.03	-1.23	2.44	-0.02	-0.008
10	1.44	1.455	-0.015	-1.04	1.45	-0.01	-0.006
11	1.61	1.586	0.024	1.49	1.58	0.03	0.01
12	1.65	1.67	-0.02	-1.21	1.66	-0.01	-0.006
13	1.85	1.81	0.04	2.16	1.82	0.03	0.01
14	1.89	1.91	-0.02	-1.05	1.91	-0.02	-0.01
15	1.92	1.962	-0.042	-2.18	1.96	-0.04	-0.02
16	2.23	2.217	0.013	0.58	2.22	0.01	0.004
17	2.28	2.285	-0.005	-0.21	2.28	0.00	0.00
18	2.33	2.306	0.024	1.03	2.29	0.04	0.01
19	1.46	1.433	0.027	1.84	1.43	0.03	0.02
20	1.52	1.519	0.001	0.06	1.50	0.02	0.01
21	1.55	1.557	-0.007	-0.45	1.55	0.00	0.00
22	1.73	1.742	-0.012	-0.69	1.75	-0.02	-0.01
23	1.78	1.796	-0.016	-0.89	1.79	-0.01	-0.005
24	1.81	1.803	0.007	0.38	1.81	0.00	0.00
25	2.05	2.104	-0.054	-2.63	2.09	-0.04	-0.01
26	2.18	2.126	0.054	2.47	2.14	0.04	0.01
27	2.10	2.101	-0.001	-0.04	2.10	0.00	0.00

4.2. Optimization

The response surface plot can help in the prediction of the surface roughness at any zone of the experimental domain. The surface plot (Fig. 7) is as follows:

f*d: This plot indicates that how variables, feed and depth of cut are related to the surface roughness while the cutting speed is held at constant at middle level. The response is at its lowest at the lightest region of the surface plot (f = 0.04 mm/rev and d = 0.1 mm).

v*d: This plot indicates that how variables, cutting speed and depth of cut are related to the surface roughness while the feed is held at constant at middle level. The response is at its lowest at cutting speed of 260 m/min and depth of cut of 0.1 mm respectively.

v*f: This plot indicates that how variables, cutting speed and feed are related to the surface roughness while the depth of cut is held at constant at middle level. The response is at its lowest when cutting speed of 260 m/min and feed of 0.04 mm/rev respectively.

From the 3D surface plots, the optimal parametric combination for lowest surface roughness is d1-f1-v3 i.e. d = 0.1 mm, f = 0.04 mm/rev and v = 260 m/min. Both have curvilinear profile in accordance to the quadratic model fitted.

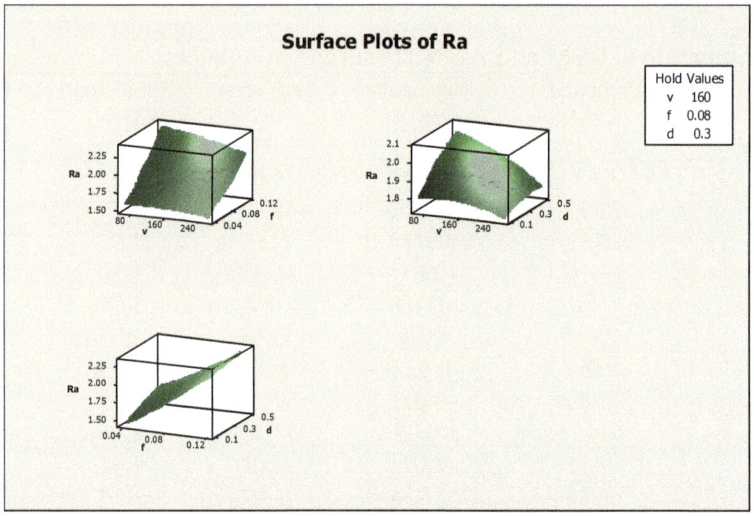

Fig. 7. Surface plots of Ra

5. Conclusions

From the above investigations, it is concluded that the full factorial design gives a comparatively accurate prediction of surface roughness averages. From RSM model, regression is significant. Regression, linear, square and interaction terms are significant with P value less than 0.05. It is evident that, feed is the significant factor affecting surface roughness followed by cutting speed and depth of cut. It is observed that the maximum error between ANN model and experimental lies between -1.27 to 0.02 % which is significantly less than the RSM model. Hence, both the proposed RSM and ANN prediction model sufficiently predicts the surface roughness accurately. However, ANN prediction model is found to be better compared to RSM model (Sehgal & Meenu, 2013). From the 3D surface plots, the optimal parametric combination for lowest surface roughness is d1-f1-v3 i.e. d = 0.1 mm, f = 0.04 mm/rev and v = 260 m/min.

References

Bagci, E., & Işık, B. (2006). Investigation of surface roughness in turning unidirectional GFRP composites by using RS methodology and ANN. *The International Journal of Advanced Manufacturing Technology*, *31*(1-2), 10-17.

Che Haron, C. H., Ghani, J. A., & Ibrahim, G. A. (2007). Surface integrity of AISI D2 when turned using coated and uncoated carbide tools. *International Journal of Precision Technology*, *1*(1), 106-114.

Dabnun, M. A., Hashmi, M. S. J., & El-Baradie, M. A. (2005). Surface roughness prediction model by design of experiments for turning machinable glass–ceramic (Macor). *Journal of Materials Processing Technology*, *164*, 1289-1293.

Davim, J. P., Gaitonde, V. N., & Karnik, S. R. (2008). Investigations into the effect of cutting conditions on surface roughness in turning of free machining steel by ANN models. *Journal of materials processing technology*, *205*(1), 16-23.

Feng, C. X. (2001). An experimental study of the impact of turning parameters on surface roughness. In *Proceedings of the Industrial Engineering Research Conference* (No. 2036, pp. 1-7).

Gillibrand, D., Sarwar, M., & Pierce, C. T. (1996). The economic benefit of finish turning with coated carbide. *Surface and Coatings Technology*, *86*, 809-813.

Gökkaya, H., & Nalbant, M. (2007a). The effects of cutting tool coating on the surface roughness of AISI 1015 steel depending on cutting parameters. *Turkish Journal of Engineering and Environmental Sciences*, *30*(5), 307-316.

Gökkaya, H., & Nalbant, M. (2007b). The effects of cutting tool geometry and processing parameters on the surface roughness of AISI 1030 steel. *Materials & design*, *28*(2), 717-721.

Horng, J. T., Liu, N. M., & Chiang, K. T. (2008). Investigating the machinability evaluation of Hadfield steel in the hard turning with Al_2O_3TiC mixed ceramic tool based on the response surface methodology. *Journal of materials processing technology*, *208*(1), 532-541.

Karayel, D. (2009). Prediction and control of surface roughness in CNC lathe using artificial neural network. *Journal of materials processing technology*,*209*(7), 3125-3137.

Lalwani, D. I., Mehta, N. K., & Jain, P. K. (2008). Experimental investigations of cutting parameters influence on cutting forces and surface roughness in finish hard turning of MDN250 steel. *Journal of materials processing technology*, *206*(1), 167-179.

Montgomery, D.C. (1997). *Design and Analysis of Experiments*. 4th ed. Wiley, New York.

Nalbant, M., Gökkaya, H., & Sur, G. (2007). Application of Taguchi method in the optimization of cutting parameters for surface roughness in turning.*Materials & design*, *28*(4), 1379-1385.

Nalbant, M., Gokkaya, H., & Toktas, I. (2007). Comparison of regression and artificial neural network models for surface roughness prediction with the cutting parameters in CNC turning. *Modelling and Simulation in Engineering*, *2007*(2), 3.

Noordin, M. Y., Venkatesh, V. C., Chan, C. L., & Abdullah, A. (2001). Performance evaluation of cemented carbide tools in turning AISI 1010 steel. *Journal of Materials Processing Technology*, *116*(1), 16-21.

Noordin, M. Y., Venkatesh, V. C., Sharif, S., Elting, S., & Abdullah, A. (2004). Application of response surface methodology in describing the performance of coated carbide tools when turning AISI 1045 steel. *Journal of Materials Processing Technology*, *145*(1), 46-58.

Özel, T., Karpat, Y., Figueira, L., & Davim, J. P. (2007). Modelling of surface finish and tool flank wear in turning of AISI D2 steel with ceramic wiper inserts. *Journal of materials processing technology*, *189*(1), 192-198.

Özel, T., & Karpat, Y. (2005). Predictive modeling of surface roughness and tool wear in hard turning using regression and neural networks. *International Journal of Machine Tools and Manufacture*, *45*(4), 467-479.

Park, Y. W. (2002). Tool material dependence of hard turning on the surface quality. *International Journal of Precision Engineering and Manufacturing*, *3*(1), 76-82.

Pal, S. K., & Chakraborty, D. (2005). Surface roughness prediction in turning using artificial neural network. *Neural Computing & Applications*, *14*(4), 319-324.

Quiza, R., Figueira, L., & Davim, J. P. (2008). Comparing statistical models and artificial neural networks on predicting the tool wear in hard machining D2 AISI steel. *The International Journal of Advanced Manufacturing Technology*,*37*(7-8), 641-648.

Risbood, K. A., Dixit, U. S., & Sahasrabudhe, A. D. (2003). Prediction of surface roughness and dimensional deviation by measuring cutting forces and vibrations in turning process. *Journal of Materials Processing Technology*,*132*(1), 203-214.

Sahin, Y., & Motorcu, A. R. (2008). Surface roughness model in machining hardened steel with cubic boron nitride cutting tool. *International Journal of Refractory Metals and Hard Materials*, *26*(2), 84-90.

Sahoo, A. K., & Sahoo, B. (2011). Surface roughness model and parametric optimization in finish turning using coated carbide insert: Response surface methodology and Taguchi approach. *International journal of industrial engineering computations*, *2*(4), 819-830.

Sahoo, A., Orra, K., & Routra, B. (2013). Application of response surface methodology on investigating flank wear in machining hardened steel using PVD TiN coated mixed ceramic insert. *International Journal of Industrial Engineering Computations*, *4*(4), 469-478.

Sahoo, A., & Mohanty, T. (2013). Optimization of multiple performance characteristics in turning using Taguchi's quality loss function: An experimental investigation. *International Journal of Industrial Engineering Computations*, *4*(3), 325-336.

Sahoo, A. (2014). Application of Taguchi and regression analysis on surface roughness in machining hardened AISI D2 steel. *International Journal of Industrial Engineering Computations*, *5*(2), 295-304.

Sehgal, A.K., (2013) Application of artificial neural network and response surface methodology for achieving desired surface roughness in end milling process of ductile iron grade 80-55-06, *International Journal of Computational Engineering & Management*, 16 (3), 2230-7893.

Suresh, P. V. S., Venkateswara Rao, P., & Deshmukh, S. G. (2002). A genetic algorithmic approach for optimization of surface roughness prediction model. *International Journal of Machine Tools and Manufacture*, *42*(6), 675-680.

Tsao, C. C., & Hocheng, H. (2008). Evaluation of thrust force and surface roughness in drilling composite material using Taguchi analysis and neural network. *Journal of materials processing technology*, *203*(1), 342-348.

Tıgıt, R., Findik, F., & Çelık, E. (2009). Performance of multilayer coated carbide tools when turning cast iron. *Turkish Journal of Engineering & Environmental Sciences*, *33*(3), 147 – 157.

Sharma, V. S., Dhiman, S., Sehgal, R., & Sharma, S. K. (2008). Estimation of cutting forces and surface roughness for hard turning using neural networks. *Journal of Intelligent Manufacturing*, *19*(4), 473-483.

A simulation study on the performance of the sign test, Mann-Whitney test, Hodges-Lehmann estimator and control charts for Normal and Weibull data

Vadhana Jayathavaj[a] and Adisak Pongpullponsak[a*]

[a]*Department of Mathematics, King Mongkut's University of Techology Thonburi, 126 Pracha-utid Road, Bangmod, Bangkok 10140 Thailand*

CHRONICLE

Keywords:
Hodges-Lehmann estimator
Mann-Whitney
Normal distribution
Sign test
Statistical process control
Weibull distribution

ABSTRACT

The new method to chart the Hodges-Lehmann estimator control chart is proposed in this study. The evaluation of the three nonparametric control charts - the Sign test (ST), Mann-Whitney (MW), and the Hodges-Lehmann estimator (HL), for the known process distribution using normal and Weibull data represent the symmetric and asymmetric shapes of the process based on the original method through the 10000 run lengths simulation. The result illustrates that the average run length performance of the ST and MW correspond to their respective test statistics but for HL's performance, the result indicates that the average run length is much greater than that derived from Wilcoxon signed rank statistics. The Hodges-Lehmann estimator control chart by the new approach for the known process distribution will be the alternative method for the process that needs to robust outliers' properties from this statistics. In addition, the simulation demonstrates that the performances of the Sign test (ST) from mean and median processes are varied in the skewed distribution, and moreover, the Sign test (ST) from the median process represents more accurate performance. Meanwhile, for the control groups, MW generated within control limits or without restriction shows slightly different performance. The performance of dual scheme for the above-mentioned variable parameters control charts also produce the weighted average values that effect from the tight control scheme to the regular control scheme.

1. Introduction

The parametric Shewhart control charts measure a quality statistics of interest (x) for the normal (or assumed to be normal) distribution process with the mean μ_X and the standard deviation σ_X, within the control limits $\mu_X \pm L\sigma_X$ where L is the distance from the center line (Montgomery, 2013). The statistics L corresponds to the Type I error probability (α) in hypothesis testing. Parametric tests, statistical tests for population parameters such as means, variances, and proportions, involve assumptions from which the samples are selected. One assumption is that these populations are normally distributed and the sample of parametric tests is Z test, t test, and the F test. However, a branch of statistics known as nonparametric statistics or distribution-free statistics is used when the population from which samples are drawn do not follow a normal distribution or normality cannot be met. The nonparametric tests are the sign test, the Wilcoxon rank sum test, the Wilcoxon signed-rank test, the Kruskal-Wallis test, the runs test, and so on (Bluman, 1998). In many statistical quality control and operations, the processes

* Corresponding author.

may have no prior knowledge of the underlying distribution or have not much data available to justify parametric assumptions especially in the start-up period. Therefore, normality is the exception rather than the rule and the assumption of normality is often not justified in the statistical practice especially in the field of health sciences (Neuhäuser, 2012). Apart from distribution-based procedures, a nonparametric model is the one in which no assumption is made about the process distribution. The only assumption made about the observations is the independence and identical distribution (i.i.d.) from an arbitrary continuous distribution. The nonparametric tests can be used when the conditions of the normality neither are met nor realizable by transformations. However, a transformation might solve a problem and, at the same time, it can deliver to another (Neuhäuser, 2012). The nonparametric tests are also used when the sample sizes are very small and violate the central limit theorem. The current computing power leads to the need for monitoring many simultaneous variables without restriction on the assumption of their probability distribution (Bersimis et al., 2007). Using the nonparametric tests, the knowledge of the precise form of the population distribution is unnecessary.

In a distribution free inference, whether for testing or estimation, the methods are based on functions of the observation, which do not depend on the specific distribution function of the population from which the sample is drawn (Gibbons, 1971). Based on the definition of the distribution-free control chart, the in control average run length (ARL_0) is available for every underlying process distribution (Bakir, 2001). While parametric tests are based on mean, the symmetric discrete distribution of the nonparametric statistics which leads to the nonparametric tests concentrate on median (the value at the center of the process distribution).

For the process that the quality control activity starts with a nonparametric control chart at the beginning (Phase I - the retrospective phase), the process distribution can be obtained from data collection and learning curve from the operation (Phase II – the perspective or monitoring phase), "What are the right performance of the nonparametric control charts?" If the distribution is known, the assumed nonparametric distribution will still produce an accurate performance. For the nonparametric knowledge together with the simulation method in computing the performance, average run length (*ARL*) of the nonparametric control charts for both symmetry and asymmetry processes with the process mean shifts in δ times of standard deviation are implemented in this study. In case the chart performance from the simulation does not correspond to the chart performance derived from the nonparametric statistics probability, the new charting technique will be proposed, and the trial variable parameters technique for the chart performance will also be demonstrated. The three different nonparametric control charts: the Sign test, the Mann-Whitney, and the Hodges-Lehmann estimator control chart for the normal data and 11 shapes of Weibull data (skewness from 0.1, 0.5, 1,2,3, …, 9) with the process mean shift in δ times of standard deviation (δ=0.25, 0.50, 0.75, 1, 1.5, 2, 2.5, and 3) are the scope of this study. Das (2009) mentioned that the nonparametric methods are not well known among many quality control practitioners because these methods are not emphasized, and perhaps are not covered in a typical engineering curriculum. This study provides both methodology and performance behaviors of the nonparametric quality control charts for the quality control practitioners in order to use them effectively when the process distribution is known.

2. Literature review

After Shewhart established his $\bar{X}$ chart in 1926 (Shewhart, 1926) and explained the five economic advantages in 1929 (Shewhart, 1930), the continuous development started from univariate parametric control charts in shifts detection of various distributions; exponentially weighted moving average (EWMA) and cumulative sum (CUSUM) in small shifts detection; variable parameters control chart for the improvement of chart performance; multivariate control charts in handling many process variables and finally leading to the monetary decision by economic design (Montgomery, 2013). The nonparametric control charts have come to play an increasingly important role in statistical process control literatures, and overviews presented by Chakraborti et al. (2001) showed many univariate nonparametric control charts.

The Sign test control chart (ST) related to several literatures are nonparametric control chart using Sign statistics (Amin et al., 1995); the combination of sign chart and conforming run length chart called the synthetic control chart (Khilare & Shirke, 2010); Sign control charts based on runs (Human et al., 2010), and Sign control charts with variable sampling intervals (Amin, 1999). For the Mann-Whitney Control chart (MW), these are nonparametric control charts based on runs and Wilcoxon-type rank-sum statistics (Balakrishnan, 2009), and the in control and out of control performances of Mann-Whitney control chart for the normal distribution. A heavy-tailed distribution such as the Laplace, or a skewed distribution such as the Gamma are studied using the control group size m = 50, 100, 500, 1000, and 2000 and the treatment group size n = 5, 10, and 25. The control limits are computed by using Lugannani-Rice-saddle point, Edgeworth, and Monte Carlo approximation for estimation (Chakraborti & Van de Wiel, 2008). The control chart based on median (Graham et al., 2010) and Signed-rank (Bakir, 2004) (Ghute & Shirke, 2012). Chakraborti and Eryilmaz (2007) developed the effective Shewhart-type chart based on the Wilcoxon signed rank statistics by incorporating some "runs" type signaling rules. Graham et al. (2010) and Jones-Farmer et al. (2009) have considered distribution-free phase I control charts. Yang et al. (2011) proposed a new nonparametric version of EWMA Sign chart for variables data to monitor the deviation from the process target, without assuming a process distribution. A nonparametric exponentially weighted moving average (NPEWMA) control chart combines the advantages of a nonparametric control chart with the better shift detection properties of a traditional EWMA chart. A NPEWMA chart for the median of a symmetric continuous distribution was introduced by Amin and Searcy (1991) using the Wilcoxon signed-rank statistic (Gibbons & Chakraborti, 2003). Graham (2011) proposed the nonparametric exponentially weighted moving average Signed-Rank (NPEWMA-SR) chart. Graham et al. (2012) presented a two-sided nonparametric Phase II exponentially weighted moving average (EWMA) control chart, based on the exceedance statistics (EWMA-EX) in detecting a shift in the location parameter of a continuous distribution. Bakir and Reynolds (1979) considered a cumulative sum chart based on the Wilcoxon signed rank statistics. Nonparametric multivariate CUSUM control charts for location and scale changes were proposed by Li et al. (2013). Cheng et al. (2000) applied the data depth in monitoring multivariate aviation safety data.

The out of control average run length of the control charts was based on the Sign test, the Hodges–Lehmann estimator and the Mann–Whitney compared their efficiency to detect the shift in location among the symmetric distributions (mesokurtic distribution). The uniform distribution (platykurtic distribution) and Laplace distribution (leptokurtic distribution) had been considered since they were different in peakedness or kurtosis. Asymmetric distribution and gamma distributions with different skewness had been considered. The simulation study was performed by taking 10,000 independent runs for sample size n=10, 12, 15 (Das, 2009).

There are very rare literatures on the variable parameters and economic design in nonparametric control charts. It may be because the in control average run length performance (α) is not depended on the population data.

The area of nonparametric control charts continues to be an area of active and ongoing research that follows the parametric control charts in every aspect. To overcome the illusory performance from the assumed nonparametric test statistics distribution that may occur, the simulation study for small sample size from the normal and Weibull data (from symmetry to asymmetry distributions) is established to investigate the performance of the three well-known nonparametric control charts; ST, MW, and HL.

3. Experimental design and Methodology

This section presents the theory of the three nonparametric tests, the control chart construction with related Type-I and Type-II probabilities, the average run length performance, and the simulation steps.

3.1 Nonparametric tests

Table 1 shows the three different nonparametric tests: a simple method - the Sign test (ST); a nonparametric competitor of the two-independent-sample t-test - the Mann-Whitney (MW), and the more calculation steps together with their complication - the Hodges-Lehmann estimator (HLE).

Table 1
The three nonparametric tests

	Nonparametric tests		
	The Sign Test (ST)	The Mann-Whitney (MW)	The Hodges-Lehmann estimator (HLE)
Hypothesis testing	The Sign test	The Wilcoxon, Mann-Whitney rank sum test	The Hodges-Lehmann estimator with associated the Wilcoxon signed rank distribution
The test statistics	The number of sign (+/-) counted and observed from the median process	The rank of observations summed from the treatment group after combined with the control group	The median of Walsh average (Walsh averages = the observed average estimation in every combination of two observations) with associated location probability. (locations come from the sum of the rank by each (+/-) sign).
Assumed process distribution	Binomial with index n and parameter ½	The Mann-Whitney statistics (The Mann-Whitney U statistics)	The Wilcoxon signed rank statistics
Range of discrete random variable for sample size = n	0 to n	0 to mn m = Number of observations in the control group	0 to $n(n+1)/2$

3.2 Nonparametric control charts

The three nonparametric control chartings are compared in Table 2, the control limits of both ST and MW come from the Sign test and the Mann-Whitney statistics respectively, but only HL, for the control limits, uses the median of Walsh averages at the determined Wilcoxon signed rank locations. For the known process distribution, the probability distribution of the order statistics can be derived from the location of that order (Gibbons, 1971) (For example, the median is always at the middle of data), but not for the HLE because the median of Walsh average estimator is not always formed from the observations at the same ranks. Instead, the HLE depends on the magnitude of the two observations. Without the probability distribution function of HLE, the HL associates the HLE to the Wilcoxon signed rank distribution in constructing the control limits (Alloway et al., 1991).

Table 2
The three nonparametric control charts

	Nonparametric control chart		
	The Sign Test (ST)	The Mann-Whitney (MW)	The Hodges-Lehmann estimator (HL)
Sample size	N	n (m for control group)	n
Control limits Lower = $-k$ Upper = $+k$	$a \in I^+[0,n]$ $+k = n-a$ $-k = a$	$a \in I^+[0,mn]$ $+k = mn-a$ $-k = a$	$a \in I^+[0,n(n+1)/2]$ $+k$ = the median of Walsh average at $n(n+1)/2-a$ $-k$ = the median of Walsh average at a
Type I error (α)	Binomial distribution α = Probability ($S^+<-k$ or $S^+>+k$)	Mann-Whitney U distribution α = Probability ($U_T<-k$ or $U_T>+k$)	Wilcoxon signed rank distribution (WSR) α = Probability ($WSR<a$ or $WSR>n(n+1)/2-a$)
Test statistics, T	S^+	U_T	H_E
Out of control condition	$S^+<-k$ or $S^+>+k$	$U_T<-k$ or $U_T>+k$	$H_E<-k$ or $H_E>+k$

The test statistics, T

The Sign test, S^+

Suppose that $x_1, x_2,\ldots, x_n$ is a random sample of size n from a continuous distribution with the median of the distribution, $\tilde{m}$.

$$S^+ = \sum_{i=1}^{n} f(x_i - \tilde{m}) \qquad \text{for } i=1,2,\ldots, n \tag{1}$$

where $f(x_i - \tilde{m}) = \begin{cases} 1, x_i - \tilde{m} > 0 \\ 0, x_i - \tilde{m} \leq= 0 \end{cases}$

The random variable S^+ gives the number of positive signs in a sample and it has a Binomial distribution with parameters n and $p=P(x_i>\tilde{m})$.

The Mann-Whitney, U_T

Suppose that $x_1, x_2,\ldots, x_n$ is a random sample of n elements from the treatment group, and $y_1, y_2,\ldots, y_m$ is a random sample of m elements from the control group,

$x_1,x_2,\ldots, x_n,y_1,y_2,\ldots, y_m$ are random samples of size $n+m$.

Let $MW = \{x_1,x_2,\ldots, x_n, y_1,y_2,\ldots, y_m\}$, and

$\downarrow MW$ = sorted elements of MW in ascending order.

If R_i is the rank of the ith element of $\downarrow MW$,

then $R_t = \sum_{i=1}^{n} R_i$ is the sum of n treatment ranks.

$$U_T = R_t - n(n+1)/2 \,. \tag{2}$$

$0 \leq U_T \leq mn$.

U_T is called the Mann-Whitney statistics, and the statistics R_t is originated by Wilcoxon (Beaumont & Knowles, 1996).

The Hodges-Lehmann estimator, H_E

Suppose that $x_1, x_2,\ldots, x_n$ is a random sample of size n from a continuous distribution.

Let $Q = n(n+1)/2$
The Walsh averages,
$W_k=(x_i+x_j)/2$ for $k = 1,2, \ldots, Q$
$i<j$
$i = 1,2, \ldots, n$
$j = 1,2, \ldots, n$

$$H_E = \begin{cases} W_{d+1} & \text{if Q is odd} \\ (W_d + W_{d+1})/2 & \text{if Q is even} \end{cases} \tag{3}$$

where,
$$d = \begin{cases} (Q-1)/2 & \text{if Q is odd} \\ Q/2 & \text{if Q is even'} \end{cases}$$

3.3 Control chart performance

The control limits in the nonparametric control charts come from the probability of the Type-1 error (α) from related statistical table. The binomial, Mann-Whitney, and Wilcoxon signed rank distributions have symmetric discrete probability mass functions, then the $\alpha/2$ and $1-\alpha/2$ for lower and upper control limits can be chosen from 0 to n, 0 to mn, and 0 to $n(n+1)/2$ respectively. The 5-digits right tail probabilities of the Mann-Whitney distribution for sample sizes m and n such as $2 \leq m \leq n \leq 15$, and the Wilcoxon signed rank statistic for sample sizes n = 1, 2, …, 20 are available in Beaumont & Knowles (1996). Both ST and MW use the Sign test statistic and Mann-Whitney statistics in hypothesis testing, but HL uses the median of Walsh averages at the Wilcoxon signed rank locations as their control limits.

The performance of the control charts are the in control average run length (ARL_0) and the out of control average run length (ARL_1). When Type-I error $=\alpha$ and Type-II error $=\beta$, then

$$ARL_0=1/\alpha \tag{4}$$
$$ARL_1=1/(1-\beta). \tag{5}$$

ARL_0 represents the average number of samples that fall within the control limits before an out of control condition occurs. ARL_1 represents the average number of samples that is counted until the first sample falls out of control limits when the process goes out of control (the mean shifts). Once the Type-I error (α) is known, ARL_0 can be computed directly by equation (1) which is the performance by using formula. Therefore, by definition, ARL_0 of the nonparametric control charts have the same result for every underlying process distribution. ARL_0 and ARL_1 can also be computed by simulating the samples from the given distribution for the in control (process mean $=\mu$) when the shifts occur (process mean $=\mu+\delta\sigma$).

The dual scheme for variable parameters control chart with variable sampling intervals (h), sample sizes (n), and control limits (action and warning limits ($\pm k$ and $\pm w$)) are introduced. The continuous process starts from the Scheme 1 ($n_1,h_1,\pm k_1,\pm w_1$).The next sample will be drawn by the Scheme 1, if the previous sample is plotted in the central region [$-w,+w$]. The next sample will be drawn by the scheme 2 ($n_2,h_2,\pm k_2,\pm w_2$), if the previous sample is plotted in the warning regions [$-k,-w$) or ($+w,+k$]. The performances of the dual scheme for variable parameters control charts are as follows (Lin & Chou, 2007).

The average number of samples to signal (ANSS) is defined as the expected value of the number of samples taken from the start of the process to the time when the chart indicates out of control signal.

The average number of observation to signal (ANOS) is defined as the expected value of the number of observations taken from the start of the process to the time when the chart indicates out of control signal.

The average time to signal (ATS) is defined as the expected value of time from the start of the process to the time when the chart indicates out of control signal.

Table 3
Skewness coefficient and shape parameter of standard Weibull distribution (the scale parameter $\theta=1$)

Skewness coefficient	Shape parameter (β)
0.1	3.2219
0.5	2.2110
1	1.5630
2	1.0000
3	0.7686
4	0.6478
5	0.5737
6	0.5237
7	0.4873
8	0.4596
9	0.4376

3.4 Process data

The process distributions in this study are the standard normal distribution ($N(0,1)$) and the standard Weibull distribution (the scale parameter $\theta = 1$).

A Weibull distribution has two parameters viz., θ and β where the value of skewness is inversely proportional to the shape parameter β. Nelson (1979) as cited in Pongpullponsak et al. (2004) computed the parameter β for the skewness coefficient from 0.1, 0.5, 1, 2, …, 9 for θ=1 as shown in Table 3.

The performance in term of average run length (*ARL*) of the three control charts for the symmetry standard normal distribution, the 11 positive skewed (more data in the right elongated tail would be expected in the normal distribution) from symmetry to asymmetry shapes of standard Weibull distribution, and the process mean shifts in δ times of standard deviation (δ = 0, 0.25, 0.50, 0.75, 1, 1.5, 2, 2.5, and 3) will be compared to investigate; which chart is the most effective within the various experiment cases. The sample sizes are 10, 10,11,12,… , 20 for the Sign test control chart and the Hodges-Lehmann estimator control chart. For the Mann-Whitney control chart, the sample sizes are only in control group m = 10 and the treatment groups are n = 10, 11, 12, … ,15 due to the availability of statistical table (Beaumont & Knowles, 1996). The sample sizes n start from 10 because the statistics for control limits can be small enough and correspond to the Type-I error (α), at least less than or equal to 0.0027 for ±3σ control limits of the normal data.

3.5 Simulation steps

The simulation methods for the average run length estimation are described as follows:

Step 1 Determine the control statistics for lower and upper action limits ($-k$, $+k$) and correspond to the desired α probability.

Step 2 Compute the 10000 run lengths

Let RL_i be the ith run length and given that $RL_i = 0$ for i= 1 to 10000

[a] For each RL_i

[b] – Generate the random number x_i for i=1,2, …,n (the sample size =n) from the given distribution with the process parameter μ+δσ

- Compute the statistic T

- Compare the statistic T with control limits

If $-k \le T \le +k$ then RL = RL + 1 and go to [b]

If $T < -k$ or $T > +k$, then if δ = 0, RL_i= RL

else if δ > 0, RL_i = RL+1.

set RL = 0 and go to [a]

Step 3 Compute the average run length

$$ARL = \sum_{i=1}^{10000} RL_i / 10000 \quad (6)$$

For the Mann-Whitney statistics, the control group of sample size m also generates randomly from the in control process with mean = μ+0σ.

The Hodges-Lehmann estimator control limits come from Walsh averages at the determined Wilcoxon signed rank locations (Das, 2009). The simulation method for HL control limits is described as follows:

Step 1 Determine the Wilcoxon signed rank statistics for lower and upper control limits

Step 2 Compute 100000 sets of Walsh averages of the sample size n from the given distribution with the process parameter μ+0σ

Step 3 Compute the median of Walsh averages at the determined Wilcoxon signed rank locations for lower and upper control limits

All models in this study are designed in MATLAB using custom scripts.

4. Results and discussion

The results of the Sign test (ST), the Mann-Whitney (MW), and the Hodges-Lehamann estimator (HL) control charts for the normal data and Weibull data are presented as follows.

4.1 The Sign test control charts

Twelve fixed parameter Sign test control charts with sample sizes from 10,10,11, ..., 20, determined control limits with α closed to 0.0027 (closed to ±3σ control limits in Shewhart $\bar{X}$ chart) denoted by $-k$ and $+k$ for action limits, and ARL_0 and ARL_1 of selected schemes for standard normal data are shown in Table 4. The ARL_0 from both α and the simulation are in the same magnitude i.e., for n=10 in the scheme R, α = 0.00195, ARL_0 from α =512, and ARL_0 from simulation = 508.01.

The dual scheme for variable parameters control charts is set from the schemes in Table 4.

Table 4
Average run length of the Sign test control chart for standard normal data

Scheme	R	T0	T1	T2	T4	T5	T6	T8	T10
N	10	10	11	12	14	15	16	18	20
Control limits									
$+k$	9	8	9	10	11	12	13	14	16
$-k$	1	2	2	2	3	3	3	4	4
α	0.00195	0.02148	0.01172	0.00635	0.01294	0.00739	0.00418	0.00754	0.00258
ARL_0=1/α	512.00	46.55	85.33	157.54	77.28	135.40	239.18	132.66	388.07
ARL from 10000 run lengths simulation									
shift (δ)									
0.00	508.01	45.12	83.94	158.80	76.15	136.39	235.67	130.73	388.01
0.25	166.48	21.16	33.05	51.17	25.24	37.34	55.04	31.12	64.93
0.50	39.83	7.36	9.63	12.99	6.90	8.79	11.52	6.87	10.80
0.75	13.17	3.30	3.97	4.87	2.85	3.28	3.86	2.56	3.31
1.00	5.56	1.92	2.17	2.43	1.63	1.79	1.90	1.47	1.65
1.50	2.01	1.16	1.21	1.23	1.07	1.08	1.09	1.03	1.04
2.00	1.25	1.02	1.03	1.03	1.00	1.01	1.01	1.00	1.00
2.50	1.06	1.00	1.00	1.00	1.00	1.00	1.00	1.00	1.00
3.00	1.01	1.00	1.00	1.00	1.00	1.00	1.00	1.00	1.00

The result shows that the regular scheme is equal to the scheme R and the tight scheme, which is smaller in central region and larger in both warning and out of control regions, when comparing to the scheme R, from T0 (tighter than R), T1, T2, T4, T5, T6, T8, and T10 as shown in Table 5. The performance of ANSS, ANOS, and ATS of the dual scheme for variable parameters Sign test control chart for the normal data are computed by 10000 runs simulation, as shown in Table 5. The ANSS of each VP scheme shows the weighted average from ARLs of the combined schemes that are reduced from the ARL of the regular principal scheme R in every combination.

For Weibull data, the Sign test statistics is calculated from median, the performance from 10000 runs simulation for selected schemes are shown in Table 6. For the skewed distribution, if the mean is used in the Sign test computation, the ARL from the simulation will be less than the sign test that uses median. For example, Weibull process skew = 2, shifts δ = 0.00, 0.25, 0.50, and 0.75 when using mean to compute the Sign test statistics, the ARL from the simulation are 95.54, 449.96, 146.97, 12.38 respectively. For the standard practice in quality control for the higher shift, the ARL should be lower. The dual scheme for variable parameters Sign test control charts for Weibull data show the combination results in the performance of ANSS as the same result having ever happened in the normal data. However, the shift rows that ARL =1 for the entire row are not shown in the table.

Table 5

ANSS, ANOS, and ATS from 10000 runs simulation of Variable parameters Sign test control chart for standard normal data (n_1=10, h_1=1)

VP Scheme	R&R	R&T0	R&T1	R&T2	R&T4	R&T5	R&T6	R&T8	R&T10
n_2	10	10	11	12	14	15	16	18	20
h_2	0.5	0.5	0.5	0.5	0.5	0.5	0.5	0.5	0.5
Scheme	R	T0	T1	T2	T4	T5	T6	T8	T10
+k	9	8	9	10	11	12	13	14	16
+w	7	6	7	8	9	10	10	11	13
-w	3	4	4	4	5	5	6	7	7
-k	1	2	2	2	3	3	3	4	4
central	0.89063	0.65625	0.77344	0.85400	0.82043	0.88153	0.69824	0.76212	0.88468
warning	0.10742	0.32227	0.21484	0.13965	0.16663	0.11108	0.29758	0.23035	0.11274
shift (δ)	**ANSS**								
0.00	505.02	211.14	313.88	405.26	308.58	392.23	452.92	378.16	494.88
0.25	167.21	63.16	90.72	117.29	77.28	101.72	118.05	83.73	125.94
0.50	39.40	11.72	16.29	21.43	12.18	15.46	17.09	10.21	17.08
0.75	12.22	3.39	4.19	5.39	2.91	3.55	3.72	2.33	3.24
1.00	4.75	1.56	1.75	2.06	1.34	1.46	1.52	1.17	1.32
1.50	1.50	1.02	1.04	1.05	1.01	1.01	1.01	1.00	1.00
2.00	1.05	1.00	1.00	1.00	1.00	1.00	1.00	1.00	1.00
2.50	1.00	1.00	1.00	1.00	1.00	1.00	1.00	1.00	1.00
3.00	1.00	1.00	1.00	1.00	1.00	1.00	1.00	1.00	1.00
shift (δ)	**ANOS**								
0.00	5050.16	2111.43	3176.79	4142.84	3227.40	4134.38	4853.18	4152.83	5484.97
0.25	1672.06	631.56	925.32	1215.50	831.55	1107.99	1326.15	981.68	1492.66
0.50	394.03	117.24	169.58	230.41	141.65	183.85	218.63	143.03	243.61
0.75	122.20	33.94	44.71	60.61	37.14	47.01	54.42	38.54	56.60
1.00	47.53	15.62	19.03	24.08	18.22	20.97	23.78	20.87	25.61
1.50	14.97	10.22	11.40	12.57	14.06	15.10	16.14	18.01	20.03
2.00	10.53	10.00	11.01	12.00	13.99	15.00	16.00	18.00	20.00
2.50	10.04	10.00	11.00	12.00	13.97	15.00	16.00	17.97	19.99
3.00	10.00	10.00	10.98	11.99	13.95	15.00	15.99	17.98	19.95
shift (δ)	**ATS**								
0.00	505.02	196.58	294.87	382.69	290.87	371.02	425.92	354.96	468.06
0.25	167.21	56.00	81.69	106.64	69.94	92.64	105.91	74.71	114.28
0.50	39.40	9.04	12.93	17.40	9.70	12.54	13.12	7.65	13.45
0.75	12.22	2.17	2.77	3.71	1.91	2.39	2.29	1.37	2.03
1.00	4.75	0.86	0.99	1.20	0.73	0.82	0.80	0.60	0.69
1.50	1.50	0.51	0.52	0.53	0.50	0.51	0.50	0.50	0.50
2.00	1.05	0.50	0.50	0.50	0.50	0.50	0.50	0.50	0.50
2.50	1.00	0.50	0.50	0.50	0.50	0.50	0.50	0.50	0.50
3.00	1.00	0.50	0.51	0.50	0.51	0.50	0.50	0.50	0.50

Table 6

Average run length of the Sign test control chart for standard Weibull data

Scheme	shift	R	T0	T1	T2	T4	T5	T6	T8	T10
Skew	n	10	10	11	12	14	15	16	18	20
0.10	0.00	510.51	45.38	84.44	155.15	75.56	134.89	234.64	134.05	393.93
	0.25	176.69	22.17	34.35	53.94	26.78	39.96	59.66	33.39	70.69
	0.50	44.14	7.96	10.66	14.25	7.41	9.80	12.55	7.39	11.97
	0.75	14.33	3.51	4.33	5.25	3.07	3.54	4.16	2.73	3.62
	1.00	6.11	2.04	2.26	2.57	1.69	1.86	2.03	1.52	1.72
	1.50	1.98	1.15	1.20	1.23	1.07	1.08	1.10	1.03	1.04
	2.00	1.18	1.01	1.01	1.01	1.00	1.00	1.00	1.00	1.00
	2.50	1.02	1.00	1.00	1.00	1.00	1.00	1.00	1.00	1.00
0.50	0.00	517.92	45.21	82.18	155.90	76.08	133.22	238.37	133.18	385.63
	0.25	172.71	21.87	34.01	53.08	25.79	38.74	56.94	32.48	67.29
	0.50	38.95	7.23	9.66	12.83	6.74	8.86	11.02	6.63	10.40
	0.75	11.85	3.08	3.64	4.39	2.63	2.97	3.43	2.35	2.95
	1.00	4.46	1.72	1.85	2.07	1.44	1.54	1.65	1.31	1.43
	1.50	1.39	1.04	1.05	1.06	1.01	1.01	1.01	1.00	1.00
1.00	0.00	509.00	46.21	84.20	151.12	75.40	136.75	235.14	132.82	390.25
	0.25	151.69	19.50	30.32	46.60	23.05	33.75	49.28	28.20	56.30
	0.50	28.18	5.76	7.38	9.62	5.11	6.41	8.04	4.98	7.32
	0.75	6.96	2.21	2.51	2.90	1.85	2.05	2.24	1.66	1.92
	1.00	2.31	1.23	1.28	1.33	1.10	1.13	1.15	1.05	1.07
2.00	0.00	496.90	45.57	84.07	159.38	76.88	135.62	240.55	131.35	384.33
	0.25	85.51	12.62	17.99	26.56	13.31	18.39	25.61	14.64	26.35
	0.50	7.00	2.21	2.49	2.86	1.84	2.03	2.24	1.63	1.91
3.00	0.00	507.93	45.18	83.94	155.08	76.06	133.76	238.93	131.65	393.91
	0.25	27.16	5.46	7.06	9.13	4.99	6.17	7.72	4.77	6.92
4.00	0.00	505.26	45.75	83.75	155.34	75.40	133.33	241.60	131.81	385.94
	0.25	2.14	1.20	1.23	1.28	1.08	1.10	1.13	1.04	1.06
5.00	0.00	509.76	45.59	84.88	155.73	75.87	134.05	231.84	134.90	383.33
6.00	0.00	512.89	45.44	83.64	157.81	77.05	133.40	238.77	130.34	391.06
7.00	0.00	506.99	46.41	86.26	156.83	76.67	133.09	239.92	132.05	384.07
8.00	0.00	509.86	46.28	85.90	157.18	75.37	135.36	240.41	132.61	387.28
9.00	0.00	497.29	45.48	84.42	154.67	76.28	135.60	237.70	132.30	383.87

Note: The shift rows that ARL =1 for the entire row are not shown.

4.2 The Mann-Whitney control charts

From the available Mann-Whitney distribution table (Beaumont & Knowles, 1996), seven fixed parameter Mann-Whitney control charts with sample sizes from control group $m = 10$ and the treatment group n = 10,10,11, …, 15, determined control limits with α closed to 0.0027 (closed to ±3σ control limits in Shewhart $\bar{X}$ chart) denoted by $-k$ and $+k$ for action limits, and ARL_0 and ARL_1 of selected schemes for standard normal data are shown in Table 7.

Table 7

Average run length of the Mann-Whitney control chart for standard normal data

Scheme	R	T0	T1	T2	T3	T4	T5
Control, m	10	10	10	10	10	10	10
Treament, n	10	10	11	12	13	14	15
Control limits							
$+k$	88	87	95	102	110	118	126
$-k$	12	13	15	18	20	22	24
Mann-Whitney U statistics probability							
89-100	0.00104	0.00144	0.00138	0.00172	0.00162	0.00153	0.00145
0-11	0.00104	0.00144	0.00138	0.00172	0.00162	0.00153	0.00145
α	0.00208	0.00288	0.00276	0.00344	0.00324	0.00306	0.00290
ARL_0=1/α	480.77	347.22	362.32	290.70	308.64	326.80	344.83
Shift(δ)	Within action limits = control group data come from within action limits only						
0.00	476.39	347.39	367.99	295.24	306.85	328.65	346.61
0.25	203.10	152.32	152.46	120.92	122.10	123.56	130.21
0.50	56.04	45.86	42.86	34.50	34.33	33.80	33.73
0.75	19.44	15.94	14.69	12.08	11.59	11.40	11.06
1.00	8.10	6.77	6.25	5.16	4.99	4.94	4.77
1.50	2.44	2.19	2.03	1.79	1.74	1.69	1.66
2.00	1.31	1.25	1.20	1.15	1.12	1.11	1.09
2.50	1.05	1.04	1.03	1.02	1.01	1.01	1.01
3.00	1.00	1.00	1.00	1.00	1.00	1.00	1.00
Shift(δ)	Without action limits restriction for control group data						
0.00	472.93	352.06	363.07	291.95	306.23	325.90	340.10
0.25	205.13	153.10	151.64	122.20	126.56	128.07	129.00
0.50	58.03	45.02	43.35	34.50	33.71	33.18	34.15
0.75	19.44	15.81	15.02	11.98	11.67	11.45	11.26
1.00	8.19	6.89	6.43	5.28	5.11	4.87	4.77
1.50	2.46	2.22	2.05	1.82	1.76	1.70	1.66
2.00	1.32	1.25	1.22	1.15	1.14	1.12	1.11
2.50	1.06	1.04	1.03	1.02	1.01	1.01	1.01
3.00	1.01	1.00	1.00	1.00	1.00	1.00	1.00

Table 7 shows that there were nearly the same between *ARL* from Type-I error (α) and the *ARL* from 10000 runs simulation for the normal data when control group sample data come from μ+0σ process parameter within only control limits and there was no restriction about the other methods.

Table 8

Average run length of the Mann-Whitney control chat for standard Weibull data

Scheme		R	T0	T1	T2	T3	T4	T5
Control, m		10	10	10	10	10	10	10
Treatment, n		10	10	11	12	13	14	15
Skew	shift (δ)							
0.1	0.00	473.19	346.11	364.23	289.41	308.18	320.40	342.47
	0.25	210.14	155.34	157.02	123.40	129.71	130.09	131.99
	0.50	61.33	47.14	45.57	36.14	36.56	35.52	35.59
	0.75	21.57	16.89	16.17	12.40	12.41	12.14	11.76
	1.00	8.74	7.24	6.83	5.52	5.30	5.22	5.02
	1.50	2.53	2.25	2.12	1.88	1.81	1.74	1.70
0.5	0.00	478.19	345.58	362.24	290.60	308.19	327.00	336.83
	0.25	205.04	151.28	152.96	120.81	122.19	121.84	124.53
	0.50	57.92	45.13	43.24	33.74	32.63	33.02	32.49
	0.75	20.00	15.99	15.08	12.00	11.33	11.10	10.55
	1.00	8.28	6.85	6.28	5.15	4.94	4.76	4.62
	1.50	2.40	2.18	2.06	1.82	1.75	1.68	1.65
1.0	0.00	473.75	344.47	360.00	292.85	302.93	324.59	346.83
	0.25	183.04	135.88	134.30	101.08	104.11	103.35	104.91
	0.50	46.99	36.65	34.08	25.86	25.33	24.42	24.12
	0.75	15.28	12.48	11.27	9.08	8.42	8.31	7.97
	1.00	6.47	5.42	5.02	4.13	3.95	3.79	3.67
	1.50	2.17	1.95	1.86	1.66	1.63	1.58	1.55
2.0	0.00	483.75	350.20	370.33	285.05	308.18	327.91	343.94
	0.25	99.04	77.70	70.84	52.29	50.89	49.57	47.99
	0.50	20.35	16.57	14.99	11.73	10.95	10.57	10.11
	0.75	7.22	6.04	5.53	4.52	4.33	4.18	4.02
	1.00	3.71	3.19	3.01	2.58	2.49	2.40	2.36

The *ARL*s result from 10000 runs simulation for standard Weibull data is shown in Table 8. The dual scheme for variable parameters Mann-Whitney control charts for both normal and Weibull data also show the combination results, as the same result having ever happened in the normal data. However, the shift rows that all ARL≤2 are not shown in the table.

Table 8

Continued

	Scheme	R	T0	T1	T2	T3	T4	T5
3.0	0.00	481.59	347.01	361.58	286.94	309.84	326.14	345.36
	0.25	44.42	34.78	30.94	23.61	22.15	21.33	20.05
	0.50	9.46	8.03	7.27	5.90	5.59	5.39	5.21
	0.75	4.11	3.68	3.41	2.93	2.80	2.69	2.62
	1.00	2.46	2.28	2.18	1.98	1.89	1.85	1.81
4.0	0.00	476.90	349.52	354.45	292.20	305.88	324.55	344.79
	0.25	21.86	17.77	15.76	12.55	11.48	11.23	10.81
	0.50	5.60	4.84	4.54	3.92	3.67	3.61	3.42
	0.75	2.88	2.60	2.52	2.27	2.18	2.10	2.06
5.0	0.00	479.43	346.76	359.80	293.78	305.25	332.95	343.87
	0.25	12.73	10.61	9.62	7.88	7.44	7.18	6.69
	0.50	3.92	3.55	3.41	2.94	2.82	2.74	2.68
	0.75	2.29	2.15	2.08	1.92	1.85	1.82	1.78
6.0	0.00	477.15	347.60	358.52	294.99	307.46	325.71	342.06
	0.25	8.65	7.50	6.74	5.61	5.42	5.17	4.97
	0.50	3.04	2.83	2.74	2.46	2.38	2.27	2.24
7.0	0.00	477.57	342.91	362.83	291.28	309.56	320.98	346.38
	0.25	6.46	5.63	5.29	4.45	4.25	4.08	3.89
	0.50	2.57	2.42	2.36	2.17	2.08	2.01	1.98
8.0	0.00	477.82	346.99	361.51	291.29	313.50	326.03	342.81
	0.25	5.07	4.54	4.36	3.71	3.55	3.44	3.34
	0.50	2.25	2.15	2.07	1.95	1.91	1.85	1.82
9.0	0.00	472.97	344.44	360.17	291.24	305.81	325.43	341.82
	0.25	4.19	3.84	3.64	3.29	3.07	3.02	2.89
	0.50	2.02	1.96	1.93	1.79	1.75	1.73	1.71

Note: The shift rows that all ARL≤2 are not shown. No restriction for control group data.

4.3 The Hodges-Lehmann estimator control charts

The *ARL* performed by 10000 run lengths simulation of the Hodges-Lehmann estimator control chart for the normal data shows very high *ARL* when comparing to the ARL_0 from the Wilcoxon signed rank statistics. The control limits, proposed by Alloway et al. (1991), are computed by the original method as shown in Table 9. For the sample size n =10, $(-k,+k)$ = (2,53), α = 0.00390, ARL_0 = 256.41, the median of Walsh averages for 100000 samples simulation at (2,53) are (-1.50027, 1.15015), by using this Hodges-Lehmann control limit the ARL_0 from 10000 run lengths simulation = 4241.49. The control limits (-1.50027, 1.15015) has the probability= 0.7703 in $N(0,1)$, α = 0.2297, ARL_0 =4.35. For the sample size n = 10, using the Wilcoxon signed rank wider control limits at (1, 54) with the probability α = 0.00196, ARL_0 = 510.20, it shows that the ARL_0 performance is better than $\pm 3\sigma$ control limit, α=0.0027, ARL_0 = 370 in Shewhart $\bar{X}$ chart, and HL control limits from 100000 sets of Walsh averages= (-1.4993, 1.2544) with the probability = 0.8283 in $N(0,1)$, α = 0.1717, ARL_0 from process distribution =5.82, but the ARL_0 from 10000 run lengths simulation = 13281.35 (this case is not shown in Table 9). For the known process distribution, the robust to outliers of the Hodges-Lehmann estimator give this very high *ARL* performance. The Hodges-Lehmann estimator is the nonparametric statistics that is very robust to the presence of outliers (Duchnowski, 2013).

For the original HL method, the sample size in HL must be started from 10 in order that the Type-I error probability is low enough (ARL_0 is high enough) from Wilcoxon signed rank statistics. But for the normal data, ARL_0 in the simulation is about 3 to 16 times of ARL_0 from Wilcoxon signed rank probability. The very high ARL_0 in the simulation leads to a chance in using the smaller sample size *n* = 9, 8, 7 when the process distribution is known.

Table 9
Average run length of the Hodges-Lehmann estimator control chart for standard normal data using the original charting technique

Scheme	R	*T0*	T1	T2	T4	T5	T6	T8	T10
n	10	*10*	11	12	14	15	16	18	20
n(*n*+1)/2	55	*55*	66	78	105	120	136	171	210
Wilcoxon Signed Rank Statistic action limits									
+*k*	53	*51*	63	73	96	108	121	150	181
-*k*	2	*4*	3	5	9	12	15	21	29
α	0.00390	*0.00896*	0.00292	0.00342	0.00306	0.00336	0.00336	0.00280	0.00272
$ARL_0 = 1/\alpha$	256.41	*111.61*	342.47	292.40	326.80	297.62	297.62	357.14	367.65
Hodges-Lehmann Estimator Control Limits from 100000 runs simulation									
+*k*	1.15015	*1.14950*	1.09318	1.01846	0.93124	0.87789	0.84133	0.80215	0.76000
-*k*	-1.50027	*-1.25569*	-1.20516	-1.08337	-0.97378	-0.91128	-0.87195	-0.82538	-0.77042
ARL from 10000 run lengths simulation									
Shift (δ)									
0.00	4241.49	*3260.34*	3401.88	2102.92	1642.85	1227.30	1079.72	1224.29	1132.42
0.25	328.55	*322.06*	288.14	197.77	145.20	108.76	91.24	86.50	74.70
0.50	42.46	*41.96*	35.19	24.28	16.96	12.71	10.68	9.33	7.76
0.75	8.90	*9.05*	7.45	5.43	3.88	3.15	2.76	2.39	2.06
1.00	3.13	*3.06*	2.61	2.09	1.69	1.47	1.37	1.26	1.17
1.50	1.16	*1.17*	1.11	1.06	1.02	1.01	1.00	1.00	1.00

Note: The shift rows that ARL ≤1 are not showed.

The new approach to find the right performance for the known process distribution is using the Hodges-Lehmann estimator at the locations corresponding to the desired Type-I error probability as the control limits. To verify with ±3σ control limits of Shewhart $\bar{X}$ chart, $\alpha = 0.00270$, $ARL_0 = 370.37$), in the new approach to HL, for $n = 10$, Type I error (α) = 0.00270, $-k = 135$ and $+k = 99865$ are the locations of control limits from the 100000 ascending order simulated Hodges-Lehmann estimator and they are the new Hodges-Lehmann control limits (-0.99573, 0.99179) with ARL_0 from 10000 run lengths simulation = 401.03. The 401.03 is also closed to 370.

The Hodges-Lehmann estimator control chart for the normal data by using the new control limits for Type-I error probability α=0.0027 (ARL_0 =370.37) with selected sample sizes from 10 to 20 present in Table 10.

Table 10
Average run length of the new Hodges-Lehmann estimator control chart for standard normal data

Scheme	Rs	*Ts*	Rs1	Rs2	Rs3	Rs4	Rs5
n	10	*10*	11	12	13	14	15
Type I error (α)	0.00270	*0.00308*	0.00270	0.00270	0.00270	0.00270	0.00270
Location at							
+*k*	99865	*99845*	99865	99865	99865	99865	99865
-*k*	135	*155*	135	135	135	135	135
Hodges-Lehmann estimator control limits from 100000 runs simulation							
+*k*	0.99179	*0.97489*	0.92749	0.89708	0.86389	0.82901	0.78779
-*k*	-0.99573	*-0.97909*	-0.93255	-0.90214	-0.87512	-0.82383	-0.79610
ARL from 10000 run lengths simulation							
shift (δ)							
0.00	401.03	*342.40*	345.64	376.66	402.13	362.69	336.38
0.25	84.20	*74.51*	66.80	67.60	61.94	55.49	46.29
0.50	15.03	*13.53*	11.72	10.93	9.65	8.49	7.08
0.75	4.42	*3.99*	3.55	3.21	2.93	2.63	2.22
1.00	1.96	*1.88*	1.70	1.57	1.48	1.36	1.26
1.50	1.06	*1.05*	1.03	1.02	1.01	1.01	1.00
2.00	1.00	*1.00*	1.00	1.00	1.00	1.00	1.00
2.50	1.00	*1.00*	1.00	1.00	1.00	1.00	1.00
3.00	1.00	*1.00*	1.00	1.00	1.00	1.00	1.00

When the sample size is increasing the control limits is also narrower, the sample size affects the control limits vis-à-vis $1/\sqrt{n}$ in the Shewhart $\bar{X}$ chart, and the ARL_0 of each scheme from simulation are 370 (in the range of 401 to 336). The tight control by using α= 0.00308 (ARL_0 = 324.37) for the Scheme *Ts* is in Table 10, and ARL_0 from the simulation= 342.40. The ARL_0 from the simulation in this new control limits does not show the very high value as the original practice presented in Table 9.

The Hodges-Lehmann estimator control chart for Weibull data by using the new control limits also shows the performance closed to the normal data in every skewness. However, the table is not presented. The dual scheme for variable parameters control charts of the Hodges-Lehmann estimator control charts for both the normal and Weibull data also show the combination results for performances of ANSS, ANOS, and ATS, the same results as having ever happened in the Sign test control charts. However, the table is not presented.

5. Conclusion

The performances of the three nonparametric control charts (ST, MW, and HL) for the known process distribution (normal and Weibull data) shown in this simulation study are as follows.

The control limits of the three nonparametric control charts are not effected from the sample sizes ($1/\sqrt{n}$ in $\bar{X}$ chart), but the Type-I error (α) probability is associated with the selected non-parametric statistics for only control limits. In the Sign test and the Mann-Whitney control charts, the ARL_0 performance follows the Type-I error probability (α) from the control statistics. For only the original Hodges-Lehmann estimator control chart, the robust to outliers of the median of Walsh averages also gives narrower control limits and the simulation also shows very large *ARL* performance when compared to the *ARL* performance from the Type-I error probability (α) which is derived from the assumed Wilcoxon signed rank statistics.

The new HL approach by using the control limits derives from the Hodges-Lehmann estimator distribution, and the *ARL* performance shows the effect of increasing sample size as the effect of $1/\sqrt{n}$ in the Shewhart $\bar{X}$ chart. At the $\pm 3\sigma$ control limits in the normal data, the ARL_0 of this new control limits also closes to 370 as that in the Shewhart $\bar{X}$ chart.

For the variable parameters, the performance of the combined dual schemes is the weighted averages between the regular scheme and the tight scheme in every non-parametric control chart.

In term of the Hodges-Lehmann estimator control chart for the known process distribution, the control limits at the given probability can be derived by the simulation, then the HL will be the alternative method for the process that needs the robust to outlier property from this statistics, and it is possible that the economic design (expected costs per unit time) will be solved.

References

Alloway, J.A. & Raghavachari, M. (1991). Control chart based on Hodges–Lehmann estimator. *Journal of Quality Technology*, 23, 336–347.

Amin, R.W., &Widmaier, O. (1999). Sign control charts with variable sampling intervals. *Communication in Statistics - Theory and Methods*, 28(8), 1961–1985.

Amin, R., Reynolds Jr, M.R., & Bakir, S.T. (1995).Nonparametric quality control charts based on the sign statistic.*Communication in Statistics - Theory and Methods*, 24, 1579–1623.

Bakir, S.T. (2001). Classification of distribution-free quality control charts, Proceedings of the Annual Meeting of the American Statistical Association, August 5-9, 2001.

Bakir, S.T. (2004). A distribution-free Shewhart quality control chart based on Signed-rank. *Quality Engineering*, 16(4),613-623.

Bakir, S.T. & Reynolds, M.R. (1979).A nonparametric for process control based on within-groups ranking. *Technometrics*, 21(2), 175-183.

Balakrishnan, N., Triantafyllou, I.S. & Koutras, M.V. (2009). Nonparametric control charts based on runs and Wilcoxon-type rank-sum statistics. *Journal of Statistical Planning and Interface*, 139, 3177-3192.

Beaumont, G.P., & Knowles, J.D. (1996). *Statistical tests An introduction with MINITAB commentary*. Hertfordshire: Prentice Hall international (UK) Limited.

Bersimis, S., Psarakis, S., & Panaretos, J. (2007). Multivariate Statistical Process Control Charts : An Overview. *Quality and Reliability Engineering International*, 23, 517-543.

Black, G., Smith, J. & Wells, S. (2011). The impact of Weibull data and autocorrelation on the performance of the Shewhart and exponentially weighted moving average control charts. *International Journal of Industrial Engineering Computations*, 2, 575-582.

Bluman, A.G. (1998). *Elementary Statistics : a step by step approach.* Boston: WCB McGraw-Hill.

Chakraborti, S.&Eryilmaz, S. (2007). A nonparametric Shewhart-type signed-rank control chart based on runs.*Communications in Statistics – Simulation and Computation*, 36(2), 335-356.

Chakraborti, S., van der Lann, P., & Bakir, S.T. (2001). Nonparametric control charts: an overview and some results. *Journal of Quality Technology*, 33(3), 304-315.

Chakraborti, S. & van de Wiel, M.A. (2008).A nonparametric control chart based on the Mann-Whitney statistic.*IMS Collections. Institute of Mathematical Statistics*, 1, 156–172.

Cheng, A.Y., Liu, R.Y. & Luxhoj, J.T. (2000).Monitoring Multivariate Aviation Safety Data by Data Depth: Control Charts and Threshold Systems. *IIE Transactions*, 32, 861-872.

Das, N. (2009). A comparison study of three non-parametric control charts to detect shift in location parameters. *The International Journal of Advanced Manufacturing Technology*, 41, 799-807.

Duchnowski R. (2013). Hodges–Lehmann estimates in deformation analyses. *Journal of Geodynamics*, 87, 873–884.

Ghute, V.B. & Shirke, D.T.(2012). A nonparametric Signed-rank control chart for bivariate process location. *Quality Technology & Quantitative Management*, 9(4), 317-328.

Gibbons, J.D. (1971). *Nonparametric Statistical Inference*. Tokyo: McGraw-Hill Kogakusha.

Graham, M.A., Human, S.W. & Chakraborti, S. (2010). A phase I nonparametric Shewhart-type control chart based on the median. *Journal of Applied Statistics*, 37(11), 1795-1813.

Graham, M.A., Chakraborti, S., & Human, S.W. (2011).A nonparametric exponentially weighted moving average signed-rank chart for monitoring location. *Computational Statistics and Data Analysis*, 55, 2490-2503.

Graham, M.A., Mukherjee, A. & Chakraborti, S. (2012). Distribution-free exponentially weighted moving average control charts for monitoring unknown location. *Computational Statistics and Data Analysis*, 56, 2539-2561.

Human, S.W., Chakraborti, S. & Smit, C.F. (2010).Nonparametric Shewhart-type Sign control charts based on runs. *Communication in Statistics - Theory and Methods*, 39(11), 2046–2062.

Jones-Farmer, L.A., Jordan, V. & Champ, C.W. (2009). Distribution-free phase I control charts for subgroup location. *Journal of Quality Technology*, 41(3), 304-316.

Khilare, S.K., & Shirke, D.T. (2010). A nonparametric synthetic control chart using Sign statistic. *Communicatins in statistics – Theory and Methods*, 39(18), 3282-3293.

Lehmann, E.L. (1963). Non-parametric confidence intervals for a shift parameter. *The Annals of Mathematical Statistics*, 34, 1507–1512.

Li, J., Zhang, X. & Jeske, D.R. (2013).Nonparametric multivariate CUSUM control charts for location and scale changes. *Journal of Nonparametric Statistics*, 25(1), 1-20.

Lin, Y.C. & Chou, C.Y. (2007). Non-normality and the variable parameters $\bar{\bar{X}}$ control charts. *European Journal of Operations Research*, 176, 361-373.

Montgomery, D.C. (2013). *Statistical quality control* (7th edition). Asia: John Wiley & Sons Singapore.

Nelson, P.R. (1979). Control Charts for Weibull Processes with Standards Given. *IEEE Transactions on Reliability*, 28, 283-288.

Neuhäuser, M. (2012). *Nonparametric Statistical tests: A computational Approach*. Florida : CRC Press.

Pongpullponsak, A., Suracherdkiati, W., & Kriweradechachai, P. (2004). The comparison of efficiency of control chart by weighted variance method, Nelson Method, Shewhart method for skewed population, Proceeding of the 5th Applied Statistics Conference of Northern Thailand; 2004 May 27-29; Chiang Mai, Thailand.

The Math WorksTM. (2009). MATLAB 7.6.0(R2009a). License Number 350306, February 12, 2009.

Yang, S., Lin, J., & Cheng, S.W. (2011). A new nonparametric EWMA Sign Control Chart. *Expert Systems with Applications,* 38, 6239-6243.

3

Numeric treatment of nonlinear second order multi-point boundary value problems using ANN, GAs and sequential quadratic programming technique

Zulqurnain Sabir[a*] and Muhammad Asif Zahoor Raja[b]

[a]*Department of Mathematics, Unique Science College (for girls) Dina, Pakistan*
[b]*Department of Electrical Engineering, COMSATS Institute of Information Technology, Attock Campus, Attock Pakistan*

CHRONICLE

Keywords:
Artificial neural networks
Genetic Algorithm
Sequential Quadratic Programming Technique
Hybrid computing techniques

ABSTRACT

In this paper, computational intelligence technique are presented for solving multi-point nonlinear boundary value problems based on artificial neural networks, evolutionary computing approach, and active-set technique. The neural network is to provide convenient methods for obtaining useful model based on unsupervised error for the differential equations. The motivation for presenting this work comes actually from the aim of introducing a reliable framework that combines the powerful features of ANN optimized with soft computing frameworks to cope with such challenging system. The applicability and reliability of such methods have been monitored thoroughly for various boundary value problems arises in science, engineering and biotechnology as well. Comprehensive numerical experimentations have been performed to validate the accuracy, convergence, and robustness of the designed scheme. Comparative studies have also been made with available standard solution to analyze the correctness of the proposed scheme.

1. Introduction

Multi-point boundary value problems (BVPs) or non-local boundary value problems were introduced by Ilin and Moiseev (1987). These BVPs have become the most important area among researchers. These days, because of its widespread applications in engineering as to model the physical problems, including vibration happening in a wire of uniform cross section and combined of material with changed densities, through porous media applications, BVPs are used in fluid flow and in elastic stability. In addition, these problems have wide applications in applied physics particularly in heat conduction (Cannon, 1984; Cannon et al., 1987) and other problems in nonlinear elasticity (Timoshenko, 1961). By using perturbation techniques, these problems have been normally solved but these techniques have some confines, e.g. the approximate solution consists of a series of very small parameters, which poses difficulty since the popularity of nonlinear problems has no minor parameters.

* Corresponding author.

These multi-point BVPs are generally limited to second order equation. Agarwal and Kinguradze (Das et al., 2010) solved higher order linear ordinary differential equation with singularity at numerous points in 2004. Cheung and Ren (Das et al., 2010) discussed multi-point BVPs in 2005. Tatari and Dehghan (Das et al., 2010) used Adomian decomposition method (ADM) to find the solution of multi-point BVP in 2006. Gupta (1992, 1994, 1997) is believed to be the first who used functional analytical technique to demonstrate the existence of the solution monitored by Eloe and Henderson (1994), Ma (1999, 2001), Liu (2002), Webb (2001), etc. Deimling, (1985), Guo and Lakshmikantham (1988) and Krasnosel'skij (1964) used commonly fixed-point theorem on cones for positive solution. The source to apply this theorem can be initiated with semi linear elliptic equations on annuli (Erbe & Wang, 1994).

Stochastic numerical techniques have been used extensively by many researchers in different fields to solve linear and nonlinear differential equations (Raja & Samar, 2012; Khan, 2009). Interest in this area is significantly enhanced with effective numerical treatment for fractional differential equation (Khan et al., 2012). The analysis is carried out further by constructing different types of neural networks models with/without satisfying the boundary conditions, exactly. Furthermore, the effect of change on number on neurons on accuracy and convergence has also been analyzed.

In the present study, computational intelligent techniques are developed for solving a nonlinear multi-point BVPs representing to model the equation with the help of universal approximation capability of feed-forward artificial neural networks (ANN) trained in an unsupervised manner with genetic algorithms (GA) technique, as a tool for effective global search optimizer, hybrid with sequential quadratic programming technique (SQPT), an efficient local search approach. The proposed schemes are evaluated on four variants of the problems to validate the correctness of the approaches. The reliability and effectiveness of the proposed scheme is analyzed based on sufficient large set of data generated from independent execution of the optimizers, i.e., GA, SQPT and GA-SQPT.

The organization of the paper is as follows: in the second section, the system model of the problem is given in details. Design methodology consists of feed-forward artificial neural networks modeling and learning procedure based on GA, SQPT and GA-SQPT is narrated in section three. Numerical experimentation of number of variant of the problem is provided in section four. Concluding remarks and few future research directions are provided in the last section.

2. General form of Multi-point BVPs

Mathematically, this problem is a second-order ordinary differential equation (ODE). The generic form or general form of multi-point boundary value problems is written as follows,

$$\begin{cases} \dfrac{d^2y}{dx^2} + h(y, y') = q(x), \quad 0 \le x \le 1, \\ y(0) = A \text{ and } y(1) = \sum_{i=1}^{m} \alpha_i y(\eta_i) + \gamma, \end{cases} \tag{1}$$

where $\eta_i \in (0,1), i = 0,1,2,..., m$, α and γ are constants

The Eq. (1) represents a standard form of multi-point BVP. The aim of studying the generalized form of the nonlinear multi-point BVP and its solutions is to develop a broader understanding of the general equations and to develop analytical tools to analyze these equations to cover more applications as they arise in the future.

3. Proposed Methodology

The brief description of designed methodology will be presented for the solution of the multi-point BVPs. In this section, the procedure consists of the development of two feed-forward unsupervised neural networks models of the equation. Moreover, brief introductory material for the optimization algorithms i.e. evolutionary computing and active set programming techniques are also given.

3.1 Neural Network Mathematical Modeling

Mathematical model for the second order multi-point boundary value problems is constructed with the strength of feed-forward ANN, in the form of following continuous mapping for the solution $y(x)$, and its first dy/dx, second d^2y/dx^2 respectively, For the activation function log-sigmoid function $g(x) = 1/(1+e^{-x})$ is used in the neural network modeling, given as:

$$\begin{cases} \hat{y}(x) = \sum_{i=1}^{k} \alpha_i g(w_i x + \beta_i) = \sum_{i=1}^{n} \alpha_i \dfrac{1}{1+e^{-(w_i x+\beta_i)}}, \\ \dfrac{d\hat{y}}{dx} = \sum_{i=1}^{k} \alpha_i \dfrac{d}{dx} g(w_i x + \beta_i) = \sum_{i=1}^{n} \alpha_i w_i \dfrac{e^{-(w_i x+\beta_i)}}{1+e^{-(w_i x+\beta_i)^2}}, \\ \dfrac{d^2\hat{y}}{dx^2} = \sum_{i=1}^{k} \alpha_i \dfrac{d^2}{dx^2} g(w_i x + \beta_i) = \sum_{i=1}^{n} \alpha_i w_i^2 \left(\dfrac{2e^{-2(w_i x+\beta_i)}}{\left(1+e^{-(w_i x+\beta_i)}\right)^3} - \dfrac{e^{-(w_i x+\beta_i)}}{\left(1+e^{-(w_i x+\beta_i)}\right)^2} \right), \end{cases} \tag{2}$$

where the vectors α, w and β are real-valued bounded unknown parameters, i.e., weights W = $[\alpha, w, \beta]$, n is the number of neurons and g is the activation function generally taken as log-sigmoid function.

The suitable combination of the networks given in the set (2) can be used to model the differential equation (1). An objective function or fitness function is developed in an unsupervised manner and it is defined by sum of two mean square error, e_1 is error function associated with differential equation (1) and it is given as:

$$\begin{cases} e = e_1 + e_2 \\ e_1 = \dfrac{1}{N} \sum_{m=1}^{N} \left(\dfrac{d^2\hat{y}_m}{dx^2} + h(\hat{y}_m, \hat{y}'_m) \dfrac{d\hat{y}_m}{dx} - q_m \right)^2, 0 \le x \le 1 \\ N = \dfrac{1}{h}, \hat{y}_m = \hat{y}(x_m), q_m = q(x_m), x_m = mh \end{cases} \tag{3}$$

Similarly, e_2 is the error function associated with boundary conditions for Eq. (1) is given as:

$$e_2 = \frac{1}{2}\left((\hat{y}_0 - A)^2 + (\hat{y}_N - B)^2\right) \tag{4}$$

A second form of feed-forward artificial neural networks modeling is also constructed such that initial and boundary conditions are exactly satisfied in order to solve boundary value problems of the multi-point BVPs. The governing equations of alternative form of artificial neural networks model for the solution $y(x)$, and its first dy/dx, second d^2y/dx^2 respectively, written as:

$$\begin{cases} \tilde{y}(x) = P(x) + Q(x)\hat{y}(x) \\ \dfrac{d\tilde{y}}{dx} = \dfrac{dP}{dx} + \dfrac{dQ}{dx}\hat{y}(x) + Q(x)\dfrac{d\hat{y}}{dx} \\ \dfrac{d^2\tilde{y}}{dx} = \dfrac{d^2P}{dx^2} + \dfrac{d^2Q}{dx^2}\hat{y}(x) + Q(x)\dfrac{d^2\hat{y}}{dx^2} \end{cases} \tag{5}$$

where $\hat{y}(x)$, $d\hat{y}/dx$, $d^2\hat{y}/dx^2$ are the networks as shown in Eq. (6). The updated neural network can be developed for solving the general nonlinear multi-point boundary value problem (1) that satisfies boundary conditions exactly by taking the approximate values of $P(x)$ and $Q(x)$.

An objective function or fitness function is developed in an unsupervised manner for introducing error function base on the sum of mean square error as:

$$\begin{cases} \varepsilon = \dfrac{1}{N}\displaystyle\sum_{m=1}^{N}\left(\dfrac{d^2\tilde{y}_m}{dx^2} + h(\tilde{y}_m, \tilde{y}'_m) - q_m\right)^2, \; x \in (0,1) \\ N = \dfrac{1}{h}, \tilde{y}_m = \tilde{y}(x_m), q_m = q(x_m), x_m = mh \end{cases} \quad (6)$$

One can only deduce that with the availability of weights of neural networks such that the objective function given in Eq. (3) or Eq. (6) approaches zero, the proposed solution will approximate the exact solution of the problem closely.

3.2 Learning Methodology

The procedure for training the designed parameters of the networks is accomplished with the help of genetic algorithms (GAs), sequential quadratic programming technique (SQPT) and hybrid computing approach GA-SQPT. The recent researches in genetic algorithms (GAs) has emphasized that the initial proposals were found incompetent of solving tough problems in a valuable and efficient way. For a large numbers of optimization problems, the time of execution of first-generation GAs increases significantly while solution quality decreases. Moreover the things such as selection schemes, encoding procedures, and self-adaptive and knowledge based operators play an important role in the optimization of well convex and stochastic nature problems. Since the beginning of the GAs, it has used for optimization of different fields of interest. In addition to the optimization problems, it is also used as an effective technique for achieving modeling, forecasting, control and simulation objectives. Traditional optimization approach start with a single candidate and search iteratively for the optimal result by using static heuristics. While, the GA techniques uses a population of candidate to seek a number of areas of a solution space, simultaneously and adaptively. The most famous methods that go beyond easy local search are GAs, simulated annealing (SA), and tabu search (TS) etc. Genetic algorithms work on a population of individuals. All individual is a potential solution to a given problem and is normally encoded as a fixed-length binary string, which is an analogy with an actual chromosome. After an initial population is randomly or heuristically generated, the algorithm evolves population through sequential and iterative application of selection, crossover, and mutation operators. A new generation is shaped after every each iteration. The strongest feature of the GA is that do not get stuck in local minimum.

Sequential quadratic programming techniques is basically a local search method which belongs to the class of efficient constrained optimization technique. The method is based on mathematical model for solving the Karush-Kuhn-Tucker (KKT) equations to get the desired Lagrange multipliers simply and consequently the global candidate solution. The SQP technique has been used in many practical important optimization problems since their origin. The interesting reader is referred to these literatures to known the history, importance, subject term, working and detail procedural step of the algorithm. The necessary procedure adopted for GA-SQPT is given in following steps:

Step 1: *Initialization*: Initial values of parameters are set in this step with random assignment and declarations. These setting are also tabulated in Table1 for important parameter of GAs.

Step 2: *Fitness Evaluation*: Calculate the fitness of each individual or chromosome of population using the Eq. (2) and Eq. (5), for first and second type of modeling, respectively.

Step 3: *Termination Criteria:* Terminate the algorithm when either of following criteria matches:

- Predefined fitness values $e \leq 10^{-15}$ is achieved.

- Predefine number of generations are executed.
- Any of termination setting given in Table 1 for GA is fulfilled.

If termination criterion meets, then go to step 5

Step 4: *Reproduction:* Create next generation on the basis of Crossover: Call for scattered function, Mutation: Call for Adaptive Feasible function, Selection: Call for Stochastic Uniform function and Elitism account is set 4 etc.

Repeat the procedure from step 2 to step 4 with newly produced population

Step 5: *Improvements:* Sequential quadratic programming technique is used for further refinement of results by taking final adaptive weights of GAs as initial weights (start point) of SQPT algorithm. SQPT is applied as per setting of parameters given in Table 2. Store also the refined final weights of the algorithm.

Step 6: *Neurons Analysis*: Repeat step 1 to 5 for by taking size of initial weights, i.e. 15, 30 and 45 for k = 5, 10 and 15 neurons, respectively. These results are used for detail analysis of algorithm later.

The parameter setting used in this paper for GA algorithm in table 1 and SQPT algorithm are given in Table 2.

Table 1

Parameters Setting for GA in simulations

Parameters	Setting	Parameters	Setting
Population Creation	Linear feasible	Bounds	[-20, 20]
Initial Population range	[-1, 1]	Derivative	Approximate by solver
Population	300 individuals	TolFun	10^{-20}
Generations	700	StallGenLimit	100
Scaling faction	Rank	Mutation	Adaptive feasible
Selection function	Stochastic Uniform	Migration interval	20
Crossover fraction	0.80	Elite Count	02
Crossover function	Heuristic	TolCon	10^{-20}
Migration fraction	0.2	Other	Defaults

Table 2

Parameter Settings of "fmincon" function for SQPT in simulations

Parameters	Settings/Values	Parameters	Settings/Values
Algorithm	active-set	Initial Weights	best weights of GA
FinDiffType	Central	Initial Weight Vector length	30
TolX	10^{-20}	Total Initial Weight Vectors	100
Iterations	700	Bounds	$\alpha_i, w_i, b_i \in (\pm 20)\ \forall$ i 1 to n
MaxFunEvals	200000	TolCon	Zero
TolFun	10^{-20}	Derivative	Approximate by solver
TolCon	0	Other	as defaults

3. Simulations and Results

In this section, three problems of multi-point boundary value problems will be presented with their multi-point boundary conditions. We compare the results of all the numerical problems for different number of neurons with exact solutions that will be provided with each problem. The error analysis showed graphically the high reliability of purposed scheme.

Problem I: consider the following nonlinear multi-point boundary value problem (Das et al., 2010)

$$\begin{cases} \dfrac{d^2y}{dx^2}+\dfrac{x^2(1-x)}{2}\dfrac{dy}{dx}-y^2(x)=x^3+2 \\ y(0)=0, \quad y(1)=\displaystyle\sum_{i=0}^{4}\left(\frac{1}{1+i}\right)y\left(\frac{i}{5}\right)+0.708667 \end{cases} \tag{7}$$

The exact solution of the problem is given as:

$$y(x)=x^2 \tag{8}$$

The proposed methodologies are applied to solve the problem by taking 10 neurons in the hidden layer of neural networks thus with a total 30 design parameter or weights, $W(\alpha, w, \beta)$.The fitness functions e and ε is formulated for this case for r ϵ (0, 1] with a step size h = 0.1 as:

$$\begin{cases} e=\dfrac{1}{10}\displaystyle\sum_{m=1}^{10}\left(\frac{d^2\hat{y}_m}{dx^2}+\frac{x_m^2(1-x_m)}{2}\frac{d\hat{y}_m}{dx}-\hat{y}_m^2-x_m^3-2\right)^2 \\ \quad +\dfrac{1}{2}\left((\hat{y}_0)^2+\left(\hat{y}_{10}-\displaystyle\sum_{i=0}^{4}\left(\frac{1}{1+i}\right)y\left(\frac{i}{5}\right)+0.708667\right)^2\right) \\ \varepsilon=\dfrac{1}{10}\displaystyle\sum_{m=1}^{10}\left(\frac{d^2\tilde{y}_m}{dx^2}+\frac{x_m^2(1-x_m)}{2}\frac{d\tilde{y}_m}{dx}-\tilde{y}_m^2-x_m^3-2\right)^2 \end{cases} \tag{9}$$

Set of trained weights with respective fitness for GA-SQPT algorithm are shown in Fig. 1

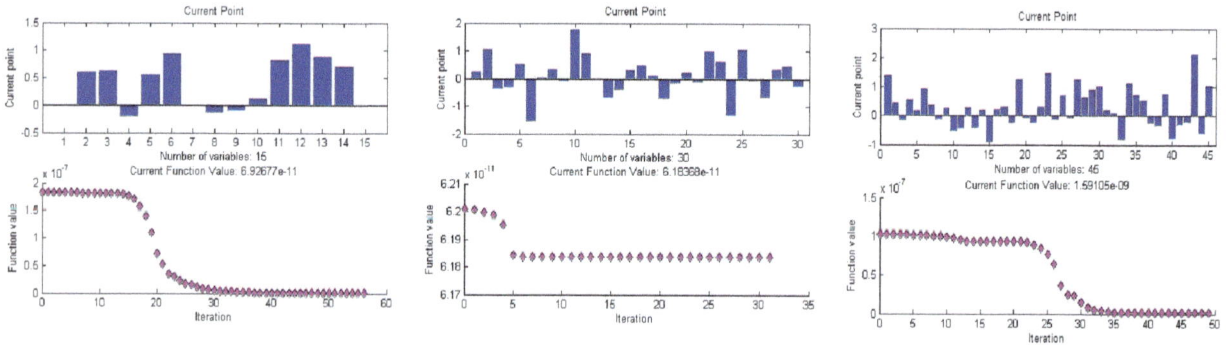

(a) (b) (c)

Fig. 1. Set of optimal weights along with parameters for problem 1 by GA-SQPT using 5, 10 and 15 numbers of neurons

The proposed solution $\hat{y}(x)$ and $\tilde{y}(x)$ of the Eq. (7) is obtained using the optimal weights of algorithms in first equation of the set (2) and (5), respectively. The results due to GA-SQPT for the case $k = 5$ are given in simplify form as:

$$\hat{Y}_{GA-SQPT}(x)=\frac{-3.67842896132752}{1+e^{-(2.34877564743t+3.219305585838)}}-\frac{1.14752400515832}{1+e^{-(4.4035182757t-0.46497078475872)}} \\ -\frac{2.39639235002620}{1+e^{-(-0.4350829368t-2.29597874248666)}}-\frac{2.35054880126743}{1+e^{-(0.52111789400447t-1.78365289124987)}}-\frac{2.29409857048802}{1+e^{-(2.0465687282029t-4.25093661709093)}} \tag{10}$$

$$\tilde{y}_{GA-SQP}(x)=x+x(x-1) \\ [\frac{-0.00916357067839}{1+e^{-(0.5913937719t-0.617416045561)}}-\frac{-0.20873044942255}{1+e^{-(0.53952271524t-0.93546047665)}} \\ -\frac{0.00455641085491}{1+e^{-(-0.13418836737t+-0.10888915790)}}+\frac{0.10796315561423}{1+e^{-(0.81207439935t+1.10333363137)}}+\frac{0.8652393033873}{1+e^{-(0.69277039883t-0.02118837096)}}] \tag{11}$$

To find the solution of the problems, we have applied the GA, SQPT and hybrid approach GA-SQPT by invoking the Matlab built in functions using the parameters setting as given in Table 1 and Table 2.

The results calculated for the both neural networks models optimized with GA-SQPT for different number of neurons, i.e., k = 5, 10 and 15, are given in the Table 3 for inputs t between 0 and 1 with a step size of 0.1. The results obtained with exact solution given in Eq. (8) are also given in the table for the same inputs. It is seen that the proposed solution match with exact solution to five to seven decimal space of the accuracy. The values of absolute error (AE) are determined for each algorithm, i.e., GA, SQPT and GA-SQPT, for both models and results are shown graphically in Fig 2

Table 3
Proposed results of the problem 1 using neural networks models with different neurons optimized with GA-SQPT

X	$Y(x)$ Exact		$\tilde{y}(x)$			$\hat{y}(x)$	
		GA	*SQPT*	*GA-SQPT*	*GA*	*SQPT*	*GA-SQPT*
0.00	0	0	0	0	0	0	0
0.10	0.01	0.010005785	0.010002356	0.010024446	0.010000081	0.01000	0.010000
0.20	0.04	0.040004076	0.040002018	0.040021325	0.040000132	0.04000	0.040000
0.30	0.09	0.09000689	0.090002685	0.090020551	0.090000205	0.09000	0.089999
0.40	0.16	0.160006592	0.160002162	0.160017598	0.160000277	0.16000	0.159999
0.50	0.25	0.250003202	0.250001204	0.250015241	0.25000031	0.25000	0.249999
0.60	0.36	0.360002446	0.36000157	0.360014615	0.360000284	0.36000	0.360000
0.70	0.49	0.490005155	0.490002722	0.490013618	0.490000212	0.49000	0.490000
0.80	0.64	0.640005664	0.640002441	0.640011193	0.640000127	0.64000	0.640000
0.90	0.81	0.810002392	0.810000901	0.810008764	0.810000061	0.81000	0.810000
1.00	1	1.000003505	1.0000016	1.000007151	1	1	1

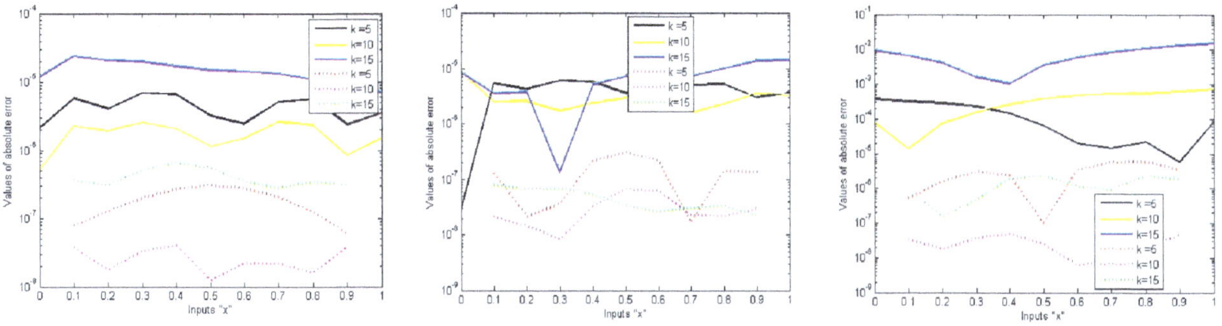

(a) (b) (c)

Fig. 2. Results based on AE for two models in case of problem I (solid and dotted lines for neural network with/without satisfying boundary condition exactly) (a) for GA (b) for SQP and (c) for GA-SQP

It is seen that the values of AE are determined for each algorithm, i.e., GA, SQPT and GA-SQPT, for both models and results are shown graphically in Fig 3. In 3(a), the values of AE for GA lies in the range 10^{-05} to 10^{-06}, 10^{-05} to 10^{-06}, and 10^{-05} to 10^{-06} for k=5, 10 and 15 respectively using first fitness function, while for fitness second function these values lies in the range 10^{-07} to 10^{-08}, 10^{06} to 10^{-07}, and 10^{-05} to 10^{-06} for k = 5, 10 and 15, respectively. Similarly it is inferred from Fig 3(b) the value of AE for SQPT lies in the range 10^{-05} to 10^{-07}, 10^{-05} to 10^{-06}, and 10^{-05} to 10^{-06} for k = 5, 10 and 15 respectively using first fitness function, while for second fitness function these values lies in the range 10^{-06} to 10^{-07} 10^{-06} to 10^{-07}, and 10^{-07} to 10^{-08} for k = 5, 10 and 15, respectively. Whereas, from Fig 3(c) the values of AE for GA-SQPT lies in the range 10^{-02} to 10^{-05}, 10^{-02} to 10^{-03}, and 10^{-03} to 10^{-05} for k = 5, 10 and 15 respectively using first fitness function, while for second fitness function these values lies in the range 10^{-06} to 10^{-08}, 10^{-05} to 10^{-07}, and 10^{-06} to 10^{-07} for k = 5, 10 and 15, respectively.

Problem II: Consider the following nonlinear multi-point boundary value problem (Das et al., 2010)

$$\begin{cases} \dfrac{d^2y}{dx^2}+xy(x)\dfrac{dy}{dx}-2y^2(x)=x^3-x^2+2 \\ y(0)=0, \quad y(1)=\displaystyle\sum_{i=0}^{4}\left(\frac{1}{1+i}\right)y\left(\frac{i}{5}\right)+0.252 \end{cases} \tag{12}$$

The exact solution of the problem is given as:

$$y(x)=x(x-1) \tag{13}$$

The proposed methodologies are applied to solve the problem by taking 10 neurons in the hidden layer of neural networks thus with a total 30 design parameter or weights, **W** (α, w, β). The fitness functions e and ε is formulated for this case for $r \in (0, 1]$ with a step size $h = 0.1$ as:

$$\begin{cases} e=\dfrac{1}{10}\displaystyle\sum_{m=1}^{10}\left(\frac{d^2\hat{y}_m}{dx^2}+x_m\hat{y}_m\frac{d\hat{y}_m}{dx}-2\hat{y}_m^2-x_m^3-x_m^2-2\right)^2 \\ \quad +\dfrac{1}{2}\left((\hat{y}_0)^2+\left(\hat{y}_{10}-\displaystyle\sum_{i=0}^{4}\left(\frac{1}{1+i}\right)y\left(\frac{i}{5}\right)+0.252\right)^2\right) \\ \varepsilon=\dfrac{1}{10}\displaystyle\sum_{m=1}^{10}\left(\frac{d^2\tilde{y}_m}{dx^2}+x_m\tilde{y}_m\frac{d\tilde{y}_m}{dx}-2\tilde{y}_m^2-x_m^3-x_m^2-2\right)^2 \end{cases} \tag{14}$$

Set of trained weights with respective fitness for GA-SQPT algorithm are shown in Fig. 3

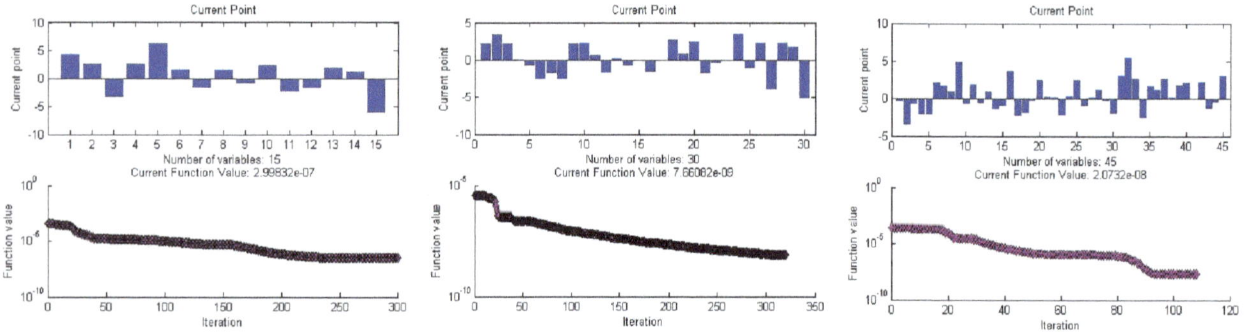

(a) (b) (c)

Fig. 3. Set of optimal weights along with parameters for problem 1 by GA-SQPT using 5, 10 and 15 numbers of neurons

The results due to GA-SQPT for the case $k = 5$ are given in simplify form as:

$$\begin{aligned} \hat{Y}_{GA-SQP}(x) = {} & \frac{2.208836555}{1+e^{(3.346487248t+2.243395633)}}+\frac{0.071721746}{1+e^{(-0.763290739t-2.46820952)}}-\frac{1.810734908}{1+e^{(-2.483154936t+2.243058379)}} \\ & -\frac{2.349373568}{1+e^{(0.636566587t-1.617782428)}}-\frac{0.209680387}{1+e^{(-0.775217641t+0.026655226)}}-\frac{1.522652644}{1+e^{(-0.111253639t+2.697695214)}} \\ & +\frac{0.789955082}{1+e^{(2.417955151t-1.836772022)}}-\frac{0.394007752}{1+e^{(-0.005227503t+3.564844228)}}-\frac{1.128676534}{1+e^{(2.389719539t-3.905731664)}} \\ & +\frac{2.34355798}{1+e^{(1.69498294t-5.121411805)}} \end{aligned} \tag{15}$$

$$\tilde{y}_{GA-SQP}(x) = x^2 - x + x(x-1)$$
$$\left[\frac{-0.216506509}{1+e^{(0.472487834t-0.246514322)}} - \frac{0.109795413}{1+e^{(0.095063987t-0.487915835)}} - \frac{0.482970033}{1+e^{(-0.305821484t+0.263233801)}} - \frac{0.018294812}{1+e^{(0.944712492t+0.484968391)}} - \frac{0.230717011}{1+e^{(0.316310172t-0.346091359)}} + \frac{0.426353657}{1+e^{(-0.201150105t+0.031234018)}} - \frac{0.427353059}{1+e^{(-0.69348194t+0.274893474)}} + \frac{0.28357977}{1+e^{(0.842677833t+0.550224316)}} - \frac{0.230940307}{1+e^{(-0.576745358t--0.000596585)}} - \frac{0.250772371}{1+e^{(0.529882133t-0.372938855)}}\right] \quad (16)$$

The results obtained for the both neural networks models of GA-SQPT for k = 5, 10 and 15, are also presented in the Table 4 along with exact solution using Eq. (13).

Table 4
Proposed results of the problem using neural networks models with different neurons optimized with GA-SQPT

X	$y(x)$ Exact	$\tilde{y}(x)$ k=5	k=10	k=15	$\hat{y}(x)$ k=5	k=10	k=15
0	0	0	0	0	0	0	0
0.1	-0.09	-0.08999763	-0.08999647	-0.08999603	-0.08999998	-0.08999988	-0.08999929
0.2	-0.16	-0.16000270	-0.15999643	-0.15999751	-0.15999990	-0.160000271	-0.15999938
0.3	-0.21	-0.20999887	-0.20999540	-0.20999636	-0.20999988	-0.210000158	-0.20999944
0.4	-0.24	-0.23999158	-0.23999535	-0.23999641	-0.23999993	-0.23999969	-0.23999948
0.5	-0.25	-0.24998915	-0.24999592	-0.24999801	-0.25000000	-0.249999367	-0.24999952
0.6	-0.24	-0.23999295	-0.23999582	-0.23999915	-0.24000004	-0.239999515	-0.23999965
0.7	-0.21	-0.20999795	-0.20999516	-0.20999915	-0.21000004	-0.210000055	-0.20999980
0.8	-0.16	-0.15999881	-0.15999515	-0.15999901	-0.16000002	-0.160000553	-0.15999985
0.9	-0.09	-0.08999632	-0.08999595	-0.08999958	-0.08999999	-0.090000531	-0.0899998
1	0	0	0	0	0	0	0

The values of absolute error AE are determined for each algorithm, i.e., GA, SQPT and GA-SQPT for both models and results are shown graphically in Fig 4.

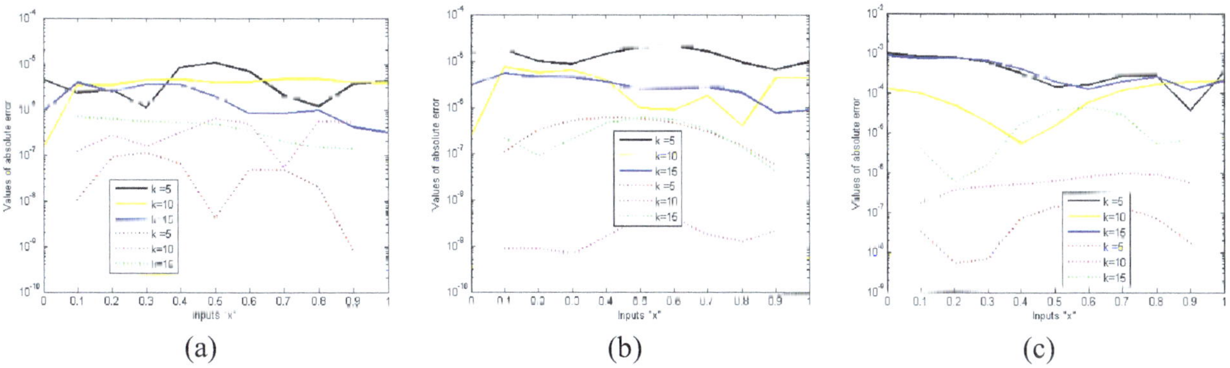

Fig. 4. Results based on AE for two models in case of problem II (solid and dotted lines for neural network with/without satisfying boundary condition exactly) (a) for GA (b) for SQPT and (c) for GA-SQPT

Problem III: Consider the following nonlinear multi-point boundary value problem (Das et al., 2010)

$$\begin{cases} \dfrac{d^2y}{dx^2} + y(x)\dfrac{dy}{dx} = (\cos x - 1)\sin x \\ y(0) = 0, \quad y(1) = \sum_{i=0}^{4}\left(\dfrac{1}{1+i}\right)y\left(\dfrac{i}{5}\right) + 0.3277 \end{cases} \tag{17}$$

The exact solution of the problem is given as:

$$y(x) = \sin x \tag{18}$$

The proposed methodologies are applied to solve the problem by taking 10 neurons in the hidden layer of neural networks thus with a total 30 design parameter or weights, $\mathbf{W}\ (\alpha, w, \beta)$. The fitness functions e and ε is formulated for this case for $r \in (0, 1]$ with a step size $h = 0.1$ as:

$$\begin{cases} e = \dfrac{1}{10}\sum_{m=1}^{10}\left(\dfrac{d^2\hat{y}_m}{dx^2} + \hat{y}_m\dfrac{d\hat{y}_m}{dx} - (\cos x_m - 1)\sin x_m\right)^2 \\ \quad + \dfrac{1}{2}\left((\hat{y}_0)^2 + \left(\hat{y}_{10} - \sum_{i=0}^{4}\left(\dfrac{1}{1+i}\right)y\left(\dfrac{i}{5}\right) + 0.3277\right)^2\right) \\ \varepsilon = \dfrac{1}{10}\sum_{m=1}^{10}\left(\dfrac{d^2\tilde{y}_m}{dx^2} + \tilde{y}_m\dfrac{d\tilde{y}_m}{dx} - (\cos x_m - 1)\sin x_m\right)^2 \end{cases} \tag{19}$$

The proposed solution $\hat{y}(x)$ and $\tilde{y}(x)$ of the Eq. (17) is obtained using the optimal weights of algorithms in first equation of the set (2) and (5), respectively. The results due to GA-SQP for the case $k = 15$ are given in simplify form as:

$$\begin{aligned} \hat{Y}_{GA-AST}(x) = {} & \frac{-0.081445879}{1+\mathrm{e}^{(-2.768026281t-0.07889657)}} + \frac{1.033908368}{1+\mathrm{e}^{(1.577421678t+0.764886671)}} + \frac{1.99603985}{1+\mathrm{e}^{(-2.261775246t+1.861122461)}} - \frac{1.159325859}{1+\mathrm{e}^{(-0.069874053t-1.296706406)}} \\ & - \frac{0.298371076}{1+\mathrm{e}^{(-0.764074296t-0.48929052)}} - \frac{2.389750629}{1+\mathrm{e}^{(1.329328249t-1.775691856)}} - \frac{0.408425054}{1+\mathrm{e}^{(-0.452390437t-0.437945435)}} + \frac{1.081451478}{1+\mathrm{e}^{(-0.69183918t-0.116530885)}} \\ & - \frac{1.118420805}{1+\mathrm{e}^{(-0.337217405t-1.205051142)}} + \frac{0.4761533}{1+\mathrm{e}^{(0.335142006t+0.432716274)}} - \frac{0.899806552}{1+\mathrm{e}^{(-3.539588497t-0.950303091)}} + \frac{0.418222187}{1+\mathrm{e}^{(0.200102379t-0.184532206)}} \\ & - \frac{0.262434241}{1+\mathrm{e}^{(0.608412449t+0.339126605)}} + \frac{0.337546906}{1+\mathrm{e}^{(-2.253966554t-0.045011958)}} + \frac{0.18163671}{1+\mathrm{e}^{(0.432918626t+0.136772046)}} \end{aligned} \tag{20}$$

$$\begin{aligned} \tilde{y}_{GA-SQP}(x) = x^2 - 0.158527384x + x(x-1) = [& \frac{0.564010455}{1+\mathrm{e}^{(0.758597564t-0.91034693)}} + \frac{0.534950738}{1+\mathrm{e}^{(-0.324178311t-0.361743894)}} \\ & - \frac{0.332320715}{1+\mathrm{e}^{(-0.257771472t-0.794779984)}} + \frac{0.392079392}{1+\mathrm{e}^{(0.011730424t-0.310811717)}} + \frac{0.126893795}{1+\mathrm{e}^{(0.021418674t-0.927117635)}} - \frac{0.666059302}{1+\mathrm{e}^{(-0.219926712t0.695773998)}} \\ & - \frac{0.438332404}{1+\mathrm{e}^{(-0.321418936t+0.273684792)}} - \frac{0.337776689}{1+\mathrm{e}^{(-0.278016426t-0.166833512)}} - \frac{0.246601324}{1+\mathrm{e}^{(-0.075388873t-0.250126438)}} + \frac{0.350453409}{1+\mathrm{e}^{-(1.171431708t-0.507170459)}} \\ & - \frac{0.128862184}{1+\mathrm{e}^{(-0.406160924t-0.195300395)}} - \frac{0.265027029}{1+\mathrm{e}^{(0.47739276t+0.196942455)}} + \frac{0.596502792}{1+\mathrm{e}^{(0.226194573t-0.353944167)}} + \frac{0.453471338}{1+\mathrm{e}^{(0.527981159t+0.856344939)}} \\ & + \frac{0.773546968}{1+\mathrm{e}^{(1.62352718t+0.590627788)}}] \end{aligned} \tag{21}$$

The results obtained for the both neural networks models of GA-SQPT for $k = 5$, 10 and 15, are also presented in the Table 4 along with exact solution using Eq. (18). The proposed solution approximately matches with exact solution up to four to six decimal places of the accuracy.

Table 4
Proposed results of the problem using neural networks models with different neurons optimized with GA-SQPT

X	$y(x)$	$\tilde{y}(x)$			$\hat{y}(x)$		
	Exact	$k=5$	$k=10$	$k=15$	$k=5$	$k=10$	$k=15$
0	0	0	0	0	0	0	0
0.1	0.099833	0.099827	0.099832	0.099834	0.099832	0.099834	0.099835
0.2	0.198669	0.198665	0.198668	0.19867	0.198669	0.198669	0.198671
0.3	0.29552	0.295515	0.295519	0.295521	0.29552	0.295521	0.295522
0.4	0.389418	0.389416	0.389417	0.389419	0.389418	0.38942	0.389421
0.5	0.479426	0.479425	0.479425	0.479426	0.479426	0.479428	0.479429
0.6	0.564642	0.564642	0.564642	0.564644	0.564644	0.564645	0.564646
0.7	0.644218	0.644216	0.644217	0.644219	0.644219	0.64422	0.64422
0.8	0.717356	0.717356	0.717356	0.717358	0.717357	0.717357	0.717358
0.9	0.783327	0.78333	0.783327	0.783329	0.783328	0.783328	0.783328
1	0.841471	0.841473	0.841472	0.841473	0.841473	0.841473	0.841473

The values of absolute error AE are determined for each algorithm, i.e., GA, SQP and GA-SQP for both models and results are shown graphically in Fig 5 as follows,

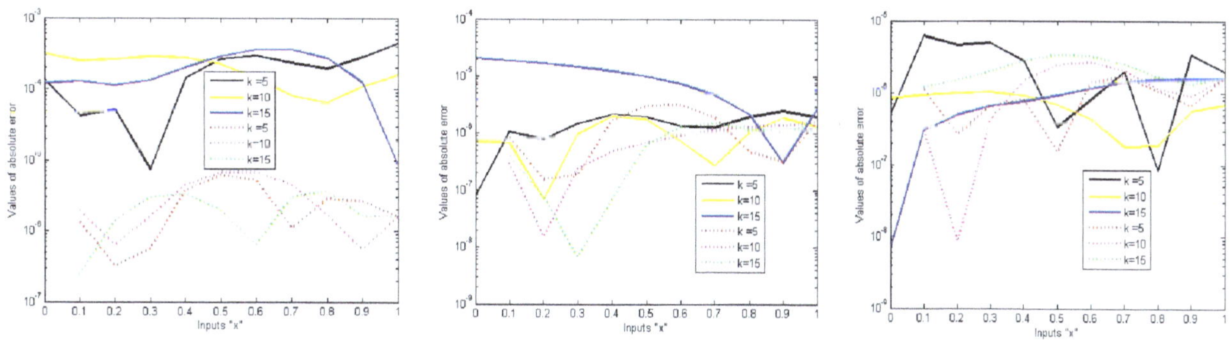

(a) (b) (c)

Fig. 5. Results based on AE for two models in case of problem III (solid and dotted lines for neural network with/without satisfying boundary condition exactly) (a) for GA (b) for SQPT and (c) for GA-SQPT

4. Conclusions

Following conclusions are drawn for our research studies:

- A new soft computing approach has been developed effectively for solving multi-point boundary value problems, in-particularly multi-point BVPs and its variants using neural networks optimized with genetic algorithm, sequential quadratic programming technique and their hybrid combination.
- The sufficient low value of absolute error has established the correctness of the designed scheme.
- By taking fewer number of neurons, the performance of method were efficient for finding the solution, however, it increased the number of neurons, one can get slightly more accurate solution with immense reliability but at the cost of more computations.

Future research directions

Following are few suggested research directions for interested readers:

- One can look for more accurate neural networks modeling by using alternate activation functions like radial basis, Mexican Hat, wavelets hat, etc.
- Change of optimization algorithm can also help us improve the accuracy and the convergence of results. In this regards, particle swarm optimization, differential evolution, genetic programming, hill climbing etc., are possible choices.

- Better hardware platform like parallel, grid and cloud computing, can help in decreasing computational time of the algorithm, considerably. Consequently, we may look for other complicated nonlinear problems to solve by our design scheme.

Acknowledgement

Authors like to thank the anonymous referees for constructive comments on this paper.

References

Cannon, J. R. (1984). The one-dimensional heat equation, volume 23 of Encyclopedia of Mathematics and its Applications.

Cannon, J. R., Esteva, S. P., & Van Der Hoek, J. (1987). A Galerkin procedure for the diffusion equation subject to the specification of mass. *SIAM Journal on Numerical Analysis*, *24*(3), 499-515.

Deimling, K. (1985). Nonlinear Functional Analysis. *Springler-Verlag, Berlin*.

Das, S., Kumar, S., & Singh, O. P. (2010). Solutions of Nonlinear Second Order Multi-point Boundary Value Problems by Homotopy Perturbation Method. *Applied Mathematics: An International Journal*, *5*(10), 1592-1600.

Erbe, L. H., & Wang, H. (1994). On the existence of positive solutions of ordinary differential equations. *Proceedings of the American Mathematical Society*, *120*(3), 743-748.

Gupta, C. P. (1992). Solvability of a three-point nonlinear boundary value problem for a second order ordinary differential equation. *Journal of Mathematical Analysis and Applications*, *168*(2), 540-551.

Gupta, C. P. (1994). A note on a second order three-point boundary value problem. *Journal of Mathematical Analysis and Applications*, *186*(1), 277-281.

Gupta, C. P., & Trofimchuk, S. I. (1997). A sharper condition for the solvability of a three-point second order boundary value problem. *Journal of Mathematical Analysis and Applications*, *205*(2), 586-597.

Guo, D., & Lakshmikantham, V. (1988). *Nonlinear Problems in Abstract Cones* (Vol. 5). San Diego: Academic press.

Eloe, P. W., & Henderson, J. (1994). Multipoint boundary value problems for ordinary differential systems. *Journal of Differential Equations*, *114*(1), 232-242.

Ilin, V. A., & Moiseev, E. I. (1987). Nonlocal boundary-value problem of the first kind for a Sturm-Liouville operator in its differential and finite difference aspects. *Differential Equations*, *23*(7), 803-810.

Khan, J. A., Zahoor, R. M. A., & Qureshi, I. M. (2009, December). Swarm intelligence for the solution of problems in differential equations. In *Environmental and Computer Science, 2009. ICECS'09. Second International Conference on* (pp. 141-147). IEEE.

Khan, A., Raja, M. A. Z., & Ijaz Mansoor Qureshi, J. (2012). An application of evolutionary computational technique to non-linear singular system arising in polytrophic and isothermal sphere. *Global Journal of Researches In Engineering*, *12*(1-I).

Krasnosel'skij, M. A. (1964). *Positive solutions of operator equations* (p. 381). L. F. Boron (Ed.). Groningen: P. Noordhoff.

Liu, B. (2002). Positive solutions of a nonlinear three-point boundary value problem. *Computers & Mathematics with Applications*, *44*(1), 201-211.

Ma, R. (1999). Positive solutions of a nonlinear three-point boundary-value problem. *Electronic Journal of Differential Equations*, *1999*(34), 1-8.

Ma, R. (2001). Positive solutions for second-order three-point boundary value problems. *Applied Mathematics Letters*, *14*(1), 1-5.

Raja, M. A. Z., & Samar, R. (2012). Neural network optimized with evolutionary computing technique for solving the 2-dimensional Bratu problem. *Neural Computing and Applications*, 1-12.

Timoshenko, S. P., & Gere, J. M. (1961). Theory of elastic stability. 1961.

Webb, J. R. L. (2001). Positive solutions of some three point boundary value problems via fixed point index theory. *Nonlinear Analysis: Theory, Methods & Applications*, *47*(7), 4319-4332.

Modified generalized linear failure rate distribution: Properties and reliability analysis

Ezzatallah Baloui Jamkhaneh*

Department of Statistics, Qaemshahr Branch, Islamic Azad University, Qaemshahr, Iran

CHRONICLE

Keywords:
Fuzzy reliability
Fuzzy MGLFR distribution
Hazard function

ABSTRACT

This paper introduces a new comprehensive four-parameter distribution called the modified generalized linear failure rate (MGLFR) distribution. The method generalizes some well-known and most commonly used distributions in reliability such as exponential, Rayleigh, linear failure rate, generalized linear failure rate and modified Weibull distribution. The study also investigates some essential properties of this new distribution and considers the problem of the evaluation of system reliability by describing the lifetimes of components based on a fuzzy MGLFR distribution and by developing fuzzy reliability characteristics. The results can be applied to determine the reliability of real objects where parameters of lifetime variable are subject to uncertainty.

1. Introduction

There are literally numerous distributions for modeling lifetime data such as exponential, Weibull, Rayleigh, linear failure rate or generalized exponential distributions. Reliability has always been a key role in designing engineering systems. The most frequently used functions in lifetime data analysis and reliability engineering are the reliability function (survival function), and hazard function. Survival function gives the probability of an item operating for a certain amount of time without failure. Exponential distribution maintains only constant hazard function whereas Rayleigh, linear failure rate and generalized exponential distribution may have only monotone hazard functions. The Weibull distribution function was introduced by Fisher and Tippett in 1928. The Swedish physicist Wallodi Weibull (1939) used this probability distribution for describing the lifetime of components with variable failure rate. Burr (1942) introduced twelve different forms of cumulative distribution functions for modeling lifetime data. Among those distributions, Burr Type X and Burr Type XII are the most popular ones.

* Corresponding author.

Surles and Padgett (2001) introduced two-parameter Burr Type X distribution and correctly named as the generalized Rayleigh (GR) distribution. They showed that the GR distribution could be used quite effectively in modeling strength data and in modeling general lifetime data. Mudholkar and Srivastava (1993) introduced the exponential Weibull family, which contains important physical interpretation. Gupta and Kundu (1999a) introduced generalized exponential distribution (GED). The two-parameter GED can have non-increasing and non-decreasing failure rates depending on the shape parameter. Sarhan and Zaindin (2009) introduced a new three-parameter distribution called the Modified Weibull distribution (MWD). This distribution generalizes the well-known (1) exponential distribution, (2) linear failure rate distribution, (3) generalized exponential distribution, and (4) generalized Rayleigh distribution. The MWD can be used to describe several reliability models. Sarhan and Kundu (2009) introduced generalized linear failure rate distribution. It can have increasing, decreasing and bathtub shaped hazard functions.

There are several methods and models in classical reliability theory, which assume that all parameters of lifetime density functions are precise. However, in the real world applications, randomness and fuzziness are often mixed up in the lifetimes of systems. However, the parameters sometimes cannot record precisely due to machine errors, experiment, personal judgment, estimation or some other unexpected situations. When parameter in the lifetime distribution is fuzzy, the conventional reliability system may have difficulty for handling reliability and hazard functions. The theory of fuzzy reliability was proposed and development by several authors (Cai et al., 1991, 1993; Cai, 1996; Chen & Mon, 1993; Hammer, 2001; Onisawa & Kacprzyk, 1995; Utkin & Gurov, 1995).

Aliev and Kara (2004) considered fuzzy system reliability analysis using time dependent fuzzy set and the concept of alpha-cut. Utkin (1994) discussed imprecise reliability models for the general lifetime distribution classes. He applied the theory of imprecise probability to reliability analysis. Wu (2006) considered fuzzy Bayesian system reliability assessment based on exponential distribution. Guo et al. (2007) proposed a credibility hazard concept associated with fuzzy lifetimes. Guo et al. (2007) considered random fuzzy variable modeling on repairable system. Yao et al. (2008) applied a statistical methodology in fuzzy system reliability analysis and provided a fuzzy estimation of reliability. Karpisek et al. (2010) described two fuzzy reliability models based on the Weibull fuzzy distribution. Baloui Jamkhaneh and Nozari (2012) investigated fuzzy system reliability analysis based on confidence interval. Garg et al. (2013) considered reliability analysis of the engineering systems using intuitionistic fuzzy set theory. Pak et al. (2013) presented a Bayesian approach to estimate the parameter and reliability function of Rayleigh distribution from fuzzy lifetime data. Baloui Jamkhaneh (2011, 2014) evaluated reliability function using fuzzy lifetime distribution.

The aim of this paper is to introduce the modified generalizes linear failure rate distribution (MGLFRD). We consider the problem of the evaluation of system reliability, in which the lifetimes of components are described using MGLFR distribution with fuzzy parameter.

2. Modified generalized linear failure rate distribution

In this section, we introduce a new four-parameter distribution function called as modified generalized linear failure rate distribution with four parameters a,b,c,θ denoted as MGLFRD(a,b,c,θ). Lifetime random variable of X with MGLFR distribution has probability density function as follows

$$f(x,a,b,c,\theta)=\theta(a+bcx^{c-1})[1-\exp(-(ax+bx^{c}))]^{\theta-1}\exp(-(ax+bx^{c})), \quad x>0,a\geq 0,b\geq 0,c\geq 0,\theta>0 \tag{1}$$

and its distribution function is as follows,

$$F(t,a,b,c,\theta)=[1-\exp(-(at+bt^{c}))]^{\theta},\quad t>0,\ a\geq 0,b\geq 0,c\geq 0,\theta>0. \tag{2}$$

It is immediate that from MGLFRD(a,b,c,θ), the following special cases can be derived:

a) Linear failure distribution $LFRD(a,b)$, when $\theta=1, c=2$

$$f(x)=(a+2bx)\exp(-(ax+bx^2)) \ , x>0, a\geq 0, b\geq 0 . \tag{3}$$

b) Generalized exponential distribution $GE(a,\theta)$, when $b=0$,

$$f(x)=\theta a[1-\exp(-(ax))]^{\theta-1}\exp(-(ax)) \ , x>0, a\geq 0, c\geq 0, \theta>0. \tag{4}$$

c) Generalized Rayleigh distribution $GRD(b,\theta)$, when $a=0, c=2$.

$$f(x)=2\theta bx[1-\exp(-(bx^2))]^{\theta-1}\exp(-(bx^2)) \ , x>0, b\geq 0, \theta>0 . \tag{5}$$

d) Exponential Weibull distribution $EW(b,c,\theta)$, when $a=0$,

$$f(x)=\theta bcx^{c-1}[1-\exp(-bx^c)]^{\theta-1}\exp(-bx^c) \ , x>0, ,b\geq 0, c\geq 0, \theta>0. \tag{6}$$

e) Weibull distribution $W(b,c)$, when $a=0, \theta=1$.

$$f(x)=bcx^{c-1}\exp(-bx^c) \ , x>0, ,b>0, c>0 \tag{7}$$

f) Exponential distribution $E(a)$, when $\theta=1, b=0$,

$$f(x)=a\exp(-ax) \ , x>0, a>0 \tag{8}$$

g) Generalized Linear Failure Rate Distribution $GLFRD(a,b,\theta)$, when $c=2$,

$$f(x)=\theta(a+2bx)[1-\exp(-(ax+bx^2))]^{\theta-1}\exp(-(ax+bx^2)) \ , x>0, a\geq 0, b\geq 0, \theta>0. \tag{9}$$

h) Modified Weibull Distribution MWD(a,b,c), when $\theta=1$,

$$f(x)=(a+bcx^{c-1})\exp(-(ax+bx^c)) \ , x>0, a\geq 0, b\geq 0, c\geq 0. \tag{10}$$

3. Statistical properties of MGLFRD

3.1 The quantile q^{th} (x_q)

The quantile q^{th} of the $MGLFRD(a,b,c,\theta)$ is given by

$$q=\int_0^{x_q} f(x,a,b,c,\theta)dx=F(x_q,a,b,c,\theta) \tag{11}$$

So, the x_q of $MGLFRD(a,b,\theta)$ can be obtained with equation as follows,

$$bx_q^c+ax_q+Ln(1-q^{\frac{1}{\theta}})=0. \tag{12}$$

i) if $c = 1$, then $x_q = \frac{-Ln(1-q^{\frac{1}{\theta}})}{a+b}$

ii) if $c = 2$, then $x_q = \frac{-a+\sqrt{a^2 - 4bLn(1-q^{\frac{1}{\theta}})}}{2b}$

iii) if $q = 0.5$ in i and ii, then we will gain distribution median.

3.2 Moments

The following Lemma gives the kth moment of $MGLFRD(a,b,c,\theta)$, when $\theta \geq 1$.

Lemma 1: If X has $MGLFRD(a,b,c,\theta)$, then the kth moment of X ($\mu^{(k)}$), is given as follows:

for $a = 0, b > 0$:

$$\mu^{(k)} = \frac{\theta \Gamma(\frac{k}{c}+1)}{b^{\frac{k}{c}}} \sum_{i=0}^{\infty} \frac{\binom{\theta-1}{i}(-1)^i}{(i+1)^{\frac{k}{c}+1}} \quad (13)$$

for $a > 0, b \geq 0$:

$$\mu^{(k)} = \sum_{i=0}^{\infty}\sum_{j=0}^{\infty} \theta \binom{\theta-1}{i} (-1)^i \frac{w_i^{(j)}(0)}{j!} [\frac{a\Gamma(k+j+1)}{[a(i+1)]^{k+j+1}} + \frac{bc\Gamma(k+j+c)}{[a(i+1)]^{k+j+c}}] \quad (14)$$

Proof: under definition of kth moment, we will have

$$\mu^{(k)} = \int_0^{\infty} x^k f(x, a, b, c, \theta) dx, \quad (15)$$

then

$$\mu^{(k)} = \int_0^{\infty} x^k \theta (a + bcx^{c-1})[1-\exp(-(ax+bx^c))]^{\theta-1} \exp(-(ax+bx^c))dx, \quad (16)$$

since $0 < \exp(-(ax+bx^c) < 1$, $x > 0$, by using the binomial series expansion we have

$$[1-\exp(-(ax+bx^c))]^{\theta-1} = \sum_{i=0}^{\infty} \binom{\theta-1}{i} (-1)^i \exp(-i(ax+bx^c)) \quad (17)$$

then

$$\mu^{(k)} = \theta \int_0^{\infty} x^k (a+bcx^{c-1}) \sum_{i=0}^{\infty} \binom{\theta-1}{i} (-1)^i \exp(-(i+1)(ax+bx^c))dx \quad (18)$$

Since the inner quantity of the summation is computable, interchanging the integration and summation yields,

$$\mu^{(k)} = \sum_{i=0}^{\infty} \binom{\theta-1}{i} (-1)^i \theta \int_0^{\infty} x^k (a + bcx^{c-1}) \exp(-(i+1)(ax+bx^c)) dx \tag{19}$$

i) if $a=0, b>0$ then

$$\int_0^{\infty} x^k (a+bcx^{c-1}) \exp(-(i+1)(ax+bx^c))dx = \int_0^{\infty} bcx^{k+c-1} \exp(-(i+1)bx^c)dx = \frac{b\Gamma(\frac{k}{c}+1)}{((i+1)b)^{\frac{k}{c}+1}} \tag{20}$$

then

$$\mu^{(k)} = \frac{\theta\Gamma(\frac{k}{c}+1)}{b^{\frac{k}{c}}} \sum_{i=0}^{\infty} \frac{\binom{\theta-1}{i}(-1)^i}{(i+1)^{\frac{k}{c}+1}} \tag{21}$$

ii) if $a>0, b\geq 0$, using the Taylor expansion of the function $\exp(-(i+1)bx^c)$ given by

$$\exp(-(i+1)bx^c) = \sum_{j=0}^{\infty} \frac{w_i^{(j)}(0)}{j!} x^j \ , \ w_i^{(j)}(0) = \frac{d^j}{dx^j} \exp(-(i+1)bx^c)\Big|_{x=0} \tag{22}$$

so

$$\begin{aligned} \mu^{(k)} &= \sum_{i=0}^{\infty}\sum_{j=0}^{\infty} \theta \binom{\theta-1}{i} (-1)^i \frac{w_i^{(j)}(0)}{j!} \int_0^{\infty} x^{k+j}(a+bcx^{c-1})\exp(-(i+1)ax)dx \\ &= \sum_{i=0}^{\infty}\sum_{j=0}^{\infty} \theta \binom{\theta-1}{i} (-1)^i \frac{w_i^{(j)}(0)}{j!} [\frac{a\Gamma(k+j+1)}{[a(i+1)]^{k+j+1}} + \frac{bc\Gamma(k+j+c)}{[a(i+1)]^{k+j+c}}]. \end{aligned} \tag{23}$$

3.3 Distribution of order statistics

Let $X_1, X_2, ..., X_n$ be a random sample from $MGLFRD(a,b,c,\theta)$. Let $Y_1 \leq Y_2 \leq ... \leq Y_n$ denote the order statistics obtained from this sample. Then PDF of Y_i is given by,

$$\begin{aligned} g_i(y) &= \frac{n!}{(i-1)!(n-i)!} f(y,a,b,c,\theta)F(y,a,b,c,\theta)^{i-1}(1-F(y,a,b,c,\theta))^{n-i} \\ &= \frac{n!}{(i-1)!(n-i)!} f(y,a,b,c,\theta)\sum_{j=0}^{n-i}\binom{n-i}{j}(-1)^j F(y,a,b,c,\theta))^{j+i-1} \\ &= \sum_{j=0}^{n-i}\frac{n!}{(i-1)!(n-i)!} \times \binom{n-i}{j}(-1)^j \times \frac{f(y,a,b,c,\theta(i+j))}{i+j} = \sum_{j=0}^{n-i} k_j(n,i) f(y,a,b,c,\theta_{i+j})) \end{aligned} \tag{24}$$

where

$$k_j(n,i) = \frac{n(-1)^j \binom{n-1}{i-1}\binom{n-i}{j}}{i+j} \ , \ \theta_r = r\theta \tag{25}$$

Lemma 2: If $X_1, X_2, ..., X_n$ be a random sample from $MGLFRD(a,b,c,\theta)$. Then Y_n follows $MGLFRD(a,b,c,n\theta)$.

Remark: Consider a parallel system of k identical and independent components, when each component has follows $MWD(a,b,c)$. In this case, the distribution function of a parallel system is as $MGLFRD(a,b,c,k)$.

Lemma 3: Let Y_i denote the ith order statistics, then the kth moment of Y_i ($\mu^{(k)}$), is given as follows:

for $a=0, b>0$:

$$\mu^{(k)} = \frac{\Gamma(\frac{k}{c}+1)}{b^{\frac{k}{c}}} \sum_{j=0}^{n-i} \sum_{m=0}^{\infty} k_j(n,i) \frac{\binom{\theta_{i+j}-1}{m}(-1)^m \theta_{i+j}}{(m+1)^{\frac{k}{c}+1}} \tag{26}$$

for $a>0, b\geq 0$:

$$\mu^{(k)} = \sum_{m=0}^{\infty} \sum_{l=0}^{\infty} \sum_{j=0}^{n-i} \theta_{i+j} k_j(n,i) \binom{\theta_{i+j}-1}{m} (-1)^m \frac{w_m^{(l)}(0)}{l!} \left[\frac{a\Gamma(k+l+1)}{[a(m+1)]^{k+l+1}} + \frac{bc\Gamma(k+l+c)}{[a(m+1)]^{k+l+c}}\right] \tag{27}$$

3.4 Stress-strength parameter

Suppose that X and Y are two independent MGLFR RVs with respective parameters (a,b,c,θ_1) and (a,b,c,θ_2) having PDFs $f_X(.)$ and $f_Y(.)$, respectively. Let X be the strength of a system, which is subjected to stress Y; therefore the stress-strength measures the system performance. Then stress-strength parameter, i.e. $R=P(Y<X)$, is as follows,

$$R = P(Y<X) = \int_0^{\infty} P(Y<X \mid Y=y) f_Y(y) dy = \int_0^{\infty} (1-F_X(y,a,b,c,\theta_1)) f_Y(y,a,b,c,\theta_2) dy = \frac{\theta_1}{\theta_1+\theta_2} \tag{28}$$

3.5 Reliability function

If X has $MGLFRD(a,b,c,\theta)$, then the reliability function at time t is given as follows:

$$S(t,a,b,c,\theta) = 1-[1-\exp(-(at+bt^c))]^{\theta}, \quad t>0, a\geq 0, c>0, b\geq 0, \theta>0. \tag{29}$$

This shows that increasing θ results upper reliability. If $\theta=1$ then $S(t)=\exp(-(at+bt^c))$, the higher values of a and b result less reliability.

3.6 Hazard function

If X has $MGLFRD(a,b,c,\theta)$, then the hazard function at time t, is given as follows:

$$h(t) = \frac{f(t)}{S(t)} = \frac{\theta(a+bct^{c-1})[1-\exp(-(at+bt^c))]^{\theta-1}\exp(-(at+bt^c))}{1-[1-\exp(-(at+bt^c))]^{\theta}}, \tag{30}$$

if $\theta=1$ then $h(t)=a+bct^{c-1}$. In addition, if $c=1$, then the hazard function is a constant function, if $c=2$, then the hazard function is an ascending line, If $c=3$, then the hazard function is ascending curve. The reversed hazard function of $MGLFRD(a,b,c,\theta)$ is:

$$r(t,a,b,c,\theta)=\frac{f(t,a,b,c,\theta)}{F(t,a,b,c,\theta)}=\frac{\theta(a+bct^{c-1})[1-\exp(-(at+bt^c))]^{\theta-1}\exp(-(at+bt^c))}{[1-\exp(-(at+bt^c))]^{\theta}}$$
$$=\frac{\theta(a+bct^{c-1})\exp(-(at+bt^c))}{[1-\exp(-(at+bt^c))]}=\theta\frac{f(t,a,b,c,1)}{F(t,a,b,c,1)}=\theta r(t,a,b,c,1) \quad (31)$$

4. Fuzzy reliability function

Sometimes we are faced with situations that the parameters of lifetime variable cannot be expressed as crisp values. They can be stated as "approximately", "around", "between", or "about". Fuzzy sets theory is a useful tool for conveying these expressions into mathematical functions. In this case, reliability theory should be considered with respect to fuzzy rules. Buckley (2006) analyzed probability density functions when their parameters are fuzzy. We may consider the MGLFR distribution with fuzzy parameters and trapezoidal fuzzy number of $\tilde{a}$ that is replaced instead of a in MGLFR distribution. In this case, we show the fuzzy probability of obtaining a value in the interval $[c^*,d^*]$, $c^*\geq 0$ is as $\tilde{P}(c^*\leq X\leq d^*)$ and compute its $\alpha-$cut as follows: (For more details, refer to Buckley, 2006)

$$\tilde{P}(c^*\leq X\leq d^*)[\alpha]=\{\int_{c^*}^{d^*} f(x,a,b,c,\theta)dx \mid a\in\tilde{a}[\alpha]\}=[P^L[\alpha],P^U[\alpha]] , \quad (32)$$

where

$$P^L[\alpha]=\min\{\int_{c^*}^{d^*} f(x,a,b,c,\theta)dx \mid a\in\tilde{a}[\alpha]\}, P^U[\alpha]=\max\{\int_{c^*}^{d^*} f(x,a,b,c,\theta)dx \mid a\in\tilde{a}[\alpha]\} . \quad (33)$$

We represent parameter $\tilde{a}$ with a trapezoidal fuzzy number as $\tilde{a}=(a_1,a_2,a_3,a_4)$ such that we can describe a membership function $\xi_{\tilde{a}}(x)$ in the following manner:

$$\xi_{\tilde{a}}(x)=\begin{cases}\dfrac{x-a_1}{a_2-a_1} , & a_1\leq x<a_2\\ 1 , & a_2\leq x\leq a_3\\ \dfrac{a_4-x}{a_4-a_3} , & a_3<x\leq a_4\\ 0 , & \text{not}\end{cases} \quad (34)$$

The $\alpha-$cut $\tilde{a}$ denote as $\tilde{a}[\alpha]=[a_1+(a_2-a_1)\alpha,a_4-(a_4-a_3)\alpha]$

Fuzzy reliability (or fuzzy survival) function ($\tilde{S}(t)$) is the fuzzy probability a unit survives beyond time t. Let the random variable X denote lifetime of a system component, also let X follow fuzzy density function $f(x,\tilde{\theta})$ and fuzzy cumulative distribution function $\tilde{F}_X(t)=\tilde{P}(X<t)$ where parameter $\tilde{\theta}$ is a fuzzy number, in these conditions the fuzzy reliability function at time t is defined as (See Baloui Jamkhaneh, 2014):

$$\tilde{S}(t)[\alpha]=\tilde{P}(X>t)[\alpha]=\{\int_t^{\infty} f(x,\theta)dx \mid \theta\in\tilde{\theta}[\alpha]\}=[S^L(t)[\alpha],S^U(t)[\alpha]] , \quad t>0, \quad (35)$$

where

$$S^L(t)[\alpha]=\min\{\int_t^{\infty} f(x,\theta)dx \mid \theta\in\tilde{\theta}[\alpha]\} \quad \text{and} \quad S^U(t)[\alpha]=\max\{\int_t^{\infty} f(x,\theta)dx \mid \theta\in\tilde{\theta}[\alpha]\} . \quad (36)$$

Therefore, fuzzy reliability function based on fuzzy MGLFRD distribution is as follows:

$$\tilde{S}(t,b,c,\theta)[\alpha]=\{\int_{t}^{\infty}\theta(a+bcx^{c-1})[1-\exp(-(ax+bx^{c}))]^{\theta-1}\exp(-(ax+bx^{c}))dx \,\big|\, a\in\tilde{a}[\alpha]\}, \tag{37}$$

$$\tilde{S}(t,b,c,\theta)[\alpha]=\{1-[1-\exp(-(at+bt^{c}))]^{\theta} \,\big|\, a\in\tilde{a}[\alpha]\},\quad t>0,c>0,b\geq 0,\theta>0. \tag{38}$$

According to the function of $1-[1-\exp(-(at+bt^{c}))]^{\theta}$ that is decreasing in terms of a, we have:

$$\tilde{S}(t,b,c,\theta)[\alpha]=[1-[1-\exp(-((a_4-(a_4-a_3)\alpha)t+bt^{c}))]^{\theta},1-[1-\exp(-((a_1+(a_2-a_1)\alpha)t+bt^{c}))]^{\theta} \tag{39}$$

Upper and lower bound of $\tilde{S}(t,b,c,\theta)[\alpha]$ are two dimensional functions in terms of α and t ($0\leq\alpha\leq 1$ and $t>0$). For any particular value of t_0, $\tilde{S}(t_0,b,c,\theta)[\alpha]$ is a fuzzy number. Finally, $\tilde{S}(t_0,b,c,\theta)[\alpha_0]=[S^{L}(t_0)[\alpha_0],S^{U}(t_0)[\alpha_0]]$ is α_0-cut of fuzzy reliability of a unit. In this method, for any particular level of α_0, upper and lower bound of $\tilde{S}(t,b,c,\theta)[\alpha_0]$ are two functions in terms of t. So, in this case reliability curve is like a band with upper and lower bound whose width depends on the ambiguity parameter (See Baloui Jamkhaneh, 2011). Fig. 1 shows $\alpha-$cut of fuzzy reliability with $\alpha=$ 0 and 1. Fig. 2 shows that by increasing of the value of c, when t is small, we may find higher reliability band and for large value of t, we may find lower reliability band.

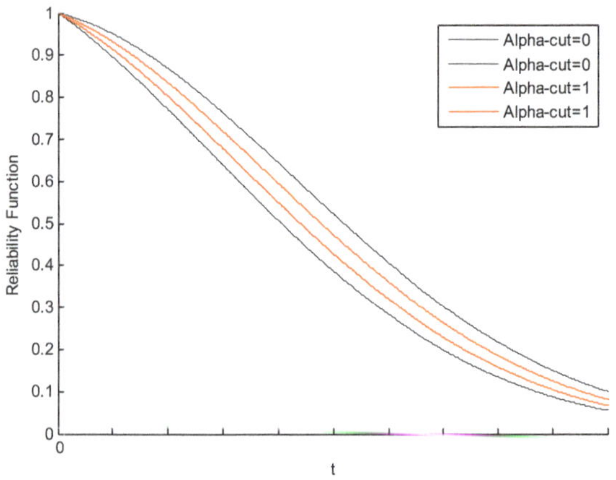

Fig. 1. $\alpha-$cut of fuzzy reliability for different t

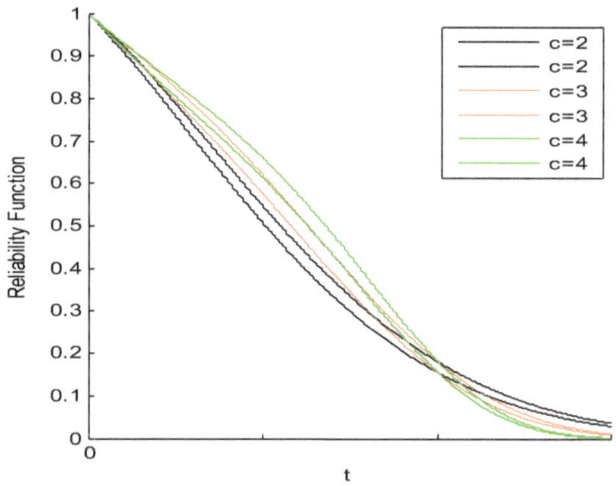

Fig. 2. $\alpha-$cut of fuzzy reliability for different c

Fig. 3 shows the behavior of reliability band $\tilde{S}(t)[0]$ with $c=b=2$ under various conditions. This figure shows that decreasing θ results lower reliability band, which means the reliability will be lower under these conditions.

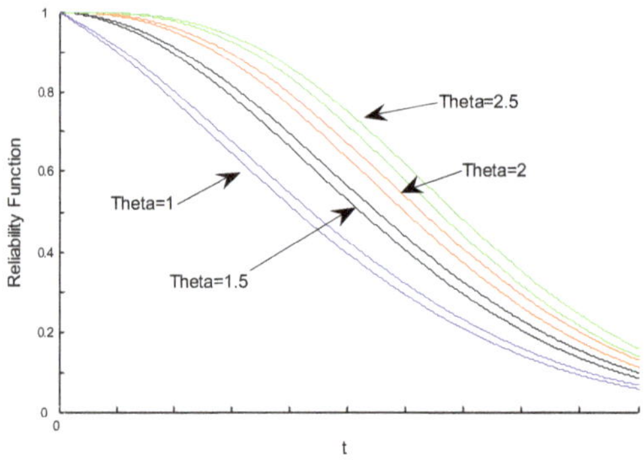

Fig. 3. $\alpha-$cut of fuzzy survival ($\alpha=0$) for different θ

If $\theta=1$ then fuzzy reliability fuzzy is as follows,

$$\tilde{S}(t)[\alpha] = [\exp(-((a_4 - (a_4 - a_3)\alpha)t + bt^c)), \exp(-((a_1 + (a_2 - a_1)\alpha)t + bt^c))]. \tag{40}$$

For t_0, reliability function is a fuzzy number and membership function of $\tilde{S}(t_0)$ is as follows,

$$\xi_{\tilde{S}(t_0)}(x) = \begin{cases} \dfrac{xe^{bt_0^c} - e^{-a_4 t_0}}{e^{-a_3 t_0} - e^{-a_4 t_0}} , & \exp\{-a_4 t_0 - bt_0^c)\} \le x < \exp\{-a_3 t_0 - bt_0^c\} \\ 1 , & \exp\{-a_3 t_0 - bt_0^c)\} \le x < \exp\{-a_2 t_0 - bt_0^c\} \\ \dfrac{e^{-a_1 t_0} - xe^{bt_0^c}}{e^{-a_1 t_0} - e^{-a_2 t_0}} , & \exp\{-a_2 t_0 - bt_0^c)\} \le x < \exp\{-a_1 t_0 - bt_0^c\} \end{cases} \tag{41}$$

for every b, c, the value of $e^{bt_0^c}$ is greater than or equal to 1 and $e^{bt_0^c}$ is a non-decreasing function of b. If $b = 0$, then fuzzy number of reliability will have its maximum value with the lowest uncertainty. As the values of b increases, we get lower values for fuzzy numbers of reliability with more uncertainty.

5. Fuzzy hazard function

Another fuzzy characterizes of the lifetime distribution is the fuzzy hazard function $\tilde{h}(t)$. This function is also known as the instantaneous failure rate function. We propose the concept of a fuzzy hazard function based on the fuzzy probability measure and named $\alpha-$cut hazard band. The fuzzy hazard function $\tilde{h}(t)$ is the fuzzy conditional probability of an item failing in the short time interval t to $(t + dt)$ given that it has not failed at time t. Mathematically, we would define the fuzzy hazard function as

$$\tilde{h}(t)[\alpha] = \lim_{\Delta t \to 0} \frac{\tilde{P}(t < X < t + \Delta t | X > t)}{\Delta t} = \{\lim_{\Delta t \to 0} \frac{S(t) - S(t + \Delta t)}{\Delta t S(t)} | a \in \tilde{a}[\alpha]\} \tag{42}$$

$$= \{\frac{-S'(t)}{S(t)} | a \in \tilde{a}[\alpha]\} = \{\frac{f(t)}{S(t)} | a \in \tilde{a}[\alpha]\}.$$

The fuzzy MGLFRD distribution has the following fuzzy hazard function,

$$h(t)[\alpha] == \{\frac{\theta(a + bct^{c-1})[1 - \exp(-(at + bt^c))]^{\theta-1} \exp(-(at + bt^c))}{1 - [1 - \exp(-(at + bt^c))]^{\theta}} | a \subset \tilde{a}[\alpha]\}, \tag{43}$$

If $\theta = 1$ then

$$h(t)[\alpha] = \{a + bct^{c-1} | a \in \tilde{a}[\alpha]\}, \tag{44}$$

and $\alpha-$cut of $\tilde{h}(t)$ is as follows,

$$h(t)[\alpha] = [a_1 + (a_2 - a_1)\alpha + bct^{c-1}, a_4 - (a_4 - a_3)\alpha + bct^{c-1}] \tag{45}$$

i) If $c = 1$, then the hazard function is a fuzzy number (see Fig. 4)

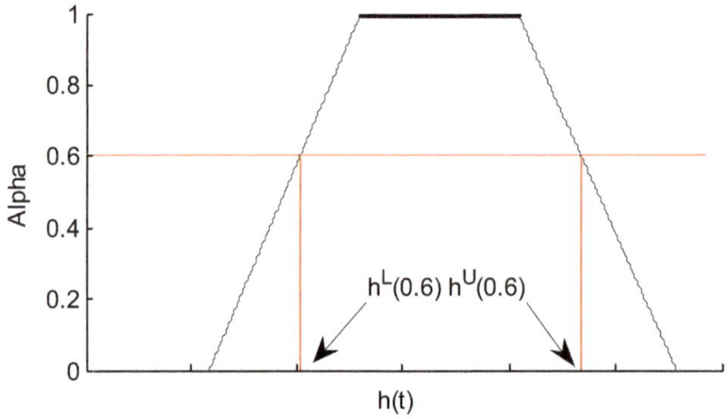

Fig. 4. membership function and $\alpha-$cut ($\alpha=0.6$) of fuzzy hazard ($c=1$)

ii) If $c=2$, then for every $\alpha-$cut, the hazard band is ascending with linear upper and lower bounds.

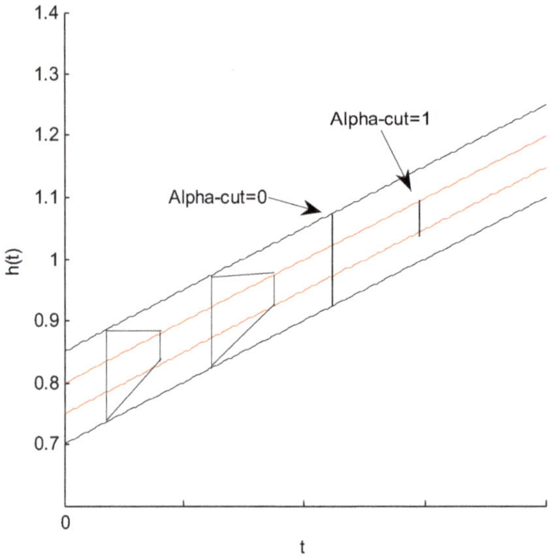

Fig. 5. $\alpha-$cut ($\alpha=0,1$) of fuzzy hazard ($c=2$)

iii) If $c=3$, then for every $\alpha-$cut, the hazard band is ascending with curve trend behavior in upper and lower bound.

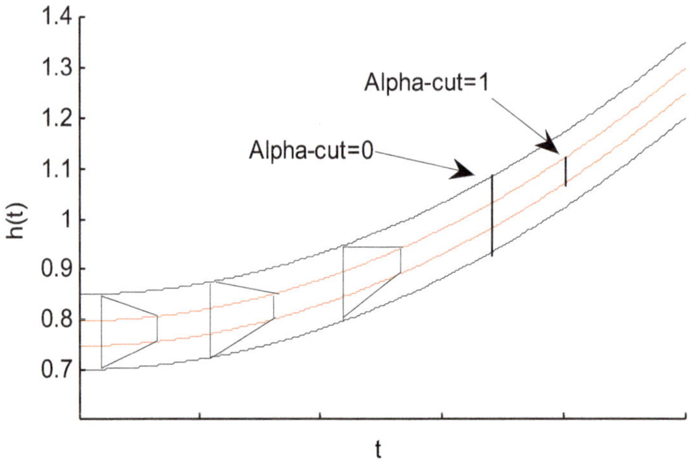

Fig. 6. $\alpha-$cut ($\alpha=0,1$) of fuzzy hazard ($c=3$)

6. Conclusions

In this paper, we have introduced a new four-parameter modified generalized linear failure rate distribution and different properties of the new model have been presented. It is observed that the proposed MGLFR distribution has several desirable properties and several existing well known distributions can be obtained as special cases of this distribution. It is observed that the MGLFR distribution can have non-decreasing, non-increasing and bathtub shaped hazard rate functions, which are quite desirable for data analysis purposes. The fuzzy probability theory has been successfully applied to the reliability system in this paper. Whenever, the lifetimes of components and parameters follow randomness and fuzziness, respectively, conventional reliability system is not feasible. Thus, we have applied successfully the fuzzy distribution to overcome this difficulty.

Acknowledgement

The author would like to thank the anonymous referees for constructive comments on earlier version of this paper.

References

Aliev, I. M., & Kara, Z. (2004). Fuzzy system reliability analysis using dependent fuzzy set. *Control and Cybernetics*, *33*, 653-662.

Baloui Jamkhaneh, E. (2011). An Evaluation of the Systems Reliability Using Fuzzy Lifetime Distribution. *Journal of Applied Mathematics, Islamic Azad University of Lahijan*, *8*(28), 73-80.

Baloui Jamkhaneh. E., & Nozari, A. (2012). Fuzzy System Reliability Analysis Based on Confidence Interval. *Advanced Materials Research*, *433*, 4908-4914.

Baloui Jamkhaneh, E. (2014). Analyzing system reliability using fuzzy Weibull lifetime distribution. *International Journal of Applied Operational Research*, 4(1), 81-90.

Buckley, J.J. (2006). *Fuzzy probability and statistics*. Springer-Verlage Berlin Heidelberg.

Burr, I.W. (1942). Cumulative frequency distribution. *Annals of Mathematical Statistics*, 13, 215-232.

Cai, K.Y., Wen, C.Y. & Zhang, M.L. (1991). Fuzzy variables as a basic for a theory of fuzzy reliability in the possibility context. *Fuzzy Set and Systems*, 42, 145-172.

Cai, K.Y., Wen, C.Y. & Zhang, M.L. (1993). Fuzzy states as for a theory of fuzzy reliability. *Microelectron Reliability*, 33, 2253-2263.

Cai, K.Y. (1996). System failure engineering and fuzzy methodology. An introductory overview. *Fuzzy Set and Systems*, 83, 113-133.

Chen, C.H., Mon, L. (1993). Fuzzy system reliability analysis by interval of confidence. *Fuzzy Set and Systems*, 56, 29-35.

Garg, H., Rani, M., & Sharma. S.P. (2013). Reliability analysis of the engineering systems using intuitionistic fuzzy set theory. *Journal of Quality and Reliability Engineering*, Article ID 943972, 10 pages.

Guo, R., Zhao R.Q., & Li, X. (2007). Reliability analysis based on scalar fuzzy variables. *Economic Quality Control*, 22(1), 55 – 70.

Guo, R., Zhao, R.Q., Guo, D., & Dunne T. (2007). Random fuzzy variable modeling on repairable system. *Journal of Uncertain Systems*, 1(3), 222-234.

Gupta, R.D., Kundu D. (1999a). Generalized exponential distributions. *Australian and New Zealand Journal of Statistics*, 41(2), 173 - 188.

Karpisek, Z., Stepanek, P., & Jurak, P. (2010). Weibull fuzzy probability distribution for reliability of concrete structures. *Engineering Mechanics*, 17(5/6), 363–372.

Mudholkar, G.S., Srivastava, D.K. (1993). Exponentiated Weibull family for analyzing bathtub failure rate data. *IEEE Transactions on Reliability*, 42, 299-302.

Pak, A., Parham Gh. A., & Saraj, M. (2013). Reliability estimation in Rayleigh distribution based on fuzzy lifetime data. *International Journal of System Assurance Engineering and Management*, published online August 2013.

Sarhan, A., & Kundu, D. (2009). Generalized linear failure rate distribution. *Communications in Statistics - Theory and Methods*, 38, 642 - 660.

Sarhan, A., & Zaindin, M. (2009). Modified Weibull distribution. *Applied Sciences*, 11, 123-136.

Surles, J.G., & Padgett, W.J. (2001). Inference for reliability and stress-strength for a scaled Burr Type X distribution. *Lifetime Data Analysis*, 7, 187-200.

Hammer, M. (2001). Application of fuzzy theory to electrical machine reliability.*Zeszyty Naukowe. Elektryka/Politechnika Śląska*, 177, 161-166.

Onisawa, T., & Kacprzyk, J. (1995). *Reliability and safety analysis under fuzziness*. Physica-Verlag Heidelberg.

Utkin, L. V. (1994). Knowledge based fuzzy reliability assessment. *Microelectronics Reliability*, *34*(5), 863-874.

Utkin, L.V. (1994). Fuzzy reliability of repairable systems in the possibility context. *Microelectron. Reliability*, 34, 1865–1876.

Utkin, L.V., & Gurov, S.V. (1995). A general formal approach for fuzzy reliability analysis in the possibility context. *Fuzzy Set and Systems*, 83, 203-213.

Wu, H.-C. (2006). Fuzzy Bayesian system reliability assessment based on exponential distribution. *Applied Mathematics Modeling*, 30, 509–530.

Yao, J.S., Su, J.S., & Shih, T.S. (2008). Fuzzy system reliability analysis using triangular fuzzy numbers based on statistical data. *Journal of information science and engineering*, 24, 1521-1535.

A deterministic inventory model for deteriorating items with selling price dependent demand and three-parameter Weibull distributed deterioration

Asoke Kumar Bhunia[a] and Ali Akbar Shaikh[b*]

[a]*Department of Mathematics, The University of Burdwan, Burdwan – 713104, West Bengal, India*
[b]*Department of Mathematics, Krishnagar Govt. College, Krishnagar-741101, West Bengal, India*

C H R O N I C L E

Keywords:
Inventory
Deterioration
Weibull distribution
Variable demand
Partially backlogged shortage
Non-linear programming

A B S T R A C T

In this paper, an attempt is made to develop two inventory models for deteriorating items with variable demand dependent on the selling price and frequency of advertisement of items. In the first model, shortages are not allowed whereas in the second, these are allowed and partially backlogged with a variable rate dependent on the duration of waiting time up to the arrival of next lot. In both models, the deterioration rate follows three-parameter Weibull distribution and the transportation cost is considered explicitly for replenishing the order quantity. This cost is dependent on the lot-size as well as the distance from the source to the destination. The corresponding models have been formulated and solved. Two numerical examples have been considered to illustrate the results and the significant features of the results are discussed. Finally, based on these examples, the effects of different parameters on the initial stock level, shortage level (in case of second model only), cycle length along with the optimal profit have been studied by sensitivity analyses taking one parameter at a time keeping the other parameters as same.

1. Introduction

According to the existing literature of inventory control system, most of the inventory models have been developed under the assumption that the life time of an item is infinite while it is in storage i.e., an item once in stock remains unchanged and fully usable for satisfying future demand. In real life situation, this assumption is not always true due to the effect of deterioration in the preservation of commonly used physical goods like wheat, paddy or any other type of food grains, vegetables, fruits, drugs, pharmaceuticals, etc. A certain fraction of these goods are either damaged or decayed or vaporized or affected by some other factors, etc. and are not in a perfect condition to satisfy the demand. As a result, the loss due to this natural phenomenon (i.e., the deterioration effect) can't be ignored in the analysis of the inventory system. Ghare and Schrader (1963) first developed an inventory model for exponentially decaying inventory. Then Emmons (1968) proposed this type of model with variable deterioration, which follows two-parameter Weibull distribution. These models were extended and improved by several researchers, viz. Covert and Philip (1973), Giri et al. (2003),Ghosh and

* Corresponding author.

Chaudhari (2004). On the other hand, Chakrabarty et al. (1998), Giri et al.(1999), Sana et al. (2004), Sana and Chaudhari (2004) and others developed inventory models for deteriorating items with there-parameter weibull distributed deterioration. Misra (1975) developed an EOQ model with weibull deterioration rate for perishable product without considering shortages. These investigations were followed by several researchers like, Deb and Chaudhari (1986), Giri et. al. (1996), Goswami and Chaudhari (1991), Mandal and Phaujdar (1989a), Padmanabhan and Vrat (1995), Pal et al.(1993), Mandal and Maiti (1997), Goyal and Gunasekaran (1995), Sarkar et al.(1997), Bhunia and Maiti (1998a,1998b), Pal et al. (2005, 2006), Mishra and Tripathy (2010), Kawale and Bansode (2012), Bhunia et al. (2013a, 2013b), Sharma and Chaudhary (2013), Amutha and Chandrasekaran (2013) etc., where a time-proportional deterioration rate was considered.

In the present competitive market, the effect of marketing policies and conditions such as the price variations and the advertisement of an item change its demand pattern amongst the public. The propaganda and canvassing of an item by advertisement in the well-known media such as Newspaper, Magazine, Radio, T. V., Cinema, etc. and also through the sales representatives have a motivational effect on the people to buy more. Also, the selling price of an item is one of the decisive factors in selecting an item for use. It is commonly observed that lower selling price causes increase in demand whereas higher selling price has the reverse effect. Hence, it can be concluded that the demand of an item is a function of displayed inventory in a show-room, selling price of an item and the advertisement expenditures frequency of advertisement, Very few OR researchers and practitioners studied the effects of price variations and the advertisement on the demand rate of items. Kotler (1971) incorporated marketing policies into inventory decisions and discussed the relationship between economic order quantity and pricing decision. Ladany and Sternleib (1974) studied the effect of price variation on selling and consequently on EOQ. However, they did not consider the effect of advertisement. Subramanyam and Kumaraswamy (1971), Urban (1992), Goyal and Gunasekaran (1995), Abad (1996) and Luo (1998), Pal et al. (2007), Bhunia and Shaikh (2011) developed inventory models incorporating the effects of price variations and advertisement on demand rate of an item.

When a purchasing manager places an order of items, it is important to realize that different types of costs including the transportation cost of the items should be taken into account. Therefore, the inventory and transportation costs are dependent to each other when the transportation cost is involved in inventory replenishment, It is well known that different transportation models have different speed, reliability and cost characteristics. In most of the existing research, the transportation cost is not considered separately, it is included in the replenishment cost which is independent of the order quantity. In realistic situation, the transportation cost is not independent of the ordered quantity. As a result, this cost cannot be ignored in the analysis of inventory system. Recently, very few researchers considered this cost into the analysis of lot-size determination. Baumol and Vinod (1970) first considered an inventory model of freight transport where by ordered quantity and transportation alternative can jointly be determined. Constable and Whybark (1978) assumed that the transportation cost per unit is independent of the order quantities. Buffa and Munn (1989) developed the model considering the transportation per unit to be a negative exponential function of the order quantity. Anily and Federgruin (1990) have considered the transportation cost in terms of truck loading cost. Krishnawamy et al. (1995) developed an EOQ model considering the transportation cost both for deterministic and stochastic demand cases. In these models, transportation cost per unit for the mode of transport (transport vehicle) is dependent on the quantity of the product. Recently, Pal et al. (2006) and Mondal et al. (2007) considered this cost under the assumption that the transportation cost is constant for transport vehicle (of a given capacity) even if the quantity shipped is less than a transport vehicle load by some quantity.

In this paper, we have developed two inventory models for deteriorating items with variable demand dependent on the selling price of items and frequency of advertisement of items. In the first model, stock-out situation is not allowed whereas in the second, it is allowed and partially backlogged with a variable rate dependent on the duration of waiting time up to the arrival of next lot. In both the models, the deterioration rate follows a three-parameter Weibull distribution and the transportation cost is considered explicitly for replenishing the order quantity. The corresponding models have been formulated and solved by considering the transportation cost for replenishing the items. Two numerical examples have been given to illustrate the results and the significant features of the result are discussed. Finally, based on these examples, the effects of different parameters on the initial stock level, shortage level (in case of second model only), cycle length along with the optimal profit, sensitivity analyses have been performed considering one parameter at a time keeping other parameters at their original values.

2. Assumptions and Notations

The following assumptions and notations are used to develop the proposed model:

(i) Replenishments are instantaneous with a known and constant lead time.
(ii) The entire lot is delivered in one batch.
(iii) The inventory planning horizon is infinite and the inventory system involves only one item and one stocking point.
(iv) The deterioration occurs when the item is effectively in-stock and its rate follows a three-parameter Weibull distribution.
(v) The deteriorated units are not replaced.
(vi) The replenishment cost (ordering cost) is constant and does not include the transportation cost for replenishing the item.
(vii) A be the frequency of advertisement in the cycle length.
(viii) The inventory carrying cost, C_1 per unit per unit time, shortage cost, C_2 per unit per unit time, the purchase cost, C_3 per unit, the ordering cost, C_4 per order, the advertisement cost C_5 per advertisement and the selling price, p are known and constants.
(ix) α, β, γ be the parameters of the Weibull distribution whose probability density function is $f(t) = \alpha\beta(t-\gamma)^{\beta-1}\exp\left\{-\alpha(t-\gamma)^{\beta}\right\}$
(x) The instantaneous rate of deterioration of the on-hand in any time t is $\theta(t)$ which obeys the three –parameter Weibull distribution.

So, $\theta(t) = \dfrac{f(t)}{1-F(t)} = \alpha\beta(t-\gamma)^{\beta-1}$ where $0 < \alpha << 1,\ \beta > 0, \gamma \geq 0$ and $F(t)$ is the distribution function of Weibull distribution.

For $\beta = 1$, $\theta(t)$ is constant and the Weibull distribution reduces to exponential distribution

$\beta > 1$, $\theta(t)$ is an increasing function of t,

$\beta < 1$, $\theta(t)$ is a decreasing function of t.

For $\gamma = 0$, the three-parameter Weibull distribution reduces to two parameter Weibull distribution.

(xi) The demand rate $D(A, p)$ is dependent on selling price (p) of an item and the frequency of advertisement (A). We assume it as follows: $D(A,p) = A^{v}(a-bp),\ a,b,v > 0$.
(xii) R be the maximum shortage level.
(xiii) $m(>1)$ be the mark-up i.e., $p=mC_3$.
(xiv) The capacity of a transportation vehicle is k units.
(xv) L be the distance between the shop and the source of the items/commodities from where items/commodities to be transported.
(xvi) C_t be the transportation cost for full load of the transport vehicle and C_{tF} be the transportation cost per unit item.

(xviii) U be the upper break point, some quantity loss than k but more than U , the transportation cost for whole quantity is C_t.

Hence $U = \frac{C_t}{C_{tF}}(<k)$ where $\left[\frac{C_t}{C_{tF}}\right]$ represents the greatest integer value which is less then or equal to C_t / C_{tF} .

3. Inventory model without shortage

Initially, an enterprise purchases an amount of stock of S units of the item. This amount will be depleted due to deterioration of item and also to meet up the customers' demand. Let $q(t)$ be the instantaneous inventory level at any time $t \geq 0$. Then the inventory level $q(t)$ at any time t satisfies the differential equation as follows:

$$\frac{dq(t)}{dt} + \theta(t)q(t) = -D(A, p), \quad 0 \leq t \leq T \tag{1}$$

with the boundary conditions

$$q(t) = S \text{ at } t = 0 \tag{2}$$

and

$$q(t) = 0 \text{ at } t = T . \tag{3}$$

Using the condition (3), the solution of the differential Eq. (1) is given by

$$q(t) = D(A, p)e^{-\alpha(t-\gamma)^\beta} \int_t^T e^{\alpha(t-\gamma)^\beta} dt \tag{4}$$

From Eq. (2), we have

$$S = D(A, p)e^{-\alpha(-\gamma)^\beta} \int_0^T e^{\alpha(t-\gamma)^\beta} dt \tag{5}$$

During the inventory cycle, deteriorated units are to be separated. The amount of inventory that has deteriorated during the cycle can be derived by integrating the product of the deterioration rate and the inventory level over the entire cycle i.e., the total number of deteriorated units is given by

$$D' = \int_0^T \theta(t)q(t)dt .$$

However, D' can be derived from the difference between the initial stock and the total selling amount during the cycle, i.e.,

$$D' = S - \int_0^T D(A, p)dt = S - D(A, p)T \tag{6}$$

Now, the total inventory holding cost C_{hol} is given by

$$C_{hol} = C_1 \int_0^T q(t)\,dt$$

where

$$\begin{aligned}\int_0^T q(t)\,dt = {} & \frac{T^2}{2} + \frac{\alpha^2 T (T-\gamma)^{2\beta+1}}{2(2\beta+1)} - \frac{\alpha (T-\gamma)^{\beta+2}}{(\beta+1)(\beta+2)} - \frac{\alpha^2 (T-\gamma)^{2\beta+2}}{2(2\beta+1)(2\beta+2)} \\ & - \frac{\alpha^2 (T-\gamma)^{2\beta+2}}{(\beta+1)^2} + \alpha(-\gamma)^{\beta}\left\{\frac{T^2}{2} - \left(\frac{\beta}{\gamma}\right)\frac{T^3}{3}\right\} \\ & + \frac{\alpha^2 (T-\gamma)^{2\beta+2}}{(\beta+1)(2\beta+2)} + \frac{\alpha^2 T (T-\gamma)^{2\beta+1}}{2(2\beta+1)} - \frac{\alpha^2 (-\gamma)^{2\beta}}{2}\left\{\frac{T^2}{2} - \left(\frac{2\beta}{\gamma}\right)\frac{T^3}{3}\right\} \\ & + \frac{\alpha\,(-\gamma)^{\beta+2}}{(\beta+1)(\beta+2)} + \frac{\alpha^2 (-\gamma)^{2\beta+2}}{2(2\beta+1)(2\beta+2)} + \frac{\alpha T (-\gamma)^{\beta+1}}{(\beta+1)} \\ & + \frac{\alpha^2 (T-\gamma)^{\beta+1}(-\gamma)^{\beta+1}}{(\beta+1)^2} - \frac{\alpha^2 (-\gamma)^{2\beta+2}}{(\beta+1)(2\beta+2)} - \frac{\alpha^2 T (-\gamma)^{2\beta+1}}{2(2\beta+1)}\end{aligned} \tag{7}$$

neglecting the powers of α higher than two as $0 < \alpha << 1$. The total advertisement cost is the product of the number of advertisement and the cost per advertisement i.e., $C_{adv} = C_5 A$

When the ordered quantity is greater than one integral transport vehicle load, the ordered quantity Q can be expressed as $Q = nk + k_1 q$ where $n = 0$ or any positive integer ; $k_1 = 0$ or 1 and $q < k$.
In that case, two situations may arise:

(i) $nk < Q \le nk + U$ (ii) $nk + U < Q \le (n+1)k$

Hence the total transportation cost is given by

$$\begin{aligned} C_{tran} &= nC_t + (Q - nk)C_{tF}, && \text{where } nk < Q \le nk + U \\ &= (n+1)C_t, && \text{where } nk + U < Q \le (n+1)k \end{aligned}$$

The total cost (TC) of the system is given by

TC = *<ordering cost>* + *<purchasing cost>* + *<inventory holding cost>* + *<advertisement cost>* + *<transportation cost>*

$$= C_4 + C_3 S + C_1 \int_0^T q(t)\,dt + C_5 A + C_{tran}$$

The net profit (X) for the entire system is the difference between the sale revenue per cycle and the total cost of the system i.e.,

$$X = pA^{v}(a - bp)T - TC \tag{8}$$

Therefore the profit function $Z(m,n,A,T)$ (average profit per unit time for the entire cycle) of the inventory system is given by

$$Z(m,n,A,T)=\frac{X}{T}$$

i.e., $$Z(m,n,A,T)=\left[pA^{v}(a-bp)-\left\{C_4+C_3.S+C_1\int_0^T q(t)\,dt+C_5A+C_{tran}\right\}\right]/T \tag{9}$$

Here the profit function is a function of two continuous variables m, T and two integer variables n, A.

Proposition: The profit function Z is an increasing function of m for any feasible values of n, A and T.

Proof: Clearly $\frac{dZ}{dm}>0$ for $a>2bp$. This condition gives the increasing property of the profit function Z.

Hence our problem is to determine the optimal values of n, A, T and S by solving the following mixed integer nonlinear optimization problem.

$$\left.\begin{array}{l}\text{Maximize } Z(n,A,T)\\ \text{subject to } n,\ A,T>0 \text{ and } n,\ A \text{ are integers}\end{array}\right\} \tag{10}$$

$$C_{tran}=nC_t+(S-nk)C_{tF},\ \ when\ \ nk<S\le nk+U$$
$$=(n+1)C_t,\ \ when\ \ nk+U<S\le(n+1)k$$

The above problem can be solved by using the well-known LINGO 8.0 software. However, the optimal solution of the above problem can be obtained with the help of the following algorithm.

Algorithm 1

Step-1: Input all the parameters.
Step-2: Calculate the value of U.
Step-3: Solve the problem (10) by taking the transportation cost for first situation $(nk<S\le nk+U)$
Step-4: If S lies in the interval $(nk<S\le nk+U)$ *, then this is the optimal policy and go to Step-7. Otherwise, go to Step-5.*
Step-5: Solve the problem (10) by taking the transportation cost for second situation $(nk+U<S\le(n+1)k)$.
Step-6: If S lies in the interval $(nk+U<S\le(n+1)k)$ *, then this is the optimal policy.*
Step-7: Stop.

4. Numerical Example

To illustrate the developed model, an example with the following data has been considered.
$C_1=\$1.5$ per unit per unit time, $C_3=\$8$ per unit, $C_4=\$250$ per order, $C_5=\$50$ per advertisement, $C_t=\$100$ per transport vehicle, $C_{tF}=\$1.25$ per unit, $\alpha=0.05$, $\beta=2$, $\gamma=2.5$, $a=250$, $b=0.3$, $k=100$ units. L=50 km, v =0.1. Though the values of different parameters are not collected from any case study, the values considered here are realistic.

According to our developed algorithm (i.e., *Algorithm 1*) of the proposed inventory system, the optimal solution has been obtained with the help of well known LINGO software for different values of m. The optimum values of n, A, T, S along with the maximum average profit are displayed in Table 1.

Table 1
Optimal solution for different values of mark-up rate m

m	A	S	T	Z
1.25	4	1300.00	5.4787	326.1550
1.27	5	1300.00	5.3887	372.4020
1.30	6	1400.00	5.61664	441.7629
1.32	7	1400.00	5.5551	489.6958
1.35	8	1400.00	5.5021	561.5950

5. Sensitivity Analysis

For the given example mentioned earlier, sensitivity analysis has been performed to study the effect of changes (under or over estimation) of different parameters like demand, deterioration parameters and mark-up rate on maximum initial stock level, cycle length, frequency of advertisement along with the maximum profit of the system. This analysis is carried out by changing (increasing and decreasing) the parameters from – 20% to + 20%, taken one or more parameters at a time and making the other parameters at their original values. The results of this analysis are shown in Table 2.

Table 2
Sensitivity analysis with respect to different parameters

Parameter	% changes of parameters	% changes in Z^*	A^*	% changes in S^*	% changes in T^*
	-20	14.83	7	-7.14	-6.48
C_1	-10	7.35	6	-7.14	-5.36
	10	-6.53	6	0	0
	20	-12.91	5	0	1.31
	-20	-47.33	4	0	2.73
C_3	-10	-24.08	5	0	1.22
	10	25.14	7	-7.14	-6.39
	20	50.87	8	-7.14	-7.27
	-20	2.12	6	-7.14	-5.35
C_4	-10	1.05	6	-7.14	-5.36
	10	-1.01	6	0	0
	20	-2.02	6	0	0
	-20	2.97	8	0	-2.07
C_5	-10	1.44	7	0	-1.11
	10	-1.03	5	-7.14	-4.04
	20	-2.08	5	-7.14	-4.04
	-20	-24.52	5	21.43	0.24
a	-10	-12.17	5	-14.29	-2.1
	10	12.69	7	7.14	-3.1
	20	25.24	7	14.29	-4.79
	-20	0.34	6	0	-0.18
b	-10	0.18	6	0	-0.09
	10	-0.16	6	-7.14	-5.27
	20	-0.3	6	-7.14	-5.18
	-20	-3.79	5	-7.14	-1.71
v	-10	-1.86	5	-7.14	-2.87
	10	2.51	7	0	-2.52
	20	4.89	8	7.14	-0.1
	-20	-52.42	2	-50	-43.58
α	-10	-28.87	4	-14.29	-9.68
	10	31.38	8	0	-0.87
	20	64.14	10	7.14	3.41
	-20	-61.12	2	-57.14	-53.28
γ	-10	-40.67	3	-35.71	-30.18
	10	62.12	12	21.43	15.34
	20	126.39	13	7.14	10.37

6. Inventory model with shortages

In this model, shortages, if any, are allowed and partially backlogged. During the shortage period, the backlogging rate is dependent on the length of the waiting time up to the arrival of fresh lot. Considering this situation, the rate is defined as $\left[1+\delta\left(T-t\right)\right]^{-1}$, $\delta>0$. In this model, it is assumed that after fulfilling the backorder quantity, the on-hand inventory level is S at $t=0$ and it declines continuously up to the time $t=t_1$ when it reaches the zero level. The decline in inventory during the closed time interval $0\le t\le t_1$ occurs due to the customer's demand and deterioration of the item. After the time $t=t_1$, shortage occurs and it accumulates at the rate $\left[1+\delta\left(T-t\right)\right]^{-1}$, ($\delta>0$) up to the time $t=T$ when the next lot arrives. At time $t=T$, the maximum shortage level is R. This entire cycle then repeats itself after the cycle length T.

Let $q\left(t\right)$ be the instantaneous inventory level at any time $t\ge 0$. Then the inventory level $q\left(t\right)$ at any time t satisfies the differential equations as follows,

$$\frac{dq(t)}{dt}+\theta(t)\,q(t)=-D\left(A,\,p\right),\qquad 0\le t\le t_1 \tag{11}$$

$$\frac{dq(t)}{dt}=\frac{-D(A,p)}{1+\delta(T-t)},\ \ t_1<t\le T \tag{12}$$

with the boundary conditions

$$q\left(t\right)=S \text{ at } t=0\ ,\ q(t)=0 \quad \text{at } t=t_1\ . \tag{13}$$

and

$$q\left(t\right)=-R \quad \text{at } t=T\,. \tag{14}$$

Also, $q(t)$ is continuous at $t=t_1$.

Using the conditions (3) and (4), the solutions of the differential equations (11)-(12) are given by

$$q(t)=D(A,p)e^{-\alpha(t-\gamma)^{\beta}}\int_{t}^{t_1}e^{\alpha(t-\gamma)^{\beta}}dt,\qquad 0\le t\le t_1$$

$$=\frac{D(A,p)}{\delta}\log\left|1+\delta(T-t)\right|-R,\quad t_1<t\le T$$

From Eq. (12), we have $q\left(t\right)=S$ at $t=0$.

Then,

$$S=D\left(A,p\right)e^{-\alpha\left(-\gamma\right)^{\beta}}\int_{0}^{t_1}e^{\alpha\left(t-\gamma\right)^{\beta}}dt \tag{15}$$

From the continuity condition, we have

$$R=\frac{D(A,p)}{\delta}\log\left|1+\delta(T-t_1)\right| \tag{16}$$

Now the total inventory holding cost for the entire cycle is given by

$$C_{hol} = C_1 \int_0^{t_1} q(t)\,dt$$

where

$$\int_0^{t_1} q(t)\,dt = \frac{t_1^2}{2} + \frac{\alpha^2 t_1 (t_1-\gamma)^{2\beta+1}}{2(2\beta+1)} - \frac{\alpha (t_1-\gamma)^{\beta+2}}{(\beta+1)(\beta+2)} - \frac{\alpha^2 (t_1-\gamma)^{2\beta+2}}{2(2\beta+1)(2\beta+2)}$$
$$\frac{-\alpha^2 (t_1-\gamma)^{2\beta+2}}{(\beta+1)^2} + \alpha(-\gamma)^{\beta}\left\{\frac{t_1^2}{2} - \left(\frac{\beta}{\gamma}\right)\frac{t_1^3}{3}\right\}$$
$$+\frac{\alpha^2 (t_1-\gamma)^{2\beta+2}}{(\beta+1)(2\beta+2)} + \frac{\alpha^2 t_1 (t_1-\gamma)^{2\beta+1}}{2(2\beta+1)} - \frac{\alpha^2(-\gamma)^{2\beta}}{2}\left\{\frac{t_1^2}{2} - \left(\frac{2\beta}{\gamma}\right)\frac{t_1^3}{3}\right\} \tag{17}$$
$$+\frac{\alpha(-\gamma)^{\beta+2}}{(\beta+1)(\beta+2)} + \frac{\alpha^2(-\gamma)^{2\beta+2}}{2(2\beta+1)(2\beta+2)} + \frac{\alpha t_1 (-\gamma)^{\beta+1}}{(\beta+1)}$$
$$+\frac{\alpha^2 (t_1-\gamma)^{\beta+1}(-\gamma)^{\beta+1}}{(\beta+1)^2} - \frac{\alpha^2(-\gamma)^{2\beta+2}}{(\beta+1)(2\beta+2)} - \frac{\alpha^2 t_1 (-\gamma)^{2\beta+1}}{2(2\beta+1)}$$

Again, the total shortage cost C_{Sho} over the entire cycle is given by

$$C_{sho} = \left(R + \frac{D(A,p)}{\delta}\right)(T-t_1) - \frac{D(A,p)}{\delta^2}\left[(1+\delta(T-t_1))\log\left|1+\delta(T-t_1)\right|\right]$$

Hence the total inventory cost (TC) of the system is given by

TC = *<ordering cost>* + *<purchasing cost>* + *<inventory holding cost>* + *<advertisement cost>* + *<transportation cost>*+*< inventory shortage cost>*

$$= C_4 + C_3(S+R) + C_1\int_0^{t_1} q(t)\,dt + C_5 A + C_{tran} + C_{sho}$$

Now, the net profit (*X*) for the entire system is given by

$$X = pA^{\nu}(a - bp)T - TC. \tag{18}$$

Therefore, the profit function $Z(m,n,A,t_1,T)$ (average profit per unit time for the entire cycle) of the inventory system is given by $Z(m,n,A,t_1,T) = \dfrac{X}{T}$

i.e., $$Z(m,n,A,t_1,T) = \left[pA^{\nu}(a-bp) - \left\{C_4 + C_3(S+R) + C_1\int_0^{t_1} q(t)\,dt + C_5 A + C_{tran} + C_{sho}\right\}\right]/T \tag{19}$$

Here the profit function is a function of three continuous variables *m*, t_1, *T* and two integer variables *n*, *A*. Clearly , the above function is an increasing function with respect to *m*. Hence our problem is to determine the optimal values of *n*, *A*, t_1, *T* and *S* by solving the following mixed integer nonlinear optimization problem.

$$\left.\begin{array}{l}\text{Maximize } Z(n,A,t_1,T) \\ \text{subject to } t_1 < T, n,\ A,\ t_1 > 0 \text{ and } n,\ A \text{ are integers}\end{array}\right\} \tag{20}$$

where

$$C_{tran} = nC_t + (S + R - nk)C_{tf} \quad when\ nk < S + R \le nk + U$$

$$= (n+1)C_t \quad when\ nk + U < S + R \le (n+1)k$$

This is a non-linear optimization problem. The optimal solution of the this problem can be obtained with the help of the following algorithm using LINGO software.

Algorithm 2

Step-1: Input all the parameters.
Step-2: Calculate the value of U.
Step-3: Solve the problem (20) by taking the transportation cost for first situation $(nk < S + R \le nk + U)$
Step-4: If S+R Satisfies the condition $nk < S + R \le nk + U$ *, then this is the optimal policy and go to Step-7. Otherwise, go to Step-5.*
Step-5: Solve the problem (20) by taking the transportation cost for second situation $(nk + U < S + R \le (n+1)k)$.
Step-6: If S+R Satisfies the condition $nk + U < S + R \le (n+1)k$ *, then this is the optimal policy.*
Step-7: Stop.

7. Numerical Example

To illustrate the model with partially backlogged shortages, a numerical example with the following data has been considered.

$C_1 = \$1.5$ per unit per unit time, C_2=\$3 per unit per unit time, $C_3 = \$8$ per unit, $C_4 = \$250$ per order, $C_5 = \$50$ per advertisement, $C_t = \$100$ per transport vehicle, $C_{tF} = \$1.25$ per unit, $\alpha = 0.05$, $\beta = 2$, $\gamma = 2.5$, a = 250, b = 0.3, k= 100 units. L=50 km, $\delta = 1.5$, $v = 0.1$.

Like first model (no-shortage case), the values of different parameters considered here are realistic, through these are not taken from any case study. According to the solution procedure (Algorithm-2), the optimal solution has been obtained with the help of LINGO software for different values of *m*. The optimum values of *n*, *A*, t_1 , *T*, *S* and *R* along with maximum average profit are displayed in Table 3.

Table 3
Optimal solution for different values of mark-up rate *m*

m	*A*	*S*	*R*	t_1	*T*	*Z*
1.25	2	783.8420	16.1580	3.7305	3.7944	197.1620
1.27	3	878.8360	21.1693	4.01352	4.0949	239.7680
1.30	3	880.2430	19.7569	4.02088	4.09658	305.7290
1.32	4	882.7820	17.2182	3.9214	3.9850	350.5670
1.35	4	883.8263	16.1736	3.9271	3.9867	418.4160

8. Sensitivity Analysis

For the given example mentioned earlier, sensitivity analysis has been performed to study the effect of changes (under or over estimation) of different parameters like demand, deterioration, inventory cost parameters and mark-up rate on maximum initial stock level, shortage level, cycle length, frequency of advertisement along with the maximum profit of the system. This analysis has been carried out by changing (increasing and decreasing) the parameters from – 20% to + 20%, taken one or more parameters at a time making the other parameters at their more parameters at a time and making the other parameters at their original values. The results of this analysis are shown in Tables 4.

Table 4
Sensitivity analysis with respect to different parameters

Parameter	% changes of parameters	% changes in Z^*	A^*	% changes in R^*	S^*	t_1^*	T^*
C_1	– 20	32.64	4	-	1.47	-0.64	-2.47
	– 10	16.16	4	-65.33	-12.03	-1.37	-2.59
	10	-15.45	2	29.71	-12.03	-12.02	-11.21
	20	-29.72	2	80.04	-24.52	-21.83	-19.64
C_2	– 20	0.04	3	12.62	-0.28	-0.27	-0.02
	– 10	0.02	3	5.93	-0.13	1.87	-0.01
	10	-0.02	3	-5.30	0.12	1.89	0.01
	20	-0.03	3	-10.06	0.23	1.90	0.02
C_3	– 20	-69.54	1	80.90	-24.54	-16.13	-13.75
	– 10	-35.57	2	28.56	-12.00	-8.40	-7.57
	10	36.99	4	-52.67	1.18	-1.52	-2.51
	20	-	-	-	-	-	-
C_4	– 20	4.40	3	-35.21	-10.57	-10.53	-11.01
	– 10	2.16	3	-36.58	-10.54	-10.5	-11.00
	10	-2.00	3	-0.57	0.01	0.01	0.00
	20	-3.99	3	-1.15	0.03	0.02	0.00
C_5	– 20	3.15	4	-7.67	0.17	-2.6	-2.75
	– 10	1.51	4	-8.29	0.19	-2.59	-2.75
	10	-1.20	3	-0.34	0.01	0.01	0.00
	20	-2.40	3	-0.69	0.02	0.01	0.00
a	– 20	-26.81	3	-29.94	-22.05	-2.2	-2.39
	– 10	-13.36	3	-14.85	-16.14	-0.97	-1.06
	10	13.70	3	-22.85	0.51	-8.65	-9.07
	20	27.73	4	-17.30	11.75	-9.65	-10.11
b	– 20	0.34	3	-0.67	0.02	-0.23	-0.24
	– 10	0.17	3	-0.34	0.01	-0.11	-0.12
	10	-0.17	3	0.34	-0.01	0.12	0.12
	20	-0.35	3	0.68	-0.02	0.23	0.24
v	– 20	-47.14	1	110.80	-47.93	-47.12	-43.41
	– 10	-	-	-	-	-	-
	10	52.07	6	-100	47.69	39.37	36.8
	20	129.58	11	-100	81.77	63.57	60.55
α	– 20	-37.29	2	88.59	-36.07	-37.66	-34.98
	10	-20.47	2	49.6	-23.83	-22.92	-21.38
	10	25.38	4	-89.9	13.38	11.72	9.83
	20	-	-	-	-	-	-
γ	– 20	-2.75	2	-24.69	-10.81	-5.72	-6.01
	– 10	-1.49	3	2.99	-0.07	1.0	1.06
	10	1.76	4	-12.46	0.28	-3.82	-4.06
	20	3.676	4	-15.89	-5.32	-5.06	-5.36
δ	– 20	0.02	3	7.72	-0.17	-0.17	-0.04
	– 10	0.01	3	3.71	-0.08	-0.08	-0.02
	10	-0.01	3	-3.46	0.08	0.08	0.02
	20	-0.02	3	-6.68	0.15	0.14	0.03

9. Concluding Remarks

In this paper, two deterministic inventory models for deteriorating items with variable demand dependent on the selling price and the frequency of advertisement of the item have been developed with and without shortages. In the formulation of the model, transportation cost is considered explicitly for replenishing the order quantity. In most of the situations, it is the buyer's cost who must bear the transportation cost for transportation of the goods purchased from the supplier. Such costs are either assumed to be fixed and are therefore included in the ordering cost or variable and include in the unit cost of the item. In real-life situations transportation costs of goods are fixed for a finite capacity of a transport mode such as a truck. A fixed cost is incurred when a truck is deployed whether it is utilized fully or partially for a ceiling quantity or more. For quantities less than the ceiling quantity, a uniform rate per unit is charged.

In both models, the demand rate is taken as $D(A,p)=A^{V}(a-bp)$. It is well known that $D(A,p)\propto(a-bp)$ for fixed A. But, why should we take $D(A,p)\propto A^{V}$ for fixed values of p? Generally, the demand of items varies due to the advertisement in the well known media such as Radio, T.V., Newspaper, Magazine, Cinema, etc. The demand of items increases with the increase of frequency of advertisement and is directly proportional to the number of advertisement. Hence, we take $D(A,p)\propto A^{V}$ for fixed p.

The present model is also applicable to the problems where the selling prices of the items as well as the advertisement of items affect the demand. It is applicable for fashionable goods also.

The problem of inventory and transportation interactions is a potential field of research. The subject offers a lot of scope for additional work based on what has been presented in this paper. The following can be potential problems that can be studied:

(i) The possibility of single truck supplying the products to more than one go down.
(ii) The possibility of inter-depot transportation can be incorporated from the following points of view.
   (a) The inventory – distribution costs can be minimized.
   (b) This provides another alternative to deal with the space constraint that is operative at some of the go downs.
(iii) The possibility of mixing up more than one product in the same truck when each factory produces more than onc product.

References

Abad, P.L. (1996). Optimal pricing and lot-sizing under of conditions of perishability and partial backordering, *Management Science*, **42**,1093-1104.

Amutha, R., & Chandrasekaran, E. (2013). An inventory model for deteriorating items with three parameter weibull deterioration and price dependent demand, *Journal of Engineering Research & Technology*, 2(5), 1931-1935.

Anily, S., & Federgruen, A. (1990). One warehouse multiple retailer systems with vehicle routing costs, Management Science, 36, 32.

Baumol, W. J., & Vinod, H. C. (1970). An inventory theoretic model of freight transport demand, *Management Science*,16, 413 – 421.

Bhunia, A.K., & Maiti, M. (1998). Deterministic inventory model for deteriorating items with finite rate of replenishment dependent on inventory level, *Computers and Operations Research,* 25, 997-1006.

Bhunia, A.K., & Maiti, M. (1998). An inventory model of deteriorating items with lot-size dependent replenishment cost and a linear trend in demand, *Applied Mathematical Modelling*, 23, 301-308.

Buffa, F., & Munn, J. (1989). A recursive algorithm for order cycle that minimizes logistic cost, *Journal of Operational Research Society*, 40, 357.

Bhunia, A.K., & Shaikh, A.A. (2011). A deterministic model for deteriorating items with displayed inventory level dependent demand rate incorporating marketing decision with transportation cost. *International Journal of Industrial Engineering Computations*, 2(3), 547-562.

Bhunia A.K., Shaikh, A.A., Maiti, A.K., & Maiti, M. (2013a). A two warehouse deterministic inventory model for deteriorating items with a linear trend in time dependent demand over finite time horizon by elitist real-coded genetic algorithm. *International Journal of Industrial Engineering Computations*, 4(2), 241-258.

Bhunia, A.K., Shaikh, A.A., & Gupta, R.K. (2013b). A study on two-warehouse partially backlogged deteriorating inventory models under inflation via particle swarm optimization, *International Journal of System Science*. Article in Press.

Chakrabarty, T., Giri, B.C., & Chaudhuri., K.S. (1998). An EOQ model for items with Weibull distribution deterioration, shortages and trend demand: An extension of Philip's model., *Computers & Operations Research,* 25, 649-657.

Constable, G.K., & Whybark, D.C. (1978). Interactions of transportation and inventory decision, *Decision Science*, 9, 689.

Covert, R.P., & Philip, G.C. (1973). An EOQ model for items with Weibull distribution deterioration, *American Institute of Industrial Engineering Transactions*, 5, 323-326.

Deb, M., & Chaudhuri, K.S. (1986). An EOQ model for items with finite rate of production and variable rate of deterioration, *Opsearch*, 23, 175-181.

Emmons, H. (1968). A replenishment model for radioactive nuclide generators. *Management Science*, 14, 263-273.

Ghare, P., & Schrader, G. (1963). A model for exponential decaying inventories, *Journal of Industrial Engineering*, 14, 238-243.

Giri, B.C. Jalan,A.K., & Chaudhuri K.S. (2003). Economic order quantity model with weibull deteriorating distribution, shortage and ram-type demand, *International journal of System Science,* 34,237-243.

Ghosh, S.K., & Chaudhury, K.S. (2004). An order-level inventory model for a deteriorating items with Weibull distribution deterioration, time-quadratic demand and shortages, *International Journal of Advanced Modeling and Optimization,* 6(1),31-45.

Giri, B.C., C hakrabarty ,T., & Chaudhuri K.S. (1999). Retailer's optimal policy for perishable product with shortages when supplier offers all-unit quantity and freight cost discounts, *Proceeding of National Academy of Sciences,* 69(A),III, 315-326.

Giri, B.C. Pal, S., Goswami A., & Chaudhuri K.S. (1996). An inventory model for deteriorating items with stock-dependent demand rate, *European Journal of Operational Research*, 95, 604-610.

Goswami, A., & Chaudhuri, K. S. (1991). An EOQ model for deteriorating items with shortage and a linear trend in demand, *Journal of the Operational Research Socity*, 42, 1105-1110.

Goyal, S.K., & Gunasekaran, A. (1995). An integrated production-inventory-marketing model for deteriorating items, Computers & Industrial Engineering, 28, 755-762.

Kawale, S., & Bansode, P. (2012). An EPQ model using weibull deterioration for deterioration item with time varying holding cost, *International Journal of Science Engineering and Technology Research*, 1(4), 29-33.

Krishnaswamy, K. N., Kulkarni, N. G., & Mathirajan, M. (1995). Inventory models with constraints and changing transportation cost structure, International Journal of Management and Systems, 11, 91 – 110.

Kotler, P. (1971). Marketing Decision Making: A Model Building Approach, Holt. Rinehart, Winston, New York.

Ladany, S., & Sternleib, A. (1974). The intersection of economic ordering quantities and marketing policies, *AIIE Trnsactions*, 6, 173-175.

Luo, W. (1998). An integrated inventory system for perishable goods with backordering, *Computers & Industrial Engineering*, 34, 685 – 693.

Mandal, B. N., & Phaujdar, S. (1989). An inventory model for deteriorating items and stock-dependent consumption rate, *Journal of Operational Research Society*, 40, 483 – 488.

Mandal, M., & Maiti, M. (1997). Inventory model for damageable items with stock-dependent demand and shortages, *Opsearch,* 34, 156-166.

Misra, R.B.(1975). Optimum Production lot-size model for a system with deteriorating inventory, *International Journal of Production Research*, 13, 495-505.

Mondal, B., Bhunia, A.K., & Maiti, M. (2007). A model of two storage inventory system under stock dependent selling rate incorporating marketing decisions and transportation cost with optimum release rule, *Tamsui Oxford Journal of Mathematical Sciences*, 23(3), 243-267.

Padmanabhan, G., & Vrat, P. (1995). EOQ models for perishable items under stock-dependent selling rate, *European Journal of Operational Research*, 86, 281-292.

Pal, S., Goswami, A., & Chaudhuri, K.S. (1993). A deterministic inventory model for deteriorating items with stock-dependent demand rate, *International Journal of Production Economics*, 32, 291-299.

Pal. P, Bhunia, A.K., & Goyal, S.K. (2007). On optimal partially integrated production and marketing policy with variable demand under flexibility and reliability consideration via Genetic Algorithm. *Applied Mathematics and Computation*, 188, 525-537.

Pal, A.K., Bhunia, A.K., & Mukherjee, R.N. (2005). A marketing oriented inventory model with three component demand rate dependent on displayed stock level (DSL), *Journal Operational Research Society*, 56, 113-118.

Pal, A.K., Bhunia, A.K., & Mukherjee, R.N. (2006). Optimal lot size model for deteriorating items with demand rate dependent on displayed stock level(DSL) and partial backordering, *European Journal of Operational Research*, 175, 977-991.

Sarkar, B.R., Mukherje,e. S., & Balan, C.V. (1997). An order-level lot-size inventory model with inventory-level dependent demand and deterioration, International Journal of Production Economics, **48**, 227-236.

Sana, S., Goyal, S.K., & Chaudhuri, K.S. (2004). A production-inventory model for a deteriorating item with trended demand and shortages, *European Journal of Operation Research,* 157, 357-371.

Sana, S., Chaudhuri, & K.S. (2004). On a volume flexible production policy for deteriorating item with stock-dependent demand rate, *Nonlinear Phenomena in Complex system,*7(1),61-68.

Sharma , V. & Chaudhary, R.R. (2013). An inventory model for deteriorating items with weibull deterioration with time dependent demand and shortages, *Research Journal of Management Sciences*, 2, 28-30.

Subramanyam, S., & Kumaraswamy, S. (1981). EOQ formula under varying marketing policies and conditions, *AIIE Transactions*, 22, 312-314.

Tripathy.,C. K.,& Mishra.,U. (2010). An inventory model for weibull deteriorating items with price dependent demand and time-varying holding cost, *Applied Mathematical Sciences*, 4, 2171-2179

Urban, T.L. (1992). Deterministic inventory models incorporating marketing decisions, *Computers & Industrial Engineering*, 22, 85-93.

A production inventory model with flexible manufacturing, random machine breakdown and stochastic repair time

S.R. Singh[a] and Leena Prasher[b*]

[a]*Department of Mathematics, D. N. College, Meerut, 250103,India*
[b]*Centre for Mathematical Sciences, Banasthali University, Banasthali, Rajasthan 304022, India*

CHRONICLE

Keywords:
Volume flexible manufacturing system
Stochastic machine breakdown
Stochastic repair time
Stock dependent demand

ABSTRACT

This paper derives a production inventory model over infinite planning horizon with flexible but unreliable manufacturing process and the stochastic repair time. Demand is stock dependent and during the period of sale it depends on reduction on selling price. Production rate is a function of demand and reliability of the production equipment is assumed to be exponentially decreasing function of time. Repair time is estimated using uniform probability density function. The objective of the study is to determine the optimal policy for production system, which maximizes the total profit subject to some constraints under consideration. The results are discussed with a numerical example to illustrate the theory.

1. Introduction

Classical economic production inventory model assumes that manufacturing systems are perfectly reliable. This assumption, however, does not hold for many real systems. Even the best and the most modern production systems face the situation of sudden machine breakdown, and the time taken in the repair of machine also sometimes depend on the type of injury occurred. Reliability of the production equipment is a crucial factor for keeping the synchronization in the production system, and may harm the organization if the existing uncertainty of the production equipment is not taken into account and is planned, accordingly. In this study, the production system is taken as flexible to produce as per the demand but is not reliable. The production equipment may breakdown at any random time and the repair time is also assumed to be stochastic in nature. During a production run, it may shift from in-control state to out-of control state, and the production process may have to be stopped at any random time. The objective of this study is to determine the expected optimal production run time with a view to maximizing the expected profit per unit time.

* Corresponding author.

2. Literature Review

The classical production inventory model assumes that manufacturing system is perfectly reliable. Such an assumption appears impractical in real system. Researchers, therefore, have been attracted towards machine breakdown effects on production inventory problem. The effects of machine breakdown and corrective maintenance were studied by Groenevelt et al. (1992). They studied two production control policies to deal with stochastic machine breakdowns. The first one assumes that the production of the interrupted lot is not resumed after a breakdown. While the second policy considers that the production of the interrupted lot will be immediately resumed after the breakdown if the current on-hand inventory level is below a certain threshold level. Incorporated preventive maintenance to production inventory model was done by Cheung and Hausman (1997). They developed a mathematical model with random machine breakdowns and considered preventive maintenance and safety stock. Wang (2004) developed an EPQ mathematical model where production shifts from an in-control state to an out-of control state with a general shift distribution.

Giri et al. (2005) developed EMQ model with machine failure and general repair time. They proposed a model to determine the production rate and production lot size to minimize the expected total cost. Giri and Dohi (2005) developed EMQ model with random variables, corrective and preventive repair. They proposed solution procedure and computational algorithms to find the optimal production rate and lot size. Lin and Gong (2006) developed EPQ model deteriorating inventory model with machine breakdown and fix repair time. Chiu et al. (2007) derived an economic production quantity (EPQ) model with scrap, rework, and stochastic machine breakdowns, assuming some portion of the defective items to be scrapped and the other part to be repairable. Leung (2007) derived a generalized geometric programming solution to an EPQ model with flexibility and reliability considerations. Chakraborty et a,. (2008) developed an EPQ model considering production system that may shift from in-control state to out-of control state or may breakdown at any random time during a production period. Ferik (2008) developed an EPQ model for unreliable manufacturing facility. Similar research for EPQ model with imperfect process has been done by Liao et al. (2009). Singh and Singh (2010) worked on supply chain model with stochastic lead time under imprecise partially backlogging for expiring items. Widyadana and Wee (2011) developed production inventory model with random machine breakdown and stochastic repair time. They proved that stochastic repair model tends to have larger optimal cost than fixed repair time model.

An increase in the shelf space can influence more customers. In this connection, the observations made by Levin et al. (1972) and Silver and Peterson (1985) was worth noting, that the presence of greater quantity of the same item tends to attract more customers. The reason behind this fact is a typical psychology of the customers. They may have the feeling of obtaining a wide range for selection when a large amount is stored/displayed. Gupta and Vrat (1986) developed models for stock dependent consumption rate. Mandal and Phaujdar (1989) developed an inventory model for deteriorating items and stock dependent consumption rate. Schweitzer and Seidmann (1991) established optimizing processing rate for flexible manufacturing systems. Giri and Chaudhuri (1998) developed deterministic model of perishable inventory with stock-dependent demand rate and nonlinear holding cost and proved that the nonlinear holding cost affected the total average cost. Sana et al. (2006) established a production-inventory model for a deteriorating item with trended demand and shortages. Teng and Chang (2005) proposed economic production model for deteriorating item with price and stock dependent demand. Singh and Jain (2009) worked on reserve money for an EOQ model in an inflationary environment under supplier credits. Singh (2010) gave an inventory model for deteriorating items with shortages and stock-dependent demand under inflation for two-shops under one management. Yadav et al. (2012) developed an inventory model of deteriorating items with stock dependent demand using genetic algorithm in fuzzy environment. Dem and Singh (2012) investigated an EPQ model for damageable items with multivariate demand and flexible manufacturing. Dem and Singh (2013) developed a production model for imperfect production process under volume flexibility.

Goyal et al. (2013) explored an inventory system with variable demand as well as production under partially backordered shortages.

3. Assumptions and Notations

The following assumptions and notations are used throughout the model.

3.1. *Assumptions*

1. The production rate is a function of demand $P = \ell D(q), \ell > 1$
2. The demand rate $D(q)$ is a function of on hand inventory level in the interval $(0, \mu)$ and is given by $D(q) = \alpha + \beta q,\ 0 < \beta < 1,\ q \geq 0$ where β denotes the shape parameter and is a measure of responsiveness of the demand to changes in the level of on hand inventory and α denotes the scale parameter.
3. After $t = \mu$, the sale starts and demands rate $D(q) = (\alpha + \beta q)(ab^r), 0 \leq r \leq 1$ is taken as function of stock displayed and reduction on the selling price.
4. The time horizon of the inventory system is infinite. Only a typical planning schedule of expected length $E(T)$ is considered, all remaining cycles are identical.
5. Machine repair time is independent of machine breakdown.

3.2 *Notations*

$q(t)$: On hand inventory level of products.
$D(q)$: Demand rate,
P : Production rate $P = \ell\ D(q)$ where ℓ is a scale parameter, $P > D(q),\ \ell > 1$
K : Set up cost
S : Selling price per item
r : Reduction (in %) of selling price of products
h : Holding cost per unit of item per unit time
T_1 : Time when production stops
T_p : Time when machine breakdown occurs
μ : Time when sale of products starts
T_2 : Time when inventory of products vanishes and shortages start to accumulate which causes lost sales
$E(T)$: Expected Duration of a production cycle
$E(PC)$: Expected production cost
$E(HC)$: Expected holding cost in the production cycle
$E(SR)$: Expected sales revenues from items in the production cycle
$E(LSC)$: Expected lost sales cost
$E(TAP)$: Expected total profit per unit time from the production cycle

4. Formulation of model

We consider a system in which the manufacturing process is flexible as long as machine is working efficiently and hence can produce as per the demand rate. Generally, reliability of the machine is assumed to be an exponentially decreasing function of time and therefore the probability density function for machine breakdown is assumed as $f\left(T_p\right)=\lambda e^{-\lambda T_p}$. The demand function for the products is assumed as stock dependent, which is $D(q)=\alpha+\beta q$ where β denotes the shape parameter and is a measure of responsiveness of the demand to changes in the level of on hand inventory and α is the deterministic factor. Many of the organizations decide to sell their goods at reduced prices after predestined time, which is normally known as sale period. The demand function during the sale period is assumed as function of stock displayed as well as discounted price for items and so the demand function during sale period is assumed as $(\alpha+\beta q)(ab^r)$, $a>0, b>1, 0\le r\le 1$, where r is the reduction in the selling price, Geometrical description is shown in Fig. 1.

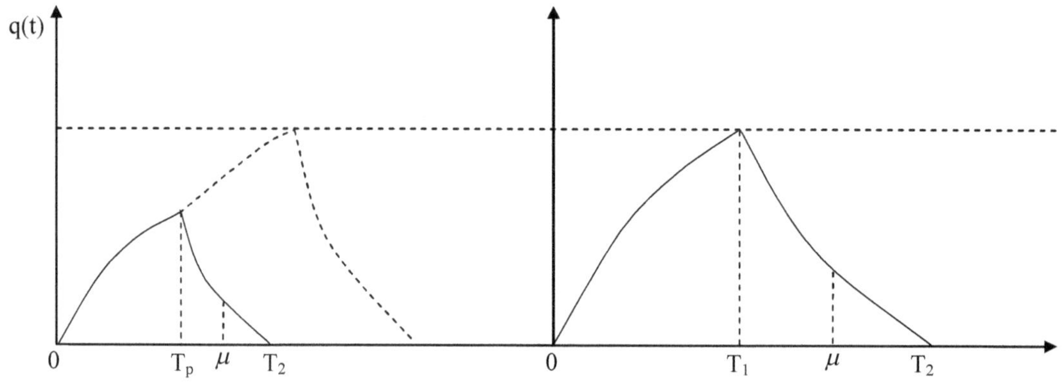

Fig. 1. Production system with lost sales.

The production cycle begins with zero inventory and starts at $t=0$. As time advances, if the machine does not breakdown in the production period $[0,T_1]$ inventory level of products pile up even after meeting market demand in the interval $0\le t\le T_1$, as shown by Eq. (1). Feasibility of this assumption implies $\ell-1$ must be greater than zero. Production is stopped at time $t=T_1$ and the

inventory level of products decreases due to demand in the interval $[T_1,\mu]$ as depicted by Eq (2). The sale period starts at $t=\mu$ and the inventory of products further decreases due to demand and reaches zero at time $t=T_2$ as shown by Eq.(3). Since the machine has a possibility of breakdown, the machine may not work the whole T_1 period. When the machine breakdown occurs, the production period stops at $t=T_p$ and machine requires repair time. As repair time is also stochastic, production may not always be possible and lost sales may occur.

Case I: When μ is less than the cycle length

$$\frac{dq}{dt}=P-D(q)\ ,\qquad q(0)=0,\qquad 0\le t\le T_1 \tag{1}$$

$$\frac{dq}{dt}=-(\alpha+\beta q),\quad q\left(T_1^+\right)=q\left(T_1^-\right),\qquad T_1\le t\le \mu \tag{2}$$

$$\frac{dq}{dt}=-(\alpha+\beta q)(ab^r),\quad q(T_2)=0,\qquad \mu\le t\le T_2 \tag{3}$$

Solving Eq. (1), Eq. (2) and Eq. (3) using appropriate boundary conditions, the inventory levels in various intervals are calculated as below

$$q(t)=\frac{\alpha\left(e^{(\ell-1)\beta t}-1\right)}{\beta}, \qquad 0\le t\le T_1 \tag{1s}$$

$$q(t)=\frac{\alpha}{\beta}\left(e^{(\ell T_1-t)\beta}-1\right),\ T_1\le t\le \mu \tag{2s}$$

$$q(t)=\frac{\alpha}{\beta}\left(e^{ab^r(T_2-t)\beta}-1\right), \qquad \mu\le t\le T_2 \tag{3s}$$

To find the relation between the variables using the Taylor series expansion of solutions and using continuity condition, we have $T_2=\dfrac{\mu\left(ab^r-1\right)+\ell T_1}{ab^r}$.

For the feasibility of practical situation assumed in case I, T_2 must be greater than μ which in turn implies $\ell T_1-\mu>0$. Total Inventory in the complete production cycle is calculated as below

$$\int_0^{T_1}\frac{\alpha}{\beta}\left(e^{(\ell-1)\beta t}-1\right)dt+\frac{\alpha}{\beta}\int_{T_1}^{\mu}\left(e^{(\ell T_1-t)\beta}-1\right)dt+\int_{\mu}^{T_2}\frac{\alpha}{\beta}\left(e^{ab^r(T_2-t)\beta}-1\right)dt \tag{4}$$

$$=\frac{\alpha}{\beta}\left[\frac{\ell e^{(\ell-1)T_1\beta}-1}{(\ell-1)\beta}+\frac{\left(1-ab^r\right)e^{(\ell T_1-\mu)\beta}-1}{\left(ab^r\beta\right)}-\frac{\left(\mu\left(ab^r-1\right)+\ell T_1\right)}{ab^r}\right]$$

If machine breakdown occurs at $t=T_p$, then (4) is formulated as below

$$E(I)=\begin{bmatrix}\dfrac{\alpha}{\beta}\left[\dfrac{\ell e^{(\ell-1)T_p\beta}-1}{(\ell-1)\beta}+\dfrac{\left(1-ab^r\right)e^{(\ell T_p-\mu)\beta}-1}{\left(ab^r\right)\beta}-\dfrac{\mu\left(ab^r-1\right)+\ell T_p}{ab^r}\right]\text{......If......}T_p<T_1\\[2ex] \dfrac{\alpha}{\beta}\left[\dfrac{\ell e^{(\ell-1)T_1\beta}-1}{(\ell-1)\beta}+\dfrac{\left(1-ab^r\right)e^{(\ell T_1-\mu)\beta}-1}{\left(ab^r\right)\beta}-\dfrac{\mu\left(ab^r-1\right)+\ell T_1}{ab^r}\right]\text{.......If......}T_p>T_1\end{bmatrix}$$

Using the machine breakdown probability density function of T_p, $f\left(T_p\right)=\lambda e^{-\lambda T_p}$, $T_p>0$, the expected inventory is calculated as:

$$\int_{T_p=0}^{T_p=T_1}E(I)\lambda e^{-\lambda T_p}dT_p++\int_{T_p=T_1}^{\infty}E(I)\lambda e^{-\lambda T_p}dT_p$$

$$\int_{T_p=0}^{T_p=T_1}\frac{\alpha}{\beta}\left[\frac{\ell e^{(\ell-1)T_p\beta}-1}{(\ell-1)\beta}+\frac{\left(1-ab^r\right)e^{(\ell T_p-\mu)\beta}-1}{\left(ab^r\right)\beta}-\frac{\mu\left(ab^r-1\right)+\ell T_p}{ab^r}\right]\lambda e^{-\lambda T_p}dT_p+\int_{T_p=T_1}^{\infty}E(I)\lambda e^{-\lambda T_p}dT_p$$

$$=\frac{\lambda\alpha}{\beta}\left[\frac{\ell\left(e^{((\ell-1)\beta-\lambda)T_1}-1\right)}{(\ell-1)\beta\left((\ell-1)\beta-\lambda\right)}+\frac{e^{-\lambda T_1}-1}{\lambda(\ell-1)\beta}+\frac{e^{-\lambda T_1}-1}{\left(ab^r\right)\beta\lambda}+\frac{\left(1-ab^r\right)\left(e^{(\ell\beta-\lambda)T_1-\mu\beta}-e^{-\mu\beta}\right)}{\left(ab^r\right)\beta\left(\ell\beta-\lambda\right)}+\right.$$

$$\frac{\mu\left(ab^{r}-1\right)\left(e^{-\lambda T_1}-1\right)}{\left(ab^{r}\right)\lambda}-\frac{\ell}{ab^{r}}\left(\frac{-T_1e^{-\lambda T_1}}{\lambda}+\frac{1-e^{-\lambda T_1}}{\lambda^2}\right)\Bigg]$$

$$+\frac{\alpha}{\beta}\left[\frac{\ell e^{(\ell-1)T_1\beta}-1}{(\ell-1)\beta}+\frac{\left(1-ab^{r}\right)\left(e^{(\ell T_1-\mu)\beta}\right)-1}{\left(ab^{r}\right)\beta}-\frac{\mu\left(ab^{r}-1\right)+\ell T_1}{ab^{r}}\right]e^{-\lambda T_1}$$

Expected holding cost in complete Production cycle, E (HC)

$$=h\left[\frac{\alpha\ell e^{((\ell-1)\beta-\lambda)T_1}}{\beta((\ell-1)\beta-\lambda)}-\frac{\lambda\alpha\ell}{(\ell-1)\beta^2((\ell-1)\beta-\lambda)}+\frac{\ell\alpha\left(1-ab^{r}\right)e^{(\ell\beta-\lambda)T_1-\mu\beta}}{\left(ab^{r}\right)\beta\left(\ell\beta-\lambda\right)}-\frac{\left(1-ab^{r}\right)e^{-\mu\beta}\lambda\alpha}{\left(ab^{r}\right)\beta^2\left(\ell\beta-\lambda\right)}\right. \tag{5}$$

$$\left.-\frac{\alpha}{\beta^2}\left(\frac{1}{\ell-1}+\frac{1}{\left(ab^{r}\right)}\right)-\frac{\mu\left(ab^{r}-1\right)\alpha}{\left(ab^{r}\right)\beta}-\frac{\ell\alpha}{\left(ab^{r}\right)\beta}\left(\frac{1-e^{-\lambda T_1}}{\lambda}\right)\right]$$

Lost sales occur when repair time exceeds T_2. Assuming that machine repair time t is a random variable and is uniformly distributed over the interval $\left[0,c\right]$.The probability density function f (t) for the repair time is given by $f\left(t\right)=\begin{cases}\frac{1}{c}, & 0\le t\le c\\ 0, & otherwise\end{cases}$

For feasibility of the practical situation considered in the model, T_2 must be less than c, otherwise there will be no lost sales interval as lost sales occur when repair time exceeds T_2. Substituting the uniform probability density function of repair time and machine breakdown probability density function, expected lost sales cost is obtained as below

Expected Lost sales cost,

$$E\ (LSC)=\frac{S\alpha}{c}\int_{T_p=0}^{T_1}\int_{t=T_2}^{c}\left(t-T_2\right)\lambda e^{-\lambda T_p}dtdT_p=\frac{\lambda S\alpha}{2c}\int_{0}^{T_1}\left(c-\frac{\mu\left(ab^{r}-1\right)+\ell T_p}{ab^{r}}\right)^2 e^{-\lambda T_p}dT_p$$

$$\frac{\lambda S\alpha}{2c}\left[\frac{A^2\left(1-e^{-\lambda T_1}\right)}{\lambda}+\frac{\ell^2}{\left(ab^{r}\right)^2}\left(\frac{-T_1^2e^{-\lambda T_1}}{\lambda}-\frac{2T_1e^{-\lambda T_1}}{\lambda^2}+\frac{2\left(1-e^{-\lambda T_1}\right)}{\lambda^3}\right)-\frac{2A\ell}{ab^{r}}\left(\frac{-T_1e^{-\lambda T_1}}{\lambda}+\frac{1-e^{-\lambda T_1}}{\lambda^2}\right)\right] \tag{6}$$

where $A=c-\frac{\mu\left(ab^{r}-1\right)}{ab^{r}}$

Next, we calculate production cost as below

$$C_p\int_0^{T_1}Pdt=C_p\int_0^{T_1}lD(q)dt=C_pl\alpha\left(\frac{e^{(l-1)\beta T_1}-1}{(l-1)\beta}\right) \tag{7}$$

When machine breakdown occurs at $t=T_p$, then Eq. (7) can be formulated as

$$PC=\begin{cases}C_pl\alpha\left(\frac{e^{(l-1)\beta T_p}-1}{(l-1)\beta}\right) & If.....T_p<T_1\\ C_pl\alpha\left(\frac{e^{(l-1)\beta T_1}-1}{(l-1)\beta}\right) & If.....T_p>T_1\end{cases}$$

Using the above formulation, expected production cost can be obtained as

$$E(PC) = \int_{T_p=0}^{T_p=T_1} C_p l\alpha\left(\frac{e^{(l-1)\beta T_p}-1}{(l-1)\beta}\right)\lambda e^{-\lambda T_p}dT_p + \int_{T_p=T_1}^{T_p=\infty} C_p l\alpha\left(\frac{e^{(l-1)\beta T_1}-1}{(l-1)\beta}\right)\lambda e^{-\lambda T_p}dT_p$$

$$= C_p l\alpha\left(\frac{e^{((l-1)\beta-\lambda)T_1}-1}{(l-1)\beta-\lambda}\right) \tag{8}$$

The expected total inventory cost consists of set up cost, expected holding cost, expected lost sales cost and expected production cost.

Expected total cost, $E(TC) = K + E(HC) + E(LSC) + E(PC)$ (9)

Next we calculate sales revenue in the complete production cycle,

$$= S\left(\int_0^{T_1}(\alpha+\beta q)dt + \int_{T_1}^{\mu}(\alpha+\beta q)dt\right) + S(1-r)\left(\int_{\mu}^{T_2}(\alpha+\beta q)(ab^r)dt\right) = S\alpha\left(\frac{e^{(\ell-1)\beta T_1}-1}{(\ell-1)\beta}+\frac{r\left(1-e^{(\ell T_1-\mu)\beta}\right)}{\beta}\right)$$

If machine break down occurs at $t = T_p$, then sales revenues are formulated as

$$SR = \begin{bmatrix} S\alpha\left(\dfrac{e^{(\ell-1)\beta T_p}-1}{(\ell-1)\beta}+\dfrac{r\left(1-e^{(\ell T_p-\mu)\beta}\right)}{\beta}\right) \text{.....If......} T_p < T_1 \\ S\alpha\left(\dfrac{e^{(\ell-1)\beta T_1}-1}{(\ell-1)\beta}+\dfrac{r\left(1-e^{(\ell T_1-\mu)\beta}\right)}{\beta}\right) \text{.....If......} T_p > T_1 \end{bmatrix}$$

Using the probability density function of machine breakdown time T_p, the expected sales revenues of complete production cycle are obtained as

$$E(SR) = \int_0^{T_1} S\alpha\left(\frac{e^{(\ell-1)\beta T_p}-1}{(\ell-1)\beta}+\frac{r\left(1-e^{(\ell T_p-\mu)\beta}\right)}{\beta}\right)\lambda e^{-\lambda T_p}dT_p + \int_{T_1}^{\infty} S\alpha\left(\frac{e^{(\ell-1)\beta T_1}-1}{(\ell-1)\beta}+\frac{r\left(1-e^{(\ell T_1-\mu)\beta}\right)}{\beta}\right)\lambda e^{-\lambda T_p}dT_p \tag{10}$$

$$= \frac{S\alpha\ell\left(e^{((\ell-1)\beta-\lambda)T_1}-1\right)}{(\ell-1)\beta-\lambda} + \frac{S\alpha r\lambda e^{-\mu\beta}}{(\ell\beta-\lambda)\beta} - \frac{S\ell\alpha r e^{(\ell\beta-\lambda)T_1-\mu\beta}}{(\ell\beta-\lambda)} + \frac{S\alpha r}{\beta}$$

The expected total replenishment time is the sum of expected production up time period, non production period and expected repair time after $t - T_2$. Therefore, Expected total time, $E(T) = E(T_2) +$ Expected Repair time

$$\int_{T_p=0}^{T_1} T_2\lambda e^{-\lambda T_p}dT_p + \int_{T_p=T_1}^{\infty} T_2\lambda e^{-\lambda T_p}dT_p + \int_{T_p=0}^{T_1}\int_{t=T_2}^{\infty}(t-T_2)f(t)\lambda e^{-\lambda T_p}dT_p \tag{11}$$

$$= \frac{\mu\left(ab^r-1\right)}{ab^r} + \frac{\ell}{ab^r}\frac{\left(1-e^{-\lambda T_1}\right)}{\lambda} + \frac{\lambda}{2c}\left[\frac{A^2\left(1-e^{-\lambda T_1}\right)}{\lambda} + \frac{\ell^2}{\left(ab^r\right)^2}\left(\frac{-T_1^2 e^{-\lambda T_1}}{\lambda} - \frac{2T_1}{\lambda^2}e^{-\lambda T_1} + \frac{2}{\lambda^3}\left(1-e^{-\lambda T_1}\right)\right)\right.$$

$$-\frac{2A\ell}{ab^r}\left(\frac{-T_1e^{-\lambda T_1}}{\lambda}+\frac{1-e^{-\lambda T_1}}{\lambda^2}\right)\Bigg]$$

Substituting all the values from Eqs. (5-11), the expected total profit, $E(TP)=E(SR)-E(TC)$ is calculated as follows,

$$\left\{\frac{S\alpha\ell\left(e^{((\ell-1)\beta-\lambda)T_1}-1\right)}{(\ell-1)\beta-\lambda}+\frac{S\alpha r\lambda e^{-\mu\beta}}{(\ell\beta-\lambda)\beta}-\frac{S\ell\alpha re^{(\ell\beta-\lambda)T_1-\mu\beta}}{(\ell\beta-\lambda)}+\frac{S\alpha r}{\beta}\right\} \quad (12)$$

$$-\left\{K+h\left(\frac{\alpha\ell e^{((\ell-1)\beta-\lambda)T_1}}{\beta((\ell-1)\beta-\lambda)}-\frac{\lambda\alpha\ell}{(\ell-1)\beta^2((\ell-1)\beta-\lambda)}+\frac{\ell\alpha\left(1-ab^r\right)e^{(\ell\beta-\lambda)T_1-\mu\beta}}{\left(ab^r\right)\beta(\ell\beta-\lambda)}-\frac{\left(1-ab^r\right)e^{-\mu\beta}\lambda\alpha}{\left(ab^r\right)\beta^2(\ell\beta-\lambda)}\right)\right\}$$

$$+\left\{\frac{h\alpha}{\beta^2}\left(\frac{1}{\ell-1}+\frac{1}{\left(ab^r\right)}\right)+\frac{h\mu\left(ab^r-1\right)\alpha}{\left(ab^r\right)\beta}+\frac{h\ell\alpha}{\left(ab^r\right)\beta}\left(\frac{1-e^{-\lambda T_1}}{\lambda}\right)-C_pl\alpha\left(\frac{e^{((l-1)\beta-\lambda)T_1}-1}{(l-1)\beta-\lambda}\right)\right\}$$

$$-\frac{\lambda S\alpha}{2c}\left\{\frac{A^2\left(1-e^{-\lambda T_1}\right)}{\lambda}+\frac{\ell^2}{\left(ab^r\right)^2}\left(\frac{-T_1^2e^{-\lambda T_1}}{\lambda}-\frac{2T_1e^{-\lambda T_1}}{\lambda^2}+\frac{2\left(1-e^{-\lambda T_1}\right)}{\lambda^3}\right)-\frac{2A\ell}{ab^r}\left(\frac{-T_1e^{-\lambda T_1}}{\lambda}+\frac{1-e^{-\lambda T_1}}{\lambda^2}\right)\right\}$$

$$\frac{dE(TP)}{dT_1}=S\alpha\ell e^{-\lambda T_1}\left(e^{(\ell-1)T_1\beta}-re^{(\ell T_1-\mu)\beta}\right)-\left\{h\left(\frac{\alpha\ell e^{((\ell-1)\beta-\lambda)T_1}}{\beta}+\frac{\ell\alpha\left(1-ab^r\right)e^{(\ell\beta-\lambda)T_1-\mu\beta}}{\left(ab^r\right)\beta}-\frac{\ell\alpha e^{-\lambda T_1}}{\left(ab^r\right)\beta}\right)\right. \quad (13)$$

$$\left.+C_p\ell\alpha e^{((\ell-1)\beta-\lambda)T_1}+\frac{\lambda S\alpha}{2c}\left(A^2e^{-\lambda T_1}+\frac{\ell^2T_1^2e^{-\lambda T_1}}{\left(ab^r\right)^2}-\frac{2A\ell T_1e^{-\lambda T_1}}{ab^r}\right)\right\}$$

$$\frac{d^2E(TP)}{dT_1^2}=\left\{S\alpha\ell\left((\ell-1)\beta e^{((\ell-1)\beta-\lambda)T_1}-r\ell\beta e^{(\ell\beta-\lambda)T_1-\mu\beta}\right)\right\}-\left\{h\alpha\ell e^{-\lambda T_1}\left((\ell-1)e^{((\ell-1)\beta)T_1}+\frac{\ell\left(1-ab^r\right)e^{(\ell T_1-\mu)\beta}}{\left(ab^r\right)}\right)\right. \quad (14)$$

$$\left.C_pl(l-1)\beta\alpha e^{((l-1)\beta-\lambda)T_1}+\frac{\lambda S\alpha}{c}\left(\frac{\ell^2T_1e^{-\lambda T_1}}{\left(ab^r\right)^2}-\frac{A\ell e^{-\lambda T_1}}{ab^r}\right)\right\}$$

Using renewal reward theorem, Expected total average profit, $E(TAP)$

$$E(TAP)=\frac{E(TP)}{E(T)}=\frac{E(SR)-E(TC)}{E(T)} \quad (15)$$

5. Optimal solution procedure:

Our objective is to determine the expected optimal value of T_1 so that $E(TAP)$ is maximized. The necessary condition for $E(TAP)$ to be maximized is $\frac{d(E(TAP))}{dT_1}=0$ and $\frac{d^2E(TAP)}{dT_1^2}<0$. The expected total profit per unit time is concave where $0\le T_2\le c$, (see Appendix A, Appendix B and Appendix C for detailed calculations).

The optimal value of T_1 has been obtained numerically using Newton Raphson Method.

The following solution procedure is used to derive the optimal values of T_1

We find the root of the equation $\frac{d(E(TAP))}{dT_1}=0$ using C^{++} program of Newton Raphson Method using the algorithm as below

Step 1: Define $f(T_1)=\frac{d(E(TAP))}{dT_1}$

Define $f^{'}(T_1)=\frac{d^2(E(TAP))}{dT_1^2}$

Step 2: Choose initial value of $T_1=t_0$ and set values for other parameters.

Step 3: Apply do-while loop

Find $p=\frac{f(t_0)}{f^{'}(t_0)}$

Store in $t_0=t_0-p$

If $|p|<0.0002$, then declare t_0 to be the required root else repeat Step 3.

Case II : When μ is greater than the cycle length

When μ is greater than the cycle length then there is no sale period and demand remains stock dependent, the governing equations take the form:

$$\frac{dq}{dt}=(\ell-1)(\alpha+\beta q),q(0)=0,0\le t\le T_1$$

$$\frac{dq}{dt}=-(\alpha+\beta q),q(T_2)=0,T_1\le t\ge T_2$$

As $\mu\to T_1$, a $\to 1$ and r$\to 0$, in case I, we can have the expected total profit in Case II as $E(TP)$ = $E(SR)-E(TC)$

$$\left\{\frac{S\alpha\ell\left(e^{((\ell-1)\beta-\lambda)T_1}-1\right)}{(\ell-1)\beta-\lambda}\right\}-\left\{K+h\left(\frac{\alpha\ell\left(e^{((\ell-1)\beta-\lambda)T_1}-1\right)}{\beta((\ell-1)\beta-\lambda)}-\frac{\ell\alpha}{\beta}\left(\frac{1-e^{-\lambda T_1}}{\lambda}\right)\right)+C_p\ell\alpha\left(\frac{e^{((\ell-1)\beta-\lambda)T_1}-1}{(\ell-1)\beta-\lambda}\right)\right\}$$
$$-\frac{s\alpha}{2c}\left\{c^2-(c-\ell T_1)^2e^{-\lambda T_1}+\frac{2\ell}{\lambda}\left((c-\ell T_1)e^{-\lambda T_1}-c\right)-\frac{2\ell^2}{\lambda^2}\left(c^{-\lambda T_1}-1\right)\right\}$$

Expected total time, $E(T)=E(T_2)+$ Expected Repair time

$$=\ell\left(\frac{1-e^{-\lambda T_1}}{\lambda}\right)+\frac{1}{2c}\left\{c^2-(c-\ell T_1)^2e^{-\lambda T_1}+\frac{2\ell}{\lambda}\left((c-\ell T_1)e^{-\lambda T_1}-c\right)-\frac{2\ell^2}{\lambda^2}\left(e^{-\lambda T_1}-1\right)\right\}$$

The expected total profit per unit time is concave where $0\le T_2\le c$,

6. Numerical example

In this part, we have presented computational results obtained by using C++ program of Newton Raphson Method which gives insight about the behavior of expected production cycle time $E(T)$, expected optimal run size E(Q) and the expected total average profit $E(TAP)$. The parametric values in the models are taken as

$\beta = 0.4, h = 2, K = 200, \lambda = 0.2, \alpha = 25, C_p = 10, S = 20, c = 5, \mu = 3, a = 0.5, b = 2$

Table 1

Effect of C_p on optimal values of $E(Q), E(T)$ and $E(TAP)$

	ℓ=1.8			
C_p	9	10	11	12
T_1	2.652	2,444	2.2103	1.931
E(Q)	53.72	50.262	46.64	42.653
E(T)	4.679	4.3379	3.9373	3.4305
E(HC)	281.131	232.846	185.957	139.670
E(LSC)	305.612	305.375	305.267	303.678
E(PC)	1706.826	1849.723	1978.426	2087.1456
E(SR)	3522.820	3514.2084	3496.94	3467.3443
E(TAP)	241.34	236.581	235.514	243.944

- As C_p increases, the production cost also increases. To balance the high production cost, production run time decreases. Consequently, inventory level also decreases and which leads to decrease in holding cost.
- Higher values of C_p leads to lower inventory level. As the demand rate is based on the inventory level and sales revenues are based on the demand, therefore, decrease in inventory level decreases the sales revenues, which also causes fall in the expected total profit.
- As C_p increases, expected cycle length, which includes repair time also decreases. It is reasonable that decrease in repair time decreases the lost sales cost also.

Table 2

Effect of h on optimal values of $E(Q), E(T)$ and $E(TAP)$

h	2.5	2	1.5	1
C_p	1.8142	2.3023	2.5263	2.782
T_1	47.505	57.748	63.161	69.963
E(T)	3.6193	4.602	5.023	5.485
E(HC)	223.097	305.534	285.737	240.78
E(LSC)	277.071	277.992	278.863	282.302
E(PC)	1321.98	1457.541	1524.323	1604.305
E(SR)	2597.82	2666.54	2684.62	2692.99
E(TAP)	214.315	135.83	118.595	103.119

- As h decreases, the productions run time increases. Rise in production run time raises the production cost.
- Lower values of h leads to higher production run time. Consequently, there is a rise in the inventory level. As the demand rate is based on the inventory level and sales revenues are based on the demand, therefore, increase in inventory level increases the sales revenues. Although there is rise in the sales revenues but total average profit falls in view of rise in some other costs.
- As h decreases, expected cycle length, which includes repair time also increases. It is reasonable that increase in repair time increases the lost sales cost also.

Table 3

Effect of ℓ on optimal values of Q, T and $E(TAP)$

ℓ	1.6	1.8	2
T_1	2.609	2.444	2.3023
E(Q)	43.005	50.262	57.748
E(T)	4.0601	4.3379	4.602
E(TAP)	826.639	236.581	135.8304

- As ℓ increases, the production runtime decrease, which is very genuine result to expect. Although in view of the increase in production rate there is increase in the inventory level.
- As production rate increases, there is increase in the cycle length.
- Higher values of ℓ leads to lower expected total average profit.
- Higher production run time and lower production rate give higher profit.

7. Conclusion

The model developed above addressed some expected realistic features that usually arose while working on the optimal production policy for stochastic models that maximized the expected profit. It was very important to take the production system as unreliable as uncertainty was very expected feature of a real system. If machine broke down, it was always not certain that it could be repaired in a fixed time period. Normally, in the supermarkets the demand was influenced by the stock displayed on their shelves. In view of the highly competitive situation in the real business, the production system could not afford to be inflexible. Keeping in view all the issues raised, we took the production system unreliable and flexible, taking production rate as a function of demand. In addition, we took a machine repair time stochastic and derived an optimal production policy for the stochastic model which could maximize the expected profit. It was observed that increase in the production rate decreased the production run time and decrease in the production rate increased the production run time. Further, it was observed that longer production up time and lower production rates provided higher expected profits as compared to shorter production uptime and higher production rates in stochastic model. It was also observed that the higher production cost per unit decreased the expected profit. Further research on the problem could be extended to consider more realistic assumptions into the proposed model, for example, imperfect quality of products, reverse manufacturing, trade credit, etc.

References

Chakraborty, T., Giri, B. C., & Chaudhuri, K. S. (2008). Production lot sizing with process deterioration and machine breakdown. *European Journal of Operational Research*, *185*(2), 606-618.

Cheung, K. L., & Hausman, W. H. (1997). Joint determination of preventive maintenance and safety stocks in an unreliable production environment. *Naval Research Logistics (NRL)*, *44*(3), 257-272.

Chiu, S. W., Wang, S. L., & Chiu, Y. S. P. (2007). Determining the optimal run time for EPQ model with scrap, rework, and stochastic breakdowns. *European Journal of Operational Research*, *180*(2), 664-676.

Dem, H., & Singh, S. R. (2012, January). Production scheduling for damageable items with demand and cost flexibility using genetic algorithm. In *Proceedings of the International Conference on Soft Computing for Problem Solving (SocProS 2011) December 20-22, 2011* (pp. 747-759). Springer India.

Dem, H., & Singh, S. R. (2013). A production model for ameliorating items with quality consideration. *International Journal of Operational Research*, *17*(2), 183-198.

El-Ferik, S. (2008). Economic production lot-sizing for an unreliable machine under imperfect age-based maintenance policy. *European Journal of Operational Research*, *186*(1), 150-163.

Giri, B. C., & Chaudhuri, K. S. (1998). Deterministic models of perishable inventory with stock-dependent demand rate and nonlinear holding cost. *European Journal of Operational Research*, *105*(3), 467-474.

Giri, B. C., Yun, W. Y., & Dohi, T. (2005). Optimal design of unreliable production–inventory systems with variable production rate. *European Journal of Operational Research*, *162*(2), 372-386.

Goyal, S. K., Singh, S. R., & Dem, H. (2013). Production policy for ameliorating/deteriorating items with ramp type demand. *International Journal of Procurement Management*, *6*(4), 444-465.

Groenevelt, H., Pintelon, L., & Seidmann, A. (1992). Production lot sizing with machine breakdowns. *Management Science*, *38*(1), 104-123.

Groenevelt, H., Pintelon, L., & Seidmann, A. (1992). Production batching with machine breakdowns and safety stocks. *Operations Research, 40*(5), 959-971.

Gupta, R., & Vrat, P. (1986). Inventory model for stock-dependent consumption rate. *Opsearch, 23*(1), 19-24.

Konstantaras, I., & Skouri, K. (2010). Lot sizing for a single product recovery system with variable setup numbers. *European Journal of Operational Research, 203*(2), 326-335.

Levin, R. I., Mclaughlin, C. P., Lamone, R. P., & Kottas, J. F. (1972). Production, Operations Management: Contemporary Policy for Managing Operation System. NewYork: McGraw-Hill.

Leung, K. N. F. (2007). A generalized geometric-programming solution to "An economic production quantity model with flexibility and reliability considerations". *European Journal of Operational Research, 176*(1), 240-251.

Liao, G. L., Chen, Y. H., & Sheu, S. H. (2009). Optimal economic production quantity policy for imperfect process with imperfect repair and maintenance.*European Journal of Operational Research, 195*(2), 348-357.

Lin, G.C., & Gong, D.C. (2006). On a production inventory system of deteriorating items subject to random machine breakdowns with a fixed repair time. *Mathematical Computational Modeling*, 43(7), 920-932.

Mandal, B.N., & Phaujdar, S. (1989). An inventory model for deteriorating items and stock dependent consumption rate. *Journal Operational Research Society*, 40, 483–488.

Peterson, R., & Silver, E. A. (1979). *Decision systems for inventory management and production planning* (pp. 799-799). New York: Wiley.

Sana, S., Goyal, S.K., & Chaudhuri K.S. (2006). An imperfect production process in a volume flexible inventory model. *International Journal of Production Economics,* 105,548-559.

Schweitzer, P. J., Seidmann, A. (1991). Optimizing, processing rate for flexible manufacturing systems. *Management Science*, 37, 454-466.

Singh, S. R., Kumar, N., & Kumari, R. (2010). An inventory model for deteriorating items with shortages and stock-dependent demand under inflation for two-shops under one management. *Opsearch, 47*(4), 311-329.

Singh, S. R., & Saxena, N. (2012). An optimal returned policy for a reverse logistics inventory model with backorders. *Advances in Decision Sciences.*

Singh, S. R., & Jain, R. (2009). On reserve money for an EOQ model in an inflationary environment under supplier credits. *Opsearch, 46*(3), 303-320.

Singh, S. R., & Singh, C. (2010). Supply chain model with stochastic lead time under imprecise partially backlogging and fuzzy ramp-type demand for expiring items. *International Journal of Operational Research, 8*(4), 511-522.

Teng, J. T., & Chang, C. T. (2005). Economic production quantity models for deteriorating items with price-and stock-dependent demand. *Computers & Operations Research, 32*(2), 297-308.

Wang, C. H. (2004). The impact of a free-repair warranty policy on EMQ model for imperfect production systems. *Computers & Operations Research, 31*(12), 2021-2035.

Widyadana, G. A., & Wee, H. M. (2011). Optimal deteriorating items production inventory models with random machine breakdown and stochastic repair time. *Applied Mathematical Modelling, 35*(7), 3495-3508.

Yadav, D., Singh, S. R., & Kumari, R. (2012). Inventory model of deteriorating items with two-warehouse and stock dependent demand using genetic algorithm in fuzzy environment. *Yugoslav Journal of Operations Research ISSN: 0354-0243 EISSN: 2334-6043, 22*(1).

Appendix A:

Derivative analysis of expected time function:

For feasibility of the practical situation considered in the model T_2 must be less than c, otherwise there will be no lost sales interval as lost sales occur when repair time exceeds T_2. So we consider the behavior of $\mathrm{E(T)}$ in interval $0 \le T_2 \le c$

$$\frac{dE(T)}{dT_1} = \left(\frac{\ell}{ab^r} + \frac{\lambda A^2}{2c} + \frac{\ell^2\lambda}{2c\left(ab^r\right)^2}T_1^2 - \frac{2A\ell\lambda T_1}{\left(ab^r\right)2c}\right)e^{-\lambda T_1} \quad \frac{d^2E(T)}{dT_1^2} = e^{-\lambda T_1}\left(\frac{\ell^2\lambda T_1}{\left(ab^r\right)^2 c} - \frac{A\ell\lambda}{\left(ab^r\right)c}\right) \qquad \text{A1)}$$

Set $T_1 = 0$, we have $\dfrac{d^2E(T)}{dT_1^2} = -\dfrac{A\ell\lambda}{\left(ab^r\right)c} < 0$

$$\frac{d^2E(T)}{dT_1^2} < 0 \text{ If } \frac{\ell^2\lambda}{\left(ab^r\right)^2 c}T_1 < \frac{A\ell\lambda}{\left(ab^r\right)c} \quad \Rightarrow T_1 < \frac{A\left(ab^r\right)}{\ell}$$

$E(T)$ is concave w.r.t. T_1, where $0 \le T_1 \le \dfrac{A\left(ab^r\right)}{\ell}$, where $A = \dfrac{c\left(ab^r\right) - \mu\left(ab^r - 1\right)}{ab^r}$

Also $0 \le T_1 \le \dfrac{A\left(ab^r\right)}{\ell} \quad \Rightarrow \quad 0 \le T_2 \le c$

Therefore, $E(T)$ is concave when $0 \le T_2 \le c$

Appendix B:

To prove, $\dfrac{d^2E(TAP)}{dT_1^2} < 0$ if $\dfrac{d^2E(TP)}{dT_1^2} < 0$ where $0 \le T_2 \le c$

$$\frac{d^2E(TAP)}{dT_1^2} = \frac{d^2\left(\dfrac{E(TP)}{E(T)}\right)}{dT_1^2} = \frac{E(T)\dfrac{d^2E(TP)}{dT_1^2} - E(TP)\dfrac{d^2E(T)}{dT_1^2}}{(E(T))^2}$$

Now $\dfrac{d^2E(TAP)}{dT_1^2} < 0$ if $E(T)\dfrac{d^2E(TP)}{dT_1^2} < E(TP)\dfrac{d^2E(T)}{dT_1^2}$

Using (A1), As $\dfrac{d^2E(T)}{dT_1^2} < 0$ in the interval $0 \le T_2 \le c$

Also $E(T) > 0$, $E(TP) > 0$,

Therefore, in the interval $0 \le T_2 \le c$, $\dfrac{d^2E(TAP)}{dT_1^2} < 0$ if $\dfrac{d^2E(TP)}{dT_1^2} < 0$ (B1)

Appendix C:

To prove $\dfrac{d^2E(TP)}{dT_1^2} < 0$

$$\frac{d(E(SR))}{dT_1} = S\alpha\ell e^{-\lambda T_1}\left(e^{(\ell-1)\beta} - re^{(\ell T_1-\mu)\beta}\right)$$

$$\frac{d^2(E(SR))}{dT_1^2} = S\alpha\ell e^{-\lambda T_1}\left(\left(\ell-1\right)\beta e^{(\ell-1)\beta T_1} - r\ell\beta\, e^{(\ell T_1-\mu)\beta}\right) - \lambda\frac{dE(SR)}{dT_1}$$

$$(\ell-1)\beta e^{(\ell-1)\beta T_1}-r\ell\beta\, e^{(\ell T_1-\mu)\beta}<0\;\; If\,\frac{(\ell-1)}{r\ell}<\frac{e^{(\ell-1)\beta T_1}}{e^{(\ell T_1-\mu)\beta}}$$

$$\Rightarrow If\,\frac{(\ell-1)}{r\ell}<e^{-(\mu-T_1)\beta T_1}<\min(e^{-(\mu-T_1)\beta T_1})=1$$

AS $l>1\Rightarrow\frac{1}{l}<1$

Therefore $\frac{d^2(E(SR))}{dT_1^2}<0$ if $(1-r)<1$ which holds true (C1)

$$\frac{d(E(TC))}{dT_1}=$$

$$\left\{h\left(\frac{\alpha\ell e^{((\ell-1)\beta-\lambda)T_1}}{\beta}+\frac{\ell\alpha\left(1-ab^r\right)e^{(\ell\beta-\lambda)T_1-\mu\beta}}{\left(ab^r\right)\beta}-\frac{\ell\alpha e^{-\lambda T_1}}{\left(ab^r\right)\beta}\right)+\frac{\lambda S\alpha}{2c}\left(A^2e^{-\lambda T_1}+\frac{\ell^2T_1^2e^{-\lambda T_1}}{\left(ab^r\right)^2}-\frac{2A\ell T_1e^{-\lambda T_1}}{ab^r}\right)\right.$$

$$\left.+C_p\left(\ell\alpha e^{((\ell-1)\beta-\lambda)T_1}\right)+\frac{\lambda S\alpha}{2c}\left(A^2e^{-\lambda T_1}+\frac{\ell^2T_1^2e^{-\lambda T_1}}{\left(ab^r\right)^2}-\frac{2A\ell T_1e^{-\lambda T_1}}{ab^r}\right)\right\}$$

$$\frac{d^2(E(TC))}{dT_1^2}=\left[h\alpha\ell e^{-\lambda T_1}\left((\ell-1)e^{((\ell-1)\beta)T_1}+\frac{\ell\left(1-ab^r\right)e^{(\ell T_1-\mu)\beta}}{\left(ab^r\right)}\right)+\frac{\lambda S\alpha}{c}\left(\frac{\ell^2T_1\,e^{-\lambda T_1}}{\left(ab^r\right)^2}-\frac{A\ell e^{-\lambda T_1}}{ab^r}\right)\right]$$

$$+C_pl(l-1)\beta\alpha e^{((l-1)\beta-\lambda)T_1}\quad-\lambda\frac{d(E(TC))}{dT_1}$$

Set $T_1=0$

$$\frac{d^2(E(TC))}{dT_1^2}>0\text{ If }\left(h\alpha\ell\left((\ell-1)+\frac{\ell\left(1-ab^r\right)e^{-\mu\beta}}{\left(ab^r\right)}\right)-\frac{\lambda S\alpha A\ell}{cab^r}+C_pl(l-1)\beta\alpha\right)>0 \tag{C2}$$

Set $T_1=\frac{A\left(ab^r\right)}{\ell}$

$$\frac{d^2(E(TC))}{dT_1^2}>0\text{ If }\;h\alpha\ell\left((\ell-1)+\frac{\ell\left(1-ab^r\right)e^{-\mu\beta}}{\left(ab^r\right)}\right)+C_pl(l-1)\beta\alpha e^{((l-1)\beta-\lambda)T_1}>0 \tag{C3}$$

Now $\frac{d^2(E(TP))}{dT_1^2}=\frac{d^2(E(SR))}{dT_1^2}-\frac{d^2(E(TC))}{dT_1^2}$

Using (C1), (C2), and (C3), we have

$\frac{d^2(E(SR))}{dT_1^2}<0$ and $\frac{d^2(E(TC))}{dT_1^2}>0$ in the interval $0\le T_2\le c$ when (C2) and (C3) are fulfilled.

Therefore, $\frac{d^2(E(TP))}{dT_1^2}<0$ which in turn implies $\frac{d^2E(TAP)}{dT_1^2}<0$ where $0\le T_2\le c$

7

Solving uncapacitated multiple allocation p-hub center problem by Dijkstra's algorithm-based genetic algorithm and simulated annealing

Masoud Rabbani* **and Seyed Mahmood Kazemi**

School of Industrial Engineering, College of Engineering, University of Tehran, Tehran, Iran

CHRONICLE

Keywords:
P-hub center problem
Dijkstra's algorithm
Genetic Algorithm
Simulated Annealing

ABSTRACT

In the existing literature, there are a huge number of studies focused on p-hub median problems and inventing heuristic or metaheuristic algorithms for solving them. But such analogous body of literature does not exist for its counterpart problem; p-hub center problem. In fact, since p-hub center has been lately introduced and has a particular objective function, minimizing the maximum cost between origin-destination nodes, there are few studies investigating the problem and the challenges for solving it. In this study, after presenting a complete definition of the uncapacitated multiple allocation p-hub center problem (UMApHCP) two well-known metaheuristic algorithms are proposed to solve the problem for small scale and large scale standard data sets. These two algorithms are one single solution-based algorithm, Simulated Annealing (SA), and one population-based metaheuristic, Genetic Algorithm (GA). Because of the particular nature of the problem, Dijkstra's algorithm has been incorporated in the fitness function calculation part of the proposed methods. The numerical results of running the GA and SA for standard test problems show that for smaller scale test problems, single solution-based SA shows greater performance versus GA but for larger scales of data sets the GA generally yield more desirable solutions.

1. Introduction

In some networks, for example, telecommunication or transportations systems, there exist many nodes whose flows should depart from one origin node and arrive in a destination node. Since establishing a direct link between every pair of nodes needs considerable investments and is financially inefficient, some nodes are chosen as hubs, which operate as switching, transshipment and sorting centers and the flow of every node is conveyed to destination points through these nodes.

The problem of optimally locating these hubs and allocating demand nodes to them is called hub location problem. There are two basic types of hub networks: single allocation and multiple allocations. Their difference is in the way of allocating non-hub nodes to hub centers. According to Alumur and Kara (2008) "In single allocation, all the incoming and outgoing traffic of every demand center is routed through a single hub; in multiple allocation, each demand center can receive and send flow through more than one hub.". Fig. 1 shows the mentioned difference of single allocation and multiple allocation hub networks.

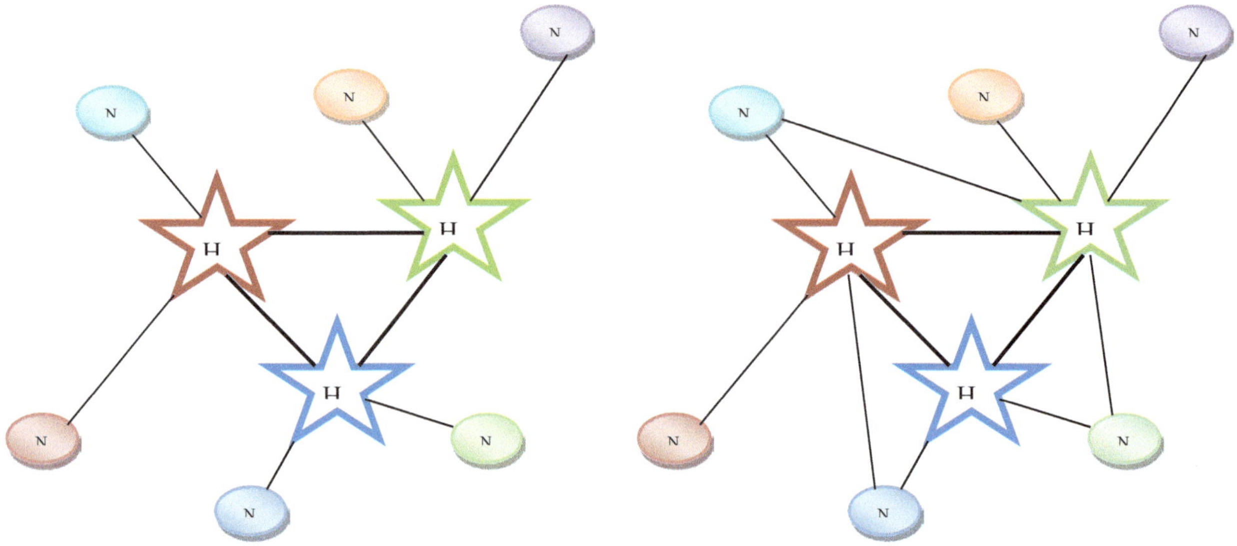

Fig. 1. A single allocation (left hand side) and multiple allocation (right hand side) hub network

The p-hub center problem is a well-known NP-hard problem (Kara & Tansel, 2000) which was firstly introduced and formulated by Campbell (1994). It is worth noting that it is a minimax type problem and is similar to the p-center problem. Campbell (1994) categorized this problem into three different types:

- The maximum cost for movement on any single link (origin-to-hub, hub-to-hub and hub-to-destination) is minimized.
- The maximum cost of movement between a hub and an origin/destination is minimized (vertex center).
- The maximum cost for any origin–destination pair is minimized.

When a hub system involves perishable or time sensitive items and because of that time is really important, we can replace cost with time and in such cases the first type of p-hub center problem becomes important. An example of the second type of p-hub is the vehicle drivers that are subject to a time limit on continuous service. Similar examples to the second type can be given for the third type problem, considering that hub-to-hub links may have some particular characteristics. Campbell (1994) presented formulations for both single and multiple allocation versions of the all three types of p-hub center problem mentioned above.

Based on the results of the study of Alumur and Kara (2008), the total number of papers on the p-hub center problem is very few compared with other hub models. The main reason is that these problems are proposed in 1994 and remain untouched until 2000. However, in the last decade this indicator is growing and the research community is giving more and more attention to the problem.

Kara and Tansel (2000) studied the computational aspects of the single-assignment p-hub center problem on the basis of Campbell's first type model and their proposed model. As reported by the authors, the new model outperformed different linearizations of the basic model regarding CPU times.

Ernst et al. (2009) developed a new formulation for the single allocation p-hub center problem. A new variable r_k was defined to model the maximum collection/distribution cost between hub k and the nodes allocated to hub k. Their model for single allocation was as follows:

$$\text{Min} \quad Z \tag{1}$$

subject to

$$\sum_k X_{ik} = 1 \qquad \forall i \tag{2}$$

$$\sum_k X_{kk} = p \qquad \forall k \tag{3}$$

$$r_k \geq C_{ik} X_{ik} \qquad \forall i, k \tag{4}$$

$$Z \geq r_k + r_m + \alpha C_{km} \qquad \forall k, m \tag{5}$$

$$X_{ik} \leq X_{kk} \qquad \forall i, k \tag{6}$$

$$X_{ik} \in \{0,1\} \qquad \forall i, k \tag{7}$$

$$r \geq 0 \qquad \forall k \tag{8}$$

Baumgartner (2003) proposed a branch-and-cut algorithm by investigating the polyhedral properties of a formulation proposed by Ernst in an unpublished report and identified some facet-defining inequalities and defined separation procedures. Pamuk and Sepil (2001) addressed the p-hub center problem. They proposed the first heuristic for the single allocation p-hub center problem as a means of generating location-allocation strategies in a reasonable amount of time, and superimposed tabu search on the underlying algorithm, so as to decrease the possibility of being trapped by local optima. Kratica and Stanimirovic (2006) proposed a genetic algorithm with binary coding for the uncapacitated multiple allocation p-hub center problems. They constructed and implemented problem-specific genetic operators in their genetic algorithm. Yaman et al. (2007) analyzed the latest arrival hub location problem with stopovers and included the transient times, the time spent for unloading, sorting and loading at hubs in their model. Campbell et al. (2007) presented complexity results and IP formulations for several versions of the p-hub center allocation problem including both capacitated and uncapacitated cases and established that some special uncapacitated cases are solvable in polynomial times.

Gavriliouk (2009) considered aggregated heuristic procedures for the hub location problems and calculated bounds for errors from such heuristics. Meyer et al. (2009) presented an exact 2-phase algorithm. In the first phase, a set of potential optimal hub locations was computed with a shortest path based B&B algorithm and in the second phase, allocation phase, the optimal allocations were computed accordingly. They also developed an ant colony optimization heuristic for the upper bound needed for the B&B. Sim et al. (2009) presented the stochastic p-hub center problem with chance constraints. To solve the problem, a two stage heuristic approach was also developed. Contreras et al. (2011) considered stochastic uncapacitated hub location problems with uncertain demands and transportation costs. They showed that if the uncertainty was associated with demands, the stochastic problem was equivalent to its expected value problem. On the contrary, if independent transportation costs were uncertain the corresponding stochastic problem would not be equivalent to its expected value problem and some other solution approaches were needed to be developed. Mohammadi et al. (2011a) considered a network with a central mine and a number of factories as customers, and tried to design and schedule transportation of raw material from the mine to its customers using a single allocation hub covering location problem. Afterward the problem was formulated as a mixed-integer programming formulation and two metaheuristics namely, genetic algorithm and shuffled frog leaping algorithm were developed. In another study, Mohammadi et al. (2011b) proposed a new model for capacitated single allocation hub covering location problem and developed a multi-objective imperialist competitive algorithm to solve the problem. Yaman and Elloumi (2012) introduced p-hub center and p-hub median problem with bounded path length. They proposed two integer programming formulations for the star p-hub center problem and three formulations for the star p-hub median problem. Furthermore, they strengthened the last formulation via specific clique inequalities and solved the considered instances to optimality within half an hour. After a while, Liang (2013) analyzed the hardness of the star p-hub center problem. Bashiri et al. (2013) considered a number of qualitative parameters for the hub location problem and proposed a GA based heuristic to solve this problem under capacitated constraints. In order to deal with uncertainty and qualitative parameters, fuzzy systems were utilized. Yang et al. (2013b) proposed a hybrid particle swarm optimization algorithm for fuzzy p-hub center problem. In their problem travel times were considered to be uncertain and modeled by normal fuzzy vectors. In a similar study, Yang et al. (2013a) considered a fuzzy p-hub center problem with fuzzy travel times and developed a genetic algorithm with local search to deal with the problem. Hult et al. (2014) proposed a reformulation for the p-hub center problem when the uncertainty of travel times was considered. Then a number of exact solution approaches based on variable reduction were developed to solve small-medium sized problems to optimality. The literature is rich enough with high-quality reviews in the context of hub location problem. In 2012, Campbell and O'Kelly (2012) provided a comprehensive review on hub location problems and discussed the present status of the literature. They also explored the shortcomings of the literature and suggested future research directions. A short after, Farahani et al. (2013) provided a latest review of models, classification, solution techniques and applications of hub location problems. To provide a concise overview of the literature review, the paramount feature of each studies mentioned above are encapsulated in Table 1.

Table 1

p-Hub center literature

Year	Authors	Notes
1994	Campbell (1994)	Different types of p-hub center formulations
2000	(Kara & Tansel, 2000)	Various linear formulations for single allocation
2001	(Pamuk & Sepil, 2001)	Heuristic for the single allocation problem
2003	(Baumgartner, 2003)	Polyhedral properties, valid inequalities and branch-and-cut algorithm
2007	(Yaman et al., 2007)	Latest arrival hub location problem with stopovers
2006	(Kratica & Stanimirovic, 2006)	GA for the uncapacitated multiple allocation problem
2007	(Campbell et al., 2007)	Complexity results and formulations for the allocation subproblem
2009	(Gavriliouk, 2009)	Heuristic procedures based on aggregation
2009	(Meyer et al., 2009)	Optimal hub locations using a shortest path based B&B and optimal allocations based on reduced size allocation; and ant colony optimization heuristic
2009	(Sim et al., 2009)	Stochastic p-hub center problems with chance constraints
2009	(Ernst et al., 2009)	Proposing integer programming formulations for both single and multiple uncapacitated hub center problems and developing a branch-and-bound approach for the multiple allocation case
2011	(Contreras et al., 2011)	Stochastic uncapacitated hub location problem by considering uncertain demands and transportation costs
2011	(Mohammadi et al., 2011a)	A two-stage capacitated single allocation hub covering location problem is considered and two metaheuristics namely, GA and Shuffled Frog leaping algorithm are proposed
2011	(Mohammadi et al., 2011b)	A new model for the capacitated single allocation hub covering location problem is proposed and a multi-objective imperialist competitive algorithm is applied
2012	(Campbell & O'Kelly, 2012)	A review of the hub location research is provided and the current status of the literature is discussed.
2012	(Yaman & Elloumi, 2012)	star p-hub center and star p-hub median problems with bounded path lengths are introduced.
2013	(Bashiri et al., 2013)	A fuzzy capacitated p-hub center problem is introduced and a genetic algorithm solution is presented.
2013	(Farahani et al., 2013)	A comprehensive survey of hub location problems is presented.
2013	(Liang, 2013)	The hardness of star p-hub center is analyzed.
2013	(Yang et al., 2013b)	A hybrid particle swarm optimization problem for p-hub center problem is developed.
2013	(Yang et al., 2013a)	Fuzzy p-hub center problem is considered and a hybrid metaheuristic consisting of a local search incorporated into a GA is proposed.
2014	(Hult et al., 2014)	For a stochastic uncapacitated single allocation p-hub center problem a number exact computational approaches are developed.
2014	(Yang et al., 2014)	Optimization of a fuzzy p-hub center problem with generalized value-at-risk criterion is considered.

In this study, our focus is on the p-hub center problem which is a minimax type problem and has the number of hubs as an exogenous parameter and previously determined p. The problem considered here is of multiple allocation type problems. Since the problem could be modeled as a graph, where the nodes represents the origin/destination or prospective location and edges represent the linkages between the nodes with weights denoting distances (or costs), Dijkstra's algorithm could be successfully used in order to find the shortest path from each node to any other node. Having the information obtained from running Dijkstra's algorithm once for each node, one can minimize the maximum length between any origin/destination nodes by incorporating this algorithm into a heuristic or metaheuristic method. Achieving this aim is exactly equivalent with solving a UMApHCP.

Hence, in essence, the objective of this study considering the literature provided above, is to propose well-qualified metaheuristic methods for solving the UMApHCP, improve the existing GA in the literature, develop SA for the first time for solving the problem and compare the results of the two algorithms for both small-scale and large-scale data sets. The rest of the paper is organized as follows: In section 2, the problem formulation is presented. In section 3, the proposed algorithms are explained in detail. The numerical experiments are illustrated in section 4. Finally, the concluding remarks are drawn in section 5.

2. Problem definition

The p-hub center multiple allocation problems is to allocate each non-hub node to one or more hubs such that the maximum travel time between any o–d pair is minimized. It is clear that the multiple allocation problems will have an objective function value no larger than that of the single allocation problem since the unique allocation constraints are relaxed in the multiple allocation problems. Thus, the solution to a multiple allocation problem can be used as a lower bound for solving a single allocation problem. Here, the model developed by Ernst et al. (2009) is presented.

$$\text{Min} \quad z \tag{9}$$

$$\sum_{k=1}^{n} z_k = p \tag{10}$$

$$\sum_{k=1}^{n}\sum_{m=1}^{n} y_{ijkm} = 1, \qquad i,j = 1,\dots,n \tag{11}$$

$$\sum_{k=1}^{n} y_{ijkm} \le z_m \qquad i,j,m = 1,\dots,n \tag{12}$$

$$\sum_{m=1}^{n} y_{ijkm} \le z_k \qquad i,j,k = 1,\dots,n \tag{13}$$

$$z \ge \sum_{k=1}^{n}\sum_{m=1}^{n} y_{ijkm}\left(c_{ik} + \alpha c_{km} + c_{mj}\right), \qquad i,j = 1,\dots,n \tag{14}$$

$$z_k, y_{ijkm} \in \{0,1\} \qquad i,j,k,m = 1,\dots,n \tag{15}$$

Constraint (10) indicates that exactly p hubs are chosen. Constraint (11) together with (15) shows that there is a unique path between each origin–destination pair. Constraints (12) and (13) imply that a node must be selected to be a hub if another node is allocated to it. Constraint (14) defines the lower bound for the objective function z, which represents the maximum transportation cost between all origin–destination pairs.

3. Proposed methods

Based on the results of the study of Alumur and Kara (2008), the total number of papers on the p-hub center problem is very few compared with other hub models. The main reason is that these problems are proposed in 1994 and remain untouched until 2000. These problems are a fairly new research area and there is still a lot of ground to cover; there is a need to develop more exact solution procedures and heuristic algorithms for these problems. To the best knowledge of authors, application of metaheuristics in p-hub center problems is very limited and has not well been studied. Therefore, in this section we propose two metaheuristics for solving UMApHCP; simulated annealing and genetic algorithm.

Because of the nature of the problem and its objective function, which makes it different from p-hub median problems, a special procedure is needed to calculate the fitness function. This procedure is based on Dijkstra's algorithm to find the maximum distance between every origin-destination pairs that is the amount of objective function value. Since the problem could be modeled as a graph, where the nodes represents the origin/destination or prospective hub location and edges represent the linkages between the nodes with weights denoting distances (or costs), Dijkstra's algorithm could be successfully used in order to find the shortest path from each node to any other node. Having the information obtained from running Dijkstra's algorithm once for each node, one can minimize the maximum length between any origin/destination nodes which is exactly equivalent with solving an UMApHCP.

3.1. Genetic Algorithm

Before explaining the main steps of the proposed GA, it is worth mentioning that it is not the first GA implemented for solving UMApHCP. Kratica and Stanimirovic (2006) proposed an efficient GA for the problem and reported the numerical results. The aim of this paper, in addition to improve the performance of their proposed GA, is comparing the performance of a population-based algorithm (GA) and a single solution-based algorithm (SA) while the fitness function calculation procedure operates based on Dijkstra's algorithm.

The pseudo code of the Dijkstra's algorithm is illustrated in Fig. 2 to provide the respected reader with a general view of the algorithm. The obtained results of the SA and GA will guide the respected reader to suitably choose between these two different categories of metaheuristics for coping with different real size problems of UMApHCP. Pseudo code for the proposed GA is presented in the following:

STEP 1: Generate Npop random solutions.

STEP 2: Calculate fitness function for each solution

> In this step a Dijkstra's algorithm is implemented to calculate the fitness of each solution. (The Dijkstra's pseudo code is shown in Fig. 2). For each solution, Dijkstra's algorithm is run by number of genes times. For example, if a chromosome has n genes (number of nodes) Dijkstra's algorithm will be run n times for that solution in order to calculate the minimum distance of every node from other nodes. The maximum of these distances is regarded as the fitness function of that solution and the goal of the GA is minimizing it.

STEP 3: Sort the solutions based on their fitness values.

STEP 4: Move the elitist solution to the new generation

STEP 5: Select good solutions by Tournament selection method and crossover a fraction of them and move to the new generation

STEP 5: Mutate a number of solutions and transfer them to the new generation.

STEP 6: Check if the termination criteria are met. If so, terminate the algorithm otherwise, go to STEP 2.

```
Function Dijkstra (Graph, Source):

        for each vertex v in Graph:
                dist[v] := infinity;
                previous pv[ := undefined;
        end for;

        dist[Source] :=0;
        Q := the set of all nodes in graph;

        While Q is not empty:
                u := vertex in Q with smallest distance in dist [];
                if dist [u] = infinity:
                        break;
                endif;

                remove u from Q;

                for each neighbor v of u:
                        alt := dist [u] + dist_between(u, v);
                        if alt < dist [v]:
                                dist[v] := alt;
                                previous [v] := u;
                                decrease-key v in Q;
                        end if;
                end for;
        end while;

    return dist[];
  end Dijkstra.
```

Fig. 2. Dijkstra's algorithm pseudo code (Taken from contributors (2014))

3.1.1. Solution representation

In this GA implementation the binary encoding of individuals is used. Each solution is represented by the binary string of length *n*. Gene 1 in the genetic code denotes that particular hub is established, while 0 shows it is not. Since users can be assigned only to open hub facilities, only array z_k is obtained from the genetic code.

3.1.2. Selection

The selection method used in this paper is Tournament selection procedure. In tournament selection, a number *Tour* of individuals is chosen randomly from the population, and the best individual from this group is selected as parent. This process is repeated as often as individuals to choose.

3.1.3. Crossover operator

The Crossover operator employed in the proposed GA is just like the operator employed by Kratica and Stanimirovic (2006). Here, the operator is elaborated in detail. Generally, crossover operator executes a swap between two random parts of a selected pair of parents producing two offsprings. However, because of the specific structure of the solution representation, where number of ones stands for number of hubs, this action will yield infeasible solution. To cope with the problem, Kratica and Stanimirovic (2006) proposed a modified version of the classical crossover operator. In this version, the operator is simultaneously tracing the genetic codes of the parents from right to left searching the position i on which the first parent has 1 and second 0. The individuals exchange genes on the found position (that is identified as crossover point), and similar process is performed starting from the left side of genetic codes. Operator seeks for the position j where the first parent is 0 and the other one is 1. Genes of the jth position are swapped while the total number of located hubs remains unaffected. The process is repeated until $j \geq i$.

3.1.4. Mutation Operator

Each offspring produced by crossover operator is mutated only one time by probability of *MutateRate*. If a random number chosen uniformly between [0,1] is less than *MutateRate*, two genes, one with value 1 and the other with value 0, are randomly selected from the chromosome and their values are exchanged. This Mutation procedure keeps the feasibility characteristics of the solutions.

3.2. Simulated annealing

Simulated annealing whose name come from annealing in metallurgy is a suitable probabilistic algorithm for finding the optimum value of a cost function that may have several local minima. This is a single solution based method that starts with an initial solution and searches the neighbors of that solution in each iteration by a local search mechanism. In fact, SA emulates the physical process of slowly cooling of a material to increase the size of its crystals and reduce their defects. One important advantage of using SA is its simple implementation. The pseudo code is really straightforward and the idea behind the algorithm could be easily understood. The pseudo code of the algorithm used in this paper is briefly presented below:

$r = 0, T = T_0, BestSol = \emptyset$

$Generate\ Initial\ solution\ X_0$

$BestSol = X_0$

$\{While\ r < R\ do\ (Outer\ loop)$

$n = 0$

$\langle While\ n < N\ do(Inner\ loop)$

$Select\ a\ move\ randomly\ and\ run\ over\ X_n\ as\ \Delta C = Cost(X_{new}) - Cost(BestSol)$

$if\ \Delta C < 0\ then$

$BestSol = X_{new}\ and\ X_n = X_{new}$

$Else$

$Generate\ a\ uniform\ random\ number\ from\ [0,1]\ and\ call\ it\ 'y'$

$Set\ Z = \exp(-\frac{\Delta C}{T_r})$

$if\ y < Z\ then\ X_n = X_{new}$

$n = n + 1\rangle$

$r = r + 1$

$T_r = Alpha \times T_{r-1}\}$

$Return\ BestSol\ as\ the\ optimum$

Remark. $Cost(X)$ denotes the objective function value of solution X. Thus, a calculation similar to that one mentioned in STEP 2 of the proposed GA is required.

Remark. In the inner loop of the proposed SA, a local search is performed on the current solution. A non-hub node of the current solution is randomly selected and changed to a hub and an arbitrarily chosen hub is changed to a non-hub node. Thus, at each inner loop iteration only two digits of the solution are changed.

The respected reader should keep in mind that the solution representation of the SA is just like the one employed in genetic algorithm. (A string of digits where 1 denotes a hub node and 0 denotes a non-hub one).

4. Results and discussions

In this section, the performance of the proposed algorithms above is assessed and compared using two sets of modified ORLIB instances. The proposed algorithms were programmed in MATLAB (R2009a) software and were run on a PC with 2.2 GHz CPU and 2.0 GB RAM. The first set of test problem instances belong to Civil Aeronautics Board (CAB) data set based on airline passenger flow between cities of the United States. The instances we used for analysis have 25 nodes, 2, 3 or 4 hubs and α values from 0.2 to 1. The other data set is of Australian Post (AP) that is drawn from study of postal delivery system. The instances used in this paper for assessment have 200 nodes, a maximum of 25 hubs and $\alpha = 0.75$.

4.1. Parameter tuning

As is known, the quality of genetic algorithm and simulated annealing solutions is significantly influenced by its parameter. Thus, considering the objective function values of these algorithms as a response of input parameters, response surface methodology (RSM) can be perfectly applied to optimize the parameter values. In most RSM applications, the form of the relationship between the response and the input variables is unknown. Therefore, finding an appropriate approximation for the true functional relationship between y (response) and the set of independent variables is the first step in RSM.

Frequently, a first-order model for beginning is sufficient because the initial parameter values are usually far from the optimum region. Then, RSM moves from the initial values using steepest descent method (if the objective is to minimize a measure) to a better area with regard to the GA response. Afterward, an ANOVA is applied to check the adequacy of a new first-order model with the new parameter values. This approach is repeated until no suitable first-order model is found; this situation usually happens in the areas near the optimum region. In such circumstances a polynomial of higher degree must be used, such as the second-order model shown in Eq. (16).

$$y = \beta_0 + \sum_{i=1}^{k} \beta_i x_i + \sum_{i=1}^{k} \sum_{i<j}^{k} \beta_{ij} x_i x_j + \sum_{i=1}^{k} \beta_{ii} x_i^2 + \varepsilon \tag{16}$$

By analyzing the second order model the optimum parameter values will be determined. The convergence of RSM is negatively affected by an increase in the number of independent variables. Thus, it is encouraging to keep the number of input variables at a minimum. To do so, we first set $N = 40, Alpha = 0.9$ for SA and Number of generations = 100 for GA using a trial-and-error approach. Afterward, we let RSM choose the optimum values of T_0, R and Elitist probability, Tour and Mutation rate for both SA and GA and for both CAB and AP data sets. Table 2 shows the initial values we considered for SA and GA parameters.

Table 2
Initial parameter values of SA and GA for RSM

SA initial parameters	T_0	30000
	R	150
GA initial parameters	Elitist probability	0.2
	Tour	4
	Mutation rate	0.1

In order to fit the second-order models, central composite design (CCD) which is a very effective design is employed. Commonly, CCD consists of a 2^kfactorial (or fractional factorial of resolution V) with n_F runs, $2k$ axial runs and $n_C$center runs. Our CCD created by MATLAB software for 3 input variables, contains $n_F = 8$ factorial runs, 6 axial runs and $n_C = 10$ center runs. Considering rotatability property, parameter α (distance of axial runs from the design center) is set to 1.6818 ($= (n_F)^{1/4} = \sqrt[4]{8}$). Rotatability is needed to have a consistent variance of the predicted response at different set of parameter values. The optimum parameter values obtained by RSM methodology for SA and GA based on the experiments designed above are shown in Table 3.

Table 3
Optimal parameter values obtained by RSM for SA and GA

SA optimal parameters for CAB data set	T_0	21760
	R	188
SA optimal parameters for AP data set	T_0	53389
	R	112
GA optimal parameters for both CAB and AP data sets	Elitist probability	0.12
	Tour	3.8
	Mutation rate	0.17

4.2. Discussions

Table 4 shows the results of the SA for different CAB data set instances. Likewise, the outputs of the GA for the same test problem instances are provided in Table 5.

Note. For each instance, each of the algorithms were run 10 times and OF average column denotes the average of obtained objective function values, OF Minimum column shows the minimum amount, the average processing time for each instance has been shown in the fifth column, the best solution already found in the literature is shown in the sixth column and in the last column our algorithm is compared against the best solution in the literature.

Table 4
Results of the SA for different CAB data set instances

α	p	OF average	OF Minimum	Avg. Time(s)	Kratica and Stanimirovic (2006) best solution	Decrease in the best solution
0.2	2	2.0495e+003	2.0495e+003	4.3746	2049.48	0
0.4	2	2.4025e+003	2.4025e+003	4.4543	2402.55	0
0.6	2	2.5587e+003	2.5587e+003	4.4305	2558.74	0
0.8	2	2.7149e+003	2.7149e+003	4.4813	2714.93	0
1	2	2.7392e+003	2.7392e+003	4.4631	2739.22	0
0.2	3	1.7729e+003	1.7651e+003	17.0272	1911.60	7.66%
0.4	3	2.0673e+003	2.0647e+003	17.5873	2064.67	0
0.6	3	2.2438e+003	2.2438e+003	18.1846	2243.77	0
0.8	3	2.5156e+003	2.5156e+003	18.9688	2515.58	0
1	3	2.7258e+003	2.7258e+003	24.5331	2725.79	0
0.2	4	1.6585e+003	1.6195e+003	28.7445	1619.48	0
0.4	4	1.8111e+003	1.7744e+003	25.4180	1774.45	0
0.6	4	2.1293e+003	2.1271e+003	28.0046	2127.13	0
0.8	4	2.4377e+003	2.4377e+003	29.1487	2437.71	0
1	4	2.7258e+003	2.7258e+003	76.9415	2725.79	0

Table 5
Results of the GA for different CAB data set instances

α	p	OF average	OF Minimum	Avg. Time(s)	Kratica and Stanimirovic (2006) best solution	Decrease in the best solution
0.2	2	2.0495e+003	2.0495e+003	6.6355	2049.48	0
0.4	2	2.4025e+003	2.4025e+003	6.6036	2402.55	0
0.6	2	2.5587e+003	2.5587e+003	6.5451	2558.74	0
0.8	2	2.7149e+003	2.7149e+003	6.6089	2714.93	0
1	2	2.7392e+003	2.7392e+003	7.2771	2739.22	0
0.2	3	1.7866e+003	1.7651e+003	7.8678	1911.60	7.66%
0.4	3	2.0885e+003	2.0647e+003	8.0270	2064.67	0
0.6	3	2.2438e+003	2.2438e+003	7.6414	2243.77	0
0.8	3	2.5156e+003	2.5156e+003	7.7504	2515.58	0
1	3	2.7258e+003	2.7258e+003	9.2883	2725.79	0
0.2	4	1.6674e+003	1.6195e+003	9.6749	1619.48	0
0.4	4	1.8669e+003	1.7744e+003	8.9404	1774.45	0
0.6	4	2.1674e+003	2.1271e+003	8.8509	2127.13	0
0.8	4	2.4499e+003	2.4377e+003	8.6370	2437.71	0
1	4	2.7258e+003	2.7258e+003	15.1055	2725.79	0

Observing the results of the proposed algorithms in Tables 4 and 5, the following conclusions can be drawn for CAB data set:

1. For α=0.2 and p=3 the proposed algorithms (both SA and GA) were able to find a value 7.66% better than the best value already found in the literature. Also, for all of the other instances both of the proposed algorithms reach to the optimum value. These experimental results imply that the proposed algorithms outperform the already proposed GA in the literature for solving UMApHCP.

2. The proposed GA is computationally more efficient than the SA because needs less time to solve larger CAB instances although for the smaller ones the SA performs better.

3. The average of obtained objective function values for the SA are less than or equal to those of the GA and hence, from the quality of solutions view point the SA shows greater performance.

For AP data set, both SA and GA were run for five times and the best obtained results are presented in Tables 6 and 7.

Table 6
Results of the GA for different AP data set instances

p	Objective function value	Time (s)	Kratica and Stanimirovic (2006) best solution	Decrease in the best solution
2	6.7083e+004	428.5157	67083.28	0
3	6.2946e+004	514.2701	62945.55	0
5	5.7419e+004	650.0875	57419.32	0
10	5.5959e+004	1.0358e+003	55958.75	0
15	5.5959e+004	1.4727e+003	55958.75	0
20	5.5959e+004	2.0195e+003	55958.75	0
25	5.5959e+004	2.2261e+003	55958.75	0

Table 7
Results of the SA for different AP data set instances

p	Objective function value	Time (s)	Kratica and Stanimirovic (2006) best solution	Decrease in the best solution
2	6.7083e+004	691.7911	67083.28	0
3	6.2550e+004	1.2726e+003	62945.55	0.63%
5	5.7419e+004	1.9504e+003	57419.32	0
10	5.5959e+004	1.6374e+003	55958.75	0
15	5.5959e+004	2.1720e+003	55958.75	0
20	5.6003e+004	3.1328e+003	55958.75	0
25	5.5959e+004	3.6111e+003	55958.75	0

As can be seen in Table 7, for AP data set, for p=3 the proposed simulated annealing was able to find a value 0.63% better than the best value already found in the literature. Comparing the obtained results for large scale instances of AP test problem, one can see that in all cases both algorithms have reached the best solution reported in the literature. Moreover, in one case the SA algorithm was able to find a solution better than the best solution reported for that specific instance in the literature. These results together with the results obtained for CAB data set imply that the both proposed algorithms perform well and are suitable for solving UMApHCP problem even for large scale instances. Also, it could be concluded that for this problem the proposed GA is computationally more efficient that could be a result of being a population-based algorithm.

5. Conclusion

Since p-hub center has been lately introduced and has a specific objective function (minimizing the maximum cost between origin-destination nodes), there are few studies investigating the problem and the challenges for solving it. Because of the specific structure of the problem Dijkstra's algorithm could be successfully used in order to find the shortest path from each node to any other node. Using the information obtained from running Dijkstra's algorithm once for each node, one can minimize the maximum length between any origin/destination nodes which is exactly equivalent with solving a UMApHCP. In this paper, two well-known metaheuristics were adapted to suit to solving the NP-hard problem. The computational results of applying the proposed algorithms (SA and GA) shows that for smaller scale test problems, single solution-based SA shows greater performance versus GA but for larger scales of data sets the GA generally yield more desirable solutions.

References

Alumur, S., & Kara, B. Y. (2008). Network hub location problems: The state of the art. *European Journal of Operational Research*, *190*(1), 1-21.

Bashiri, M., Mirzaei, M., & Randall, M. (2013). Modeling fuzzy capacitated p-hub center problem and a genetic algorithm solution. *Applied Mathematical Modelling*, *37*(5), 3513-3525.

Baumgartner, S. (2003). *Polyhedral analysis of hub center problems* (Doctoral dissertation, Technische Universität Kaiserslautern).

Campbell, A. M., Lowe, T. J., & Zhang, L. (2007). The p-hub center allocation problem. *European Journal of Operational Research*, *176*(2), 819-835.

Campbell, J. F. (1994). Integer programming formulations of discrete hub location problems. *European Journal of Operational Research*, *72*(2), 387-405.

Campbell, J. F., & O'Kelly, M. E. (2012). Twenty-five years of hub location research. *Transportation Science*, *46*(2), 153-169.

Contreras, I., Cordeau, J. F., & Laporte, G. (2011). Stochastic uncapacitated hub location. *European Journal of Operational Research*, *212*(3), 518-528.

Contributors, W. (2014). Dijkstra's algorithm. Wikipedia, The Free Encyclopedia. .

Ernst, A. T., Hamacher, H., Jiang, H., Krishnamoorthy, M., & Woeginger, G. (2009). Uncapacitated single and multiple allocation p-hub center problems.*Computers & Operations Research*, *36*(7), 2230-2241.

Farahani, R. Z., Hekmatfar, M., Arabani, A. B., & Nikbakhsh, E. (2013). Hub location problems: A review of models, classification, solution techniques, and applications. *Computers & Industrial Engineering*, *64*(4), 1096-1109.

Gavriliouk, E. O. (2009). Aggregation in hub location problems. *Computers & Operations Research*, *36*(12), 3136-3142.

Hult, E., Jiang, H., & Ralph, D. (2014). Exact computational approaches to a stochastic uncapacitated single allocation p-hub center problem. *Computational Optimization and Applications*, *59*(1-2), 185 200.

Kara, B. Y., & Tansel, B. C. (2000). On the single-assignment p-hub center problem. *European Journal of Operational Research*, *125*(3), 648-655.

Kratica, J., & Stanimirović, Z. (2006). Solving the uncapacitated multiple allocation p-hub center problem by genetic algorithm. *Asia-Pacific Journal of Operational Research*, *23*(04), 425-437.

Liang, H. (2013). The hardness and approximation of the star -hub center problem. *Operations Research Letters*, 41, 138-141.

Meyer, T., Ernst, A. T., & Krishnamoorthy, M. (2009). A 2-phase algorithm for solving the single allocation p-hub center problem. *Computers & Operations Research*, *36*(12), 3143-3151.

Mohammadi, M., Tavakkoli-Moghaddam, R., Ghodratnama, A., & Rostami, H. (2011). Genetic and Improved Shuffled Frog Leaping Algorithms for a 2-Stage Model of a Hub Covering Location Network.

Mohammadi, M., Tavakkoli-Moghaddam, R., & Rostami, H. (2011b). A multi-objective imperialist competitive algorithm for a capacitated hub covering location problem. *International Journal of Industrial Engineering Computations*, 2, 671-688.

Pamuk, F. S., & Sepil, C. (2001). A solution to the hub center problem via a single-relocation algorithm with tabu search. *IIE Transactions*, *33*(5), 399-411.

Sim, T., Lowe, T.J., & Thomas, B.W. (2009). The stochastic -hub center problem with service-level constraints. *Computers & Operations Research* 36(12), 3166-3177.

Yaman, H., & Elloumi, S. (2012). Star p-hub center problem and star p-hub median problem with bounded path lengths. *Computers & Operations Research,* 39, 2725-2732.

Yaman, H., Kara, B.Y., & Tansel, B.Ç. (2007). The latest arrival hub location problem for cargo delivery systems with stopovers. *Transportation Research Part B: Methodological,* 41, 906-919.

Yang, K., Liu, Y.-K., & Yang, G.-Q. (2013a). Solving fuzzy p-hub center problem by genetic algorithm incorporating local search. *Applied Soft Computing,* 13, 2624-2632.

Yang, K., Liu, Y., &Yang, G. (2013b). An improved hybrid particle swarm optimization algorithm for fuzzy p-hub center problem. *Computers & Industrial Engineering,* 64, 133-142.

Yang, K., Liu, Y., & Yang, G. (2014). Optimizing fuzzy p-hub center problem with generalized value-at-risk criterion. *Applied Mathematical Modelling*, 38, 3987-4005.

Generalized exponential distribution: A Bayesian approach using MCMC methods

Jorge Alberto Achcar[a,b], Fernando Antônio Moala[a*] and Juliana Boleta[b]

[a]*Departamento de Matemática, Estatística e Computação, UNESP, Universidade Estadual Paulista, Presidente Prudente, SP, Brazil*
[b]Departamento de Medicina Social, FMRP, Universidade de São Paulo, Avenida Bandeirantes, 3900, CEP: 14048-900, Ribeirão Preto, SP, Brasil

CHRONICLE

Keywords:
Generalized exponential distribution
Non-informative priors
Bayesian analysis
MCMC methods

ABSTRACT

The generalized exponential distribution could be a good option to analyse lifetime data, as an alternative for the use of standard existing lifetime distributions as exponential, Weibull or gamma distributions. Assuming different non-informative prior distributions for the parameters of the model, we introduce a Bayesian analysis using Markov Chain Monte Carlo (MCMC) methods. Some numerical illustrations considering simulated and real lifetime data are presented to illustrate the proposed methodology, especially the effects of different priors on the posterior summaries of interest.

1. Introduction

A generalized exponential distribution (see Gupta & Kundu, 1999) can be a good alternative for the use of the popular gamma or Weibull distributions to analyse lifetime data (see also, Raqab, 2002; Raqab & Ahsanullah, 2001; Zheng, 2002; Sarhan, 2007; Gupta & Kundu, 2001, 2007). The generalized exponential distribution with two parameters has density given by,

$$f(t; \alpha, \lambda) = \alpha\lambda[1 - \exp(-\lambda t)]^{\alpha-1}\exp(-\lambda t), \quad (1)$$

where $t > 0$; $\alpha > 0$ and $\lambda > 0$ are respectively, shape and scale parameters. Let us denote this model as GE(α, λ). The density function given in Eq. (1) has great flexibility of fitting depending on the shape parameter α: if $\alpha < 1$, we have a decreasing function and if $\alpha > 1$, we have a unimodal function with mode given by $\lambda^{-1}\log\alpha$. Observe that if $\alpha = 1$, we have an exponential distribution with parameter λ. The survival and hazard function associated with Eq. (1) are given Eq. (2) and Eq. (3), respectively, as follows,

$$S(t; \alpha, \lambda) = P(T > t) = 1 - [1 - \exp(-\lambda t)]^{\alpha}, \quad (2)$$

and

* Corresponding author.

$$h(t;\alpha,\lambda) = \frac{f(t;\alpha,\lambda)}{S(t;\alpha,\lambda)} = \frac{\alpha\lambda[1-\exp(-\lambda t)]^{\alpha-1}\exp(-\lambda t)}{1-[1-\exp(-\lambda t)]^{\alpha}}. \tag{3}$$

Observe that the hazard function h(t; α, λ) has a non-deceasing trend from 0 to λ when α > 1; a non-increasing trend from ∞ to 1 when α < 1 and constant with α = 1. This behavior of the hazard function given in Eq. (3) is similar to the behavior of the hazard function of a gamma distribution. Also observe that the median lifetime obtained from S(t; α, λ) = 1/2 is given by,

$$t_{med} = -\frac{1}{\lambda}\log\left(1-\left(\frac{1}{2}\right)^{1/\alpha}\right). \tag{4}$$

The moment generating function for a random variable T with a generalized exponential distribution and density of Eq. (1) is as follows, (see Gupta & Kundu, 2008)

$$M(s) = E(e^{sT}) = \frac{\Gamma(\alpha+1)\Gamma\left(1-\frac{s}{\lambda}\right)}{\Gamma\left(\alpha-\frac{s}{\lambda}+1\right)}. \tag{5}$$

From Eq. (5), we find all moments of interest. The mean and variance are given, respectively, by

$$E(T) = \frac{1}{\lambda}[\psi(\alpha+1)-\psi(1)],\ var(T) = \frac{1}{\lambda^2}[\psi'(1)-\psi'(\alpha+1)], \tag{6}$$

where ψ(.) is a digamma function given by $\psi(x) = \frac{d}{dx}\log(\Gamma(x)) = \frac{\Gamma'(x)}{\Gamma(x)}$ and Γ(x) is a gamma function. In this paper, we develop a Bayesian analysis for the generalized exponential distribution using Markov Chain Monte Carlo (MCMC) methods (see for example, Gelfand & Smith, 1990; Chib & Greenberg, 1995) to obtain the posterior summaries of interest.

The paper is organized as follows: in Section 2, we introduce the likelihood function; in Section 3, we present a Bayesian analysis considering different non-informative priors for the parameters; in Section 4, we present inference for the survival function at a specified time; in Section 5, we introduce two numerical illustrations; finally, in Section 6, we present some conclusions.

2. The Likelihood Function

Suppose we have identically distributed lifetimes $\mathbf{t} = (t_1, ..., t_n)'$ from a GE(α, λ) distribution. The likelihood function in the parameters α and λ, based on $\mathbf{t}$ is then

$$L(\alpha,\lambda\,|\,t) = \alpha^n\lambda^n\left[\prod_{i=1}^{n}[1-\exp(-\lambda t_i)]^{\alpha-1}\right]\exp\left(-\lambda\sum_{i=1}^{n}t_i\right). \tag{7}$$

The logarithm of the likelihood function given in Eq. (7) is given by,

$$l(\alpha,\lambda) = \log L(\alpha,\lambda\,|\,t) = n\log(\alpha) + n\log(\lambda) - \lambda\sum_{i=1}^{n}t_i + (\alpha-1)\sum_{i=1}^{n}\log[1-e^{-\lambda t_i}]. \tag{8}$$

The maximum likelihood estimators (MLE) for α and λ are obtained from ∂l/∂α = 0 and ∂l/∂λ = 0, where,

$$\frac{\partial}{\partial\alpha}l(\alpha,\lambda) = \frac{n}{\alpha} + \sum_{i=1}^{n}\log[1-e^{-\lambda t_i}] = 0$$
$$\frac{\partial}{\partial\lambda}l(\alpha,\lambda) = \frac{n}{\lambda} - \sum_{i=1}^{n}t_i + (\alpha-1)\sum_{i=1}^{n}\frac{t_i e^{-\lambda t_i}}{1-e^{-\lambda t_i}} = 0 \tag{9}$$

From Eq. (9), we find the MLE for α given by,

$$\hat{\alpha} = -\frac{n}{\sum_{i=1}^{n} \log[1 - e^{-\hat{\lambda} t_i}]}. \tag{10}$$

The MLE for λ is obtained by solving the nonlinear equation,

$$\frac{n}{\hat{\lambda}} - n\bar{t} + (\hat{\alpha} - 1)\sum_{i=1}^{n} \frac{t_i e^{-\hat{\lambda} t_i}}{1 - e^{-\hat{\lambda} t_i}} = 0. \tag{11}$$

where $\hat{\alpha}$ is given by Eq. (10) and $n\bar{t} = \sum_{i=1}^{n} t_i$. Observe that we need to use an iterative method to find the MLE $\hat{\lambda}$ from Eq. (11). The second derivatives of $l(\alpha, \lambda)$ are given, respectively, by

$$\begin{aligned} \frac{\partial^2 l}{\partial \alpha^2} &= -\frac{n}{\alpha^2} \\ \frac{\partial^2 l}{\partial \lambda^2} &= -\frac{n}{\lambda^2} - (\alpha - 1)\sum_{i=1}^{n} \frac{t_i^2 e^{-\lambda t_i}}{(1 - e^{-\lambda t_i})^2}. \\ \frac{\partial^2 l}{\partial \alpha \partial \lambda} &= \sum_{i=1}^{n} \frac{t_i e^{-\lambda t_i}}{1 - e^{-\lambda t_i}} \end{aligned} \tag{12}$$

Hypotheses tests and confidence intervals for α and λ can be obtained using the asymptotical normal distribution for $\hat{\alpha}$ and $\hat{\lambda}$, that is

$$(\hat{\alpha}, \hat{\lambda}) \overset{a}{\sim} N\left((\alpha, \lambda), I_0^{-1}\right), \tag{13}$$

where I_0 is the observed Fisher information matrix given by,

$$I_0 = \begin{pmatrix} -\dfrac{\partial^2 l}{\partial \alpha^2} & -\dfrac{\partial^2 l}{\partial \alpha \partial \lambda} \\ -\dfrac{\partial^2 l}{\partial \alpha \partial \lambda} & -\dfrac{\partial^2 l}{\partial \lambda^2} \end{pmatrix}. \tag{14}$$

3. A Bayesian Analysis

For a Bayesian analysis of the GE(α, λ) distribution, we assume different prior distributions for α and λ. The Jeffreys non-informative prior (see for example, Box & Tiao, 1973) for α and λ is given by

$$\Pi_1(\alpha, \lambda) \propto [\det \mathbf{I}(\alpha, \lambda)]^{1/2}, \tag{15}$$

where $\mathbf{I}(\alpha, \lambda)$ is the Fisher information matrix given by,

$$I(\alpha, \lambda) = \begin{pmatrix} E\left(-\dfrac{\partial^2 l}{\partial \alpha^2}\right) & E\left(-\dfrac{\partial^2 l}{\partial \alpha \partial \lambda}\right) \\ E\left(-\dfrac{\partial^2 l}{\partial \alpha \partial \lambda}\right) & E\left(-\dfrac{\partial^2 l}{\partial \lambda^2}\right) \end{pmatrix} \tag{16}$$

where,

$$\begin{aligned} &E[-\frac{\partial^2 l}{\partial \alpha^2}] = \frac{n}{\alpha^2}, \quad E[-\frac{\partial^2 l}{\partial \lambda \partial \alpha}] = \frac{n}{\lambda}\left\{[\psi(\alpha+1) - \psi(1)] - \frac{\alpha}{\alpha-1}[\psi(\alpha) - \psi(1)]\right\} \\ &E[-\frac{\partial^2 l}{\partial \lambda^2}] = \frac{n}{\lambda^2}\{1 + \frac{\alpha(\alpha-1)}{\alpha-2}\left[[\psi'(1) - \psi'(\alpha-1)] + [\psi(\alpha-1) - \psi(1)]^2\right] - \alpha\left[\psi'(1) - \psi'(\alpha) + [\psi(\alpha) - \psi(1)]^2\right]\} \end{aligned} \tag{17}$$

(see Gupta & Kundu, 1999). Let us denote the prior Eq. (15) as "Jeffreys1". A possible simplification is to consider a non-informative prior from $\Pi(\alpha, \lambda) = \Pi(\lambda|\alpha)\Pi_0(\alpha)$. Using the Jeffreys'rule, we have,

$$\pi_2(\alpha,\lambda) = \left[E\left(-\frac{\partial^2 l}{\partial \lambda^2}\right)\right]^{\frac{1}{2}} \pi_0(\alpha) \tag{18}$$

where $E\left(-\frac{\partial^2 l}{\partial \lambda^2}\right)$ is given in Eq. (17) and $\pi_0(\alpha)$ is a non-informative prior given by $\pi_0(\alpha) \propto 1/\alpha$, $\alpha > 0$. In this way,

$$\pi_2(\alpha,\lambda) = \frac{1}{\alpha\lambda} A^{1/2}(\alpha) \tag{19}$$

where $A(\alpha) = 1 + \frac{\alpha(\alpha-1)}{\alpha-2}\left[\psi'(1) - \psi'(\alpha-1)] + [\psi(\alpha-1) - \psi(1)]^2\right] - \alpha[\psi'(1) - \psi'(\alpha) + [\psi(\alpha) - \psi(1)]^2]$.

Let us denote the prior Eq. (19) as "Jeffreys2". A third non-informative prior distribution is assumed considering independence between α and λ, that is,

$$\pi_3(\alpha,\lambda) \propto \frac{1}{\alpha\lambda}, \tag{20}$$

where $\alpha > 0$ and $\lambda > 0$. Let us denote the prior (20) as "Jeffreys3". Assuming dependence between the random quantities α and λ, we could assume a bivariate prior distribution for α and λ derived from copula functions (see for example, Nelsen, 1999; Trivedi & Zimmer, 2007). A special case is given by the Farlie-Gumbel-Morgenstern Copula (see Morgenstern, 1956) given by,

$$c(u, v) = uv[1 + \delta(1 - u)(1 - v)], \tag{21}$$

where $u = F_1(\alpha)$ (marginal distribution function for α) and $v = F_2(\lambda)$ (marginal distribution function for λ). The joint distribution function for α and λ is given (from (21)) by,

$$F(\alpha, \lambda) = c(F_1(\alpha), F_2(\lambda)) = F_1(\alpha)F_2(\lambda)[1 + \delta(1 - F_1(\alpha))(1 - F_2(\lambda))], \tag{22}$$

where the parameter δ is associated to the dependence between α and λ. If $\delta = 0$, we have independence between α and λ. The joint prior density for α and λ, obtained from $\partial^2 F(\alpha, \lambda)/\partial\alpha\partial\lambda$, is given by,

$$\Pi_4(\alpha, \lambda|\delta) = f_1(\alpha)f_2(\lambda) + \delta f_1(\alpha)f_2(\lambda)[1 - 2F_1(\alpha)][1 - F_2(\lambda)], \tag{23}$$

where $f_1(\alpha)$ and $f_2(\lambda)$ are the marginal densities for α and λ. Assuming marginal exponential distributions with known hyperparameters a_1 and a_2, we have, conditional on the hyperparameter δ,

$$\pi_4(\alpha,\lambda|\delta) \propto \frac{1}{a_1 a_2}\exp\left(-\frac{\alpha}{a_1} - \frac{\lambda}{a_2}\right)\left[1 + \delta(2e^{-\frac{\alpha}{a_1}} - 1)(2e^{-\frac{\lambda}{a_2}} - 1)\right]. \tag{24}$$

Let us denote Eq. (24) as "Farlie-Gumbel" or "Copula prior". The specification of Eq. (24) must be completed by a prior distribution for δ, $\Pi(\delta)$. A suggestion for this prior could be a uniform U [−1, 1] distribution on the interval [−1, 1]. Other prior specifications also could be considered, as independent informative Gamma distributions, that is,

$$\Pi_\alpha(\alpha) \sim \text{Gamma}(a_\alpha, b_\alpha) \qquad \Pi_\lambda(\lambda) \sim \text{Gamma}(a_\lambda, b_\lambda), \tag{25}$$

where a_α, b_α, a_λ and b_λ are known hyperparameters and Gamma(a,b) denotes a gamma distribution with mean a/b and variance a/b^2.

3.1 The joint posterior distribution for α and λ assuming the Farlie-Gumbel-Morgenstern prior

Assuming the "Farlie-Gumbel-Morgenstern" prior $\Pi_4(\alpha, \lambda|\delta)$ introduced in Eq. (24), the statistical model and prior model together form an ordered structure in which the distribution of the data is written conditionally on the parameters (α, λ) as $f(\mathbf{t}|\alpha, \lambda)$; the distribution of (α, λ) is written conditionally on the hyperparameter δ as $\Pi_4(\alpha,\lambda|\delta)$ and is completed by the distribution of δ, Π(δ). The full joint distribution of all random quantities in the problem is hierarchically written as,

$$f(\mathbf{t}|\alpha, \lambda, \delta) = f(\mathbf{t}|\alpha, \lambda)\Pi_4(\alpha, \lambda|\delta)\Pi(\delta) \tag{26}$$

In a three-level hierarchy with the form Eq. (26), inference about (α, λ) and δ is simply obtained through their joint posterior distribution,

$$\Pi(\alpha, \lambda, \delta|\mathbf{t}) \propto L(\alpha, \lambda|\mathbf{t})\Pi_4(\alpha, \lambda|\delta)\Pi(\delta), \tag{27}$$

and inference about (α, λ) and δ are given by their marginal posteriors. Therefore, the joint posterior for the GE(α, λ) distribution parameters (α, λ) and the hiperparameter δ is given by

$$\Pi(\alpha,\lambda,\delta\,|\,\mathrm{t}) \propto \frac{\alpha^n\lambda^n}{a_1a_2}\left[\prod_{i=1}^{n}[1-\exp(-\lambda t_i)]^{\alpha-1}\right]\exp\left(-\frac{\alpha}{a_1}-\lambda\left(\frac{1}{a_2}+\sum_{i=1}^{n}t_i\right)\right)\left[1+\delta(2e^{-\frac{\alpha}{a_1}}-1)(2e^{-\frac{\lambda}{a_2}}-1)\right]\pi(\delta) \tag{28}$$

The next step is to specify a prior distribution for the parameter δ and a convenient prior proposed by Box and Tiao (1973) for correlation parameter in bivariate normal data is given by,

$$\Pi(\delta) \propto (1-\delta^2)^c, \tag{29}$$

for an appropriated choice of "c". If we do not have any information from previous studies, a common choice is c = 0, that is, $\pi(\delta) \propto 1$. We decided to use c = −1/2, based on MCMC convergence rate and mathematics convenience, providing the joint posterior

$$\Pi(\alpha,\lambda,\delta\,|\,\mathrm{t}) \propto \alpha^n\lambda^n\left[\prod_{i=1}^{n}[1-\exp(-\lambda t_i)]^{\alpha-1}\right]\exp\left(-\frac{\alpha}{a_1}-\lambda\left(\frac{1}{a_2}+\sum_{i=1}^{n}t_i\right)\right)\left[1+\delta(2e^{-\frac{\alpha}{a_1}}-1)(2e^{-\frac{\lambda}{a_2}}-1)\right]/\sqrt{1-\delta^2} \tag{30}$$

In our study, the aim is to specify the posterior marginal distributions of the parameters α and λ. Thus, to estimate the parameters of interest, we use the marginal posterior distributions by integrating out the nuisance parameter δ from the joint density Eq. (30). Solving the integral above for the parameter δ and considering the integral results,

$$\int_{-1}^{1}\frac{1+\delta(2e^{-\frac{\alpha}{a_1}}-1)(2e^{-\frac{\lambda}{a_2}}-1)}{\sqrt{1-\delta^2}}d\delta = \int_{-1}^{1}\frac{1}{\sqrt{1-\delta^2}}d\delta + (2e^{-\frac{\alpha}{a_1}}-1)(2e^{-\frac{\lambda}{a_2}}-1)\int_{-1}^{1}\frac{\delta}{\sqrt{1-\delta^2}}d\delta$$ but $\int_{-1}^{1}\frac{1}{\sqrt{1-\delta^2}}d\delta = \pi$

and $\int_{-1}^{1}\frac{\delta}{\sqrt{1-\delta^2}}d\delta = 0$; in this way, we have the joint posterior distribution for α and λ given by

$$\Pi(\alpha,\lambda\,|\,\mathrm{t}) \propto \alpha^n\lambda^n\left[\prod_{i=1}^{n}[1-\exp(-\lambda t_i)]^{\alpha-1}\right]\exp\left(-\frac{\alpha}{a_1}-\lambda\left(\frac{1}{a_2}+\sum_{i=1}^{n}t_i\right)\right), \tag{31}$$

which is the same posterior obtained if we have used $\pi(\delta) \propto 1$. Samples of the joint posterior distributions of Eq. (30) can be simulated by using MCMC methods. In this way, we simulate α from the conditional posterior distribution $\Pi(\alpha|\lambda, t)$ and λ from the conditional distribution $\Pi(\lambda|\alpha, t)$ using the Metropolis-Hastings algorithm (see for example, Chib and Greenberg, 1995).

4. Survival function S

In applications, we usually have interest in the survival function *S*, given by Eq. (2), that is, if X represents the lifetime of a patient under a given treatment then S represents the probability of this patient "survives" for at least a specified time t (or longer). Next, we compare the posterior densities of the survival function *S(t)* by using the priors discussed in this paper. We note that Eq. (2) is a function of α and λ and hence it is a parameter itself with a posterior distribution $\Pi(S \mid t)$. To derive this

posterior we first transform (α, λ) to (S, W) where W = α and S = $S_0 = 1-[1-\exp(-\lambda t_0)]^{\alpha}$

To derive this posterior we first transform (α, λ) to (*S*, *W*) where $W = \alpha$ and $S = S_0$.
As Jeffreys and gamma priors are invariant to 1-1 transformation then the posterior distribution for the new parameters can be derived by the Jacobian transformation, that is,

$$\Pi(S, W|\mathbf{t}) \propto \Pi(\alpha, \lambda|\mathbf{t})|\mathbf{J}| \tag{32}$$

for $\alpha = W$ and $\lambda = -\frac{1}{t_0}\log\left(1-(1-S)^{1/W}\right)$. The Jacobian matrix *J* of this transformation with respect to the parameters *W* and *S* is given by:

$$J = \begin{pmatrix} 0 & 1 \\ -\frac{1}{t_o W}\left(\frac{(1-S)^{1/W-1}}{1-(1-W)^{1/W}}\right) & \frac{\partial \lambda}{\partial W} \end{pmatrix}, \tag{33}$$

where $\frac{\partial \lambda}{\partial W}$ is the derivative of $\lambda = -\frac{1}{t_0}\log\left(1-(1-S)^{1/W}\right)$ with respect to W.

Note that although the prior distribution of Eq. (24) belongs to the copula Farlie-Gumbel family the prior resulting from transformation S and W does not belong to the same family, that is, this prior is not invariant under nonlinear transformations. Marginal posterior of S could be obtained by integrating $\Pi(S, W \mid t)$ with respect to the auxiliar variable W, but this is complicated. We prefer the MCMC approach to get this posterior density. From Eq. (2), the MLE of survival function $S = S(t_0)$ is given by $\hat{S} = 1-[1-\exp(-\hat{\lambda} t_0)]^{\hat{\alpha}}$ where $\hat{\alpha}$ and $\hat{\lambda}$ are the MLE of α and λ, respectively.

5. Numerical Illustrations

In this section, we introduce two examples to illustrate the proposed method.

5.1 Simulated data

First of all, we present and discuss Bayesian inferences based on simulated samples of size n = 5, 25 and 50 generated from the GE distribution with parameters $\alpha = 1.5$ and $\lambda = 3.5$. The data set are given in Table 1.

Table 1

Random samples of 5, 25 and 50 observations from GE $f(x|\alpha, \lambda) = f(x \mid 1.5, 3.5)$

0.1294211	0.326627	0.288136	0.282337	0.155691
0.3328912	0.554069	0.6331775	0.1971299	0.4895222
0.4033831	0.2053582	0.1210208	0.3974832	0.1764692
0.043011	1.1469335	1.3916718	0.3462968	0.2938541
0.0908279	0.4975098	1.8754314	0.2369877	0.1198675
0.0320994	0.744982	0.020457	0.1040829	0.5089536
0.0872934	0.1195056	0.044733	0.097142	0.4601925
0.5188672	0.561651	0.346562	2.4052356	1.0941212
0.2344864	0.6629314	0.4760794	0.1884854	0.4192122
0.0781923	0.1524062	0.2121481	0.0503638	0.572726
0.3789628	0.2159233	0.0170265	1.3900206	0.7825544
0.3015115	0.1670891	0.1216162	0.9102928	0.3033985
0.1272576	0.5586492	0.167599	0.3013364	0.1478698
0.0347033	0.2230028	0.3697116	0.1550103	0.1998605
0.1243817	0.7130682	0.0123715	0.1804198	0.1135168
0.2553322	0.0556948	0.0847322	0.2095519	0.5097356

In Fig. 1, we have contour plots for the likelihood function (7) for α and λ considering the simulated data sets of Table 1 and the parameterizations (α, λ), $(\varphi_1, \varphi_2) = (\log\alpha, \log\lambda)$ and $(\psi_1, \psi_2) = (1/\alpha, 1/\lambda)$, respectively.

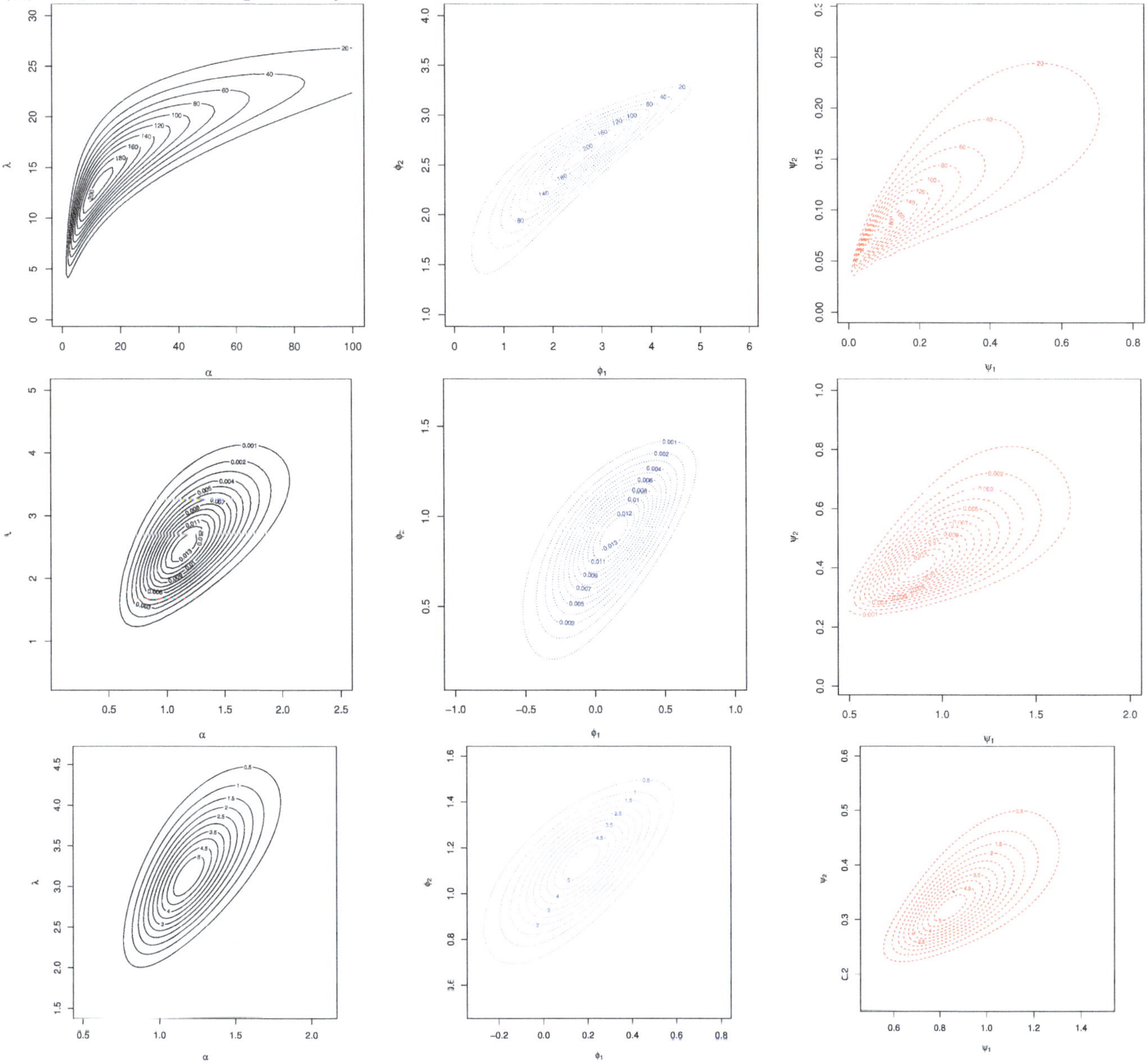

Fig. 1. Contours of likelihood on different parameterizations (α, λ), $(\varphi_1, \varphi_2) = (\log \alpha, \log\lambda)$ and $(\psi_1, \psi_2) = (1/\alpha, 1/\lambda)$ for sample sizes n = 5, n = 25 and n = 50.

From the plots of Fig. 1, we observe that the contour plots are strongly affected by the different parameterizations, especially for small sample sizes as the case of n = 5 observations. In this case, we need to be careful to assume classical asymptotical inference results. For comparison of the different priors proposed in this paper, the joint posterior contours are given in Fig. 2, Fig. 3 and Fig.4 considering the data sets introduced in Table 1 with n = 5, 25 and 50, respectively. Observe that the contour plots are similar considering the different non- informative prior distributions for α and λ, specially for large sample sizes (n = 25 and n = 50). For small sample sizes (n = 5), we observe that the choice of non-informative priors for α and λ could be an important issue in the Bayesian analysis of GE(α, λ) distributions. We also need to appeal to numerical procedures to extract characteristics of marginal posterior distributions such as Bayes estimator, mode and credible intervals. We can then use MCMC algorithm to obtain a sample of values of α and λ from the joint posterior.

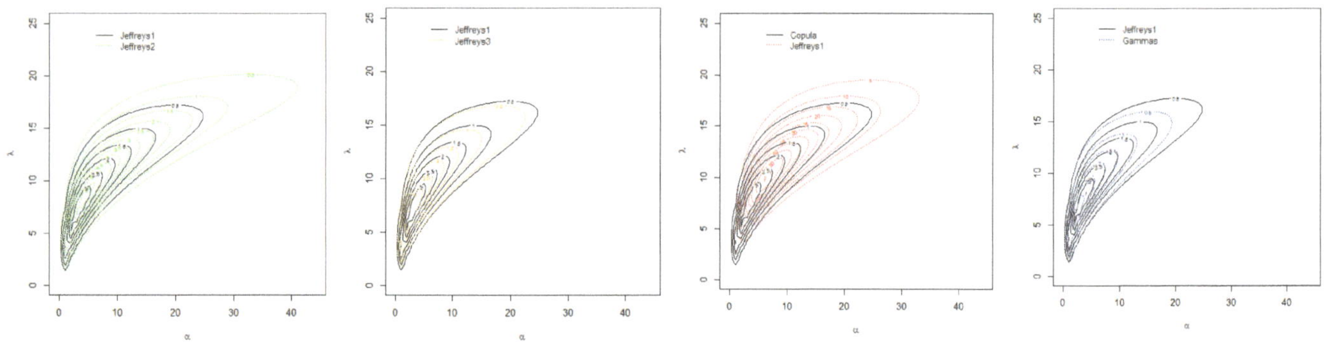

Fig. 2. Contours of posterior on (α, λ) for sample size n = 5

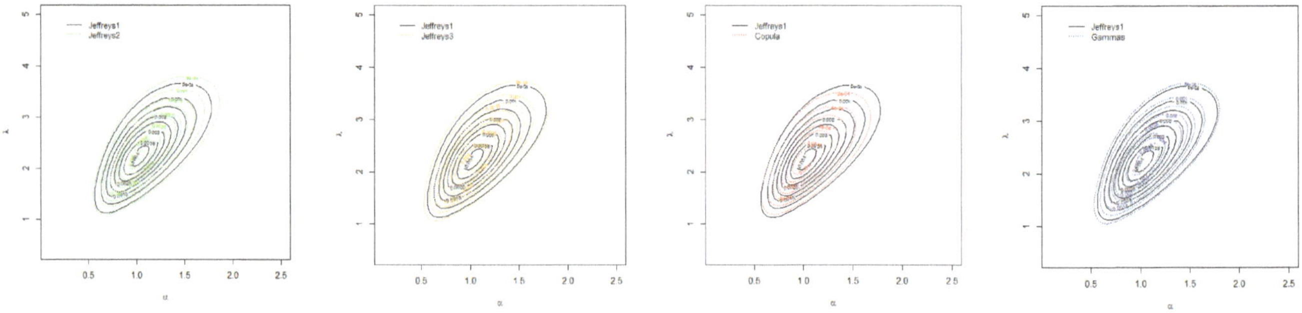

Fig. 3. Contours of posterior on (α, λ) for sample size n = 25

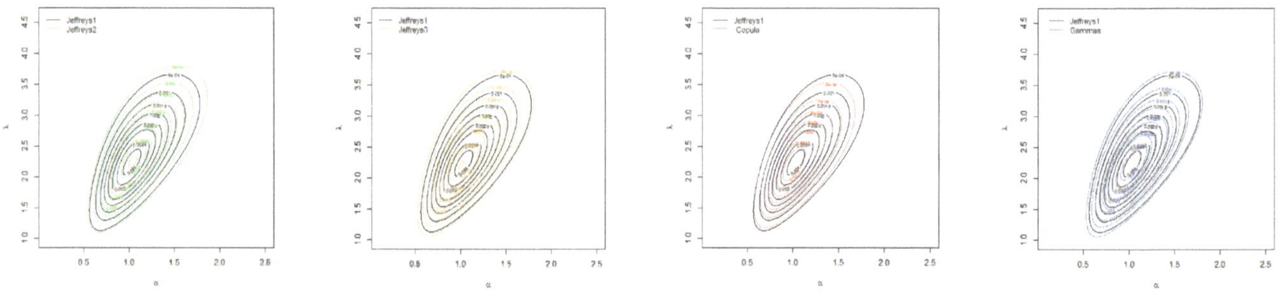

Fig. 4. Contours of posterior on (α, λ) for sample size n = 50

The chain is run for 25,000 iterations with a burn-in period of size 5,000. The MCMC traceplots for the posterior distribution are shown in Fig. 5, Fig. 6 and Fig. 7, and the resulting marginal distributions are plotted in Fig. 8, Fig. 9 and Fig. 10. It is important to point out that we have used the hyperparameter values $a_\alpha = b_\alpha = a_\lambda = b_\lambda = 0.01$ for the gamma priors (25) and $a_1 = 1$ and $a_2 = 1$ for the "Farlie-Gumbel" prior Eq. (28). We also have used the prior (31) for the parameter δ.

The MCMC plots suggest we have achieved convergence and the algorithm also showed a rate of acceptance around 25-35%.

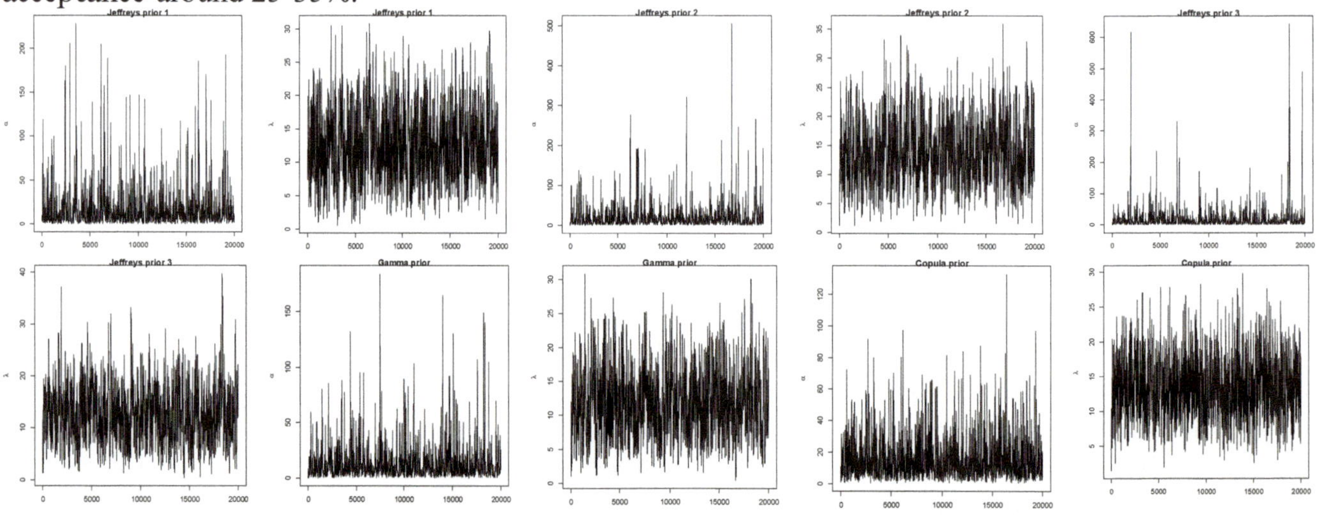

Fig. 5. The MCMC output of posterior on (α, λ) for sample size n = 5

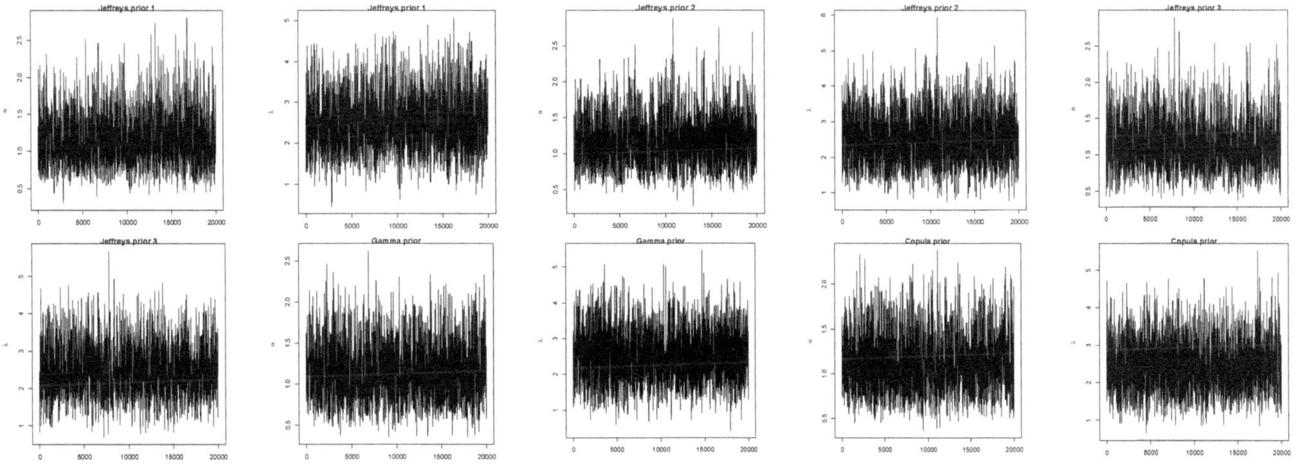

Fig. 6. The MCMC output of posterior on (α, λ) for sample size n = 25

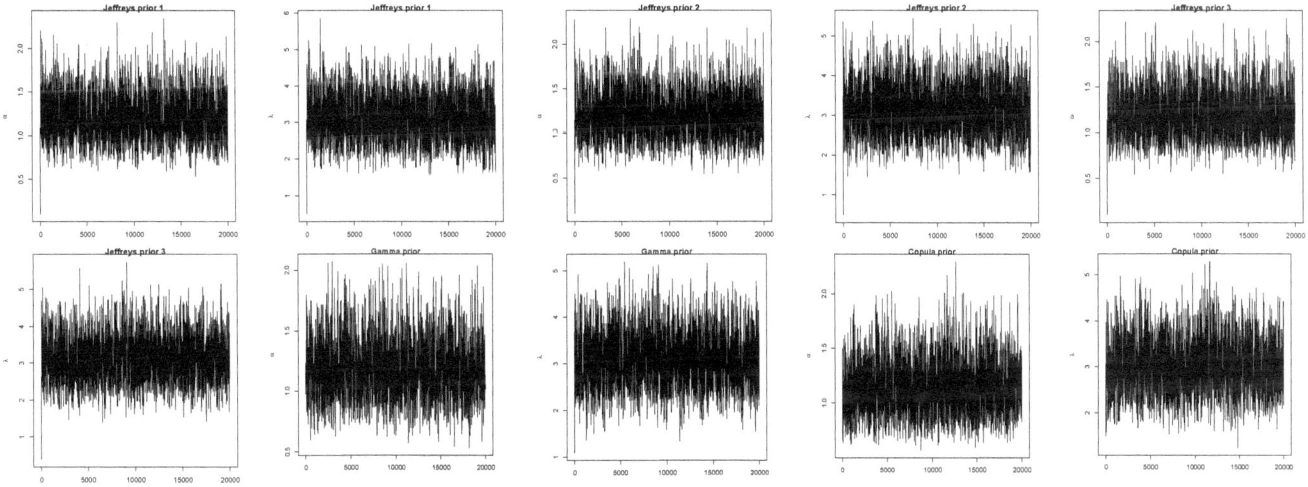

Fig. 7. The MCMC output of posterior on (α, λ) for sample size n = 50

Now we examine the performance of the priors by considering several point estimates for parameters α and λ. The maximum likelihood estimate (MLE) is also evaluated (see Tables 2 and 3). From the results of Tables 2 and 3, we observe that the Bayesian posterior means for α and λ are very different from the values α = 1.5 and λ = 3.5 used to simulate the data sets considering a small sample size (n = 5). Also observe that in this case, the estimated variances are very large.

Table 2

Posterior mean and variance for the parameter α using the data of Table 1

	Jeffreys1	Jeffreys2	Jeffreys3	Copula	Gammas	MLE
n = 5	15.69 (397.11)	20.00 (703.64)	17.54 (1274.7)	13.90 (112.62)	12.56 (194.07)	12.66
n = 25	1.14 (0.10)	1.15 (0.10)	1.13 (0.10)	1.10 (0.08)	1.13 (0.10)	1.14
n = 50	1.20 (0.05)	1.21 (0.06)	1.19 (0.05)	1.14 (0.04)	1.18 (0.05)	1.19

(The values between parentheses express the posterior variance)

Table 3

Posterior mean and variance for the parameter λ using the data of Table 1

	Jeffreys1	Jeffreys2	Jeffreys3	Copula	Gammas	MLE
n = 5	12.36 (25.63)	13.61 (26.80)	12.50 (28.45)	12.93 (15.70)	11.63 (22.80)	13.24
n = 25	2.46 (0.39)	2.47 (0.41)	2.43 (0.40)	2.40 (0.36)	2.44 (0.40)	2.48
n = 50	3.11 (0.32)	3.14 (0.34)	3.11 (0.32)	3.02 (0.27)	3.07 (0.30)	3.121

(The values between parentheses express the posterior variance)

Obviously, other posterior summaries can be evaluated as well. For example, one may want to derive the posterior intervals for comparison. The 95% posterior intervals for each parameter α and λ obtained using the different non-informative priors are displayed in Tables 4 and 5.

Table 4

95% posterior credible intervals for the parameter α using the data of Table 1

	Jeffreys1	Jeffreys2	Jeffreys3	Copula	Gammas	Confidence Interval
n = 5	(1.23, 69.11)	(1.79, 89.45)	(1.11, 77.02)	(2.38, 41.02)	(1.13, 52.09)	(-12.58, 37.91)
n = 25	(0.64, 1.86)	(0.64, 1.84)	(0.61, 1.84)	(0.63, 1.74)	(0.61, 1.83)	(0.54, 1.74)
n = 50	(0.79, 1.71)	(0.79, 1.71)	(0.80, 1.71)	(0.78, 1.61)	(0.78, 1.69)	(0.74, 1.63)

Table 5

95% posterior credible intervals for the parameter λ using the data of Table 1

	Jeffreys1	Jeffreys2	Jeffreys3	Copula	Gammas	Confidence Interval
n = 5	(3.71, 23.68)	(4.76, 24.68)	(3.68, 24.09)	(5.70, 21.34)	(3.53, 21.83)	(3.11, 23.36)
n = 25	(1.36, 3.78)	(1.35, 3.77)	(1.32, 3.80)	(1.36, 3.68)	(1.30, 3.75)	(1.25, 3.71)
n = 50	(2.08, 4.27)	(2.07, 4.37)	(2.11, 4.28)	(2.04, 4.14)	(2.06, 4.18)	(2.04, 4.20)

From the results of Tables 4 and Table 5, we observe that the 95% credible intervals for α and λ are very large considering a small sample size (n = 5 observations). We also observe that with the different non-informative priors for α and λ, we have similar results. The comparison of the marginal posterior densities is given in Figures 8, 9 and 10 assuming the different prior distributions.

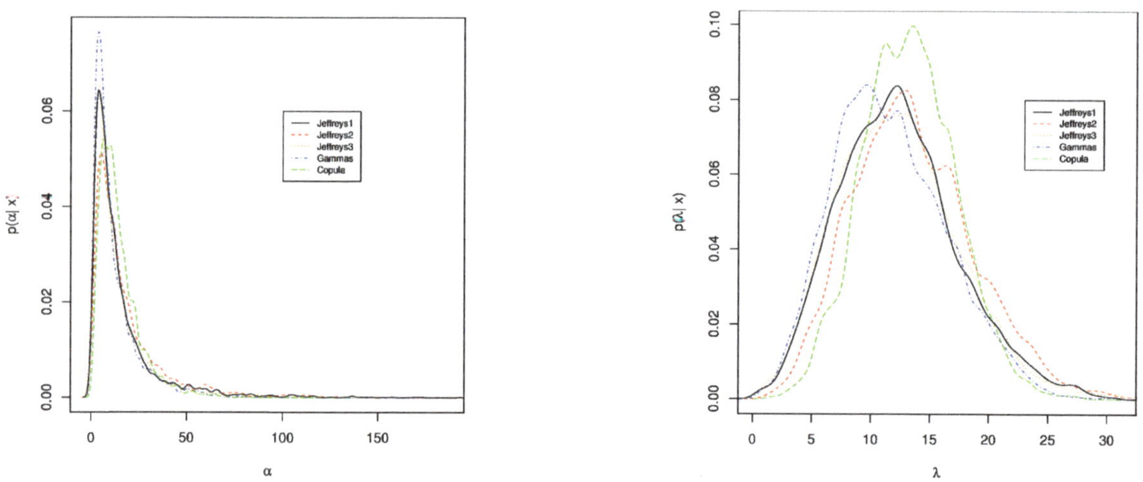

Fig. 8. Marginal posterior densities of parameters α and λ for n = 5 and simulated data with (α, λ)=(1.5, 3.5)

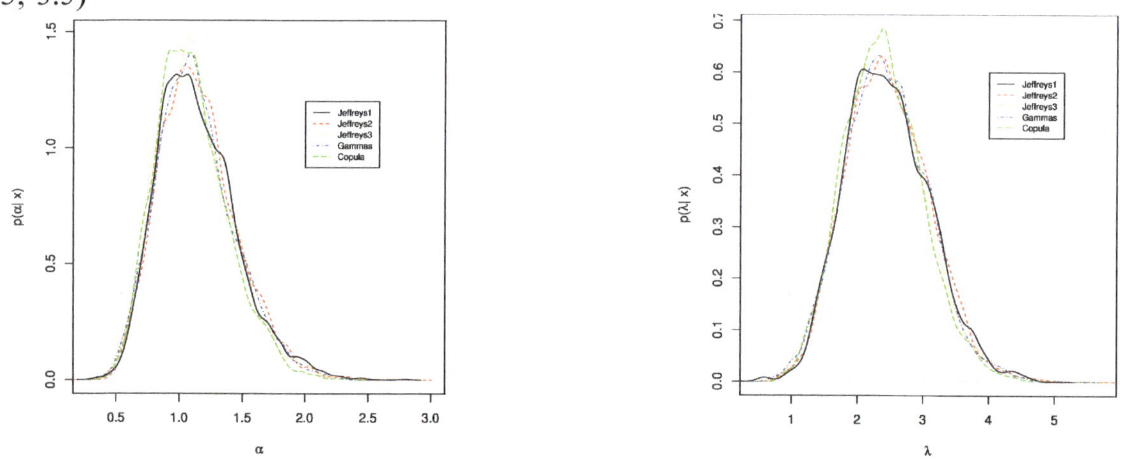

Fig. 9. Marginal posterior densities of parameters α and λ for n = 25 and simulated data with (α, λ)=(1.5, 3.5)

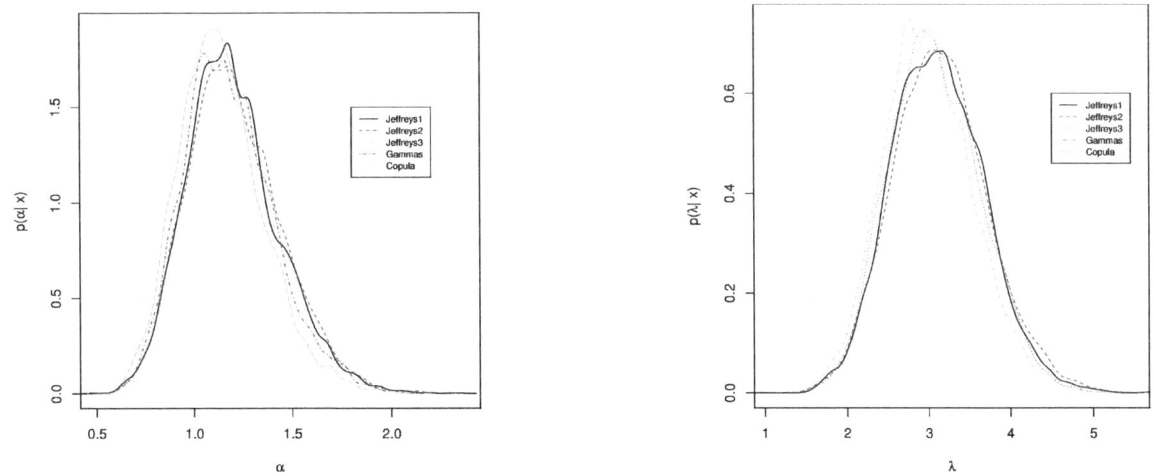

Fig. 10. Marginal posterior densities of parameters α and λ for n = 50 and simulated data with (α, λ)=(1.5, 3.5)

From the results of Figs. (8-10), we observe that the marginal posterior densities for α and λ become more similar assuming the different non-informative priors for α and λ, as the data sample size increases (n = 25 and n = 50). Assuming t = 0.2, the survival function given the parameter values α = 1.5 and λ = 3.5 is given by S(0.2) = 0.64. Assuming the three simulated data sets of Table 1, we have in Figs. (11-13), the marginal posterior distributions for S(0.2) obtained from the 20,000 simulated Gibbs samples for the joint posterior distribution of α and λ, considering the different non-informative priors introduced in Section 3. From the plots of Figs. (11-13), we observe that the choice of non-informative priors for the parameters α and λ of the GE(α, λ) distribution could be very important to obtain accurate Bayesian inferences for the survival function, since with the use of the "Farlie-Gumbel (copula)" prior we have more accurate Bayesian inferences for S(0.2). In Tables 6 and Table 7, we have the posterior summaries of interest for S(0.2) assuming the different non-informative priors for α and λ. We also observe more accurate Bayesian inferences for the survival function S(0.2), assuming the "Farlie-Gumbel" prior distribution for the parameters α and λ.

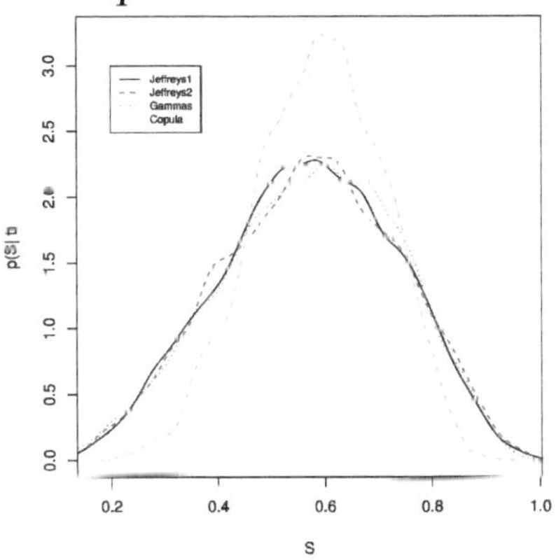

Fig. 11. Posterior densities of survival function S for n = 5

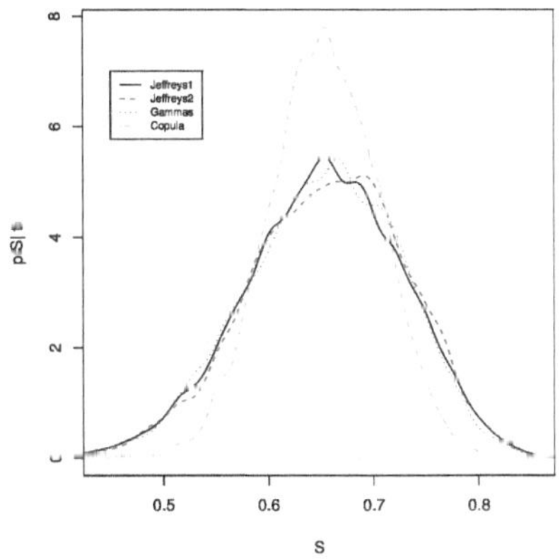

Fig. 12. Posterior densities of survival function S for n = 25

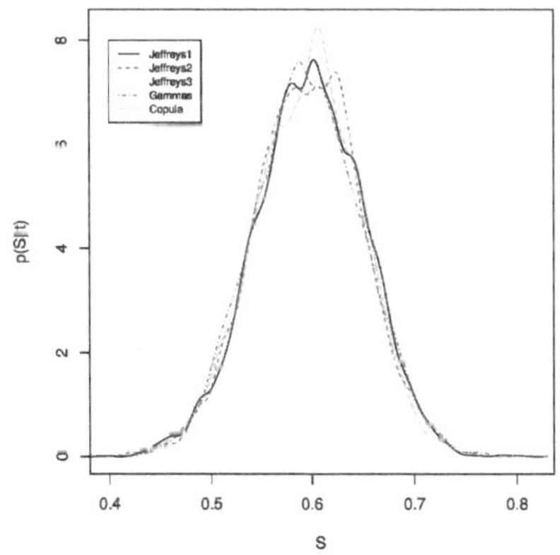

Fig. 13. Posterior densities of survival function S for n = 50

Table 6
Posterior mean and variance for the parameter S

	Jeffreys1	Jeffreys2	Jeffreys3	Copula	Gammas	Confidence Interval
n = 5	0.57 (0.027)	0.57 (0.027)	0.57 (0.026)	0.59 (0.014)	0.57 (0.027)	0.60
n = 25	0.65 (0.006)	0.65 (0.006)	0.65 (0.005)	0.65 (0.003)	0.65 (0.005)	0.66
n = 50	0.60 (0.003)	0.60 (0.003)	0.60 (0.003)	0.59 (0.001)	0.59 (0.003)	0.60

(The values between parentheses express the posterior variance)

Table 7
95% posterior intervals for the parameter S

	Jeffreys1	Jeffreys2	Jeffreys3	Copula	Gammas
n = 5	(0.25, 0.86)	(0.24, 0.87)	(0.24, 0.86)	(0.35, 0.80)	(0.23, 0.86)
n = 25	(0.50, 0.79)	(0.50, 0.79)	(0.49, 0.79)	(0.55, 0.75)	(0.50, 0.78)
n = 50	(0.49, 0.70)	(0.49, 0.70)	(0.49, 0.70)	(0.52, 0.66)	(0.49, 0.70)

(The values between parentheses express the posterior variance)

5.2 An example with literature data

In this section, let us consider a data set related to the lifetime of components (data set introduced in Lawless, 1982, page 228): 17.88; 28.92; 33.0; 41.52; 42.12; 45.60; 48.80; 51.84; 51.96; 54.12; 55.56; 67.80; 68.64; 68.64; 68.88; 84.12; 93.12; 8.64; 105.12; 105.84; 127.92; 128.04 and 173.40. Let us denote this data as "Lawless data". This data set represents the numbers (in million) of cycles until failure of the component. Let us assume a generalized exponential distribution with density (1) to analyse the data. The maximum likelihood estimators for α and λ (see (10) and (11)) are given, respectively, by where $\hat{\alpha}$ =5.2836 and $\hat{\lambda}$= 0.0323, with 95% confidence interval (1.2714; 9.2653) and (0.0197; 0.0448) for α and λ, respectively. For a Bayesian analysis of the data let us assume the prior distribution (15), (19), (20) and (24) and the Gamma priors (25) for α and λ assuming the hyperparameter values $a_\alpha = b_\alpha = a_\lambda = b_\lambda = 0.01$. Using the software R we first simulated 5,000 Gibbs samples ("burn-in-samples") for the joint posterior distribution for α and λ that were discarded to eliminate the effect of the initial values for the random quantities α and λ used in the iterative simulation method; after this "burn-in-period", we simulated other 20,000 Gibbs samples. The convergence of the Gibbs sampling algorithm was monitored from traceplots of the simulated samples. The posterior summaries of interest considering the different prior distributions are given in Tables 8 and 9. Observe that we have used $a_1 = 1$ and $a_2 = 2$ for the copula prior (28) and the prior (31) for the parameter δ.

Table 8
Posterior summaries for α (Lawless data)

Priors	Posterior mean	Posterior variance	95% posterior interval
Jeffreys1	5.451	4.856	(2.286, 10.833)
Jeffreys2	5.614	5.340	(2.481, 11.085)
Jeffreys3	5.289	4.470	(2.202, 10.602)
Copula	5.229	3.540	(2.365, 9.701)
Gammas	5.307	4.575	(2.312, 10.596)

Table 9
Posterior summaries for λ (Lawless data)

Priors	Posterior mean	Posterior variance	95% posterior interval
Jeffreys1	0.0321	4.118436e-05	(0.0202, 0.0453)
Jeffreys2	0.0323	4.146039e-05	(0.0211, 0.0459)
Jeffreys3	0.0316	4.09938e-05	(0.0195, 0.0443)
Copula	0.0316	3.499097e-05	(0.0205, 0.0438)
Gammas	0.0317	4.10683e-05	(0.0203, 0.0449)

From the obtained inference results of Table 9, we observe similar results. The comparison of the marginal posterior densities is given in Fig. 14.

Table 10

Posterior summaries for S (Lawless data)

Priors	Posterior mean	Posterior variance	95% posterior interval
Jeffreys1	0.6797	0.0055	(0.529, 0.815)
Jeffreys2	0.6867	0.0055	(0.533, 0.821)
Jeffreys3	0.6791	0.0057	(0.522, 0.816)
Copula	0.6854	0.0029	(0.573, 0.786)
Gammas	0.6759	0.0060	(0.515, 0.816)

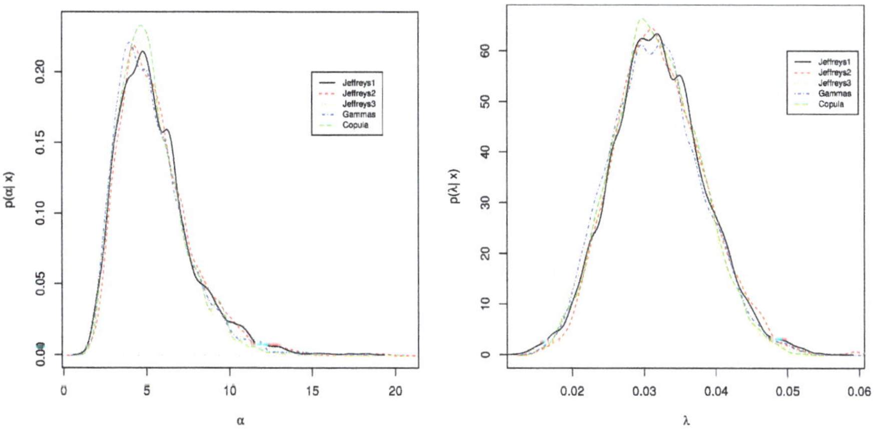

Fig. 14. Marginal posterior densities of parameters α and λ (Lawless data)

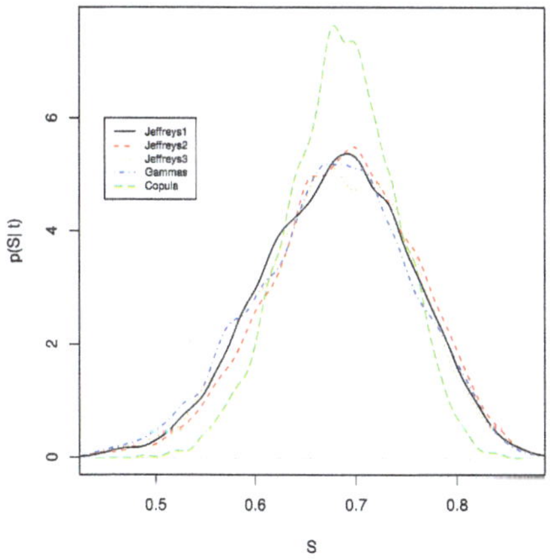

Fig. 15. Posterior density of survival for t = 50 (Lawless data)

In Fig. 16, we have the plots of the empirical and fitted survival functions modeled by the generalized exponential for $\hat{\alpha} = 5.23$ and $\hat{\lambda} = 0.031$ considering distribution with density given in Eq. (1) and assuming the Bayesian estimators b the copula prior distribution for α and λ (see Tables 8 and 9). From Fig. 16, we observe a good fit of the generalized exponential distribution for the data (Lawless data).

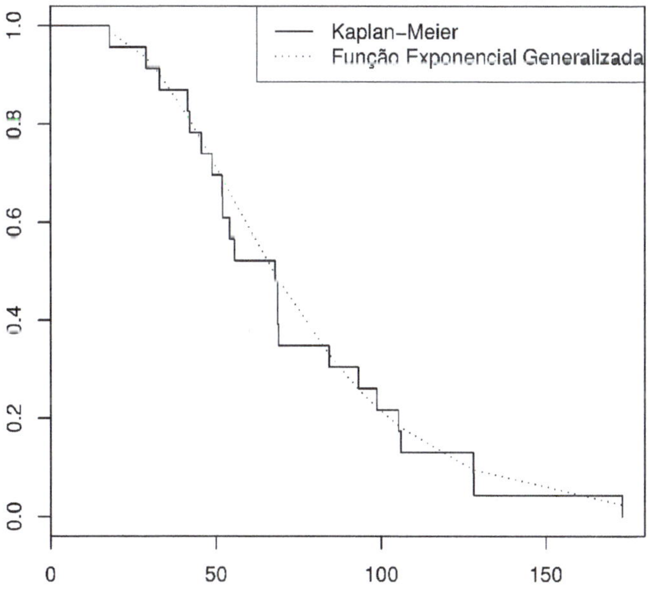

Fig. 16. Empirical and fitted survival for t = 50 (Lawless data)

6. Conclusion

The use of the generalized exponential distribution with density (1) could be a good alternative to analyse lifetime data, in comparison to the popular gamma distribution. Observe that the survival function (see (2)) for the GE(α, λ) distribution presents a closed analytical form and the survival function for the gamma distribution presents an incomplete gamma function. In this way, since lifetimes of medical or engineering applications present censored data, the use of GE(α, λ) can have good computational advantages. Accurate inference for the parameters of the GE(α, λ) could be obtained using MCMC methods for a Bayesian analysis of the model. In this way, we need to choose an appropriate prior distribution for the parameters of the model, especially in the situations where we do not have expert opinion to build our prior. From the results of this paper we observe that the use of copula prior distributions for the random quantities α and λ could improve our inference results, especially considering the survival function at specified time t. These results are of great interest in applications.

References

Box, G. E., & Tiao, G. C. (2011). *Bayesian inference in statistical analysis* (Vol. 40). John Wiley & Sons.

Chib, S., & Greenberg, E. (1995). Understanding The Metropolis-Hasting Algorithm. *The American Statistician*, 49, 327-335.

Gelfand, A. E., & Smith, A. F. (1990). Sampling-based approaches to calculating marginal densities. *Journal of the American statistical association*, *85*(410), 398-409.

Gupta, R. D., & Kundu, D. (1999). Theory & methods: Generalized exponential distributions. *Australian & New Zealand Journal of Statistics*, *41*(2), 173-188.

Gupta, R. D., & Kundu, D. (2001). Generalized exponential distribution: different method of estimations. *Journal of Statistical Computation and Simulation*, *69*(4), 315-337.

Gupta, R. D., & Kundu, D. (2007). Generalized exponential distribution: Existing results and some recent developments. *Journal of Statistical Planning and Inference*, *137*(11), 3537-3547.

Kundu, D., & Gupta, R. D. (2008). Generalized exponential distribution: Bayesian estimations. *Computational Statistics & Data Analysis*, *52*(4), 1873-1883.

Morgenstern, D. (1956). Einfache beispiele zweidimensionaler verteilungen. *Mitteilingsblatt Math Statistik*, 8, 234–235.

Nelsen, R. B. (1999). *An introduction to copulas*. Springer.

Raqab, M. Z. (2002). Inferences for generalized exponential distribution based on record statistics. *Journal of statistical planning and inference*, *104*(2), 339-350.

Raqab, M. M., & Ahsanullah, M. (2001). Estimation of the location and scale parameters of generalized exponential distribution based on order statistics. *Journal of Statistical Computation and Simulation*, *69*(2), 109-123.

Sarhan, A. M. (2007). Analysis of incomplete, censored data in competing risks models with generalized exponential distributions. *Reliability, IEEE Transactions on*, *56*(1), 132-138.

Trivedi, P. K., & Zimmer, D. M. (2007). *Copula modeling: an introduction for practitioners*. Now Publishers Inc.

Zheng, G. (2002). On the Fisher information matrix in type II censored data from the exponentiated exponential family. *Biometrical Journal*, *44*(3), 353-357.

9

An experimental investigation and statistical modelling for trim cutting operation in WEDM of Nimonic-90

Vinod Kumar[a], Vikas Kumar[b] and Kamal Kumar Jangra[c*]

[a]*Research Scholar, Department of Mechanical Engineering, YMCA University of Science and Technology, Faridabad, India*
[b]*Department of Mechanical Engineering, YMCA University of Science and Technology, Faridabad, India*
[c]*Department of Mechanical Engineering, PEC University of Technology, Chandigarh, India*

C H R O N I C L E

Keywords:
Nimonic-90
Wire electrical discharge machining
Trim cutting
Response surface methodology (RSM)
Desirability function

A B S T R A C T

Trim cutting operation in wire electrical discharge machining (WEDM) is considered as a probable solution to improve surface characteristics and geometrical accuracy by removing very small amount of work materials from the surface obtained after a rough cutting operation. In this study, an attempt has been made to model the surface roughness and dimensional shift in trim cutting operations in WEDM process through response surface methodology (RSM). Four process parameters; namely pulse-on time (Ton), servo voltage (SV), wire depth (W_d) and Dielectric flow rate (FR) have been considered as input parameters in trim cutting operations for modelling. Desirability function has been employed to optimize multi performance characteristics. Increasing the value of Ton, W_d and FR increases the surface roughness and dimensional shift but increasing SV decreases both surface roughness and dimensional shift. Quadratic models have been proposed for both the performance characteristics. In present experimentation, thickness of recast layer was observed in the range of 6μm to 12μm for low to high value of discharge parameters.

1. Introduction

Machining of high strength-heat resisting alloys and metal matrix composites with high precision is the main challenge for manufacturing industries. While machining of different materials with various machine tools, it is essential to satisfy the surface integrity of the machined surface. Nickel alloys are specially used for combustion chamber in aero-engines and other components for commercial and military aircrafts (Choudhury & Baradie, 1998; Ezugwu, 2005). These alloys possess excellent mechanical and chemical properties at elevated temperature and high corrosion resistance (Guo et al., 2009). Machinability of these materials with conventional machining processes is a great challenging task due to complex nature of material properties. Due to low thermal conductivity, Ni alloys leads to work hardening during machining and increasing temperature of tool tip results in quick wear of tool tip/ rack face and adhesion of work piece material to the cutting edge due to high thermal affinity (Choudhury & Baradie, 1998; Ulutan & Ozel, 2011). Surface drag, material pull out, cracking and tearing of work surface occur during machining of Ni based alloys with conventional machining processes (Wei, 2002;

Arunachalam et al., 2004; Sharman et al., 2004; Krain et al., 2007; Hood et al., 2011; Kortabarria et al., 2011; Soo et al., 2011).

Wire electrical discharge machining (shown in Fig. 1) is an electro thermal process, which removes electrical conductive materials by mean of repetitive electric sparks across a spark gap between a continuous moving conductive wire and work piece. Each discharge melts or vaporizes a small amount of materials from the machined surface, which is flushed away by the dielectric fluid flowing between wire electrode and work surfaced. WEDM provides the best alternatives for machining the exotic, conductive and hard materials with the scope of generating intricate shape and profile (Cheng et al., 2014).

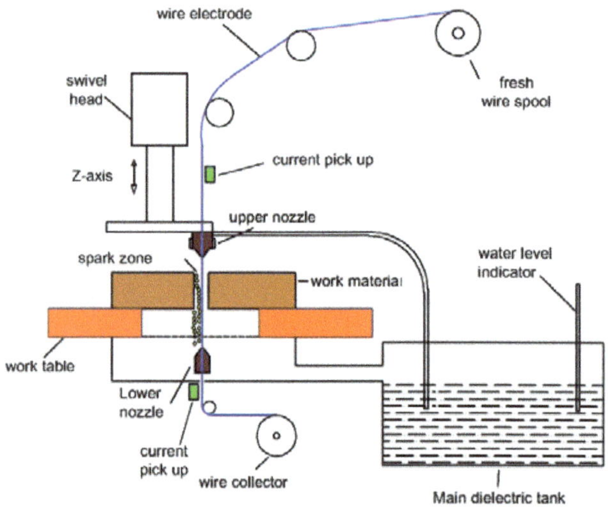

Fig. 1. Schematic representation of WEDM process

Jangra et al. (2011) utilized the grey based Taguchi method to optimize the MRR and SR for WEDM of WC-Co composite. Results revealed that taper angle, pulse on time (Ton) and pulse off time (Toff) are the most significant process parameters. Yang et al. (2012) proposed a hybrid method including RSM and back – propagation neural network (BPNN) integrated simulated annealing algorithm (SAA) to determine an optimal setting for machining of pure Tungsten in WEDM. RSM and BPNN/SAA methods were effective tools for the optimization of parameters in WEDM process. Jangra et al. (2011) developed a mathematical model using digraph and matrix method to evaluate the machinability of tungsten carbide composite on WEDM. Factors affecting the machinability of tungsten carbide composite were grouped in five broad categories namely work material, machine tool, tool electrode, cutting conditions, and geometry to be machined. Kumar et al. (2012) presented the influence of WEDM parameters on machinability of Nimonic-90. Influence of WEDM parameters namely discharge current (Ip), pulse-on time (Ton), pulse-off time (Toff), servo voltage (SV) and wire feed rate (W_F) were investigated on cutting speed. The experiments were conducted by varying a single variable at a time while keeping other parameters at constant level on 5 axis sprint cut (ELPUSE-40) wire EDM manufactured by Electronic M/C Tool LTD India. Experimental results showed that the Ip, Ton and Toff produces noticeable influence on Cutting speed.

Khanna and Singh (2013) developed a mathematical model for cryogenic treated D-3 material by means of RSM and then solved the optimization problem by desirability function. Bobbili et al. (2014) carried out a study for optimising the WEDM process parameters like pulse on time (Ton), pulse off time (Toff), wire feed rate (W_F), flushing pressure and servo voltage (SV) during the machining of high strength Armor steel. Results show that Ton, Toff and SV are significant variables to both material removal rate (MRR) and SR. Bhuyan and Yadava (2014) investigated the effect of input process variable on MRR and Kerf width during machining of Borosilicate Glass using a hybrid machining process "Travelling wire electrochemical spark machining" (TWECSM). MRR and Kerf width increase with increase in applied voltage, pulse on time and electrolyte concentration. Gupta and Jain (2014) investigated the behaviour of the micro geometry parameters of miniature spur gears produced by WEDM process and optimized the process parameters for minimizing the total profile and accumulated pitch deviation using response surface methodology. The various experimental and theoretical studies show that process capability of WEDM could be improved significantly by correct selection of machining parameters for a given material. Sharma et al. (2013) optimized the process parameters of WEDM using response surface methodology. Desirability approach has been adopted for multi response (i.e. CS and dimensional deviation) optimization. Ton is the most significant factor for multi response optimization, while two way interactions also played significant role in the process.

1.1 Trim Cutting Operation

The majority of past research works focus on rough cutting operation in WEDM. Damaged surface layer with poor surface integrity, micro cracks, heat affected zone are the major shortcoming in rough cutting operation (Lee & Li, 2003; Wang et al., 2009; Jangra, 2012). The defects are due to high heat energy generated across the electrodes and re-solidification of melted debris's that do not flushed out quickly out of a narrow spark gap (Puri & Bhattacharyya, 2003; Rebelo et al., 1998; Sarkar et al., 2011). Trim cutting is considered as a probable solution to improve the surface integrity, geometrical accuracy and fatigue life by removing the degraded materials on the machined surface. In trim cutting operation, wire electrode trace back the same wire path of first cut with low discharge energy and certain values of wire offset (Huang et al., 1999) as shown in Fig. 2. Wire offset (WO) is the distance between the center of electrode and work surface after rough cut. Wire depth (W_d) is the distance travelled perpendicular and inside the work piece during trim cutting operation. The wire depth (W_d) is related to wire offset value. Increasing wire offset value decreases the W_d.

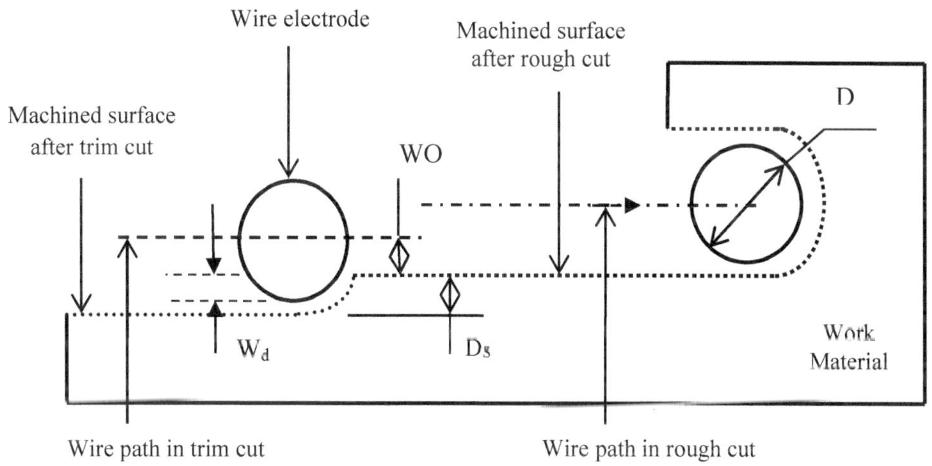

Fig. 2. Terminology used in trim cutting operation

Han et al. (2007) explained the influence of machining parameters namely Ton, Ip, sustained pulse time, pulse-interval time, polarity effect, work material and dielectric, on surface roughness after a single trim cut of WEDM. Sarkar et al. (2008) developed a second order mathematical model in term of machining parameters for surface finish, dimensional shift and cutting speed in trim cutting of γ-titanium aluminide using response surface methodology (RSM) on WEDM. Machining parameters namely pulse-on time, peak current, dielectric flow rate and effective wire offset were considered for a single trim cutting operation in WEDM. The minimum value of surface roughness obtained was 1.28μm. Klink et al. (2011) presented the comparison of the surface finish, microstructure, micro hardness and residual stresses after rough and trim cuts in WEDM.

Jangra et al. (2014) conducted an experimental study on rough and trim cutting operation in WEDM of four hard to machine materials namely WC-Co composite, HCHCr steel alloy, Nimonic-90 and Monel-400. Result shows that using single trim cutting operation with correct machining parameters and appropriate wire offset, surface characteristics could be improved irrespective of the rough cutting operation. Jangra KK (2015) investigated the multi-pass cutting operation in WEDM of WC-Co composite. Trim cuts were performed using Taguchi method to investigate the influence of rough cut history, discharge current, pulse-on time, wire offset and number of trim cuts for two performance characteristics namely surface roughness and depth of material removed. A technological data has provided for rough and trim cut on WEDM for efficient machining of WC-5.3%Co composite.

Despite many research works on WEDM, investigation on WEDM of Nimonic 90 is still missing. Nimonic-90 is a nickel-chromium-cobalt based alloy, most widely used in the aerospace and air craft industries in the manufacturing of turbine blades and combustion chamber, valve in turbo motors and disc in gas turbine. This material possesses excellent strength at extreme pressure and temperature. In present work, investigation on trim cutting operation in WEDM of Nimonic-90 has been presented. Machining parameters namely pulse on time, servo voltage, dielectric flow rate and wire depth have been investigated on surface characteristics and dimensional shift in trim cutting operation. A standard second order experimental design called face centered Central Composite Design (CCD) in term of machining parameter has been adopted using response surface methodology (RSM). Desirability function has been employed to optimize two performance characteristics simultaneously.

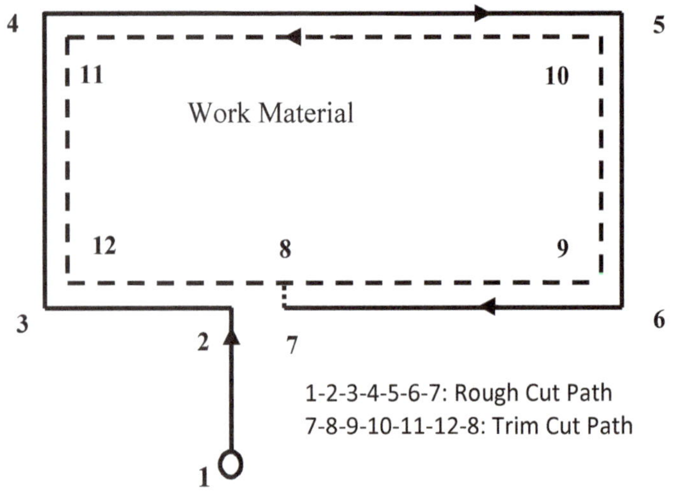

Fig. 3. Cutting operations in WEDM process

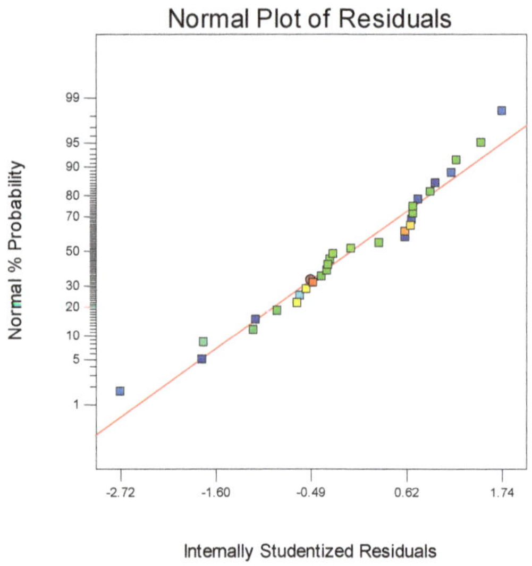

Fig. 4. Residuals plot for SR

2. Experimentation procedure

In present work, Nimonic-90 has been selected for conducting experiments on 5 axis sprint cut (ELPUSE-40) Wire EDM manufactured by Electronic M/C Tool LTD India. Nimonic-90, a nickel based super alloy containing 60% Ni, 19.3% Cr, 15% Co, 3.1% Ti, and 1.4% Al, hot forged in rectangular plate of 12.5 mm thickness; has been selected as work piece material. It has density; 8.18 g/cm^3, melting point; 1370 ^{0}C, hardness; 365 HV, thermal conductivity; 11.47 W/mĊ and modulus of elasticity; 220MPa. The major characteristic of Nimonic-90 is its high rupture strength and creep resistance at high temperature (upto 900^{0}C).

In present experimentation, trim cutting operations were performed at different combination of process parameters after a rough cut performed at constant parameters. Using WEDM, work material was machined and samples were obtained in the form of rectangular punches of dimension 6 mm × 10 mm × 12.5 mm. Fig. 3 shows the schematic diagram of the cutting operation performed in present work. According to path programme (Fig. 3), firstly, a rough cut (1-2-3-4-5-6-7) was performed at constant value of discharge parameters and zero wire offset value. The machine was halted at point 7 to change the input machining parameters and then subsequently trim cut (7-8-9-10-11-12-8) was performed according to the experimental plan mentioned in Table 3. Dimensional shift (Ds) was calculated after measuring the dimensions of punch with the help of an optical microscope. To measure the punch width (PW) after rough cut, a rough cut path; 1-2-3-4-5-6-7-2 was followed to remove the punch out of work material. Rough cut were repeated at same parameter setting to obtain an average value of PW after rough cut. Ds can be obtained as

Ds : (Punch width after rough cut – Punch width after trim cut)/2.

In case of trim cutting, the prime objective is to improve surface roughness and to reduce dimensional inaccuracy. Therefore, high discharge energy parameters combination providing maximum cutting rate has been selected in rough cutting operation, while in trim cutting operation low discharge energy parameters resulting, low surface roughness, has been selected. Fixed Machining parameters setting for rough cutting and trim cutting operation are shown in Table 1. A zinc coated brass wire having a fixed diameter of 0.25mm has been selected as wire electrode. Distilled water having conductivity 20 mho has been used as a dielectric fluid.

Table 1
Fixed machining parameters in rough & trim cutting operation

Rough cut parameters	
Pulse on Time, Ton = 118 μs	Wire Tension W_T = 10 N
Pulse off Time, Toff = 35 μs	Discharge Current, Ip = 150 machine unit
Dielectric Flow Rate, FR=12L/min	Servo Voltage, SV = 30 V
Wire Feed rate, W_F = 5 mm/min	Servo Feed, SF=150mm/min
Trim cut parameters	
Pulse off time, Toff = 30 μs	Work material thickness =12.5 mm
Discharge current, Ip =110 machine unit	Wire feed rate, W_F = 2mm/min
Wire tension, W_T = 8N	Servo feed, SF = 150

The pulse on time (Ton), servo voltage (SV), wire depth (W_d) and dielectric flow rate (FR) have been considered as main process parameters in trim cutting operation for investigation. Dimensional shift (Ds) and surface roughness (SR) are two response parameters. Table 2 shows the process parameters and their levels for trim cutting operation. Value of wire depth (Wd) was varied by varying the wire offset in trim cut. Experiments were performed according to the layout of experimental design for Face CCD of second order shown in Table 3.

Table 2
Variable process parameters and their levels for Trim cutting conditions

Parameter	Units	Levels	
Pulse on Time (Ton)	μs	104	112
Servo Voltage (SV)	V	20	40
Wire depth (W_d)	μm	10	30
Dielectric Flow Rate (FR)	L/min	2	6

3. Response Surface Methodology and Experimental Design

Response surface methodology (RSM) is a collection of mathematical and experimental techniques that requires sufficient number of experimental data to analyse the engineering problem and to develop mathematical models for several input variables and output performance characteristics (Myers & Montgomery, 1995; Jangra & Grover, 2012). By using the design of experiments and applying regression analysis, the modelling of the desired response (*Y*) to several independent input variables (x_i) can be gained. In RSM, the quantitative form of relationship between desired response and independent input variables could be represented as:

$$Y = \Phi(x_1, x_2, \dots \dots \dots.., x_k) \pm e_r \qquad (1)$$

The function Φ is called response surface or response function. The residual e_r measures the experimental errors (Cochran & Cox, 1962). In applying the RSM, the dependent variable is viewed as a surface to which a mathematical model is fitted. For the development of regression equations related to various performance characteristics of WEDM process, the second order response surface has been assumed as:

$$Y = b_0 + \sum_{i=1}^{k} b_i X_i + \sum_{i=1}^{k} b_{ii} X_i^2 + \sum_{i<j=2}^{2} b_{ij} X_i X_j \pm e_r \qquad (2)$$

where Y is the corresponding response variables i.e. surface roughness and dimensional shift produced by various process variables of WEDM. b_0 is constant and b_i, $b_{ii,}b_{ij}$ are the coefficient of linear, quadratic and cross product terms. The model parameters can be estimated most effectively if proper experimental designs are used to collect the data. The objective of this study was to identify an optimal setting for process parameters that can be minimizing the surface roughness and dimensional shift of a WEDM process in trim cutting operation.

Table 3

The layout of experimental design for Face CCD of second order and experimental results

Exp. No.	Ton	SV	W_d	FR	SR (μm)	Ds (μm)
1	104	20	10	2	1.31	14
2	112	20	10	2	2.03	17
3	104	40	10	2	1.1	16
4	112	40	10	2	1.51	14
5	104	20	30	2	1.25	38
6	112	20	30	2	2.45	38
7	104	40	30	2	1.22	43
8	112	40	30	2	2.22	45
9	104	20	10	6	1.18	22
10	112	20	10	6	2.41	29
11	104	40	10	6	1.11	17
12	112	40	10	6	1.97	28
13	104	20	30	6	1.25	40
14	112	20	30	6	2.9	48
15	104	40	30	6	1.3	46
16	112	40	30	6	2.69	54
17	104	30	20	4	1.32	23
18	112	30	20	4	2.53	27
19	108	20	20	4	2.03	23
20	108	40	20	4	1.81	27
21	108	30	10	4	1.86	20
22	108	30	30	4	2.2	47
23	108	30	20	2	1.72	27
24	108	30	20	6	2	36
25	108	30	20	4	2.03	28
26	108	30	20	4	2.08	27
27	108	30	20	4	2.09	27
28	108	30	20	4	2.06	29
29	108	30	20	4	2.08	30
30	108	30	20	4	2.12	27

4. Results and Discussions

In present study, on the basis of inputs process parameters and their level as listed in Table 2, a standard second order experimental design called face centred Central Composite Design (CCD) has been adopted for analysing and modelling the WEDM parameters for average value of surface roughness and dimensional shift is illustrated in Table 3. Surface roughness value (SR) was measured in terms of mean absolute deviation (Ra) using the digital surface tester Mitutoyo 201P. Regression equations have been developed for correlating the input process parameters with response parameters using RSM. To analyze the experimental data, Design expert (DX7), a statistical tool, has been utilized. Analysis of Variance (ANOVA) has been performed on the experimental data to test the goodness of fit of the model. This includes the test for significance of the regression model, test for significance on model coefficients and test for lack of fit model adequacy.

4.1 Analysis of Surface roughness (SR)

Table 4 shows the fit summary for SR, after backward elimination process. The Model F-value of 232.85 implies the model is significant. There is only a 0.01% chance that a large "Model F-Value" could occur due to noise. In this case A, B, C, D, AB, AC, AD, BC, A^2, B^2, D^2 are significant model terms. Values greater than 0.05 indicate the model terms are not significant. Selected model would be statistically significant, if *p*-value for the model terms are less than 0.05 (i.e. $\alpha = 0.05$, or 95% confidence level) (Myers & Montgomery, 1995). Using backward elimination process, insignificant terms (*p*-value > 0.05) have been eliminated from the reduced quadratic model. Table 4 shows that the *p*-value for quadratic model is significant, which shows that the terms in the model have significant effect on output response. In present case, the value of R^2 and R^2 (adj.), called coefficient of determination, is over 99%. When R^2 approaches unity, the better the response model fits the actual data. Also, test of 'lack of fit' shows insignificant effect, which is desirable for selecting the models. Fig. 4 shows that the residuals are normally distributed about a straight line, which means that the errors are normally distributed. Consequently, the proposed model for SR can be considered as significant for fitting and predicting the experimental results. The final response equation after eliminating the non-significant terms for surface roughness is given below:

Final Equation in Terms of actual factors:

$$\text{Surface roughness} = -63.92711 + 1.12996 \times Ton + 0.22186 \times SV - 0.33958 \times Wd - 1.17592 \times FR - 1.78125E{-}003 \times Ton \times SV + 3.15625E{-}003 \times Ton \times Wd + 0.014063 \times Ton \times FR + 5.12500E{-}004 \times SV \times Wd - 4.91477E{-}003 \times Ton^2 - 8.36364E{-}004 \times SV^2 - 0.035909 \times FR^2 \quad (3)$$

In order to analyse the influence of WEDM parameters on SR, response surface graphs have been plotted as shown in Fig. 5a-5d. Fig. 5a-5d shows the noticeable influence of process parameters on surface roughness. Surface roughness increases with increasing the value of Ton, W_d and FR while it decreases with increasing value of SV. The influence of FR is non-symmetric. The curved plots show the interaction among the input parameters. The parameter namely Ton, SV, W_d, FR and their interactions are highly significant for SR as shown by ANOVA Table 4.

Table 4
ANOVA table for fitted model for SR

Source	Sum of Square	Degree of Freedom	Mean Square	F-Value	Prob > F	
Model	7.25	11	0.66	232.85	< 0.0001	**significant**
A-Ton	5.19	1	5.19	1835.66	< 0.0001	
B-SV	0.2	1	0.2	69.38	< 0.0001	
C-Wd	0.5	1	0.5	176.68	< 0.0001	
D-FR	0.22	1	0.22	78.52	< 0.0001	
AB	0.081	1	0.081	28.7	< 0.0001	
AC	0.26	1	0.26	90.11	< 0.0001	
AD	0.2	1	0.2	71.55	< 0.0001	
BC	0.042	1	0.042	14.85	0.0012	
A^2	0.018	1	0.018	6.2	0.0228	
B2	0.02	1	0.02	7.02	0.0163	
D2	0.059	1	0.059	20.69	0.0002	
Residual	0.051	18	2.83E-03			
Lack of Fit	0.046	13	3.57E-03	3.94	0.0697	**not significant**
Pure Error	4.53E-03	5	9.07E-04			
Cor Total	7.3	29				
	R-Squared		0.9930	**Pred R-Squared**		0.9773
	Adj R-Squared		0.9887	**Adeq Precision**		54.7377

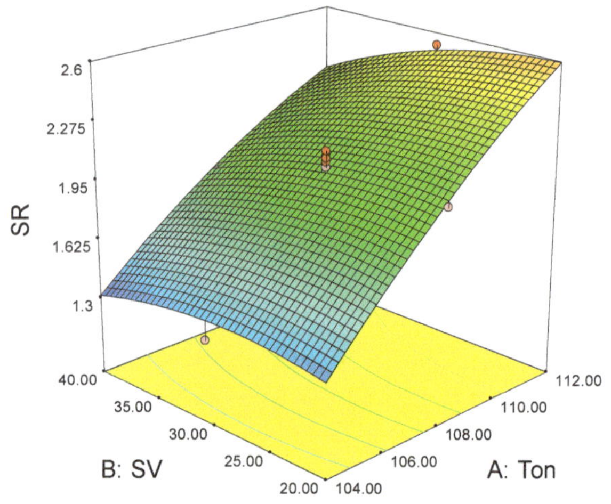

Fig. 5a. Combined effect of SV and Ton on SR

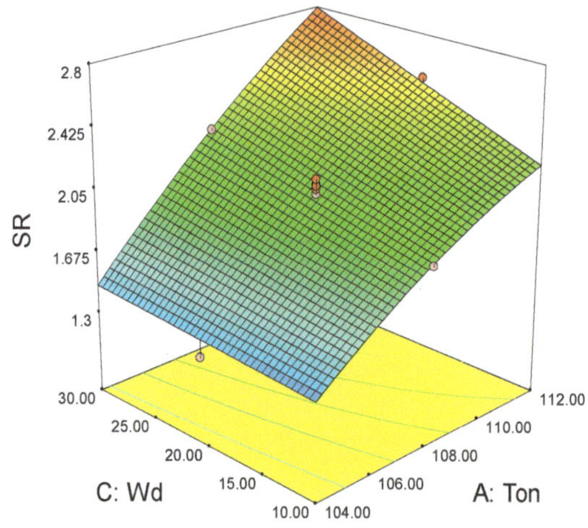

Fig. 5b. Combined effect of W_d and Ton on SR

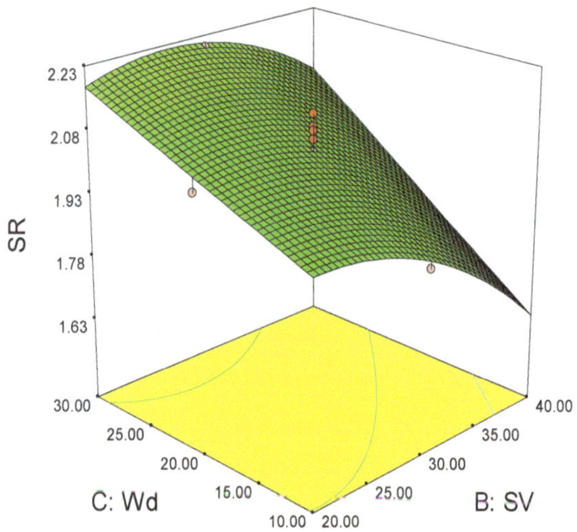

Fig. 5c. Combined effect of W_d and SV on SR

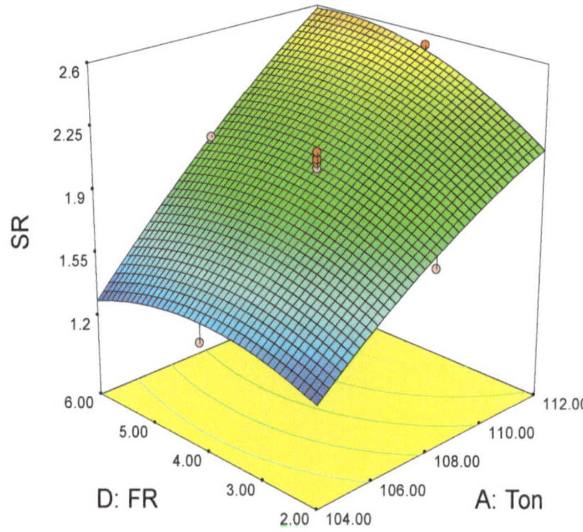

Fig. 5d. Combined effect of FR and Ton on SR

High discharge energy due to high value of Ton results into overheating and evaporation of molten metal resulting into high pressure energy that creates large size craters on work surface. The diameter and depth of crater increases with increasing of pulse-on time and hence increases the surface roughness. Increasing the value of wire depth (W_d) decreases the gap between wire electrode and work surface which increases the effective sparking on work surface and hence melting and erosion of the surface material increases. This causes increases in SR.

Surface roughness decreases with increasing the value of servo voltage as shown in Fig. 5c. Increasing SV increases the gap between work material and wire electrode that result into low ionization of dielectric medium and hence low discharge energy get generated. At low dielectric flow rate (FR), laminar dielectric flow is maintained that results into effective spark generation in trim cutting operation which removes the surface irregularities completely after the rough cutting operation. Therefore, low FR results into lower surface roughness. In order to examine the extent of surface damage (Recast layer) on machined surface, specimen were polished to have mirror finish on the transverse section and observation through scanning electron microscope (SEM) was made. Recast layer (RCL) is a hard skin on the work surface formed due to the re-solidification of melted residual material which was not completely expelled during the process (Puri & Bhattacharyya, 2005). The morphology of recast layer is much different from bulk material and it adversely affects the working life of machined component (Liao et al., 2004; Soo et al., 2013) Fig. 6a-6d shows the SEM micrographs of transverse section of sample correspond to sample no 3, 4, 15 and 26 respectively.

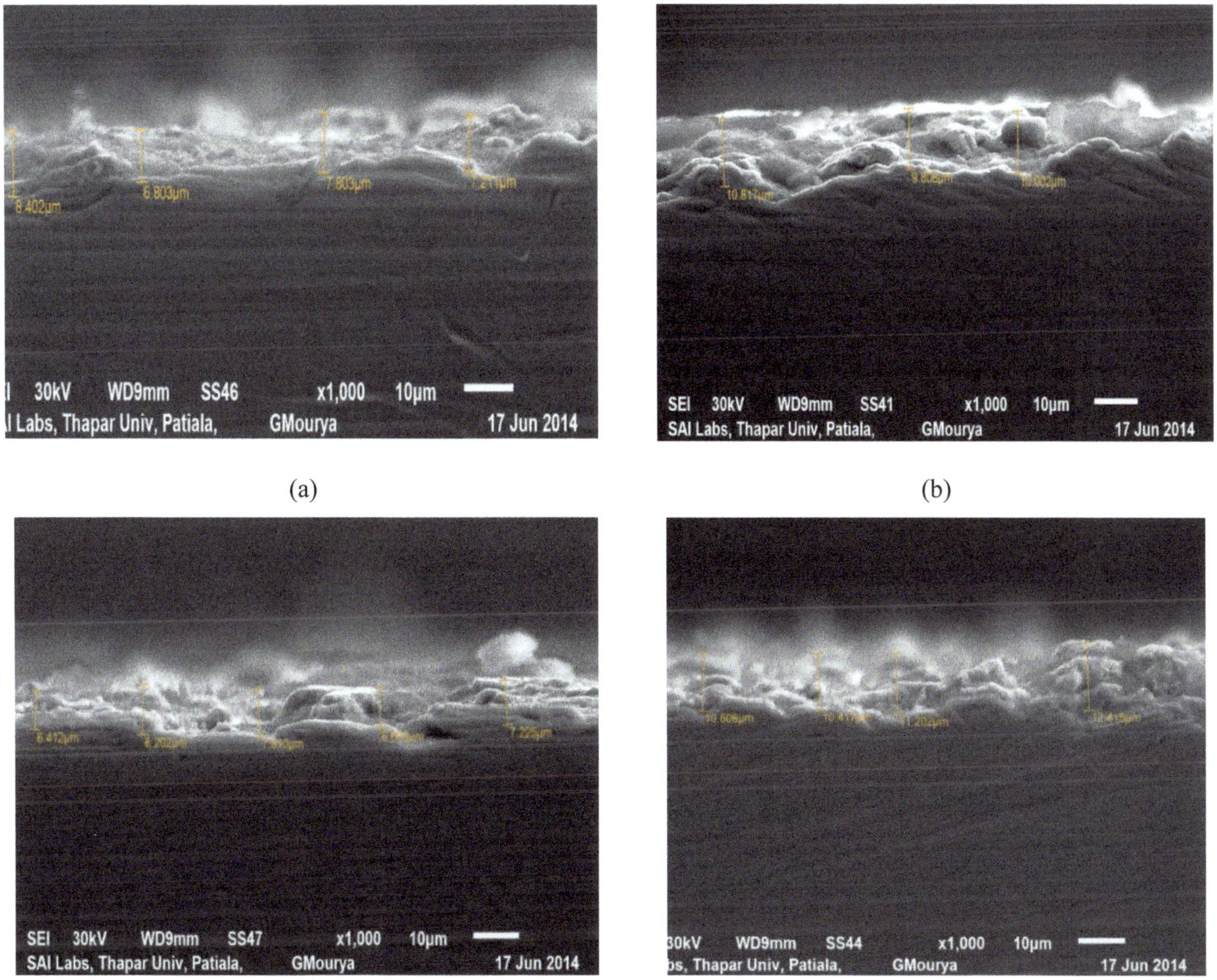

(a) (b) (c) (d)

Fig. 6. SEM images showing recast layer on machined surface correspond to (a) exp. trial 3; (b) exp. trial 4; (c) exp. trial 15; (d) exp. trial 26

Recast layer (RCL) was observed which was discontinuous and non-uniform and the average thickness of damaged surface varies from 6μm to 12μm. This thickness of RCL is low as compared to rough cutting operation. In trim cutting operation, RCL is mostly influenced by pulse on time and wire depth. At high discharge energy, melting and evaporation of material causes high pressure energy in plasma channel (Li et. al., 2013) which plough out the material from the work surface and create large size irregularities on work surface. Therefore, low value of Ip and Ton is suggested for trim cutting operation.

4.2 Analysis of Dimensional Shift (Ds)

Table 5 shows the fit summary for Ds, after backward elimination process. The Model F-value of 193.29 implies the model is significant. There is only a 0.01% chance that a large "Model F-Value" could occur due to noise. Values of "Prob > F" less than 0.050 indicate model terms are significant. In this case A, B, C, D, AD, BC, CD, A^2, B^2, C^2, D^2 are significant model terms. The "Lack of Fit F-value" of 1.02 implies there is a 953.58 % chance that a large "Lack of Fit F-value" could occur due to noise. The "Pred R-Squared" of 0.9916 is in reasonable agreement with the "Adj R-Squared" of 0.9865. "Adeq Precision" measures the signal to noise ratio. A ratio greater than 4 is desirable. Fig. 7 shows that the residuals are normally distributed about a straight line which means that the errors are normally distributed. The final response equation after eliminating the non – significant terms for surface roughness is given below:

Final Equation in Terms of actual factors:

$$\text{Dimensional Shift} = -1963.695 + 37.021 \times \text{Ton} + 1.392 \times \text{SV} - 1.501 \times W_d - 31.036 \times \text{FR} - 0.173 \times \text{Ton}^2 - 8.0454\,\text{E} - 0.0277 \times \text{SV}^2 + 0.0572 \times W_d^2 + 0.932 \times \text{FR}^2 + 0.242 \times \text{Ton} \times W_d + 0.0193 \times \text{SV} \times W_d - 0.0343 \times W_d \times \text{FR} \quad (4)$$

Table 5
ANOVA table for Ds (after backward elimination)

Source	Sum of Squares	Degree of Freedom	Mean Square	F Value	Prob > F	
Model	3444.21	11	313.11	193.29	< 0.0001	**significant**
A-Ton	93.38	1	93.39	57.65	< 0.0001	
B-SV	24.5	1	24.5	15.12	< 0.0011	
C-Wd	2738	1	2738	1690.27	< 0.0001	
D-FR	256.88	1	256.88	158.58	< 0.0001	
AD	60.06	1	60.06	37.07	< 0.0001	
BC	60.06	1	60.06	37.07	< 0.0001	
CD	7.56	1	7.56	4.66	0.0444	
A^2	19.90	1	19.91	12.28	0.0025	
B^2	19.90	1	19.91	12.28	0.0025	
C^2	85.01	1	85.01	52.47	< 0.0001	
D^2	36.01	1	36.01	22.23	0.0002	
Residual	29.16	18	1.62			
Lack of Fit	21.16	13	1.63	1.017189	0.5358	**not significant**
Pure Error	8.00	5	1.60			
Cor Total	3473.37	29				

R-Squared	0.9916	**Pred R-Squared**	0.9751
Adj R-Squared	0.9865	**Adeq Precision**	50.503

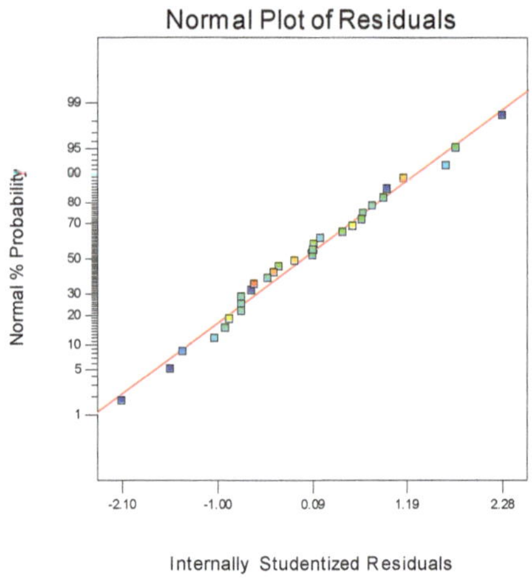

Fig. 7. Residuals plot for SR

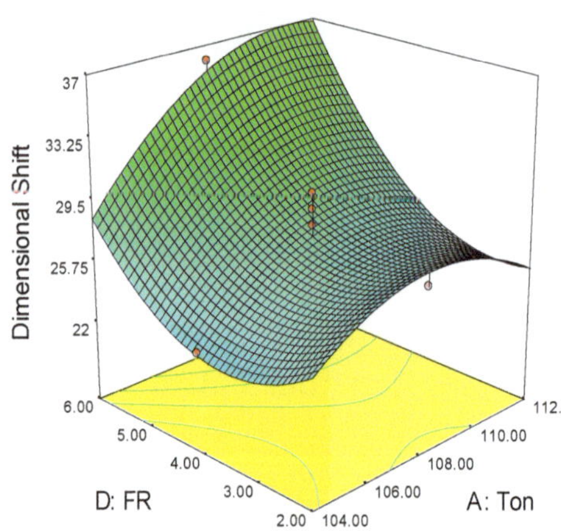

Fig. 8a. Combined effect of FR and Ton on D_S

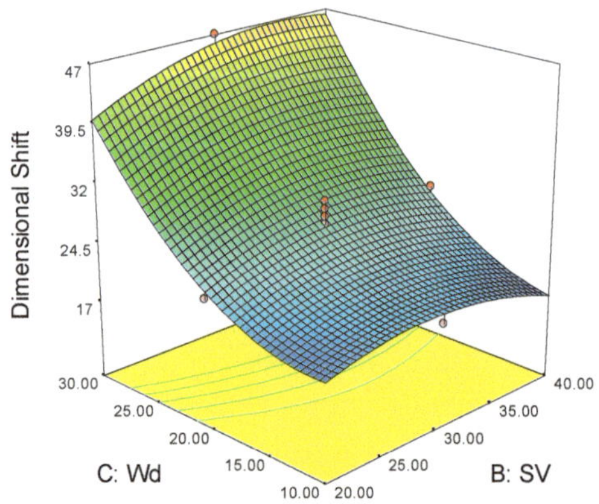

Fig. 8b. Combined effect of W_d and SV on D_S

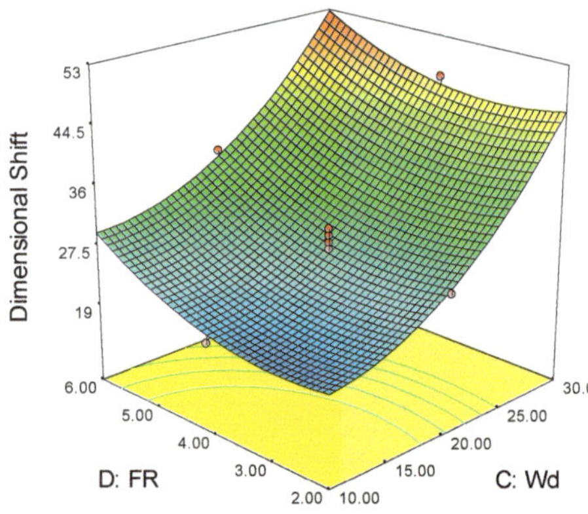

Fig. 8c. Combined effect of FR and W_d on D_S

Dimensional shift (D_s) is the thickness of material removed perpendicular to the cutting direction of wire electrode in trim cutting operation only. It depends on the melting, evaporation and flushing out of the surface material. Increase in the value of Ton results into high heat generation that increases the melting and evaporation of work material and hence the value of D_s increases as shown by response surface plot in Fig. 8a. D_s increases with decrease in the value of servo voltage as shown in Fig. 8b. Increasing the value of wire depth (W_d) increases the effective sparking on work surface and hence melting and erosion of the surface material increases as a result, D_s increases as shown in Fig. 8c. Increase in FR increases the flushing rate of eroded particles and hence D_s increases with increasing FR and Ton as shown in Fig. 8a. The interaction among the parameters can be noticed by the contour plot on 3D surface plot.

5. Multi performance optimization through Desirability function approach

In order to obtain an optimum parametric setting for two performance characteristics, desirability function has been utilised. Derringer and Suich (1980) proposed a multiple response optimization techniques approach called Desirability function. The general approach is to first convert each response $y_i(x)$ into an individual desirability function (d_i) and varied over the range $0 \leq d_i \leq 1$. The simultaneous objective function is a geometric mean of all converted responses. In the present study, Design Expert 7 has been used to optimize the response variables. Derringer and Suich (1980) defined the three types of desirability function depending on the type of response characteristics as:

(I) For the "larger- the-better" type:

$$d_i = \begin{cases} 0 & y_i \leq y_i^* \\ \left[\dfrac{y_i - y_i^*}{y_i' - y_i^*}\right] & y_i^* \leq y_i \leq y_i' \\ 1 & y_i \geq y_i' \end{cases} \tag{5}$$

where y_{i^*} is the minimum acceptable value of y_i, y_i' is the highest value of y_i; t is the shape function for desirability.

(II) For the smaller-the-better type:

$$d_i = \begin{cases} 0 & y_i \leq y_i'' \\ \left[\dfrac{y_i^* - y_i}{y_i^* - y_i''}\right]^r & y_i' \leq y_i \leq y_i' \\ 1 & y_i \geq y_i^* \end{cases} \tag{6}$$

where y_i'' is the lowest value of y_i, y_i^* is the maximum acceptable value of y_i; r is the shape function for desirability.

(III) For the nominal-the-best type:

$$d_i = \begin{cases} \left[\dfrac{y_i - y_i^*}{C_i - y_i''}\right]^s & y_i^* \leq y_i \leq c_i \\ \left[\dfrac{y_i - y_i^*}{c_i - y_i''^*}\right]^t & c_i' \leq y_i \leq y_i^* \\ 1 & y_i > y_i^* \text{ or } y_i^* > y_i \end{cases} \tag{7}$$

where C_i is the most acceptable or target value and s and t are the exponential parameters that determine the shape of desirability function. Overall desirability function of the multi-response system can be measured by combining the individual desirability functions. It can be represented as $D = (d_1^{w1}.d_2^{w2} \ldots..d_n^{wn})$; where w_j ($0 < w_j < 1$) is the weight value given for the importance of jth response variable and $\sum_{j=1}^{n} w_j = 1$. The parameters settings with maximum overall desirability value are considered to be the optimal parameter combination. In this study, the objective is to find optimal parameters setting that maximize the overall desirability function for minimum surface roughness value and dimensional shift. The ranges and targets of inputs parameters namely Ton, SV, W_d and FR and the response characteristics surface roughness and dimensional shift are given in Table 6.

Table 6

Range of Input Parameters; SR and D_S for Desirability

Constraint	Goal	Lower Limit	Upper Limit	Important
Pulse-on Time (Ton)	in range	104	112	3
Servo voltage (SV)	in range	20	40	3
Wire depth (W_d)	In range	10	30	3
Dielectric flow rate (FR)	In range	2	6	3
SR (μm)	Minimize	1.12	3.52	3
D_S (μm)	Minimize	14	54	3

Table 7 shows the possible combination of WEDM process parameters that give the high value of desirability. Corresponding to highest desirability, optimal combination of WEDM parameters for multi performance characteristics are Ton 104μs; SV 40V; W_d 10μm and FR 2 L/min. Experimental value obtained corresponding to optimal setting for SR and D_S were 1.1 μm and 16 μm that are closer to the predicted values in Table 7.

Table 7

Process parameters combination for high value of desirability

Number	Process Parameters				Predicted Response		Desirability
	Ton	SV	Wd	FR	SR	DS	
1	104.05	39.96	10.02	2.03	1.08917	13.9156	1.000
2	104.01	39.97	10.27	2.09	1.09519	13.8076	1.000
3	104	40	11.08	2.09	1.09999	14.1202	0.998
4	104	39.97	11.4	2.06	1.09999	14.3722	0.995
5	104	40	11.97	2.37	1.14347	14	0.988
6	104	39.99	10	2.72	1.16272	12.6019	0.982
7	104	40	10	2.88	1.17614	12.4514	0.979
8	104	40	10	4.64	1.2051	13.8867	0.970

6. Conclusions

In this study, trim cutting operation in WEDM has been performed on Nimonic 90: a nickel based super alloy. Two performance characteristics namely surface roughness (SR) and dimensional shift (D_S) for WEDM of Nimonic-90 have been modelled and analyzed using Response Surface Methodology (RSM) for trim cutting operation. Trim cutting operation has been performed to improve the machined surface characteristics and dimensional accuracy after a rough cutting operation. Four process parameters namely Ton, SV, W_d and FR have been selected as variable parameters; while other parameters were kept fixed for trim cutting operation. Face centered central composite design has been adopted to carry out experimental study.

Quadratic model has been proposed to determine the optimal combination of surface roughness and dimensional shift. Using response surface graphs, the developed mathematical models are able to explain the effect of process variables on performance characteristics efficiently. Increasing the value of Ton, W_d and FR increases the surface roughness and dimensional shift but increases of SV decreases the both surface roughness and dimensional shift. Using desirability function, a scale free quantity called desirability has been obtained for two performance characteristics to optimize multi-performance characteristics. Correspond to highest desirability, the optimal combination of discharge parameters was Ton: 110 μs; SV 40V; W_d10 μm and FR 2 L/min. Confirmation experiments have proven the goodness of the proposed models and desirability function approach.

Using SEM micrographs, effect of discharge energy on surface morphology has been examined. Average thickness of recast layer varies from 6 μm to 12 μm was found on the machines surfaced after trim cutting operation Present research approach is useful for achieving high productivity while maintain surface roughness and geometrical accuracy within desire limits for machining complex and intricate shapes in hard and exotic materials. Machining of Nimonic-90 with WEDM at optimized setting yields better performance and more economic as compared to conventional processes that proves the potential of WEDM in aerospace industries.

References

Arunachalam, R.M., Mannan, M.A., & Spowage, A.C. (2004). Surface integrity when machining age hardened Inconel 718 with coated carbide cutting tools. *International Journal of Machine Tools & Manufacture*, 44(14), 1481-1491.

Bhuyan, B.K., &Yadava, V. (2014). Experimental Study of Travelling Wire Electrochemical Spark Machining of Borosilicate Glass. *Materials and Manufacturing Processes*, 29(3), 298-304.

Bobbili, R., Madhu, V., & Gogia, A.K. (2013).Effect of Wire-EDM Machining Parameters on Surface Roughness and Material Removal Rate of High Strength Armor Steel. *Materials and Manufacturing Processes*, 28(4), 364–368.

Cheng, X., Yang, X.H., Huang, Y.M., Zheng, G.M., & Li, L. (2014).Helical surface creation by wire electrical discharge machining for micro tools. *Robotics and Computer-Integrated Manufacturing*, 30(3), 287–294.

Choudhury, I.A., & El-Baradie, M.A. (1998). Machinability of nickel-base super alloys- a general review. *Journal of Materials Processing Technology*, 77(1-3), 278-284.

Cochran, G., & Cox, G.M. (1962). Experimental Design. *Asia Publishing House*, New Delhi.

Deringer, G.,& Suich, R. (1980). Simultaneous optimization of several response variables. *Journal of Quality Technology*, 12(4), 214-219.

Ezugwu, E.O. (2005). Key improvements in the machining of difficult-to-cut aerospace alloys. *International Journal of Machine Tools & Manufacture*, 45(12-13), 1353-1367.

Guo, Y.B., Li, W., & Jawahir, I.S. (2009). Surface integrity characterization and prediction in machining of hardened and difficult-to-machine alloys-a state-of-art research review and analysis. *Journal of Machine Science & Technology*, 13(4), 437- 470.

Gupta, K., & Jain, N.K. (2014). Analysis and optimization of micro-geometry of miniature spur gears manufactured by wire electric discharge machining. *Precision Engineering*, 38(4), 728-737.

Han, F., Jiang, J., & Yu, D. (2007). Influence of machining parameters on surface roughness in finish cut of WEDM. *International Journal of Advance Manufacturing Technology*, 34(5-6), 538-546.

Hewidy, M.S., El-Taweel, T.A., & El-Safty, M.F. (2005). Modeling the machining parameters of wire electrical discharge machining of Inconel 601 using RSM. *Journal of Materials Processing Technology*, 169(2), 328–336.

Hood, R., Soo, S.L., Aspinwall, D.K., Andrews, P., & Sage, C. (2011). Twist drilling of Haynes 282 Superalloy, *Procedia Engineering*, 19, 150-155.

Huang, J.T., Liao, Y.S., & Hsue, W.J. (1999). Determination of finish- cutting operation and machining – parameters setting in wire electrical discharge machining. *Journal of Materials Processing Technology*, 87(1-3), 69-81.

Jangra, K., Grover, Chan FTS, &Aggarwal, A. (2011). A Digraph and matrix method to evaluate the machinability of tungsten carbide composite with wire EDM. *International Journal of Advance Manufacturing Technology*, 2(3), 959-974.

Jangra, K., Grover, S., & Aggarwal, A. (2011). Simultaneous optimization of material removal rate and surface roughness for WEDM of WC-Co composite using grey relational analysis along with Taguchi method. *International Journal of Industrial Engineering Computations*, 2(3), 479–490.

Jangra, K. (2012). Study of unmachined area in intricate machining after rough cut in WEDM. *International Journal of Industrial Engineering Computations*, 3(5), 887-892.

Jangra, K., & Grover, S. (2012). Modeling and experimental investigation of process parameters in WEDM of WC- 5.3% Co using response surface methodology. *Mechanical Science*, 3, 63-72.

Jangra, K.K., Kumar, V., Kumar, V. (2014). An experimental and comparative study on rough and trim cutting operation in WEDM of hard to machine materials. *Procedia Materials Science*, 5, 1603 – 1612.

Jangra, K.K. (2015). An experimental study for multi-pass cutting operation in wire electrical discharge machining of WC- 5.3% Co composite. *International Journal of Advance Manufacturing Technology*, 76, 971-982.

Khanna, R., & Singh, H. (2013) Performance analysis for D-3 material using response surface methodology on WEDM. *International Journal of Machining and Machinability of Materials*, 14, 45 – 65.

Klink, A., Guoa, Y.B., & Klocke, F. (2011).Surface integrity evolution of powder metallurgical tool steel by main cut and finishing trim cuts in wire-EDM. *Procedia Engineering*, 19, 178-183.

Kortabarria, A., Madariaga, A., Fernandez, E., Esnaola, J.A., & Arrazola, P.J. (2011).A comparative study of residual stress profiles on Inconel 718 induced by dry face turning, *Procedia Engineering*, 19, 228 – 234.

Krain, H.R., Sharman, A.R.C., & Ridgway, K. (2007). Optimisation of tool life and productivity when end milling Inconel 718 TM. *Journal of Material Processing Technology*, 189(1-3), 153-161.

Kumar, V., Jangra, K., & Kumar, V. (2012). Effect of WEDM parameters on machinability of Nimonic-90.*Proceedings of the National Conference on Trends and Advances in Mechanical Engineering (TAME), YMCA University of Science and Technology*, 511-516.

Lee, S.H., & Li, X.P. (2003).Study of the surface integrity of the machined workpiece in the EDM of tungsten carbide. *Journal of Materials Processing Technology*, 139(1-3), 315-321.

Li, L., Guo, Y.B., Wei, X. T., & Li, W. (2013). Surface integrity characteristics in wire-EDM of Inconel 718 at different discharge energy. *Procedia CIRP*, 6, 221 – 226.

Liao, Y.S., & Yu, Y.P. (2004). The energy aspect of material property in WEDM and its application. *Journal of Materials Processing Technology*, 149(1-3), 77–82.

Myers, R.H., & Montgomery, D.H. (1995). Response surface methodology. Wiley, New York.

Puri, A.B., & Bhattacharyya, B. (2003). An analysis and optimisation of the geometrical inaccuracy due to wire lag phenomenon in WEDM. *International Journal Machine Tools & Manufacturing*, 43(2), 151-159.

Puri, A.B., & Bhattacharyya, B. (2005). Modelling and analysis of white layer depth in a wire cut EDM process through response surface methodology. *International Journal of Advance Manufacturing Technology,* 25(3-4), 301-307.

Rebelo, J.C., Morao Dias, A., Kremer, D., & Lebrun, J.L. (1998). Influence of EDM pulse energy of on the surface integrity of martensitic steel. *Journal of Materials Processing Technology*, 84(1-3) , 90-96.

Sarkar, S., Sekh, M., Mitra, S., & Bhattacharyya, B. (2008). Modeling and optimization of wire electrical discharge machining of γ- TiAl in trim cutting operation. *Journal of Materials Processing Technology*, 205(1-3), 376-387.

Sarkar, S., Mitra, M., & Bhattacharyya, B. (2011). A novel method of determination of wire lag for enhanced profile accuracy in WEDM. *Precision Engineering*, 35(2), 339-347.

Sharman, A.R.C., Hughes, J.I., & Ridgway, K. (2004). Workpiece Surface Integrity and Tool Life Issues When Turning Inconel 718 TM Nickel Based Superalloy. *Journal of Machine Science & Technology*, 8(3), 399-414.

Sharma, N., Khanna, R., Gupta, R. D., & Sharma, R. (2013). Modeling and Multiresponse optimization on WEDM for HSLA by RSM. *International Journal of Advance Manufacturing Technology*, 67(9-12), 2269-2281.

Soo, S.L., Hood, R., Aspinwall, D.K., Voice, W.E., & Sage, C. (2011). Machinability and surface integrity of RR1000 nickel based super alloy. *CIRP Annals- Manufacturing Technology*, 60(1), 89–92.

Soo, S.L., Antar, M.T., Aspinwall, D.K., Sage, C., Cuttell, M., Perez, R., & Winn, A.J. (2013).The effect of wire electrical discharge machining on the fatigue life of Ti-6Al-2Sn-4Zr-6Mo aerospace alloy. *Procedia CIRP*, 6, 216-220.

Ulutan, D., &Ozel, T. (2011). Machining induced surface integrity in Titanium and Nickel Alloys-A review. *International Journal of Machine Tools & Manufacture*, 51(3), 250-280.

Wang, C.C., Chow, H.M., Yang, L.D., & Lu, C.T. (2009). Recast layer removal after electrical discharge machining via Taguchi analysis: a feasibility study. *Journal of Materials Processing Technology*, 209(8), 4134-4140.

Wei, X. (2002). Experimental study on the machining of a shaped hole Ni based super heat resistant alloy. *Journal of Material Processing Technology*, 129(1), 143-147.

Yang, R.T., Tzeng, C.J., Yang, Y.K., & Hsieh, M.H. (2012).Optimization of wire electrical discharge machining process parameters for cutting tungsten. *International Journal of Advance Manufacturing Technology*, 60(1-4), 135-147.

A new model for deteriorating items with inflation under permissible delay in payments

R.P. Tripathi[a*] **and Manoj Kumar**[b]

[a]*Department of Mathematics, Graphic Era University, Dehradun (U.K.) India*
[b]*Department of Mathematics, Shivalik College of Engineering, Dehradun (U.K.) India*

CHRONICLE

Keywords:
Inventory model
Exponential demand rate
Deterioration rate
Inflation

ABSTRACT

Inflation is an important factor influencing traditional economic order quality models. Marketing strategy depends on inflation due to public demand and availability of the materials. This paper presents an optimal inventory policy for deteriorating items using exponential demand rate under permissible delay in payments. Mathematical model has been derived under two cases: case I: cycle time is greater than or equal to permissible delay period, case II: cycle time is less than permissible delay period by considering holding cost as a function of time. Numerical examples and sensitivity analysis are given to reflect the numerical results. Mathematica software is used for finding optimal solutions.

1. Introduction

The objective of many inventory management problems is to deal with the minimization of inventory carrying expenditures (Donalson, 1977). Thus, it is necessary to determine the optimal inventory level as well as optimal time of replenishment of inventory to meet any future demand. Among the classical inventory management models, there are many cases on solving the optimal order quantity by ignoring the type of payment. At present scenario, it is observed that supplier offers a certain fixed period to settle the account for stimulating retailers demand. During the credit period when the payment is made, some items can be sold and revenue can be accumulated to earn interest. This paper investigates inventory model for deteriorating items with exponential time dependent demand rate. In recent years, deteriorating inventory models have been widely studied. In real life situations, it is observed that demand for a particular product can be influenced by internal factor such as inflation, price and availability. The change in the demand is responsible for the change in inventory is commonly referred to as demand elasticity. Generally, inventory model considers a case in which depletion of inventory is caused by demand rate and deterioration. Most of the items deteriorate over time and this phenomena plays essential role for decision making in modern organization. During the past few decades, many researchers have developed inventory models for deteriorating items.

* Corresponding author.

The analysis of deteriorating model is discussed by Ghare and Schrader (1963) with constant rate of deterioration. In the earlier period, researchers have discussed various demand patterns fitting the stage of product lifecycle. Resh et al. (1976) and Donaldson (1977) considered the situation and linearly time varying demand and established an algorithm to determine the optimal number of replenishments and timing. Henery (1976) further generalized the demand rate by considering a concave demand function increasing with time. Harris (1913) first introduced the basic economic order quantity (EOQ) model. Several interesting research papers are associated with deterioration, which are based on constant demand without any deterioration function (e.g. Sachan, 1984; Dave & Patel, 1981; Goyal & Giri, 2001; Liao & Haung, 2010; Sana, 2010; Lin et al., 2010; Sarkar, 2012; etc.). Covert and Phillip (1973) extended Ghare and Schrader's model by considering variable rate of deterioration.

Data and Pal (1988) developed an EOQ model by introducing a variable deterioration rate and power demand pattern. Chung and Tang (1994) determined the replenishment schedules for deteriorating items with time proportional demand. However, in real life, the demand may increase or decrease in the course of time. Many researchers considered the varying demand (e.g. Sana, 2010; Sana & Chaudhuri, 2008; Donaldson, 1977; Goyal, 1986; Kharna & Chaudhuri, 2003; Silver & Meal, 1969; Haringa, 1996; Goyal et al., 1986).

Various researchers have developed the inflanatory effects on the inventory policy. Liao et al. (2001) developed an inventory for initial stock dependent consumption rate when a delay in payment is permissible. Hou (2006) derived an inventory model for deteriorating items with stock dependent consumption rate and shortages under inflation and time discounting over a finite planning horizon. Buzacolt (1975) developed an inventory model with inflation. Vrat and Padmanabhan (1990) developed an inventory model under a constant inflation rate and initial stock dependent consumption rate. Datta and Pal (1991) developed a model with linear time dependent demand rate and shortages to investigate the effects of inflation with time value of money on ordering policy over a finite time horizon.

Recently, Teng et al. (2012) developed an EOQ model with trade credit financing for non–decreasing demand and fundamental theoretical results obtained. Sarkar (2011) developed an EOQ model with delay in payment for time varying deterioration rate and obtained a function for maximization of profit. Pricing and lot sizing policies for deteriorating items with partial backlogging under inflation was presented by Hsieh and Dye (2010) by considering pricing and lot sizing policies for deteriorating items with partial backlogging under inflation.

In this paper, demand rate is exponential time dependent and holding cost is time dependent. The present model is discussed by using truncated Taylor's series. The conditions for convexity of optimality are obtained and numerical examples and sensitivity analysis are given.

The rest of the paper is organized as follows: In the next section assumptions and notations are given. In section 3 mathematical formulations with maximization of total inventory cost is given. In section 4 numerical examples for the cases I and II are given. In section 5 sensitivity analysis with various parameters is given to validate the inventory cost function. Finally conclusion and future research directions are given in the last section 6.

2. Assumptions and Notations

The mathematical model of inventory for deteriorating items is based on the following assumptions:

(i) Demand rate is exponential and Inflation is constant

(ii) Shortages are not allowed and lead time is zero

(iii) During the permissible delay period the sales revenue generated is deposited in an interest bearing account. At the end of the trade credit period the customer pays off all units ordered and begins paying for the interest charged on the items in stock.

(iv) There is no repair or replenishment of deteriorated items during the given cycle.

(vii) Holding cost is time dependent i.e. $h(t) = ht, \quad 0 \le t \le T$

The following notations are used throughout the manuscript:

h	: Holding cost per unit
$p(t) = p_0 e^{rt}$	: Instantaneous selling price per unit
p_0	: Selling price per unit at $t = 0$
C	: Purchasing price per unit at $t = 0$
$C(t) = C_0 e^{rt}$	: Instantaneous ordering cost per order
C_0	: Ordering cost per order at $t = 0$
H	: Length of finite planning horizon
I_c	: Interest charged
I_e	: Interest earned per annum by the retailer
T	: Optimum length of cycle time , H = nT
T_1	: Allowable delay period during settlement of the account
Q	: Optimum ordering quantity
r	: Constant rate of inflation
$I(t)$	: Instantaneous level of inventory
$R = Ae^{-\alpha t}$	: Demand rate, $0 < \alpha < 1$
A	: Demand at $t = 0$
θ	: Constant deterioration rate ($\theta < \alpha$)
O_C	: Ordering cost
C_D	: Cost of deterioration
I_{HC}	: Inventory holding cost
Z_1, Z_2	: Total cost for case 1 and 2 respectively

3. Mathematical Formulation

The level of inventory I(t) decreases gradually mainly to meet demands and due to deterioration. Thus, the variation of inventory with respect to time can be described by the following differential equation:

$$\frac{dI(t)}{dt} + \theta\, I(t) = -Ae^{-\alpha t}, \quad 0 \le t \le T \tag{1}$$

The solution of equation is given by

$$I(t) = \frac{A}{\theta - \alpha}\left[e^{(\theta-\alpha)T-\theta t} - e^{-\alpha t}\right] \tag{2}$$

and order quantity

$$Q = \frac{A}{\theta - \alpha}\left[e^{(\theta-\alpha)T} - 1\right] \tag{3}$$

Since *I(t)* is a periodic function with period *T* hence we have *I(kT + t) = I(t),* therefore,

$$I(kT + t) = \frac{A}{\theta - \alpha}\left[e^{(\theta-\alpha)T-\theta t} - e^{-\alpha t}\right] \tag{4}$$

Ordering Cost: Instantaneous ordering cost per order

$$O_C = \sum_{k=0}^{n-1} C_0 e^{krt} = C_0(e^{rH} - 1)\left(\frac{1}{rT} + \frac{rT}{4} - \frac{1}{2}\right) \tag{5}$$

(6)

The number of deteriorated units = $Q - \int_0^T Ae^{-\alpha t}\,dt$

The cost of total deteriorated units

$$C_D = C\left[\frac{A}{\theta-\alpha}\left\{e^{(\theta-\alpha)T} - 1\right\} + \frac{1}{\alpha}\left(e^{-\alpha T} - 1\right)\right] = \frac{1}{2}AC\theta T^2 \tag{7}$$

Inventory Holding Cost I_{HC} is given by

$$I_{HC} = \frac{Ah}{\theta - \alpha}\sum_{k=0}^{n-1} C_0 e^{rkT}\int_0^T \left\{e^{\theta T-(\theta+\alpha)t} - e^{-\alpha t}\right\} t\,dt = \frac{AhC_0(e^{rH} - 1)\theta T}{r(\alpha^2 - \theta^2)} \tag{8}$$

Depending on the customer's choice and the length of cycle time *T* two possible cases are taken into account:

Case I $T \ge T_1$

Optimal cycle time T is greater than the permissible delay time T_1, the interest charged IC_1 during the period [0, H] is given by

$$IC_1 = I_c \sum_{k=0}^{n-1} C(kT)\int_{T_1}^{T} I(kT+t)\,dt = \frac{AI_c C_0(e^{rH} - 1)}{(\theta^2 - \alpha^2)r}\alpha T_1\left(\frac{T_1}{T} - 1\right) \tag{9}$$

Interest earned IE_1 during the period [0, H] is given by

$$IE_1 = I_e \sum_{k=0}^{n-1} P(kT)\int_0^{T_1} Ae^{-\alpha t}.t\,dt = P_0 A I_e \frac{(e^{rH}-1)}{2rT}\left(\frac{T_1^2}{2} - \frac{\alpha}{2}T_1^3\right) \tag{10}$$

Total Inventory Cost $Z_1(T) = \frac{1}{T}\left[O_C + C_D + I_{HC} + IC_1 - IE_1\right]$

$$= \frac{1}{T}\left[C_0(e^{rH}-1)\left(\frac{1}{rT}+\frac{rT}{4}-\frac{1}{2}\right)+\frac{1}{2}AC\theta T^2 - \frac{AhC_0(e^{rH}-1)\theta T}{r(\theta^2-\alpha^2)} + \frac{AI_cC_0(e^{rH}-1)\alpha T_1\left(\frac{T_1}{T}-1\right)}{r(\theta^2-\alpha^2)} - \frac{P_0AI_e(e^{rH}-1)\left(\frac{T_1^2}{2}-\frac{\alpha}{2}T_1^3\right)}{rT^2}\right] \tag{11}$$

Differentiating $Z_1(T)$ with respect to 'T' two times we get

$$\frac{\partial Z_1}{\partial T} = C_0(e^{rH}-1)\left(-\frac{2}{rT^3}+\frac{1}{2T^2}\right)+\frac{1}{2}AC\theta + \frac{AI_cC_0(e^{rH}-1)\alpha T_1}{r(\theta^2-\alpha^2)}\left(-\frac{2T_1}{T^3}+\frac{1}{T^2}\right) + \frac{P_0AI_e(e^{rH}-1)}{rT^3}\left(T_1^2-\alpha T_1^3\right) \tag{12}$$

$$\frac{\partial^2 Z_1}{\partial T^2} = C_0(e^{rH}-1)\left(\frac{6}{rT^4}-\frac{1}{T^3}\right)+\frac{AI_cC_0(e^{rH}-1)\alpha T_1}{r(\theta^2-\alpha^2)}\left(\frac{6T_1}{T^4}-\frac{2}{T^3}\right)+\frac{3P_0AI_e(e^{rH}-1)(\alpha T_1^3-T_1^2)}{rT^4} > 0 \tag{13}$$

Optimal (minimum) solution is obtained by solving $\frac{\partial Z_1}{\partial T} = 0$, yields

$$\frac{AC\theta}{2}T^3 + \left\{2C_0(e^{rH}-1)+\frac{AC_0I_c(e^{rH}-1)\alpha T_1}{(\theta^2-\alpha^2)}\right\}T + \frac{P_0AI_e(e^{rH}-1)(T_1^2-\alpha T_1^3)}{r} - \frac{2C_0(e^{rH}-1)}{r} - \frac{2AI_cC_0(e^{rH}-1)\alpha T_1^2}{(\theta^2-\alpha^2)} = 0 \tag{14}$$

Case II $T < T_1$

In this case, the retailer pays the procurement cost to the supplier prior to expiration of the delay period T_1 provided by the supplier. Hence, the interest charged IC_2 will be zero. Since cycle time T is less than permissible delay time T_1, the interest earned IE_2 during [0, H] is given by

$$IE_2 = I_e\sum_{k=0}^{n-1}P(kT)\left[\int_0^T tAe^{-\alpha t}dt + (T_1 - T)\int_0^T Ae^{-\alpha t}dt\right] - P_0I_eA\frac{(e^{rH}-1)}{r}\left(T_1 - \frac{1}{2}T - \frac{1}{2}\alpha TT_1\right) \tag{15}$$

Total Inventory Cost in this case $Z_2(T) = \frac{1}{T}\left[O_C + C_D + I_{HC} - IE_2\right]$

$$Z_2 = \frac{1}{T}\left[C_0(e^{rH}-1)\left(\frac{1}{rT}+\frac{rT}{4}-\frac{1}{2}\right)+\frac{1}{2}AC\theta T^2 - \frac{AhC_0(e^{rH}-1)\theta T}{r(\theta^2-\alpha^2)} - \frac{P_0AI_e(e^{rH}-1)}{r}\left(T_1-\frac{1}{2}T-\frac{1}{2}\alpha T_1T\right)\right] \tag{16}$$

Differentiating partially (16) w.r.t. 'T' two times yields

$$\frac{\partial Z_2}{\partial T} = C_0(e^{rH}-1)\left(-\frac{2}{rT^3}+\frac{1}{2T^2}\right)+\frac{1}{2}AC\theta+\frac{P_0AI_e(e^{rH}-1)}{r}\frac{T_1}{T^2}$$

$$\frac{\partial^2 Z_2}{\partial T^2} = C_0(e^{rH}-1)\left(\frac{6}{rT^4}-\frac{1}{T^3}\right)-\frac{2P_0AI_e(e^{rH}-1)}{r}\frac{T_1}{T^3}>0$$

Optimal (minimum) solution is obtained by solving $\frac{\partial Z_2}{\partial T}=0$, yields the following

$$\frac{AC\theta}{2}T^3+\left\{\frac{C_0(e^{rH}-1)}{2}+\frac{P_0AI_e(e^{rH}-1)}{r}T_1\right\}T-\frac{2C_0(e^{rH}-1)}{r}=0 \tag{17}$$

Note: Truncated Taylor's series in exponential terms i.e $e^{\alpha T}\approx 1+\alpha T+\frac{1}{2}\alpha^2T^2+$ ...etc. is used from Eqs. (5-17) for finding closed form solution.

4. Numerical Example 1

Let

$$A=100,\quad \theta=0.01\quad r=0.01\ to\ 0.05,\quad \alpha=0.1,\quad H=1,\quad h=0.02,\quad C_0=10$$
$$I_e=0.12,\ C=15,\quad I_c=0.15,\quad P_0=20,\ T_1=15,30,45,60,75\ and\ 90\ days$$

Optimal solution for different values of parameters associated with model for $T\geq T_1$ is given in Table 1 as follows,

Table 1
The results of optimal solution for different values of $T > T_1$

		T_1 (Days)					
r	*Parameters*	15	30	45	60	75	90
0.01	*T(years)*	1.37847	1.34582	1.28789	1.19730	1.05657	0.807657
	Q(units)	129.639	126.751	121.605	113.505	100.789	77.90000
	Z($)	79.8319	122.78	175.643	209.926	271.264	353.7040
0.02	*T(years)*	1.37967	1.34311	1.2774	1.17236	1.00147	0.641322
	Q(units)	130.626	127.347	121.430	111.906	96.2403	62.51480
	Z($)	80.1079	123.476	168.433	218.617	282.468	394.3190
0.03	*T(years)*	1.38100	1.34080	1.26790	1.14934	0.947806	0.329037
	Q(units)	131.635	127.980	121.326	110.432	91.7048	32.52770
	Z($)	80.3821	124.153	170.096	222.682	294.314	338.4250

Numerical Example 2

$$Let\ A=100,\quad \theta=0.01,\quad r=0.01\ to\ 0.05,\quad \alpha=0.1,\quad H=1,\quad h=0.02,\quad I_e=0.02,$$
$$T_1=225, 240, 255, 270, 285\ \text{and}\ 300\ days$$

Optimal solution for different values of parameters associated with model for $T<T_1$

Table 2
The results of optimal solution for different values of $T < T_1$

		T_1(Days)					
r	*Parameters*	225	240	255	270	285	300
	T(years)	0.60691	0.58707	0.56792	0.54947	0.53173	0.51470
0.01	*Q(units)*	59.4199	57.5173	55.6782	53.9042	52.1960	50.5538
	Z(Dollars)	87.6304	84.9451	82.1664	79.2914	76.3174	73.2419
	T(years)	0.60680	0.58694	0.56776	0.54930	0.53154	0.51449
0.02	*Q(units)*	59.4095	57.5042	55.6630	53.8870	52.1773	50.5340
	Z(Dollars)	87.9197	85.2203	82.4269	79.5366	76.5466	73.5443
	T(years)	87.9197	85.2203	82.4269	79.5366	76.5466	73.5443
0.03	*Q(units)*	59.3990	57.4911	55.6475	53.8696	52.1584	50.5138
	Z(Dollars)	88.2111	85.4976	82.6894	79.7836	76.7775	73.6684
	T(years)	0.60658	0.58666	0.56744	0.54893	0.53115	0.51407
0.04	*Q(units)*	59.3883	57.4776	55.6318	53.8521	52.1394	50.4936
	Z(Dollars)	88.5047	85.7770	82.9538	80.0324	77.0101	73.8841
	T(years)	0.60647	0.58652	0.56728	0.54875	0.53095	0.51386
0.05	*Q(units)*	59.3774	57.4641	55.6161	53.8345	52.1202	50.4733
	Z(Dollars)	88.8006	86.0584	83.2202	80.2831	77.2444	74.1014

5. Sensitivity Analysis: Case I

When θ and α are allowed to vary by using $T_1 = 15, 30, 45, 60, 75\, and\, 90$ days. We get different values of parameters as shown in Table 3 as follows,

Table 3
The results of optimal solution for different values of θ

		θ					
α	*Parameters*	0.01	0.02	0.03	0.04	0.05	0.06
	T_1 *(Days)*	15	30	45	60	75	90
	T(years)	1.25623	0.97230	0.81087	0.68160	0.55175	0.37573
0.2	*Q(units)*	111.756	89.1972	75.7469	64.5750	52.9536	36.6021
	Z(Dollars)	44.8472	94.0812	146.748	201.516	254.443	260.742
	T(years)	1.25676	0.97432	0.81564	0.69134	0.57162	0.42688
0.3	*Q(units)*	105.320	85.2724	73.2114	85.0612	53.2657	40.5738
	Z(Dollars)	33.9366	68.2219	103.366	138.058	169.279	180.020
	T(years)	1.25704	0.97544	0.81833	0.69687	0.58266	0.45193
0.4	*Q(units)*	99.3651	81.5068	70.6055	61.6334	52.7090	41.8925
	Z(Dollars)	28.9211	56.3023	83.5749	109.697	132.318	141.359
	T(years)	1.25723	0.97620	0.82023	0.70085	0.59061	0.46915
0.5	*Q(units)*	93.8617	77.9389	68.0628	59.9099	51.8637	42.3895
	Z(Dollars)	26.0511	49.4608	72.2592	93.6252	111.656	119.040

Case II: When θ and r are allowed to vary by using $T_1 = 225, 240, 255, 270, 285$ and 300 days. We get different values of parameters as shown in Table 4 as follows,

Table 4
The results of optimal solution for different values of θ

		θ					
r	*Parameters*	0.03	0.04	0.05	0.06	0.07	0.08
	T_1 *(Days)*	225	240	255	270	285	300
0.01	*T(years)*	0.60691	0.56002	0.52335	0.49336	0.46807	0.44626
	Q(units)	59.4199	55.0715	51.6565	48.8530	46.4806	44.4280
	Z(Dollars)	87.6304	118.694	158.066	213.142	300.834	471.514
0.02	*T(years)*	0.60680	0.55999	0.52336	0.49340	0.46813	0.44633
	Q(units)	59.4095	55.0683	51.6575	48.8565	46.4857	44.4342
	Z(Dollars)	87.9107	119.116	158.665	214.000	302.115	473.637
0.03	*T(years)*	0.60669	0.55995	0.52337	0.49344	0.46818	0.44638
	Q(units)	59.3990	55.0050	51.6582	48.8598	46.4906	44.4401
	Z(Dollars)	88.2111	119.542	159.270	214.864	303.405	475.774
0.04	*T(years)*	0.66658	0.55991	0.52338	0.49347	0.46823	0.44645
	Q(units)	59.3883	55.0614	51.6589	48.8631	46.4955	44.4461
	Z(Dollars)	88.5047	119.971	159.878	215.734	304.704	477.925
0.05	*T(years)*	0.60647	0.55988	0.52338	0.49350	0.46827	0.44651
	Q(units)	59.3774	55.0578	51.6594	48.8662	46.5002	44.4518
	Z(Dollars)	88.8006	120.402	160.322	216.609	306.011	480.091

From the above tables we conclude the following results:

From Table 1, we observe that:

Increase in T_1 results decrease in T, Q and increase in Z, keeping θ, α and r constant and increase in r results increase in T, Q and Z keeping T_1 constant.

From Table 2, we observe that:
Increase in T_1 results decrease in T, Q and Z keeping r constant and increase in r results increase in T, Q and Z keeping T_1 constant.

From Table 3, we observe that:
Increase in deterioration rate θ results decrease in T, Q and increase in Z keeping α constant. An increase in α results increase in T and decrease in Q and Z keeping θ and T_1 constant.

From Table 4, we observe that:
Increase in θ results decrease in T, Q and increase in Z keeping r constant. An increase in r results increase in T, Q and Z.

6. Conclusion

In this paper, an inventory model has been developed for deteriorating items under permissible delay in payments. Optimal solutions were obtained for both cases i.e. case I and II. Numerical examples and sensitivity analysis have been presented to obtain optimal cycle time and optimal total average cost per unit time. The sensitivity analysis is quite sensitive to the managerial point of view.

The proposed model can be extended in several ways for instance we may consider the demand rate as quadratic time dependent or stock dependent patterns as well as discount demand. We could extend the model for non – deteriorating demand function to stock dependent demand function. In addition, we could generate the model to allow shortages, finite capacity and others.

References

Buzacott, J. A. (1975). Economics order quantities with inflation. *Operational Research Quarterly*, 26, 553 – 558.

Covert, R.P., & Phillip, G.C. (1973). An EOQ model with Weibull distribution deterioration. *AIIE Transportations*, 5, 323 – 326.

Chung, K.J., & Ting, P.S. (1994). On replenishment schedule for deteriorating items with time – proportional demand. *Production Planning and Control*, 5(4), 392 – 396.

Dutta, T.K., & Pal, A.K. (1991). Effects on inflation and time value of money on an inventory model with linear time – dependent rate and shortages. *European Journal of Operational Research*, 52, 326 – 333.

Dave, U., & Patel, L.K. (1981). (T,S_i) policy inventory model for deteriorating items with time proportional demand. *Journal of Operation Research Society*, 32, 137 –142.

Donalson, W. A. (1977). Inventory replenishment policy for a linear trend in demand. An analytical solution. *Operational Research Quarterly*, 28, 663 – 670.

Donaldson, W.A. (1977). Inventory replenishment policy for a linear trend in demand, an analytical solution. *Operations Research Quarterly*, 28, 663 – 670.

Dutta, T.K., & Pal., A.K. (1988). Order level inventory system with power demand pattern for items with variable rate of deterioration. *Indian Journal of Pure and Applied Mathematics* 19, 1043 – 1053.

Ghare P.M., & Schrader, S.K. (1963). A model for exponentially decaying inventory. *Journal of Industrial Engineering,* 14 (5), 238 – 243.

Goyal, S.K. (1986). On improving replenishment policies for real trend in demand. *Eng. Cost prod. Econ.* 10, 73 – 76.

Goyal, S.K., Kusy, M., & Soni, R. (1986). A note on economic order intervals for an item with linear trend demand Eng. *Costs Prod. Econ.* 10, 253 – 255.

Harris, F.W. (1913). How many parts to make at once. *Factory Mag. Manage*, 135 – 136-152.

Henery, R.J. (1976). Inventory replenishment policy for increasing demand. *Journal of the Operational Research Society*, 30(7), 611 – 617.

Haringa, M. (1996). Optimal EOQ models for deteriorating items with time – varying demand. *Journal of the Operational Research Society*, 47, 1228 – 1246.

Hou, K.L. (2006). An inventory model for deteriorating items with stock dependent consumption rate and shortages under inflation and time discounting. *European Journal of Operational Research*, 168, 463 – 474.

Hsieh, T.P., & Dye, C.Y. (2010). Pricing and lot sizing policies for deteriorating items with partial backlogging under inflation. *Expert Systems with Applications*, 37, 7234 – 7242.

Kharna, K.S., & Chaudhuri. (2003). A note on an order – level inventory model for a deteriorating item with time dependent quadratic demand. *Computer and Operations Research*, 30, 1901–1916.

Goyal, S.K., & Giri, B.C. (2001). Recent trends in modeling of deteriorating inventory. *European Journal of Operational Research*. 134, 1 – 16.

Lin, J.J., & Haung K.N. (2010). Deteriorating Inventory model deteriorating items with trade credits financing and capacity constraints. *Computational and Industrial Engineering* ,59, 611 – 618.

Lin, Y.H., Lin. C., & Lin, B. (2010). On conflict and cooperation in a two – echelon inventory model for deteriorating items. *Computers and Industrial Engineering*, 59, 703 – 711.

Liao, H.C. Tsai, C.H., & Su, C.T. (2001). An inventory model for deteriorating items under inflation when a delay in payment is permissible. *International Journal of Production Economics*, 63, 207 – 214.

Resh, M., Friedman, M., & Barbosa, L.C. (1976). On a general solution of the deterministic lot size problem with time – proportional demand. *Operations Research* 24, 718 – 725.

Sachan, R.S., (1984). On (T,S_i). policy inventory model for deteriorating items with time proportional demand. *Journal of Operation Research Society*, 35, 1013 – 1019.

Sana, S.S. (2010). Optimal selling price and lot size with varying deterioration and partial backlogging. *Applied Mathematics and Computation*, 217, 185 – 194.

Sarkar, B. (2011). An EOQ model with delay in payments and time varying deterioration rate. *Mathematical and Computer Modeling (Article in press).*

Sarkar, B. (2012). An EOQ model with delay in payments and time varying deterioration rate. *Mathematical and Computer Modeling*, 55, 367 – 377.

Sana, S., & Chaudhuri, K.S. (2008). A deterministic EOQ model with delays in payments and price discount offers. *European Journal Operational Research*, 184, 509 – 533.

Silver, E.A., & Meal, H.C. (1969). A simple modification of the EOQ for the case of varying demand rate. *Production and Inventory Management* ,10, 52 – 65.

Teng, J.T., Min, J., & Pan, Q. (2012). Economic order quantity model with trade credit financing for non – decreasing demand. *Omega*, 40, 328 – 335.

Vrat, P., & Padmanabhan, G. (1990). An inventory model under inflation for stock dependent consumption rate items. *International Journal of Production Economics*, 19, 379 – 383.

11

Web service and dynamic pricing competition

Ehram Safari* **and Masoud Babakhani**

Department of Industrial Engineering, Iran University of Science and Technology, Tehran, Iran

C H R O N I C L E

Keywords:
Differential game
Dynamic pricing
E-commerce
Revenue Management
Nonlinear Programming
Service supply chain

A B S T R A C T

Web services have become quite popular over the last few years as they allow easier development and integration of business applications. In this paper, we consider a web service pricing problem where two providers compete through dynamic pricing. Each provider offers access to a web service with different quality classes where users may buy their required web service through a reservation system. They would like to adjust the prices of their web services over a pre-specified time horizon to manage demand and to maximize profit. Users have the right with no obligation to cancel their services as long as they pay a penalty. We consider a dynamic setting where the web service classes share a capacity. We first develop a time continuous model for competitive pricing of a web service and then we provide some insights about the equilibrium condition of the problem using open-loop differential game and propose an algorithm to obtain the optimal pricing policy for providers. Moreover, we conduct numerical analyses to examine the impacts of some parameters on control and state variables.

1. Introduction

In recent years, web services have become a useful and efficient technology for developing and integrating of web applications (Zhao & Cheng, 2005). According to the Stencil Group, "web services are loosely coupled, reusable software components that semantically encapsulate discrete functionality and are distributed and programmatically accessible over standard Internet protocols'' (Gottschalk et al., 2002, Ferris & Farrell, 2003, Kreger, 2003). In spite of developed or licensed packaged applications, web services include specific business functionalities that can be rented over the internet. Web services break business processes into granular modules and hence let customers choose the services based on customers' requirements. Using existing systems and outsourcing standard components, a firm can decline the cost of software implementation. Service providers usually create and publish modules with particular functionalities. Service users who need certain functionality can invoke the service using standard protocols by paying a fee (Bachlechner et al., 2006). In fact, Irrespective of the functionalities of the web services, it is necessary for the web service providers to design and to implement an appropriate pricing model for managing the demand as well as the capacity.

* Corresponding author.

This paper deals with the problem in which the optimal dynamic pricing strategy is obtained for two web service providers who compete with each other to sell a web service included different service classes (i.e. with different quality of service (QoS)) through a reservation system. Users may buy their required web service and use it in the future date. It is necessary to know that users have the right with no obligation to cancel their services as long as they pay a penalty. Furthermore, for a provider, a capacity is shared among all of the web service classes. The demand of each web service class for a provider depends on his/her price and competitor's price and time, this dynamic pricing competition can be modeled by the differential game theory.

Users who would like to buy a web service consider not only costs but also QoS (Wu, 2008, Pan et al., 2009, Zhang et al., 2009). Therefore, this matter motivates us to study a web service pricing problem in which providers want to offer different service classes to fulfil various customers in the web service domain. Each of the web service classes has particular QoS, which is defined as a group of service measures representing the degree of user agreement of the service. Common measures of QoS are response time, availability, reliability, accessibility, and versioning (Mani & Nagarajan, 2002, Ahluwalia & Varshney, 2009, Khaled, 2009). Without a suitable pricing strategy for the web service, any QoS based web service classes are unusable; if we determine no price for any classes, all of users would choose some classes with high priority QoS. In other words, identifying an appropriate price for any web service classes should give users an encouragement to link the "right" web service class.

The availability of demand data and the simplicity of changing prices for analysing demand data for the web service induce us to consider dynamic pricing method as an efficient access control method to offer incentives to users so that they choose proper service levels (Tripathi & Mishra, 2014; Rahchamandi & Fallahi, 2014; Rezaei-Malek & Tavakkoli-Moghaddam, 2014; Bitran & Caldentey, 2003; Elmaghraby & Keskinocak, 2003). Lin et al. (2005) conducted a pilot study to demonstrate the use of dynamic pricing scheme to manage the web service resources. Schwind (2007) extensively studied dynamic pricing and automated resource allocation for complex information services. Wu (2008) proposed a QoS-driven dynamic pricing method for a web service, which makes services price vary dynamically with corresponding factors.

Pan et al. (2009) considered a dynamic pricing strategy for a provider who offers a web service with different several service classes to satisfy requirements of different customers. In this paper, provider only has one price-change in selling period. They provided a closed form solution to obtain the price and capacity. Furthermore, their model has no constraints on web service capacity. Guerrero-Ibáñeza et al. (2011) surveyed simple QoS-based dynamic pricing approach for service provisioning in a heterogeneous wireless access network environment.

This paper considers two web service providers who offer a web services included different service classes through a reservation system. In a non-monopolistic setting, the decisions taken by a web service provider may affect other provider's profit and feasible strategies. Such problem has been studied in the literature in economic (Redondo, 2003), revenue management (Talluri & Ryzin, 2006), supply chain management (Cachon & Netessine, 2004, Kogan & Tapiero, 2007, Taheri et al., 2014, Li & Liu, 2014, Elyasi et al., 2014, Alirezaei & khoshAlhan, 2014). Some important applications of game theorem on information technology can be described as: Key and McAuley (1999) looked at ways of providing QoS to users based on a simple pricing scheme. Moreover, a framework for assessing schemes and algorithms via a distributed game was presented. Gibbens et al. (2000) studied the duopoly price competition for packet-based networks and proved that the unique equilibrium outcome for both networks was to offer a single service class which was characterized by the congestion level. Wierstra et al. (2001) presented the impacts of basic elements of business strategies on the relative competitive position of selected types of ISPs. Altman (2006) summarized different modelling and solution concepts of networking games as well as the number of different applications in telecommunications using networking games. Jia and Zhang (2008) studied a duopoly situation, where two wireless service providers participate in bandwidth competition in spectrum buying and price competition to attract users. Zhang et al. (2008) studied the price competition in packet-switching networks with a quality-of-service (QoS) guarantee in terms of an expected per-packet delay. They proposed a framework in which service providers offer multi-class priority-based services price competition to maximize profit. Zhang et al. (2009) addressed the competition between two providers that they make available the similar web services. Each provider should offer a service level (standard or premium) and charge a price for the chosen service level to meet the QoS guarantee.

This paper develops a time continuous model for competitive pricing of a web service. We use open loop differential game method as an important tool to solve and understand the behaviour of price, reservation level and sales revenue of web service classes over the planned time horizon. The study of differential game was started by Isaacs (1965). After developing Pontryagin's maximum principal, the connection between differential game and optimal control was created. However, differential game is more complex than optimal control in the sense that it is no longer clear what constitutes a solution; see Starr and Ho (1969), Mehlmann (1988), Berkovitz (1994), Basar et al. (1995), Dockner (2000), Sethi and Thompson (2000), Jørgensen and Zaccour (2007), Friesz (2010), Buckdahn et al (2011). The stream literature of differential game and dynamic pricing can be mentioned as follows: Dockner (1984) used differential game to obtain optimal pricing of new products over a finite planning period in a duopolistic market.

Jørgensen (1986) determined optimal production and pricing policies of a manufacturing firm which is supplying a retailer. The problem was modeled as a two-player nonzero-sum differential game with the inventory levels as the state variables. Jørgensen and Zaccour (2004) studied applications of differential game in marketing. Furthermore, they surveyed pricing, advertising, marketing channels and other marketing applications of differential game. Karray and Martın-Herran (2009) studied relationship between the pricing and advertising decisions in a channel where a national brand is competing with a private label. He et al. (2009) and Benchekroun et al. (2009) used differential game to study a myopic pricing behaviour in the distribution channel. Kogan and Tapiero (2008) and Xu et al. (2011) investigated the effects of the supply- side cost learning effect on dynamic pricing strategies.

The remainder of this paper is organized as follows: Section 2 defines the model formulation. In Section 3, we provide some analysis on the structure of the equilibrium point. In Section 4, we provide a heuristic algorithm to obtain the equilibrium prices. In Section 5, we perform numerical analysis to study the effect of maximum demand, and price sensitivity on control and state variables.

2. Problem statement

2.1 Notations

Inputs:

k	provider k,
k^{-1}	provider k 's competitor,
T	Advance selling period,
n	Number of web service classes,
$c_{k,i}$	Unit cost of provider k 's web service class i,
Ca_k	Provider k 's shared capacity for his web service,
$e_{k,i}(t)$	Cancellation rate of provider k 's web service class i at time t,
$cap_{k,i}$	Unit capacity of provider k 's web service class i,
$\alpha_{k,i}(t), \beta_{k,i}(t), \delta_{k,i}(t)$	Coefficients used for provider k 's web service class i in the demand function $d_{k,i} = \alpha_{k,i}(t) - \beta_{k,i}(t)p_{k,i}(t) + \delta_{k,i}(t)p_{k^{-1},i}(t)$.

Output:

$p_{k,i}(t)$ Unit selling price of provider k 's web service class i at time t (control variable),

$SR_{k,i}(t)$ Sales revenue function of provider k's web service class i at time t (state variable).

$RL_{k,i}(t)$ Reservation level of provider k's web service class i at time t (state variable).

2.2 Model description

Following Jia and Zhang et al. (2009) and Pan et al. (2009), the demand rate for i^{th} web service class of a given provider k is modelled in terms of the provider's price and the competitor's price for the same web service class as follows:

$$d_{k,i} = \alpha_{k,i}(t) - \beta_{k,i}(t)p_{k,i}(t) + \delta_{k\ ,i}(t)p_{k^{-1},i}(t) \quad \forall t \in [0,T], k = 1,2, i = 1,..,n$$

where $\alpha_{k,i}(t)$, $\beta_{k,i}(t)$ and $\delta_{k\ ,i}(t)$ show maximum demand rate of provider k 's web service class i, the demand sensitivity of provider k 's web service class i with respect to price of web service class i applied by provider k and the demand sensitivity of provider k 's web service class i with respect to price of web service class i applied by provider k *'s* competitor, respectively.

Assumption 1. The following inequalities hold $0 < \delta_{k\ ,i}(t) < \beta_{k,i}(t)$ and $0 < \delta_{k^{-1},i}(t) < \beta_{k,i}(t)$, *k=1,2.*

Assumption 2. The following inequalities hold $0 \le e_{k,i}(t) < 1$ and $\alpha_{k,i}(t) > 0$.

Users who cancel their orders are wanted to charge the penalty. The penalty at time t depends on the passed time t. This penalty policy on the reservation cancellation is not uncommon because the fee of cancellation often increases as the consumption day is due. Consequently, for provider k's web service class i, Cancellation revenue over the planned time horizon *[0,T]* can be given $\int_0^T \frac{\theta_{k,i}t}{T} SR_{k,i}(t)e_{k,i}(t)dt$, where $\theta_{k,i}$ is cancellation penalty coefficient, since we suppose the canceled orders at time t uniformly spread across the interval *[0, t]*, we can multiply $\frac{\theta_{k,i}t}{T}$ by $SR_{k,i}(t)e_{k,i}(t)$ to find the penalty of users who cancel their reservation for provider k 's web service class i at time t. The provider k 's optimization problem in this case may be formulated as follows:

$$J_k = \max \sum_{i=1}^{n} SR_{k,i}(T) + \sum_{i=1}^{n} \int_0^T \frac{\theta_{k,i}t}{T} SR_{k,i}(t)e_{k,i}(t)dt - \sum_{i=1}^{n} c_{k,i} RL_{k,i}(T) \tag{1}$$

subject to

$$\dot{SR}_{k,i}(t) = \alpha_{k,i}(t)p_{k,i}(t) - \beta_{k,i}(t)p_{k,i}(t)^2 + \delta_{k\ ,i}(t)p_{k^{-1},i}(t)p_{k,i}(t) - e_{k,i}(t)SR_{k,i}(t), \forall t \in [0,T], k = 1,2, i = 1,.. \tag{2}$$

$$\dot{RL}_{k,i}(t) = \alpha_{k,i}(t) - \beta_{k,i}(t)p_{k,i}(t) + \delta_{k\ ,i}(t)p_{k^{-1},i}(t) - e_{k,i}(t)RL_i(t), \forall t \in [0,T], k = 1,2, i = 1,...,n \tag{3}$$

$$\sum_{i=1}^{n} cap_{k,i} RL_{k,i}(T) \le Ca_k \quad k = 1,2 \tag{4}$$

$$c_{k,i} \le p_{k,i}(t) \le \frac{\delta_{k,i}(t)\alpha_{k^{-1},i}(t) + \beta_{k^{-1},i}(t)\alpha_{k\ ,i}(t)}{-\delta_{k,i}(t)\delta_{k^{-1},i}(t) + \beta_{k^{-1},i}\beta_{k,i}} \forall t \in [0,T], k = 1,2, i = 1,...,n \tag{5}$$

$$SR_{k,i}(0) = 0, RL_{k,i}(0) = 0 \qquad k = 1,2, i = 1,...,n \tag{6}$$

In this formulation, objective function of provider k (Eq. (1)) defines the profit by adding sales revenue of all web service classes at time T, and cancellation revenue over the planned time horizon, and subtracting the cost of all the web service classes at time T. the cost of each web service class is equal to the web service class unit cost multiplied by the reservation level at time T. The state Eqs. (2-3) illustrate the provider k 's change of the revenue and reservation level at time t, respectively, provider k 's revenue level change rate for the web service class i at time t is equal to the revenue that obtain from selling the web service to $d_{k,i}(t)$ users at price $p_{k,i}(t)$ minus the revenue that provider misses due to users cancellation. Since it is supposed that the canceled orders at time t uniformly spread across the interval *[0, t]*, we use expression $SR_{k,i}(t)e_{k,i}(t)$ to calculate the provider missed revenue. Provider k 's reservation level change rate for the web service class i at time t is equal to the demand $d_{k,i}(t)$ minus the orders that canceled by users at time t. Constraint (4) is to make sure that the sum of sold capacity for provider k 's all of the web service classes over the planned time horizon is less than his shared web service capacity. Constraint (5) is used to confirm that price is more than web service unit cost and demand is non-negative. The constraint $p_{k,i}(t) \le \frac{\delta_{k,i}(t)\alpha_{k^{-1},i}(t) + \beta_{k^{-1},i}(t)\alpha_{k,i}(t)}{-\delta_{k,i}(t)\delta_{k^{-1},i}(t) + \beta_{k^{-1},i}\beta_{k,i}}$ comes from the fact that provider k 's feasible pricing strategies for the web service class i depend on the pricing strategies of the competitor. In other words, for the web service class i, providers 1 , 2 have the following conditions for the feasible pricing strategies:

$$d_{1,i} = \alpha_{1,i}(t) - \beta_{1,i}(t)p_{1,i}(t) + \delta_{1,i}(t)p_{2,i}(t) \ge 0 \qquad \forall t \in [0,T],$$
$$d_{2,i} = \alpha_{2,i}(t) - \beta_{2,i}(t)p_{2,i}(t) + \delta_{2,i}(t)p_{1,i}(t) \ge 0 \qquad \forall t \in [0,T],$$

Combing feasibility conditions from above inequalities gives rise upper bound mentioned in Eq. (5). In specific, this equation demonstrates that the feasible price is bounded with an upper bound independent of the competitor's strategy. Initial value of the state variables is denoted by Eq. (6).

3. Analysis

In order to analyse the problem, we use ideas from differential game theory. Since we want to analyse the problem with open loop differential game, firstly, we dualize capacity constraint (4) and then define the Hamiltonian function by connecting adjoint variables to the state Eq. (2) and Eq. (3) and use Rosen (1965)'s theorem to show existence of equilibrium point for this problem. Finally, some results to get equilibrium point and to analyse the impact of some parameters are presented.

3.1 Nonzero-Sum Differential Games

In this section, the nonzero-sum differential games will be expressed. For further facts see reference (Sethi & Thompson, 2000; Weber, 2011).

Let us consider that we have M players. Let $u_m(t) = (u_{m,1}(t),..., u_{m,N}(t)) \in U_m$, $m = 1,..., M$ denote the control variable for the mth player, where U_m is the set of controls from which the mth player may select. Let state equation be defined as $\dot{x}(t) = f(x(t),u_1(t),...,u_M(t),t)$.

The objective function which the mth player wants to maximize may be written as follows:

$$J_m = \max \int_0^T F_m(x(t),u_1(t),...,u_M(t),t)dt + S_m(x(T))$$

In this case, a Nash solution is expressed by a set of M admissible trajectories $\{u_1^*(t),...,u_M^*(t)\}$ with the following property:

$$J_m(u_1^*,u_2^*,...,u_M^*) = \max J_m(u_1^*,...,u_{m-1}^*,u_m,u_{m+1}^*...,u_M^*), \text{ for } m = 1,..., M .$$

To obtain the open-loop Nash solution, the Hamiltonian functions may be defined as follows:

$$H_m = F_m + \lambda_m f , \text{ for } m = 1,..., M , \text{ with } \lambda_m \text{ satisfying } \dot{\lambda}_m = -\frac{\partial H_m}{\partial x} , \ \lambda_m(T) = \frac{\partial S_m(x(T))}{\partial x} .$$

The Nash control u_m^* for the mth player may be obtained by maximizing the mth Hamiltonian H_m with respect to u_m, i.e., u_m^* must fulfil

$$H_m(x^*,u_1^*,...,u_{m-1}^*,u_m^*,u_{m+1}^*,...,u_M^*,\lambda_m,t)\geq H_m(x^*,u_1^*,...,u_{m-1}^*,u_m^*,u_{m+1}^*,...,u_M^*,\lambda_m,t)\,\forall t\in[0,T],$$

for all $u_m(t)\in U_m$, $m=1,...,M$.

3.2 Analysis of equilibrium condition

In order to use nonzero-sum differential games for obtaining equilibrium point, we first dualize only the difficult constraint, i.e. the shared capacity constraint (4). Therefore, objective function for provider *k* may be written as follows:

$J_k=\sum_{i=1}^{n}SR_{k,i}(T)+\sum_{i=1}^{n}\int_0^T\frac{\theta_{k,i}t}{T}SR_{k,i}(t)e_{k,i}(t)dt-\sum_{i=1}^{n}c_{k,i}RL_{k,i}(T)+\gamma_k(Ca_k-\sum_{i=1}^{n}cap_{k,i}RL_{k,i}(T))$, complementary slackness condition on T gives rise to $\gamma_k\geq 0,\gamma_k(Ca_k-\sum_{i=1}^{n}cap_{k,i}RL_{k,i}(T))=0.$

Now, The Hamiltonian function for this problem can be defined as follows:

$$\begin{aligned}H_k(SR(t),RL_k(t),RL_{k^{-1}}(t),\lambda_k(t),\lambda'_k(t),t)=\sum_{i=1}^{n}\frac{\theta_{k,i}t}{T}R_{k,i}(t)e_{k,i}(t)+\sum_{i=1}^{n}\lambda_{k,k,i}(t)(d_{k,i}(t)p_{k,i}(t)-e_{k,i}(t)SR_{k,i}(t))\\+\sum_{i=1}^{n}\lambda_{k,k^{-1},i}(t)(d_{k^{-1},i}(t)p_{k^{-1},i}(t)-e_{k^{-1},i}(t)SR_{k^{-1},i}(t))+\sum_{i=1}^{n}\lambda'_{k,k,i}(t)(d_{k,i}(t)-e_{k,i}(t)RL_{k,i}(t))+\sum_{i=1}^{n}\lambda'_{k,k^{-1},i}(t)(d_{k^{-1},i}(t)-e_{k^{-1},i}(t)RL_{k^{-1},i}(t))\end{aligned}\tag{7}$$

where $SR(t)=(SR_k(t),SR_{k^{-1}}(t))$ and $RL(t)=(RL_k(t),RL_{k^{-1}}(t))$, the adjoint variable $\lambda_k(t)=(\lambda_{k,k,1},...,\lambda_{k,k,n},\lambda_{k,k^{-1},1},...,\lambda_{k,k^{-1},n})$ and $\lambda'_k(t)=(\lambda'_{k,k,1},...,\lambda'_{k,k,n},\lambda'_{k,k^{-1},1},...,\lambda'_{k,k^{-1},n})$ dualize, respectively, the state Eq. (2) and Eq. (3) at time *t*.

The Hamiltonian function (7) may be understood as the instantaneous profit rate, which includes the cancellation revenue rates, sales revenue rates and cost of reservation rates. The adjoint variables $\lambda_k(t)$ and $\lambda'_k(t)$ are shadow prices and show the net profit from increasing unit sales revenue and the net profit from decreasing unit reservation level at time *t*, respectively. For every $t\in[0,T]$, the continuous vector of adjoint variable $\lambda_k(t)$ fulfils the following differential equation:

$$\dot{\lambda}_{k,k,i}(t)=-e_{k,i}(t)(\frac{\theta_{k,i}t}{T}-\lambda_{k,k,i}(t)),\lambda_{k,k,i}(T)=1\tag{8}$$

$$\dot{\lambda}_{k,k^{-1},i}(t)=e_{k^{-1},i}(t)\lambda_{k,k^{-1},i}(t),\lambda_{k,k^{-1},i}(T)=0\tag{9}$$

For every $t\in[0,T]$, following differential equation holds for the adjoint vector $\lambda_k'(t)$:

$$\dot{\lambda}'_{k,k,i}(t)=e_{k,i}(t)\lambda'_{k,k,i}(t),\lambda'_{k,k,i}(T)=-(c_i+\gamma_k cap_{k,i}),$$

$$\dot{\lambda}'_{k,k^{-1},i}(t)=e_{k^{-1},i}(t)\lambda'_{k,k^{-1},i}(t),\lambda'_{k,k^{-1},i}(T)=0.$$

Proposition 1: $\forall t\in[0,T]$, the optimal trajectory $\lambda_{k,k,i}(t)$ is given by:

$\lambda_{k,k,i}(t)=\frac{1}{m_{k,i}(t)}(m_{k,i}(T)+\int_t^T\frac{\theta_{k,i}s}{T}e_{k,i}(s)m_{k,i}(s)ds)$, where $m_{k,i}(t)=e^{-\int e_{k,i}(t)dt}$.

Proof: Eq. (8) denotes a linear first order differential equation for $\lambda_{k,k,i}(t)$ as a function of *t*. Its standard form is $\dot{\lambda}_{k,k,i}(t) - e_{k,i}(t)\lambda_{k,k,i}(t) = -\frac{\theta_{k,i}t}{T}e_{k,i}(t)$, based on available standard solution for the first order differential equation in reference (Thomas & Finney, 1996), we have $\lambda_{k,k,i}(T)m_{k,i}(T) - \lambda_{k,k,i}(t)m_{k,i}(t) = -\int_t^T \frac{\theta_{k,i}s}{T}e_{k,i}(s)m_{k,i}(s)ds$, where $m_{k,i}(t) = e^{-\int e_{k,i}(t)dt}$, substituting $\lambda_{k,k,i}(T) = 1$ gives $\lambda_{k,k,i}(t) = \frac{1}{m_{k,i}(t)}(m_{k,i}(T) + \int_t^T \frac{\theta_{k,i}s}{T}e_{k,i}(s)m_{k,i}(s)ds)$. □

Proposition 2: $\forall t \in [0,T]$, the optimal trajectory $\lambda_{k,k^{-1},i}(t)$ may be obtained by $\lambda_{k,k^{-1},i}(t) = 0$.

Proof: From differential Eq. (9), we have $\frac{\dot{\lambda}_{k,k^{-1},i}(t)}{\lambda_{k,k^{-1},i}(t)} = e_{k^{-1},i}(t)$, Integrating this term with respect to t gives $\ln(\lambda_{k,k^{-1},i}(t))\Big|_t^T = \int_t^T e_{k^{-1},i}(s)ds$, substituting $\lambda_{k,k^{-1},i}(T) = 0$ gives. $\lambda_{k,k^{-1},i}(t) = 0$. □

Proposition 3: $\forall t \in [0,T]$, provider k, and web service class i, the optimal trajectory $\lambda'_{k,k,i}(t)$ may be given by:

$$\lambda'_{k,k,i}(t) = -(c_i + \gamma_k cap_{k,i})e^{-\int_t^T e_i(s)ds}.$$

The proof is similar to proposition 2. □

Proposition 4: $\forall t \in [0,T]$, the optimal trajectory $\lambda'_{k,k^{-1},i}(t)$ is given by $\lambda'_{k,k^{-1},i}(t) = 0$.

The proof is similar to proposition 2. □

Proposition 5: For provider k, Hamiltonian function H_k may be rewritten as follows:

$$H_k(SR(t), RL(t), \lambda_k(t), \lambda'_k(t), t) = \sum_{i=1}^{n} \frac{\theta_{k,i}t}{T} SR_{k,i}(t)e_{k,i}(t) + \sum_{i=1}^{n} \lambda'_{k,k,i}(t)(d_{k,i}(t) - e_{k,i}(t)RL_{k,i}(t)) +$$
$$\sum_{i=1}^{n} \lambda_{k,k,i}(t)(d_{k,i}(t)p_{k,i}(t) - e_{k,i}(t)SR_{k,i}(t)).$$

Proof: By replacing $\lambda_{k,k^{-1},i}(t) = 0$ and $\lambda'_{k,k^{-1},i}(t) = 0$ in Hamiltonian function (7), the proof is completed. □

Rosen (1965) considered a constrained n-person game in which the constraints for each player, as well as his payoff function, is determined based on the strategies of other players. The existence of an equilibrium point for such a game was proved by him. In this paper, Rosen's results is used to prove the existence of equilibrium point at each time t. Now, we express Rosen 's theorem for concave n person game as follows:

Theorem 1 (Rosen 1965): An equilibrium point exists for every concave n-person game. According to Rosen's paper, a game is called concave if payoff functions are concave.

Proposition 6: For every $t \in [0,T]$, an equilibrium point exists.

Proof: For a given t, according to theorem 1, it is sufficient to show that H_k is concave in p_k. H_k is concave iff Hesian matrix (HM_k) of H_k is negative definite for every $p_{k,i}$. Matrix $HM_k = (hm_{k,i,j})_{i,j=1,\dots,n}$ can be described as:

$$hm_{k,i,j} = \begin{cases} -2\beta_{k,i}\lambda_{k,k,i}(t) & i = j \\ 0 & i \neq j \end{cases},$$

since this matrix is diagonal and its terms are all negative, thus we clearly conclude that it is negative definite for every $p_{k,i}$. □

Proposition 7: At each time $t \in [0,T]$, for provider k 's web service class i, the equilibrium price $p^*_{k,i}$ can be given by:

$$p^*_{k,i} = \begin{cases} c_{k,i} & c_{k,i} \geq A_{k,i} \\ A_{k,i} & c_{k,i} < A_{k,i} \leq B_{k,i} \\ B_{k,i} & A_{k,i} > B_{k,i} \end{cases}$$

where $A_{k,i} = \dfrac{2\beta_{k^{-1},i}(\frac{\beta_{k,i}\lambda'_{k,k,i}}{\lambda_{k,k,i}} - \alpha_{k,i}) + \delta_{k,i}(\frac{\beta_{k^{-1},i}\lambda'_{k^{-1},k^{-1},i}}{\lambda_{k^{-1},k^{-1},i}} - \alpha_{k^{-1},i})}{\delta_{k^{-1},i}\delta_{k,i} - 4\beta_{k,i}\beta_{k^{-1},i}}$ and $B_{i,k} = \dfrac{\delta_{k,i}(t)\alpha_{k^{-1},i}(t) + \beta_{k^{-1},i}(t)\alpha_{k,i}(t)}{-\delta_{k,i}(t)\delta_{k^{-1},i}(t) + \beta_{k^{-1},i}\beta_{k,i}}$.

In order to obtain equilibrium point $p^*_{k,i}$, it is necessary to compute first partial derivative of Hamiltonian functions H_k and $H_{k^{-1}}$,respectively, with respect to control variables $p_{k,i}$, $p_{k^{-1},i}$ as follows:

$$\frac{\partial H_k}{\partial p_{k,i}} = \lambda_{k,k,i}(t)(\alpha_{k,i}(t) - \beta_{k,i}(t)p_{k,i}(t) + \delta_{k,i}(t)p_{k^{-1},i}(t)) - \lambda'_{k,k,i}(t)\beta_{k,i}(t)$$

$$\frac{\partial H_{k^{-1}}}{\partial p_{k^{-1},i}} = \lambda_{k^{-1},k^{-1},i}(t)(\alpha_{k^{-1},i}(t) - \beta_{k^{-1},i}(t)p_{k^{-1},i}(t) + \delta_{k^{-1},i}(t)p_{k,i}(t)) - \lambda'_{k^{-1},k^{-1},i}\beta_{k^{-1},i}(t),$$

setting these partial derivatives to zero and solving these system of two equations, we have:

$$p^*_{k,i} = A_{i,k} = \frac{2\beta_{k^{-1},i}(\frac{\beta_{k,i}\lambda'_{k,k,i}}{\lambda_{k,k,i}} - \alpha_{i,k}) + \delta_{k,i}(\frac{\beta_{k^{-1},i}\lambda'_{k^{-1},k^{-1},i}}{\lambda_{k^{-1},k^{-1},i}} - \alpha_{k^{-1},i})}{\delta_{k^{-1},i}\delta_{k,i} - 4\beta_{k,i}\beta_{k^{-1},i}}.$$

Since above mentioned system of the equations are linear, obtained solution is unique. If the obtained solution locates on the set of feasible controls (defined by constraints (5), it is assumed as equilibrium point. Otherwise, upper bound ($B_{i,k}$) of $p_{k,i}$ or $c_{k,i}$ is allowed as equilibrium point. □

Note, that setting $\gamma_k = 0$, we can obtain the lower bound of the equilibrium point. Clearly, this case is corresponding to the proposed problem without shared capacity constraint.

Proposition 8: if $e1_{k,i}(t)$ and $e2_{k,i}(t)$ are different cancellation rate for provider k 's web service class i such that $e1_{k,i}(t) \leq e2_{k,i}$, $\forall t \in [0,T]$, then for the corresponding lower bound prices $p1_{k,i}(t)$ and $p2_{k,i}(t)$, we have: $p1_{k,i}(t) \geq p2_{k,i}(t)$

Proof: According to proposition 1 and proposition 3, corresponding adjonit variables for $p1_{k,i}(t)$ are $\lambda1_{k,k,i}(t)$ and $\lambda1'_{k,k,i}(t)$ and for $p2_{k,i}(t)$ are $\lambda2_{k,k,i}(t)$ and $\lambda2'_{k,k,i}(t)$. Therefore, $p1_{k,i}(t)$ and $p2_{k,i}(t)$ can be given by:

$$p1_{k,i}=\frac{2\beta_{k^{-1},i}\left(\frac{\beta_{k,i}\lambda 1^{'}_{k,k,i}}{\lambda 1_{k,k,i}}-\alpha_{k,i}\right)+\delta_{k,i}\left(\frac{\beta_{k^{-1},i}\lambda^{'}_{k^{-1},k^{-1},i}}{\lambda_{k^{-1},k^{-1},i}}-\alpha_{k^{-1},i}\right)}{\delta_{k^{-1},i}\delta_{k,i}-4\beta_{k,i}\beta_{k^{-1},i}},\; p2_{k,i}=\frac{2\beta_{k^{-1},i}\left(\frac{\beta_{k,i}\lambda 2^{'}_{k,k,i}}{\lambda 2_{k,k,i}}-\alpha_{k,i}\right)+\delta_{k,i}\left(\frac{\beta_{k^{-1},i}\lambda^{'}_{k^{-1},k^{-1},i}}{\lambda_{k^{-1},k^{-1},i}}-\alpha_{k^{-1},i}\right)}{\delta_{k^{-1},i}\delta_{k,i}-4\beta_{k,i}\beta_{k^{-1},i}}.$$

Clearly, to prove the result of this proposition, it necessary to show that $\frac{\lambda 1^{'}_{k,k,i}}{\lambda 1_{k,k,i}}\geq\frac{\lambda 2^{'}_{k,k,i}}{\lambda 2_{k,k,i}}$.

Since $$\frac{\lambda 1^{'}_{k,k,i}}{\lambda 1_{k,k,i}}=\frac{c_{k,i}e^{-\int e1_{k,i}(t)dt}}{\frac{1}{e^{-\int e1_{k,i}(t)dt}\big|_{t=t}}\left(e^{-\int e1_{k,i}(t)dt}\big|_{t=T}+\int_t^T\frac{\theta_{k,i}e1_{k,i}(t)}{T}e^{-\int e1_{k,i}(t)dt}\big|_{t=t}dt\right)},$$

it follows that $\frac{\lambda 1^{'}_{k,k,i}}{\lambda 1_{k,k,i}}=\frac{c_{k,i}}{(1+\int_t^T\frac{\theta_{k,i}e1_{k,i}(t)}{T}e^{\int e1_{k,i}(t)dt}dt)}$ and $\frac{\lambda 2^{'}_{k,k,i}}{\lambda 2_{k,k,i}}=\frac{c_{k,i}}{(1+\int_t^T\frac{\theta_{k,i}e2_{k,i}(t)}{T}e^{\int e2_{k,i}(t)dt}dt)}$. furthermore, since $e1_{k,i}(t)\leq e2_{k,i}$, it is clearly concluded that

$$\frac{\lambda 2_{k,k,i}}{\lambda 2^{'}_{k,k,i}}=\frac{1+\int_t^T\frac{\theta_{k,i}e2_{k,i}(t)}{T}e^{\int e2_{k,i}(t)dt}dt}{c_{k,i}}\geq\frac{1+\int_t^T\frac{\theta_{k,i}e1_{k,i}(t)}{T}e^{\int e1_{k,i}(t)dt}dt}{c_{k,i}}=\frac{\lambda 1_{k,k,i}}{\lambda 1^{'}_{k,k,t}}.\square$$

Using differential Eq. (2), Eq. (3), the following propositions are developed to get optimal reservation level and sales revenue.

Proposition 9: For provider k 's web service class i at time t, the optimal sales revenue path $SR^*_{k,i}(t)$ is given by $SR^*_{k,i}(t)=\frac{1}{m_{k,i}(t)}\int_0^t d^*_{k,i}(s)p^*_{k,i}(s)m_{k,i}(s)ds$, where $m^{'}_{k,i}(t)=e^{\int e_{k,i}(t)dt}$ and $d^*_{k,i}(t)$ is optimal demand rate at time t.

Proof: according to the differential Eq. (2) we have $S\dot{R}^*_{k,i}(t)=d^*_{k,i}(t)p^*_{k,i}(t)-e_{k,i}(t)SR^*_{k,i}(t)$, Thus, $SR^*_{k,i}(s)m^{'}_{k,i}(s)\Big|_0^t=\int_0^t d^*_{k,i}(s)p^*_{k,i}(s)m^{'}_{k,i}(s)ds$, Where $m^{'}_{k,i}(t)=e^{\int e_{k,i}(t)dt}$, therefore

$SR^*_{k,i}(t)m^{'}_{k,i}(t)-SR^*_{k,i}(0)m^{'}_{k,i}(0)=\int_0^t d^*_{k,i}(s)p^*_{k,i}(s)m^{'}_{k,i}(s)ds$, since $R^*_{k,i}(0)=R_{k,i}(0)=0$, thus

$SR^*_{k,i}(t)=\frac{1}{m^{'}_{k,i}(t)}\int_0^t d^*_{k,i}(s)p^*_{k,i}(s)m^{'}_{k,i}(s)ds.\square$

Proposition 10: For provider k 's web service class i at time t, the optimal reservation level path $RL^*_{k,i}(t)$ is given by $RL^*_{k,i}(t)=\frac{1}{m^{''}_{k,i}(t)}\int_0^t d^*_{k,i}(s)m^{''}_{k,i}(s)ds$. where $m^{''}_{k,i}(t)=e^{\int e_{k,i}(t)dt}$ and $d^*_{k,i}(t)$ is optimal demand rate at time t.

The proof of this proposition is similar to Proposition 9. □

We can see the impact of the problem parameters changes on equilibrium prices as follows:

Proposition 11: Price of provider k 's web service class i at time t will be increased by increasing provider and his competitor's maximal demand ($\alpha_{k,i}(t),\alpha_{k^{-1},i}(t)$).

Proof: from appendix A we can conclude that $\frac{\partial p_{k,i}}{\partial \alpha_{k,i}(t)}, \frac{\partial p_{k,i}}{\partial \alpha_{k^{-1},i}(t)} > 0$ □.

Proposition 12: Price of provider k 's web service class i at time t will be decreased by increasing the demand sensitivity of provider k 's web service class i with respect to price of provider k 's web service class i ($\beta_{k,i}(t)$) and the demand sensitivity of provider k^{-1} 's web service class i with respect to price of provider k^{-1} 's web service class i ($\beta_{k^{-1},i}(t)$).

Proof: from appendix A we can conclude that $\frac{\partial p_{k,i}}{\partial \beta_{k,i}(t)}, \frac{\partial p_{k,i}}{\partial \beta_{k^{-1},i}(t)} < 0$ □.

Proposition 13: Price of provider k 's web service class i at time t will be increased by increasing the demand sensitivity of provider k 's web service class i with respect to price of provider k^{-1} 's web service class i and the demand sensitivity of provider k^{-1} 's web service class i with respect to price of provider k's web service class i ($\delta_{k,i}(t), \delta_{k^{-1},i}(t)$).

Proof: from appendix A we can conclude that $\frac{\partial p_{k,i}}{\partial \delta_{k,i}(t)}, \frac{\partial p_{k,i}}{\partial \delta_{k^{-1},i}(t)} > 0$ □.

4. Heuristic Algorithm

In what follows, we offer an algorithm to find equilibrium prices for under study problem. The proposed algorithm first uses an iterative trial and error based on Everett (1963)'s approach for identifying multiplier $\gamma_k, k = 1,2$. It then utilizes the proposition 3 to obtain the optimal trajectory $\lambda'_{k,k,i}(t), k = 1,2$. By substituting $\lambda'_{k,k,i}(t)$, $\lambda_{k,k,i}(t)$ and other pre-specified parameters into proposition 7, we can easily obtain equilibrium point for providers. If the capacity constraints (4) and complementary slackness condition $\gamma_k(Ca_k - \sum_{i=1}^{n} cap_{k,i} RL_{k,i}(T)) = 0$ are satisfied, the algorithm ends. In other words, we stop when the complementary slackness condition $\left|\gamma_k(Ca_k - \sum_{i=1}^{n} cap_{k,i} RL_{k,i}(T))\right| < \vartheta_k$ is satisfied. Otherwise, it is necessary to update the value of the multiplier γ_k, and repeat the algorithm. As a result, the proposed heuristic algorithm has the following steps:

Step 1: Set parameters $n, T, c_k(.), cap_{k,i}(t), Ca_k, \alpha_{k,i}(.), \beta_{k,i}(.), e_{k,i}(.), \delta_{k,i}, \varepsilon_k > 0, 0 < \kappa_k < 1, \vartheta_k, k = 1,2, i = 1,...,n;$
Step 2: Set $\gamma_k = 0$ and calculate $\lambda_{k,k,i}(t), \lambda'_{k,k,i}(t) k = 1,2, i = 1,...,n$ using proposition 1, 3;
Step 3: Calculate price of provider k for the web service class i, ($p_{k,i}, k = 1,2, i = 1,...,n$) using proposition 7;
Step 4: Compute the reservation level of providers for the web service classes using proposition 10;
Step 5: If $\sum_{i=1}^{n} cap_{k,i} RL_{k,i}(T) \le Ca_k, \forall k \in \{1,2\}$ go to 18;
Step 6: Set $l_k = \sum_{i=1}^{n} cap_{k,i} RL_{k,i}(T) - Ca_k, \forall k \in \{1,2\}$;
Step 7: If $l_k > 0$ set $\gamma_k = \varepsilon_k$; else set $\gamma_k = 0$; $\forall k \in \{1,2\}$
Step 8: Calculate $\lambda'_{k,k,i}(t), k = 1,2, i = 1,...,n$ using proposition 3;
Step 9: Calculate the price of the provider k 's web service class i, ($p_{k,i}, k = 1,2, i = 1,...,n$) using proposition 7;
Step 10: Compute the reservation level of web service classes using proposition 10;
Step 11: Set $u_k = \sum_{i=1}^{n} cap_{k,i} RL_{k,i}(T) - Ca_k; \forall k = 1,2$;
Step 12: Set $k=1$;

Step 13: if $\gamma_k \le 0$ then go to 14 else go to 15;

Step 14: If $u_k \le 0$ then $\gamma_k = 0$; go to 16; else $\gamma_k = \varepsilon_k$; go to 16;

Step 15: If $u_k . I_k < 0$ then set $\varepsilon_k = -\kappa\varepsilon_k$, $I_k = u_k$, $\gamma_k = \gamma_k + \varepsilon_k$; else if $u_k . I_k > 0$ then set $I_k = u_k$, $\gamma_k = \gamma_k + \varepsilon_k$; else if $u_k . I_k = 0$ then if $u_k > 0$ then $\gamma_k = \gamma_k + \varepsilon_k$;

Step 16: If $k \le 2$ go to 13 else go to 17;

Step 17: If $|\gamma_k u_k| < \vartheta_k; \forall k = 1,2$ go to 18; else go to 8;

Step 18: End;

5. Numerical Result

We implement the proposed algorithm on the time horizon [0,*10*]. We apply the algorithm for two web service classes (*n*=*2*) and consider the impact of parameters i.e. the maximal demand, $\alpha_{k,i}(t)$ and the demand sensitivity of provider *k* 's web service class *i* with respect to price of provider *k* 's web service class *i* , $\beta_{k,i}(t)$ on control and state variables. The proposed heuristic has been coded in Maple 15 on a PC with an AMD Dual core (2.31 GHz) CPU and 1 GB of RAM. Furthermore, we use parameters $\varepsilon_k = 0.1, \kappa_k = 0.1$ and $\vartheta_k = 10^{-5}$ in the proposed algorithm.

To clarify the effect of the considered parameters, we firstly create example 1(Table 1) and then use it to make other examples. In other words, other examples distinct from example 1 in a parameter which we want to know its impact. In this example, similar to some related dynamic pricing literature (see Gaimon, 1988), demand peak ($\alpha_{k,i}(t)$) is assumed to be non-decreasing during the first half of the time horizon and non-increasing during the second half.

Table 1
Value of input parameters for example 1

	$\beta_{k,i}(t)$	$\delta_{k,i}(t)$	$c_{k,i}$	$e_{k,i}$	$cap_{k,i}$	$\theta_{k,i}$	$\alpha_{k,i}(t)$
Web service class 1	2	0.5	2	0.2	0.4	0.3	$20+5t-\frac{1}{2}t^2$
Web service class 2	1	0.25	4	0.1	0.8	0.6	$20+5t-\frac{1}{2}t^2$

5.1 Impact of a demand peak

We consider three following examples which are different than example 1 in parameters $\alpha_{1,1}(t)$ and $\alpha_{1,2}(t)$ as follows:

Example 2: $\alpha_{1,1}(t) = 1.5*(20+5t-\frac{1}{2}t^2), \alpha_{1,2}(t) = 1.5*(20+5t-\frac{1}{2}t^2)$

Example 3: $\alpha_{1,1}(t) = 2(20+5t-\frac{1}{2}t^2), \alpha_{1,2}(t) = 2(20+5t-\frac{1}{2}t^2)$

Example 4: $\alpha_{1,1}(t) = 3(20+5t-\frac{1}{2}t^2), \alpha_{1,2}(t) = 3(20+5t-\frac{1}{2}t^2)$

Denoted curves in the figures are labelled as follows: *pkij* optimal pricing path for the example *k*, the provider *i* and the web service class *j*; *Ikij* optimal reservation level path for the example *k*, the provider *i* and the web service class *j*; *Rkij* optimal sales revenue path for the example *k*, the provider *i* and the web service class *j*. In general, increasing in the maximum demand of the web service may show that the web service become more attractive to the users, for example due to providing effective features for the web service by a provider. The results can be seen in Fig. 1 to Fig. 3. These figures show the optimal price path, reservation level path and sales revenue for each provider's both web service classes over the time horizon.

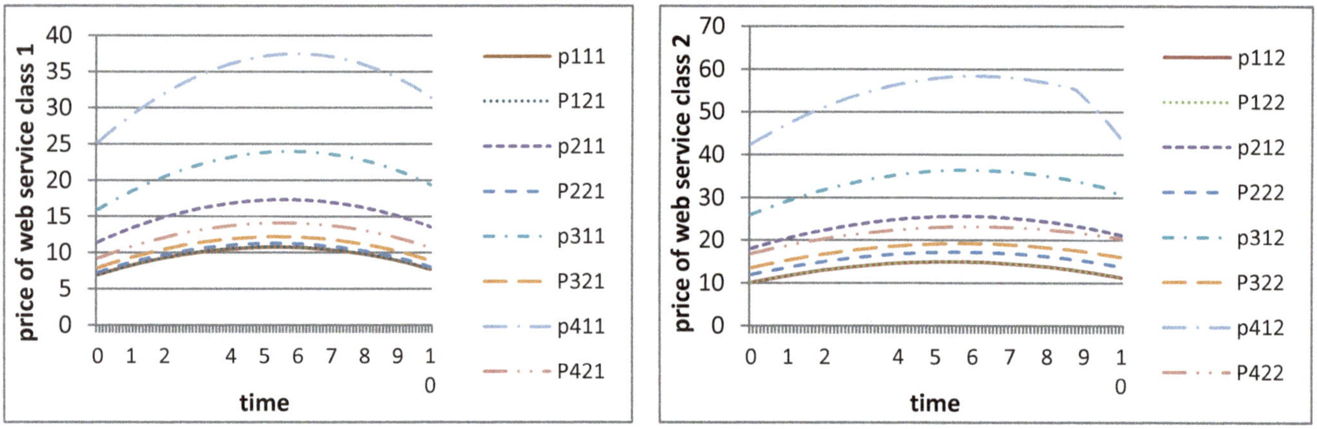

Fig. 1. Optimum prices path for example 1-4 over the considered time horizon

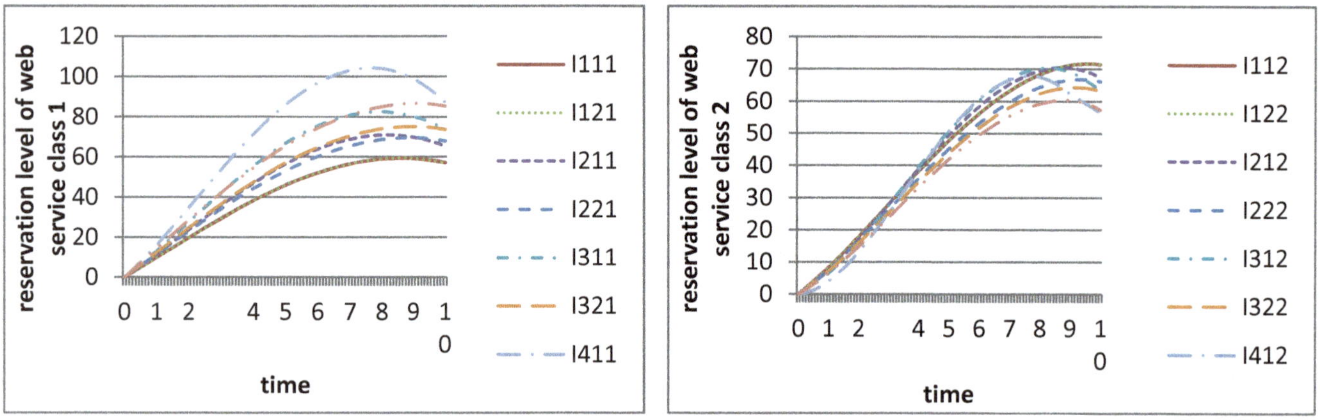

Fig. 2. Optimum reservation level path for example 1-4 over the considered time horizon

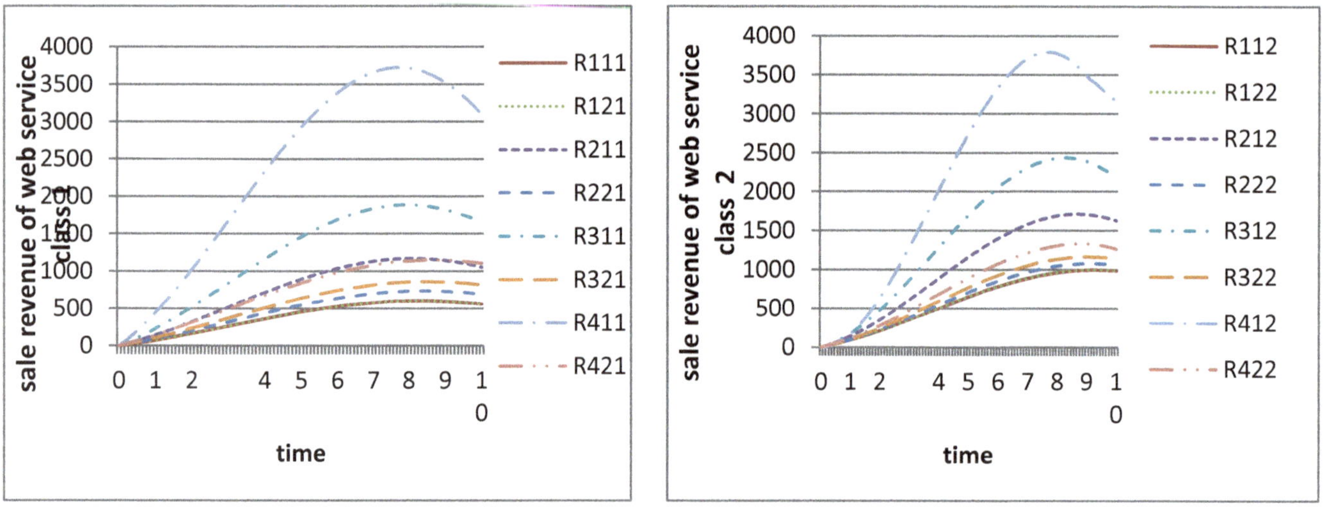

Fig. 3. Optimum sales revenue path for example 1-4 over the considered time horizon

The price of the web service classes of the example 1-4 is increased on the first half of the time horizon and decreased on the second half of time horizon. As the maximal demand for the provider 1 increases in value for both web service classes, the price path for provider 1 also increases. Increasing price for provider 1, some users try to buy their required service from provider 2, in response to this, provider 2 increases his\her prices in order to manage limited capacity. For this case, since demand for the web service classe2 decreases as the maximum demand increases, the reservation level for the web service class 2 decreases in the value. Furthermore, increasing in the demand maximum, sales revenue of providers for both web service classes increases. From Table 1, the cancellation revenue, sales revenue, total revenue and profit of providers increase as the maximum demand rises by 50%, 100%, and 200%, respectively, there are 100%, 174% and 373% increase in provider 1's cancellation revenue and 14%, 27% and 56% increase in provider 2's cancellation revenue, there are 100%, 149% and 304% increase in provider 1's sales revenue and 13%, 27% and 53% increase in provider 2's sales revenue, there are 100%, 149% and 306% increase in provider 1's total revenue and 13%, 27% and 53% increase in provider 2's total revenue, There are 66%, 200% and 410% increase in provider 1's profit and 18%, 36% and 71% increase in provider 2's profit.

Table 2

Optimum value of cancellation revenue, sales revenue, total revenue, cost and profit for example 1-4

	Example 1		Example 2		Example 3		Example 4	
	provider 1	provider 2	provider 1	provider 2	provider 1	provider 2	provider 1	provider 2
Cancellation revenue	39	39	78	44	107	50	185	61
Sales revenue	1543	1543	3086	1750	3834	1955	6238	2364
Total revenue	1582	1582	3164	1794	3941	2004	6422	2425
profit	1182	1182	1964	1394	3541	1604	6023	2025

5.2 Impact of $\beta_{k,i}(t)$

In this section, we take into account two following examples which are different than example 1 in parameters $\beta_{1,k}(t)$, *k=1, 2.*

Example 5: $\beta_{1,1}(t) = 2.5$, $\beta_{1,2}(t) = 2$ Example 7: $\beta_{1,1}(t) = 2 + 0.05t$, $\beta_{1,2}(t) = 1.5 + 0.05t$

Example 6: $\beta_{1,1}(t) = 3$, $\beta_{1,2}(t) = 2.5$ Example 8: $\beta_{1,1}(t) = 2 + 0.1t$, $\beta_{1,2}(t) = 1.5 + 0.1t$

Increasing demand sensitivity of the web service with respect to its price denotes that the web service become less attractive to the customers, for example due to appearing newer web services which can serve as substitute. Results are shown Fig. 6 and Fig. 7.

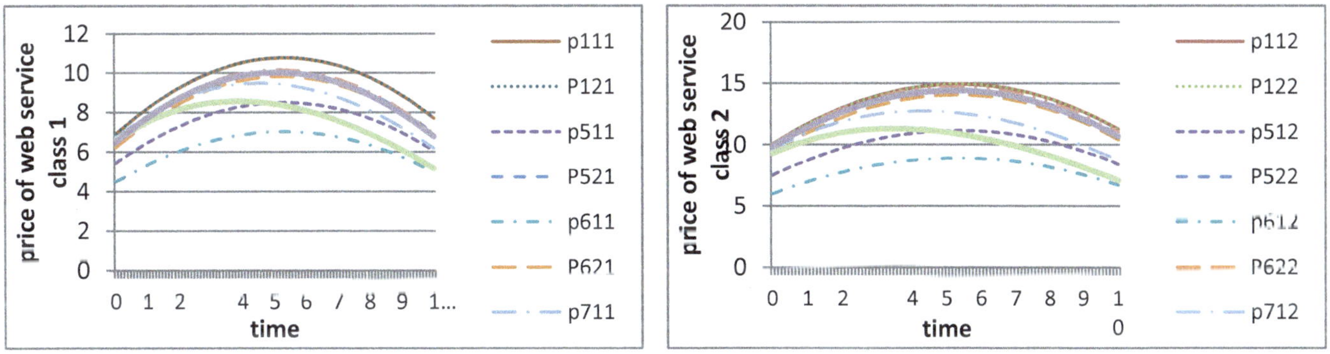

Fig. 4. Optimum prices path for examples 1, 5-8 over the considered time horizon

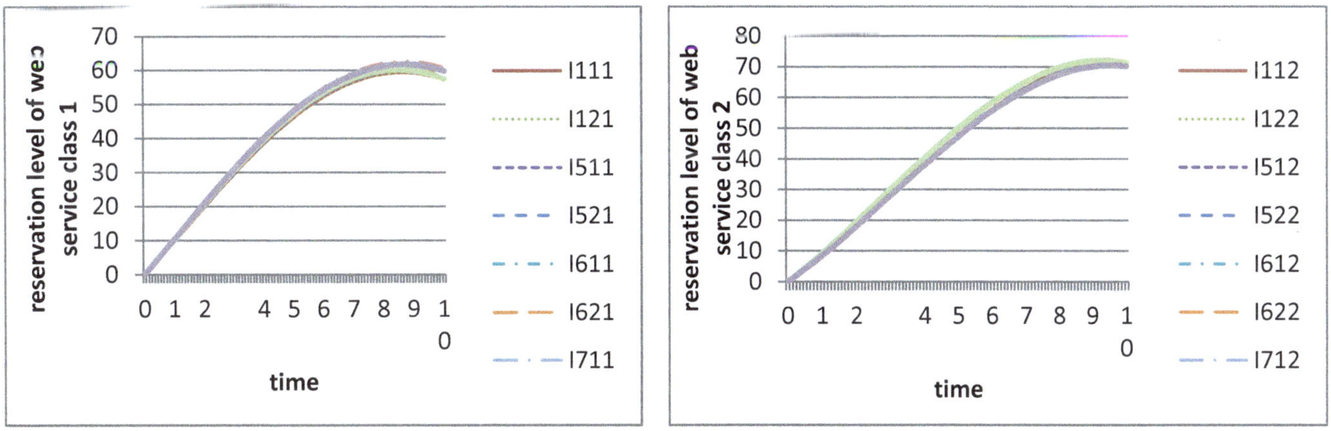

Fig. 5. Optimum reservation level path for examples 1, 5-8 over the considered time horizon

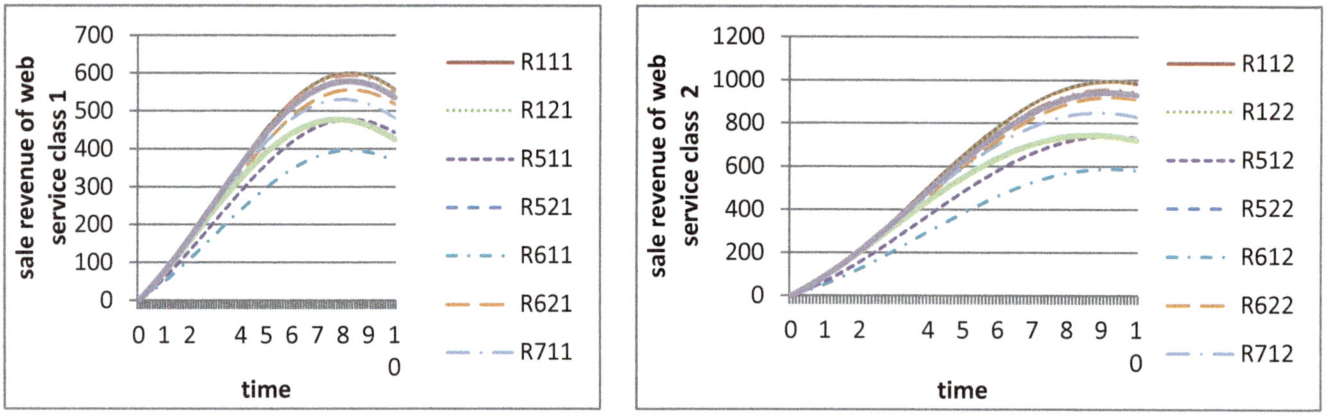

Fig. 6. Optimum sales revenue path for examples 1, 5-8 over the considered time horizon

As the demand sensitivity of provider 1's web service class 1 with respect to price of provider 1's web service class 1 increases in value, the prices path for provider 1 decreases. In response to this, provider 2 decreases his\her prices in order to prevent users from moving to provider 1. For this case, an increase in the demand sensitivity of provider 1 could slightly change reservation levels for both web service classes, but sales revenue path of providers for both web service classes decreases in the value. Table 3 denotes that the cancellation revenue, sales revenue, total revenue and profit of providers decrease when the demand sensitivity of the web service classes increases.

Table 3
Optimum value of cancellation revenue, sales revenue, total revenue, cost and profit for examples 1, 5-8

	Example 1		Example 5		Example 6		Example 7		Example 8	
	provider 1	provider 2	provider 1	provider 2	provider 1	provider 2	provider 1	provider 2	provider 1	provider 2
Cancellation revenue	39	39	30	37	24	36	35	38	31	37
Sales revenue	1543	1543	1176	1474	951	1431	1311	1499	1147	1467
Total revenue	1582	1582	1206	1512	975	1467	1345	1537	1178	1504
profit	1182	1182	806	1111	575	1067	945	1137	778	1104

6. Conclusion

In this paper, we have considered a web service pricing problem where two providers compete through dynamic pricing. Each provider offers access to a web service with different quality classes where users may buy their required web service through a reservation system. They would like adjust price of web service classes over a pre-specified time horizon to manage demand and maximize profit. Users have the right with no obligation to cancel their services as long as they pay a penalty. We have considered a dynamic setting where the web service classes share a capacity and develop a model where the demand of a service class depends on the price of provider and price of his competitor and time. We firstly have developed a time continuous model for competitive pricing of a web service and then we have studied the equilibrium condition of problem based on differential game and proposed an algorithm to obtain the optimal pricing policy for providers. Analytical analyses have provided the impact of some parameters (demand peak and price sensitivities) on the price of the web service classes. Furthermore, numerical analyses of the model have offered intuitions about the impact of the demand peak and the demand sensitivity of the provider's web service class with respect to its price on competitive price, reservation level and sales revenue of web service classes. Results have indicated that the cancellation revenue, sales revenue, total revenue and profit of providers increase as the maximum demand rises. Increasing in demand sensitivity of providers with respect to their prices leads to decrease in the cancellation revenue, sales revenue, total revenue and profit of providers.

References

Ahluwalia, P., & Varshney, U. (2009). Composite quality of service and decision making perspectives in wireless networks. *Decision Support Systems*, *46*(2), 542-551.

Alirezaei, A., & khoshAlhan, F. (2014). Coordination of pricing and co-op advertising models in supply chain: A game theoretic approach. *International Journal of Industrial Engineering Computations*, *5*(1), 23-40.

Altman, E., Boulogne, T., El-Azouzi, R., Jiménez, T., & Wynter, L. (2006). A survey on networking games in telecommunications. *Computers & Operations Research*, *33*(2), 286-311.

Bachlechner, D., Siorpaes, K., Fensel, D., & Toma, I. (2006, January). Web service discovery-a reality check. In *3rd European Semantic Web Conference* (Vol. 308).

Basar, T., Olsder, G. J., Clsder, G. J., Basar, T., Baser, T., & Olsder, G. J. (1995). *Dynamic noncooperative game theory* (Vol. 200). London: Academic press.

Benchekroun, H., Martín-Herrán, G., & Taboubi, S. (2009). Could myopic pricing be a strategic choice in marketing channels? A game theoretic analysis. *Journal of Economic Dynamics and Control*, *33*(9), 1699-1718.

Berkovitz, L. D. (1994). A theory of differential games. In *Advances in dynamic games and applications* (pp. 3-22). Birkhäuser Boston.

Bitran, G., & Caldentey, R. (2003). An overview of pricing models for revenue management. *Manufacturing & Service Operations Management*, *5*(3), 203-229.

Buckdahn, R., Cardaliaguet, P., & Quincampoix, M. (2011). Some recent aspects of differential game theory. *Dynamic Games and Applications*, *1*(1), 74-114.

Cachon, G. P., & Netessine, S. (2004). Game theory in supply chain analysis. In *Handbook of Quantitative Supply Chain Analysis* (pp. 13-65). Springer US.

Dockner, E. (1985). Optimal pricing in a dynamic duopoly game model. *Zeitschrift für Operations Research*, *29*(2), B1-B16.

Dockner, E. (Ed.). (2000). *Differential games in economics and management science*. Cambridge University Press.

Elmaghraby, W., & Keskinocak, P. (2003). Dynamic pricing in the presence of inventory considerations: Research overview, current practices, and future directions. *Management Science*, *49*(10), 1287-1309.

Elyasi, M., Khoshalhan, F., & Khanmirzaee, M. (2014). Modified economic order quantity (EOQ) model for items with imperfect quality: Game-theoretical approaches. *International Journal of Industrial Engineering Computations*, *5*(2), 211-222.

Everett III, H. (1963). Generalized Lagrange multiplier method for solving problems of optimum allocation of resources. *Operations research*, *11*(3), 399-417.

Ferris, C., & Farrell, J. (2003). What are web services?. *Communications of the ACM*, *46*(6), 31.

Friesz, T. L. (2010). *Dynamic optimization and differential games* (Vol. 135). New York: Springer.

Gaimon, C. (1988). Simultaneous and dynamic price, production, inventory and capacity decisions. *European Journal of Operational Research*, *35*(3), 426-441.

Gibbens, R., Mason, R., & Steinberg, R. (2000). Internet service classes under competition. *Selected Areas in Communications, IEEE Journal on*, *18*(12), 2490-2498.

Gottschalk, K., Graham, S., Kreger, H., & Snell, J. (2002). Introduction to web services architecture. *IBM systems Journal*, *41*(2), 170-177.

Guerrero-Ibáñez, A., Contreras-Castillo, J., Barba, A., & Reyes, A. (2011). A QoS-based dynamic pricing approach for services provisioning in heterogeneous wireless access networks. *Pervasive and Mobile Computing*, *7*(5), 569-583.

He, X., Prasad, A., & Sethi, S. P. (2009). Cooperative advertising and pricing in a dynamic stochastic supply chain: feedback Stackelberg strategies. *Production and Operations Management*, *18*(1), 78-94.

He, X., & Sethi, S. P. (2008). Dynamic slotting and pricing decisions in a durable product supply chain. *Journal of Optimization Theory and Applications*, *137*(2), 363-379.

Isaacs, R. (1965). *Differential Games*. Wiley.

Jia, J., & Zhang, Q. (2008, May). Competitions and dynamics of duopoly wireless service providers in dynamic spectrum market. In *Proceedings of the 9th ACM international symposium on Mobile ad hoc networking and computing* (pp. 313-322). ACM.

Jørgensen, S. (1986). Optimal production, purchasing and pricing: A differential game approach. *European Journal of Operational Research, 24*(1), 64-76.

Jørgensen, S., & Zaccour, G. (2004). *Differential games in marketing* (Vol. 15). Springer.

Jørgensen, S., & Zaccour, G. (2007). Developments in differential game theory and numerical methods: economic and management applications. *Computational Management Science*, *4*(2), 159-181.

Karray, S., & Martín-Herrán, G. (2009). A dynamic model for advertising and pricing competition between national and store brands. *European Journal of Operational Research, 193*(2), 451-467.

Key, P. B., & McAuley, D. R. (1999). Differential QoS and pricing in networks: Where flow control meets game theory. *IEE Proceedings-Software*, *146*(1), 39-43.

Khaled, M. K. (2009). *Managing Web Service Quality: Measuring Outcomes and Effectiveness*. Information Science Reference.

Kogan, K., & Tapiero, C. (2008). Vertical pricing competition in supply chains: the effect of production experience and coordination. *International Transactions in Operational Research, 15*(4), 461-479.

Kogan, K., & Tapiero, C. S. (2007). *Supply Chain Games: Operations Management and Risk Valuation: Operations Management and Risk Evaluation* (Vol. 113). Springer.

Kreger, H. (2003). Fulfilling the Web services promise. *Communications of the ACM, 46*(6), 29-ff.

Lin, Z., Ramanathan, S., & Zhao, H. (2005). Usage-based dynamic pricing of Web services for optimizing resource allocation. *Information Systems and E-Business Management*, *3*(3), 221-242.

Li, Q., & Liu, Z. (2014). An investigation on research and development cost reduction and channel strategies in competing supply chains. *International Journal of Industrial Engineering Computations*, *5*(3), 387-394.

Mani, A ., &Nagarajan, A . (2002). Understating quality of service for web services. URL: http://www-128.ibm.com/developerworks /webservices/library/ws-qual-ity.html .

Mehlmann, A. (1988). *Applied Differential Games*. Plenum.

Pan, W., Yu, L., Wang, S., Hua, G., Xie, G., & Zhang, J. (2009). Dynamic Pricing Strategy of Provider with Different QoS Levels in Web Service. *Journal of Networks*, *4*(4), 228-235.

Rahchamandi, E., & Fallahi, K. (2014). An investigation on logistics outsourcing on exports of minerals goods. *Uncertain Supply Chain Management*, *2*(3), 163-166.

Rezaei-Malek, M & Tavakkoli-Moghaddam, R. (2014). Robust humanitarian relief logistics network planning. *Uncertain Supply Chain Management*, 2(2), 73-96.

Vega-Redondo, F. (2003). *Economics and the Theory of Games*. Cambridge university press.

Rosen, J. B. (1965). Existence and uniqueness of equilibrium points for concave n-person games. *Econometrica: Journal of the Econometric Society*, 520-534.

Schwind, M. (2007). *Dynamic Pricing and Automated Resource Allocation for Complex Information Services*. Springer-Verlag Berlin Heidelberg.

Sethi, S. P., &Thompson, G. L. (2000). *Optimal control theory applications to management science and economics*. Springer.

Starr, A. W., & Ho, Y. C. (1969). Nonzero-sum differential games. *Journal of Optimization Theory and Applications*, *3*(3), 184-206.

Taheri, M., Ebrahimi, S & Khoshalhan, F. (2014). Game-theoretic analysis of supply chain coordination under advertising and price dependent demand. *International Journal of Industrial Engineering Computations,* 5(3), 395-406.

Talluri, K. T., & Van Ryzin, G. J. (2006). *The theory and practice of revenue management* (Vol. 68). springer.

Thomas, G. B., Finney, R. L. (1996). *Calculus and Analytic Geometry.* Addison-Wesley Publishing Company.

Tripathi, R & Mishra, S. (2014). Inventory model with inventory-dependent demand for deteriorating items in a single warehouse system. *Uncertain Supply Chain Management*, 2(4), 209-218.

Weber, T. A. (2011). Optimal control theory with applications in economics. *MIT Press Books, 1*.

Wierstra, E., Kulenkampff, G., & Schaffers, H. (2001). A framework for analysing strategies of Internet Service Providers. *Netnomics, 3*(1), 35-65.

Wu, J. (2008, August). Mechanism of Pricing Dynamically for Web Services. In *Web-based Learning, 2008. ICWL 2008. Seventh International Conference on* (pp. 9-13). IEEE.

Xu, K., Chiang, W. Y. K., & Liang, L. (2011). Dynamic pricing and channel efficiency in the presence of the cost learning effect. *International Transactions in Operational Research, 18*(5), 579-604.

Zhang, Z., Dey, D., & Tan, Y. (2008). Price and QoS competition in data communication services. *European Journal of Operational Research, 187*(3), 871-886.

Zhang, Z., Tan, Y., & Dey, D. (2009). Price competition with service level guarantee in web services. *Decision Support Systems, 47*(2), 93-104.

Zhao, J. L., & Cheng, H. K. (2005). Web services and process management: a union of convenience or a new area of research?. *Decision Support Systems, 40*(1), 1-8.

Appendix A

In this section, we would like to show that $\frac{\partial p_{k,i}}{\partial \alpha_{k,i}(t)}, \frac{\partial p_{k,i}}{\partial \alpha_{k^{-1},i}(t)}, \frac{\partial p_{k,i}}{\partial \delta_{k,i}(t)}, \frac{\partial p_{k,i}}{\partial \delta_{k^{-1},i}(t)} > 0$, $\frac{\partial p_{k,i}}{\partial \beta_{k,i}(t)}, \frac{\partial p_{k,i}}{\partial \beta_{k^{-1},i}(t)} < 0.$

Proof: $\frac{dp_{k,i}}{d\alpha_{k,i}} = \frac{-2\beta_{k^{-1},i}}{\delta_{k^{-1},i}\delta_{k,i} - 4\beta_{k,i}\beta_{k^{-1},i}}$, since $-2\beta_{k^{-1},i} < 0$ and $\delta_{k^{-1},i}\delta_{k,i} - 4\beta_{k,i}\beta_{k^{-1},i} < 0$, so that $\frac{\partial p_{k,i}}{\partial \alpha_{k,i}(t)} > 0$.

$\frac{dp_{k,i}}{d\alpha_{k^{-1},i}} = \frac{-\delta_{k^{-1},i}}{\delta_{k^{-1},i}\delta_{k,i} - 4\beta_{k,i}\beta_{k^{-1},i}}$, since $-\delta_{k^{-1},i} < 0$ and $\delta_{k^{-1},i}\delta_{k,i} - 4\beta_{k,i}\beta_{k^{-1},i} < 0$, so that $\frac{\partial p_{k,i}}{\partial \alpha_{k^{-1},i}(t)} > 0.$

$$\frac{dp_{k,i}}{d\beta_{k,i}} = -2\beta_{k^{-1},i}\left(\frac{-\lambda'_{k,k,i}\lambda_{k^{-1},k^{-1},i}\delta_{k^{-1},i}\delta_{k,i} + 4\alpha_{k,i}\beta_{k^{-1},i}\lambda_{k,k,i}\lambda_{k^{-1},k^{-1},i}}{\lambda_{k,k,i}\lambda_{k^{-1},k^{-1},i}(\delta_{k^{-1},i}\delta_{k,i} - 4\beta_{k,i}\beta_{k^{-1},i})^2} + \frac{-2\delta_{k,i}\lambda_{k,k,i}\beta_{k^{-1},i}\lambda'_{k,^{-1}k^{-1},i} + 2\alpha_{k^{-1},i}\delta_{k,i}\lambda_{k,k,i}\lambda_{k^{-1},k^{-1},i}}{\lambda_{k,k,i}\lambda_{k^{-1},k^{-1},i}(\delta_{k^{-1},i}\delta_{k,i} - 4\beta_{k,i}\beta_{k^{-1},i})^2}\right),$$

since $-\lambda'_{k,k,i}\lambda_{k^{-1},k^{-1},i}\delta_{k^{-1},i}\delta_{k,i} > 0$, $4\alpha_{k,i}\beta_{k^{-1},i}\lambda_{k,k,i}\lambda_{k^{-1},k^{-1},i} > 0$, $-2\delta_{k,i}\lambda_{k,k,i}\beta_{k^{-1},i}\lambda'_{k,^{-1}k^{-1},i} > 0$ and $2\alpha_{k^{-1},i}\delta_{k,i}\lambda_{k,k,i}\lambda_{k^{-1},k^{-1},i} > 0$, thus sum of these expression is non-negative, Also $-2\beta_{k^{-1},i} < 0$, provide that numerator expression of $\frac{dp_{k,i}}{d\beta_{k,i}}$ is non-positive. Furthermore, since $\lambda_{k,k,i}\lambda_{k^{-1},k^{-1},i}(\delta_{k^{-1},i}\delta_{k,i} - 4\beta_{k,i}\beta_{k^{-1},i}) > 0$, so that $\frac{dp_{k,i}}{d\beta_{k,i}} < 0.$

$$\frac{dp_{k,i}}{d\beta_{k^{-1},i}} = -\delta_{k,i}\left(\frac{-2\lambda'_{k,k,i}\lambda_{k^{-1},k^{-1},i}\delta_{k^{-1},i}\beta_{k,i} + 2\alpha_{k,i}\delta_{k^{-1},i}\lambda_{k,k,i}\lambda_{k^{-1},k^{-1},i}}{\lambda_{k,k,i}\lambda_{k^{-1},k^{-1},i}(\delta_{k^{-1},i}\delta_{k,i} - 4\beta_{k,i}\beta_{k^{-1},i})^2} + \frac{-\delta_{k,i}\lambda_{k,k,i}\delta_{k^{-1},i}\lambda'_{k,^{-1}k^{-1},i} + 4\alpha_{k^{-1},i}\beta_{k,i}\lambda_{k,k,i}\lambda_{k^{-1},k^{-1},i}}{\lambda_{k,k,i}\lambda_{k^{-1},k^{-1},i}(\delta_{k^{-1},i}\delta_{k,i} - 4\beta_{k,i}\beta_{k^{-1},i})^2}\right),$$ since

$-2\lambda'_{k,k,i}\lambda_{k^{-1},k^{-1},i}\delta_{k^{-1},i}\beta_{k,i} > 0$, $2\alpha_{k,i}\delta_{k^{-1},i}\lambda_{k,k,i}\lambda_{k^{-1},k^{-1},i} > 0$, $-\delta_{k,i}\lambda_{k,k,i}\delta_{k^{-1},i}\lambda'_{k,^{-1}k^{-1},i} > 0$ and $\alpha_{k^{-1},i}\beta_{k,i}\lambda_{k,k,i}\lambda_{k^{-1},k^{-1},i} > 0$, so that sum of these expressions is non-negative. Also, since $-\delta_{k,i} < 0$ and $\lambda_{k,k,i}\lambda_{k^{-1},k^{-1},i}(\delta_{k^{-1},i}\delta_{k,i} - 4\beta_{k,i}\beta_{k^{-1},i}) > 0$, thus $\frac{dp_{k,i}}{d\beta_{k^{-1},i}} < 0.$

$$\frac{dp_{k,i}}{d\delta_{k,i}} = 2\beta_{k^{-1},i}\left(\frac{-2\lambda'_{k^{-1},k^{-1},i}\lambda_{k,k,i}\beta_{k^{-1},i}\beta_{k,i} + 2\alpha_{k^{-1},i}\beta_{k,i}\lambda_{k,k,i}\lambda_{k^{-1},k^{-1},i}}{\lambda_{k,k,i}\lambda_{k^{-1},k^{-1},i}(\delta_{k^{-1},i}\delta_{k,i} - 4\beta_{k,i}\beta_{k^{-1},i})^2} + \frac{-\beta_{k,i}\lambda_{k^{-1},k^{-1},i}\delta_{k^{-1},i}\lambda'_{k,k,i} + \alpha_{k,i}\delta_{k^{-1},i}\lambda_{k,k,i}\lambda_{k^{-1},k^{-1},i}}{\lambda_{k,k,i}\lambda_{k^{-1},k^{-1},i}(\delta_{k^{-1},i}\delta_{k,i} - 4\beta_{k,i}\beta_{k^{-1},i})^2}\right),$$ since

$-2\lambda'_{k^{-1},k^{-1},i}\lambda_{k,k,i}\beta_{k^{-1},i}\beta_{k,i} > 0$, $2\alpha_{k^{-1},i}\beta_{k,i}\lambda_{k,k,i}\lambda_{k^{-1},k^{-1},i} > 0$, $-\beta_{k,i}\lambda_{k^{-1},k^{-1},i}\delta_{k^{-1},i}\lambda'_{k,k,i} > 0$ and $\alpha_{k,i}\delta_{k^{-1},i}\lambda_{k,k,i}\lambda_{k^{-1},k^{-1},i} > 0$, so that sum of these expressions is non-negative. Furthermore, since $2\beta_{k^{-1},i} > 0$ and

$\lambda_{k,k,i}\lambda_{k^{-1},k^{-1},i}(\delta_{k^{-1},i}\delta_{k,i} - 4\beta_{k,i}\beta_{k^{-1},i}) > 0$, so that $\frac{dp_{k,i}}{d\delta_{k,i}} > 0.$

$$\frac{dp_{k,i}}{d\delta_{k^{-1},i}} = \delta_{k,i}\left(\frac{-2\lambda'_{k,k,i}\lambda_{k^{-1},k^{-1},i}\beta_{k^{-1},i}\beta_{k,i} + 2\alpha_{k,i}\beta_{k^{-1},i}\lambda_{k,k,i}\lambda_{k^{-1},k^{-1},i}}{\lambda_{k,k,i}\lambda_{k^{-1},k^{-1},i}(\delta_{k^{-1},i}\delta_{k,i} - 4\beta_{k,i}\beta_{k^{-1},i})^2} + \frac{-\delta_{k,i}\lambda_{k,k,i}\beta_{k^{-1},i}\lambda'_{k^{-1},k^{-1},i} + \alpha_{k^{-1},i}\delta_{k,i}\lambda_{k,k,i}\lambda_{k^{-1},k^{-1},i}}{\lambda_{k,k,i}\lambda_{k^{-1},k^{-1},i}(\delta_{k^{-1},i}\delta_{k,i} - 4\beta_{k,i}\beta_{k^{-1},i})^2}\right),$$

Since $-2\lambda'_{k,k,i}\lambda_{k^{-1},k^{-1},i}\beta_{k^{-1},i}\beta_{k,i} > 0$, $2\alpha_{k,i}\beta_{k^{-1},i}\lambda_{k,k,i}\lambda_{k^{-1},k^{-1},i} > 0$, $-\delta_{k,i}\lambda_{k,k,i}\beta_{k^{-1},i}\lambda'_{k^{-1},k^{-1},i} > 0$ and $\alpha_{k^{-1},i}\delta_{k,i}\lambda_{k,k,i}\lambda_{k^{-1},k^{-1},i} > 0$, so that sum of these expressions is non-negative. Also, since $\delta_{k,i} > 0$ and $\lambda_{k,k,i}\lambda_{k^{-1},k^{-1},i}(\delta_{k^{-1},i}\delta_{k,i} - 4\beta_{k,i}\beta_{k^{-1},i}) > 0$, thus $\dfrac{dp_{k,i}}{d\delta_{k^{-1},i}} > 0$.

12

Sensitivity analysis for casting process under stochastic modelling

Amit Kumar[a], Aman Kumar Varshney[b] and Mangey Ram[a*]

[a]*Department of Mathematics, Graphic Era University Dehradun-248002, Uttarakhand, India*
[b]*Department of Mechanical Engineering, Graphic Era University Dehradun-248002, Uttarakhand, India*

CHRONICLE

Keywords:
System Safety
Sensitivity Analysis
Casting Model
Foundry Work
Cost-effectiveness

ABSTRACT

The present paper studies the reliability analysis of the casting process in foundry work using a probabilistic approach. As foundry industries in many developing countries suffer from poor quality of casting due to improper management, lack of resources and wrong working methods followed, which results in the decrement of productivity. Hence, to ensure the quality and productivity, favorable steps must be taken. The considered casting system has four main types of defects; namely mold shift, shrinkage, cold shut and blowholes. The complete casting system can fail due to the misalignment of the mold and combination of defects such as shrinkage and blow holes and can also fail by defects of shrinkage, blow holes and cold shut, simultaneously. The system is analyzed with the help of the supplementary variable technique and Laplace transformation. The availability, reliability, mean time to failure, sensitivity analysis and cost-effectiveness have been evaluated for the considered system. The results have been shown with the help of graphs, which predicts the behavior of the casting process system when any one of the defect or more than one defect appears.

1. Introduction

Casting is a process of pouring molten metal into a mold cavity and allowing it to solidify to obtain a desired product. By this process, intricate part can be given strength and rigidity, which is not frequently obtained by other methods.

Casting is generally based on a number of parameters such as mold, cavity, temperature of molten material and the most important is the experience of the designer. In casting many unquantifiable factors such as shrinkage, mold shift, cold shut, blow holes, porosity lead to conservative design rules. Unquantifiable factors are the ones with an unknown state of defect. The foundry industry suffers from poor quality and productivity due to a large number of parameters affecting it such as shortage of skilled labor, the poor working process followed, etc. Casting defect result in increased unit cost and lower morale of shop floor personnel. Close control and standardization of all aspects of production technique offer the best protection against casting defect. Due to a wide range of possible factors, reasonable classification of casting defect is difficult.

The ability and efficiency of the casting process can be predicted by using the concept of reliability. Redundancies play essential role in increasing the reliability characteristics of systems (Ram & Kumar, 2014). High reliability of the system increases the efficiency of the production (Kumar & Ram, 2013). Reliability measures are the foremost concern in the planning, design, and operation of any system or equipment. Many researchers, including Pan (1997) discussed a multi-stage production system with one machine/tool in active state and *n* spares in standby state. Pan found that when the operating machine/tool breaks down, a switching device detects the machine failure via the sensor and the defective tool is replaced with a functional spare, so the system can resume its operations. Cavalca (2003) presented an availability optimization problem of an engineering system assembled in series configuration, by using genetic algorithm. Barabady and Kumar (2007) defined availability importance measures in order to calculate the criticality of each component or subsystem from the availability point of view and also demonstrated the application of such important measures for achieving optimal resource allocation to arrive at the best possible available. Filieri et al. (2010) focused on a CB software system that operates in safety-critical environment, where a relevant quality factor is the system reliability, defined as a probabilistic measure of the system's ability to successfully carry out its own task.

The other authors also (Ram & Singh, 2008, 2010; Ram, 2010, Ram et al., 2013) analyzed and evaluated the reliability measures for various engineering models under the concept of Gumbel-Hougaard family copula with different repair policies. Gupta and Sharma (1993) developed different models and analyzed the failure by computing the reliability measures such as availability, cost estimation, mean time to failure. Sutaria et al. (2012) discussed the capability to predict the temporal evolution of the interface and to identify that multiple hotspots is validated with an industrial aluminum-alloy lug casting. Venkatesan et al. (2005) discussed and developed a program for finite element modelling of casting solidification. The salient features of the program are: facility to incorporate latent heat through enthalpy method, incorporation of air gap by coincident node technique, ability to handle non-linear transient heat conduction through temperature dependent material properties, and object oriented programming. Tzong and Lee (1992) presented an investigation that an enthalpy formulation could be applied to the solidification process of an arbitrarily shaped casting in a mold-casting system. The effect of thermal contact resistance existing at the mold-casting interface was also studied. Joshi and Ravi (2010) defined shape complexity factor using weighted criteria based on part geometry parameters such as number of cored features, volume and surface area of the part, core volume, section thickness and draw distance.

Mares and Sokolowski (2010) evaluated the level of improvement in the metal casting analysis by the means of the Artificial intelligence-Based control system and found that the accuracy, reliability and timelines were significantly increased to a high level. Wu et al. (2010) developed a process to fabricate turbine blades with abnormal film cooling holes by combining stereo lithography technology with gelcasting technology. To decrease the drying shrinkage, the freeze-drying technique was applied to treat the wet ceramic casting mold green body surrounded by stereo lithography mold and the proper sintering process parameters was determined for lowering the sintered shrinkage. Hojjati-Emami et al. (2012) proposed a model that analyses the interaction between human and advanced driver assistance system (ADAS) for reducing human error in road accidents. Soltani (2014) discussed about reliability optimization including redundancy allocation, reliability allocation and reliability redundancy allocation. Yang and Li (2010) provided a useful understanding of chip formation process and also helped in optimizing machining parameters and process of high speed milling of alloy cast iron. Sakalli et al. (2011) proposed a chance-constrained stochastic programing approach for the blending problem in the brass casting industry to handle the statistical variation in raw material. Qi and Li (2012) investigated metadynamic recrystallization of the as cast 42CrMo steel after normalizing and tempering during the hot compression. Zhang and Li (2013) provided a work, which focuses on the determination of interfacial heat transfer coefficient between the casting and metal chill during casting solidification. The proposed method is established based on the least square technique and sequential function specification method and can be applied to calculate heat fluxes and interfacial heat transfer coefficient for other alloys. Yourui et al. (2014) presented the reliability modelling and optimization of die casting. The authors applied finite element analysis to simulate the process of die-casting, and the quadratic response surface to represent the multidisciplinary optimization model of die-casting, in which they used evidence theory to represent the epistemic uncertainty. It is also well known that casting is an economical and efficient technology for producing metal parts. In the present scenario, casting technology is in its advanced form due the development of CAD engineers (Cleary, 2010). To prevent the defect and to increase productivity, various techniques like linear programing, Melt conditioner, Twin-roll strip casting and Auto-Cast-X software were used by different authors (Choudhari et al., 2014; Haghayeghi et al., 2010; Wang et al., 2010; Park & Yang, 2011).

Nowadays, several types of composite material exist, which play wide and extensive roles in manufacturing engineering components (Li et al., 2010; Thomas et al., 2014; Moses et al., 2014, Onat, 2010). Akhil et al. (2014) reported the cooling characteristics of cast components with varying section size and investigated how cooling rate and mechanical properties vary with varying section size. Tabibian et al. (2010) defined a thermo-mechanical fatigue criterion in order to predict the failure of cylinder heads issued with the lost foam casting process. Hamasaiid et al. (2010) proposed an analytical model to predict the time varying thermal conductance at the casting-die interface during solidification of light alloy during high pressure die-casting. System reliability occupies progressively more significant use in casting, manufacturing system, standby systems etc. Maintaining a high or required level of accuracy is often an essential requirement of the system. The study of the repairmen is an essential part of the repairable system and can affect the economy of the system directly or indirectly. Therefore, his/her action and work frames are vital in improving the reliability of repairable system.

2. Problem Statement

In the present paper, we deal with the reliability analysis of the casting process in foundry work. This research is intended to explain how much a defect can affect the casting system and its performance. Casting is done to provide strength and rigidity to the parts or system for bearing mechanical impacts. So, the reliability measures of the product are important criteria of judging the product life. There are four common defects, which affect the shape and size of the cast during casting, namely, mold shift, shrinkage, cold shut and blow holes. The state transition diagram of the proposed model has been shown in Fig. 1.

2.1 Causes and Repairing Technique of Casting Defect

2.2.1 Mold Shift

It results in a mismatching of top and bottom part of a casting, usually at the parting line. It occurs due to the following reasons:

(a) Misalignment of pattern parts, due to worn or damaged patterns,
(b) Misalignment of molding box or flask equipment.

This defect can be eliminated by ensuring proper alignment of the pattern, molding boxes and providing proper shrinkage and draft allowances etc.

2.2.2 Shrinkage

It is a defect when the thick metal solidifies. Generally, this defect occurs at hot spots. This is due to the following reasons:

(a) Improper location and size of gates and runners,
(b) Incorrect metal composition,
(c) Incorrect pouring temperature.

This defect can be eliminated by the use of feeders and chills at proper locations to promote directional solidification.

2.2.3 Cold Shut

Cold shut is a crack with round edges form due to the low melting temperature or poor gating system. This is due to the following reasons:

(a) Too small gates,
(b) Too many restrictions on gating system,
(c) Lack of fluidity in molten metal.

This defect can be eliminated by the proper use of a runner, riser and pouring temperature.

2.2.4 Blowholes

It is a defect which is caused by air and gases entrapped in the solidifying metal. This is due to the following reasons:

(a) Low gas permeability of the core sand,
(b) Improper ramming.

This defect can be eliminated by changing the hardness of mold, use of appropriate sand with adequate green compact strength.

2.3 Inspection of Casting

Casting is inspected thoroughly to find the presence of internal flaws as well as well external defects. The various methods of inspecting casting are

(i) Visual examination,
(ii) Sound or percussion test,
(iii) Pressure test,
(iv) Magnetic and fluorescent powder inspection,
(v) Radiographic examination,
(vi) Ultrasonic testing.

3. Assumptions and Notations

The following assumptions have been taken throughout the model:

(i) Initially, the casting system is free from defects.
(ii) The casting system can consist of four defects.
(iii) Each defect is either present or absent.
(iv) After repair or remedies, casting system is free from defects.
(v) When the major defect occurs in the casting system the cast component fails.

Further, the following notations are used:

○	Indicates that the system is in good condition,
▱	Indicates that the system is in a degraded condition,
▭	Indicate that the system has failed condition,
$P_0(t)$	The probability that at time t system is working to full capacity,
$P_1(t)$	The probability that at time t system is failed due to defect of mold shift,
$P_2(t)$	The probability that at time t system is in a degraded state with blowholes defect,
$P_3(t)$	The probability that at time t system is in a degraded state with blowholes and shrinkage defect,

$P_4(t)$	The probability that at time t system is in a degraded state with blowholes and cold shut defect,
$P_5(t)$	The probability that at time t system is failed due to defect of shrinkage, blowholes and cold shut,
$P_6(t)$	The probability that at time t system is failed due to defect of mold shift, blowholes and cold shut,
λ_0	Failure rate of shrinkage and blowholes,
λ_c	Failure rate of mold shift,
λ_n	Failure rate of cold shut,
μ_0	Repair rate of shrinkage,
η	Repair rate of blowholes,
μ	Repair rate of remaining units,
K_1	Revenue per unit time,
K_2	Service cost per unit time.

4. State Transition Diagram

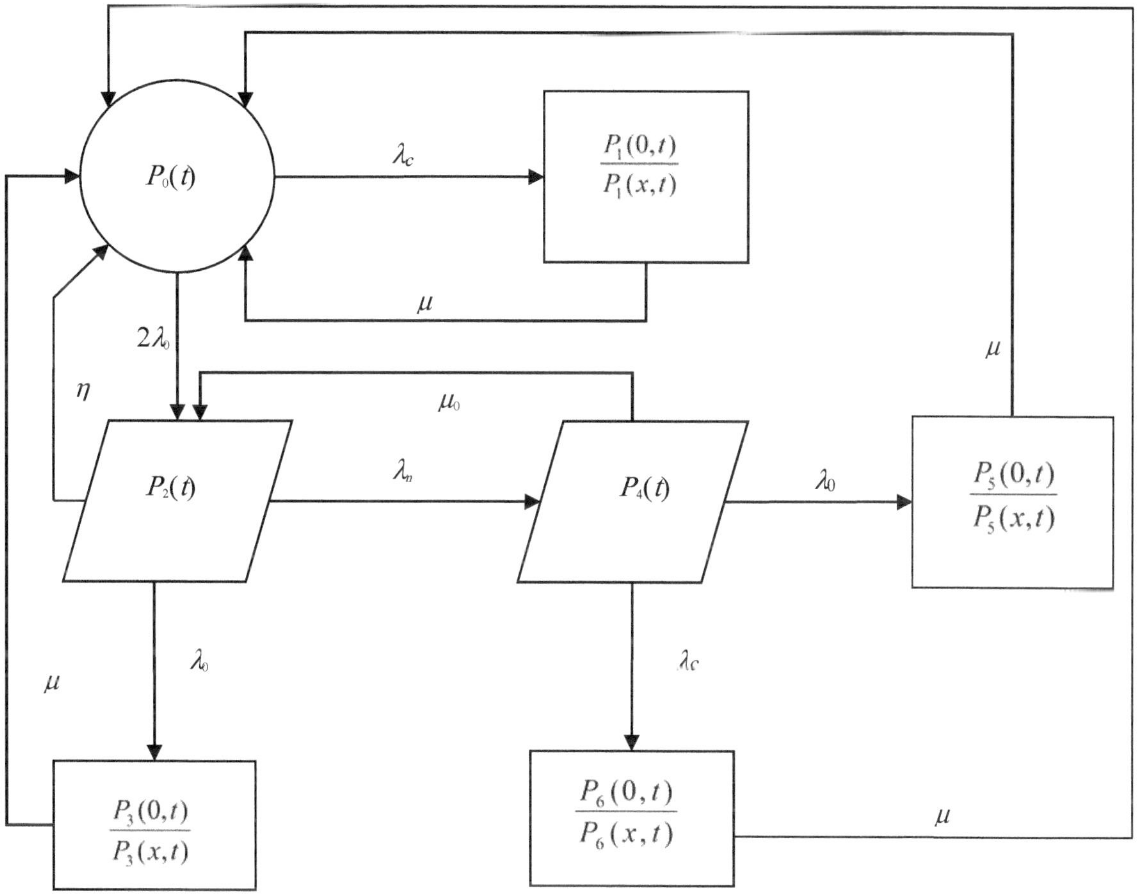

Fig. 1. State Transition Diagram

5. Mathematical Formulation and Solution of the Model

By the probability considerations and continuity arguments we can obtain the following set of difference differential equations governing the present mathematical model

$$\left(\frac{\partial}{\partial t}+2\lambda_0+\lambda_c\right)P_0(t)=\eta P_2(t)+\sum_{i=1,3,5,6}\int_0^\infty \mu P_i(x,t)dx \tag{1}$$

$$\left(\frac{\partial}{\partial t}+\eta+\lambda_0+\lambda_n\right)P_2(t)=2\lambda_0 P_0(t)+\mu_0 P_4(t) \tag{2}$$

$$\left(\frac{\partial}{\partial t}+\mu_0+\lambda_0+\lambda_c\right)P_4(t)=\lambda_n P_2(t) \tag{3}$$

$$\left(\frac{\partial}{\partial x}+\frac{\partial}{\partial t}+\mu\right)P_i(x,t)=0, i=1,3,5,6 \tag{4}$$

Boundary Conditions

$$P_1(0,t)=\lambda_c P_0(t) \tag{5}$$

$$P_3(0,t)=\lambda_0 P_2(t) \tag{6}$$

$$P_5(0,t)=\lambda_0 P_4(t) \tag{7}$$

$$P_6(0,t)=\lambda_c P_4(t) \tag{8}$$

Initial condition

$P_0(0)=1$ and all state probabilities are zero at $t = 0$. (9)

Taking Laplace transformation from Eq. (1) to Eq. (8).

$$(s+2\lambda_0+\lambda_c)\overline{P}_0(s)=1+\eta\overline{P}_2(s)+\sum_{i=1,3,5,6}\int_0^\infty \mu\overline{P}_i(x,s)dx \tag{10}$$

$$(s+\eta+\lambda_0+\lambda_n)\overline{P}_2(s)=2\lambda_0\overline{P}_0(s)+\mu_0\overline{P}_4(s) \tag{11}$$

$$(s+\mu_0+\lambda_0+\lambda_c)\overline{P}_4(s)=\lambda_n\overline{P}_2(s) \tag{12}$$

$$\left(\frac{\partial}{\partial x}+s+\mu\right)\overline{P}_i(x,s)=0; i=1,3,5,6 \tag{13}$$

$$\overline{P}_1(0,s)=\lambda_c\overline{P}_0(s) \tag{14}$$

$$\overline{P}_3(0,s)=\lambda_0\overline{P}_2(s) \tag{15}$$

$$\overline{P}_5(0,s)=\lambda_0\overline{P}_4(s) \tag{16}$$

$$\overline{P}_6(0,s)=\lambda_c\overline{P}_4(s) \tag{17}$$

Solving the Eqs. (10-13) with the help of Eqs. (14-17) and Eq. (9), one can obtain

$$\overline{P}_0(s)=\frac{1}{(s+\lambda_c+2\lambda_0)-H_1-H_2\overline{T}_1(s)-\overline{T}_1(s)\lambda_c-H_2\overline{T}_1(s)} \tag{18}$$

$$\overline{P}_1(s)=\frac{\lambda_c\overline{P}_0(s)}{(s-\mu)} \tag{19}$$

$$\overline{P}_2(s)=\frac{2\lambda_0\overline{P}_0(s)(s+\mu_0+\lambda_0+\lambda_c)}{H_4} \tag{20}$$

$$\overline{P}_3(s)=\frac{2\lambda^2{}_0\overline{P}_0(s)(s+\mu_0+\lambda_0+\lambda_c)}{(s-\mu)H_4} \tag{21}$$

$$\overline{P}_4(s) = \frac{2\lambda_0 \lambda_n \overline{P}_0(s)}{H_4} \tag{22}$$

$$\overline{P}_5(s) = \frac{2\lambda^2{}_0 \lambda_n \overline{P}_0(s)}{(s-\mu) H_4} \tag{23}$$

$$\overline{P}_6(s) = \frac{2\lambda_0 \lambda_n \lambda_c \overline{P}_0(s)}{(s-\mu) H_4} \tag{24}$$

where

$$H_1 = \frac{2\lambda_0 \eta (s+\mu_0+\lambda_0+\lambda_c)}{H_4},\ H_2 = \frac{2\lambda^2{}_0 (s+\mu_0+\lambda_0+\lambda_c)}{H_4},\ H_3 = \frac{2\lambda_0 \lambda_n (\lambda_c+\lambda_0)}{H_4},$$

$$H_4 = (s+\eta+\lambda_0+\lambda_n)(s+\mu_0+\lambda_0+\lambda_c) - \mu\lambda_0 .$$

The Laplace transformation of the probabilities that the system is in the up (i.e. good or degraded) and down (i.e. failed) state at any time is as follows

$$\overline{P}_{up}(s) = \overline{P}_0(s) + \overline{P}_2(s) + \overline{P}_4(s) \tag{25}$$

$$\overline{P}_{down}(s) = \overline{P}_1(s) + \overline{P}_3(s) + \overline{P}_5(s) + \overline{P}_6(s) \tag{26}$$

6. Particular Cases and Numerical Computations

6.1 Availability Analysis

Taking the values of different parameters as $\lambda_c = 0.2, \lambda_0 = 0.25, \lambda_n = 0.1, \mu = 1, \mu_0 = \eta = 1$ in Eq. (25) taking inverse the Laplace transform, we get the availability of the system

$$P_{up}(t) = \begin{pmatrix} 0.8206686930 + 0.1793313070e^{-1.275t} \cos(0.1391194109t) \\ +0.205891151e^{-1.275t} \sin(0.1391941091t) \end{pmatrix} \tag{27}$$

Now, taking t=0 to 10 units of time in Eq. (27), one can get the Table 1 and Fig. 2 respectively.

Table 1
Availability as function of time

Time (t)	0	1	2	3	4	5	6	7	8	9	10
Availability	1.00000	0.87827	0.83854	0.82606	0.82225	0.82112	0.82079	0.82070	0.82067	0.82067	0.82066

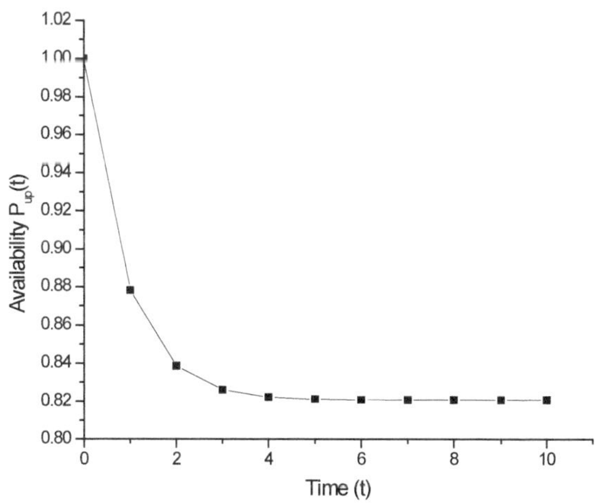

Fig. 2. Availability as function of time

6.2 Reliability Analysis

Taking all repair rates equal to be zero and failure rates $\lambda_c = 0.2, \lambda_0 = 0.25, \lambda_n = 0.1$ in Eq. (25) and then taking the inverse Laplace transform, the reliability of the system is given as

$$R(t) = 1.571428571e^{(-0.7t)} + 2.857142857e^{(-0.525t)} \sinh(0.175t) + 1.428571429e^{(-0.35t)} - 2e^{(-0.45t)} \tag{28}$$

Now, taking t=0 to 10 units of time in the Eq. (28), we get the Table 2 and Fig. 3 respectively.

Table 2
Reliability as function of time

Time (t)	0	1	2	3	4	5	6	7	8	9	10
Availability	1.00000	0.80907	0.64090	0.49883	0.38265	0.29001	0.21606	0.16191	0.11962	0.08785	0.06419

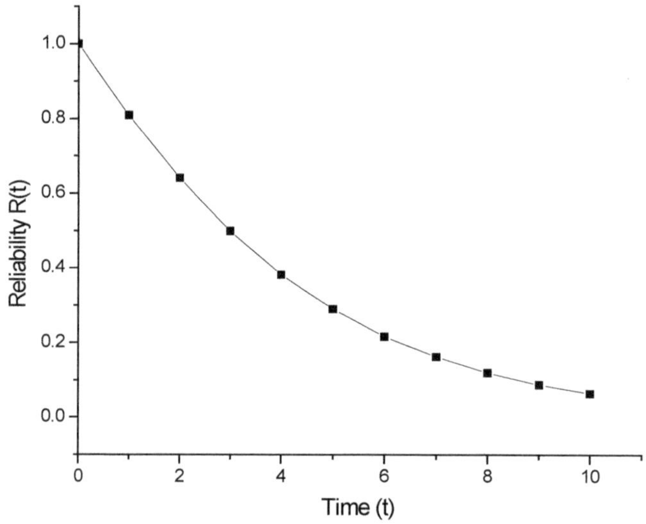

Fig. 3. Reliability as function of time

6.3 Mean Time to Failure (MTTF) Analysis

Taking all repair rates to be zero in Eq. (25) and taking s tends to zero; one can obtain the mean time to failure (MTTF) of the system as

$$MTTF = \frac{1}{(\lambda_c + 2\lambda_0)} + \frac{2\lambda_0}{(\lambda_c + 2\lambda_0)(\lambda_0 + \lambda_n)} + \frac{2\lambda_0\lambda_n}{(\lambda_c + 2\lambda_0)(\lambda_0 + \lambda_n)(\lambda_c + \lambda_0)} \tag{29}$$

Setting $\lambda_c = 0.2, \lambda_0 = 0.25, \lambda_n = 0.1$ and varying λ_c, λ_0, λ_n one by one from 0.1 to 0.9 in Eq. (29), we get the following Table 3 and Fig. 4.

Table 3
MTTF as function of failure rates

Variation in	0.1	0.2	0.3	0.4	0.5	0.6	0.7	0.8	0.9
λ_c	4.72789	3.92290	3.36038	2.94261	2.61904	2.36058	2.14912	1.97278	1.823425
λ_0	5.83333	5.55555	4.10714	3.24444	2.67676	2.27629	1.97916	1.75018	4.53703
λ_n	3.92290	5.27777	5.00000	4.83333	4.72222	4.64285	4.58333	1.56842	4.50000

6.4 Sensitivity Analysis

The sensitivity of the reliability is a demanding input factor, which is most regularly defined as the partial derivative of the reliability with respect to that factor. This measure is then used to estimate the outcome of factor changes on the model result without requiring a full model solution for each factor change. These input factors are mostly failure rates. In similar fashion, one can define sensitivity of MTTF with respect to input factor.

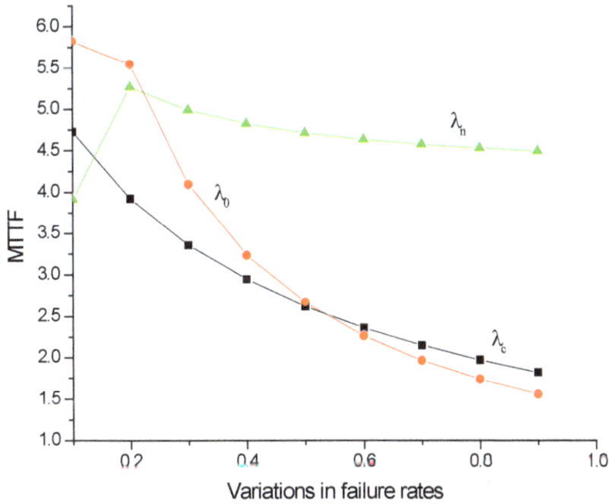

Fig. 4. MTTF as function of failure rates

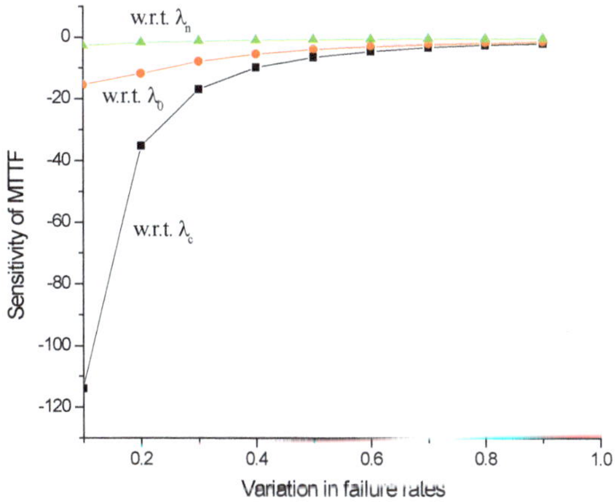

Fig. 5. Sensitivity of MTTF as function of failure rates

6.4.1 Sensitivity of MTTF

Sensitivity analysis for changes in MTTF resulting from changes in system parameters i.e. system failure rates λ_c, λ_0, λ_n. By Differentiating (29) with respect to failure rates λ_c, λ_0, λ_n respectively, we get the values of $\frac{\partial(MTTF)}{\partial\lambda_c}, \frac{\partial(MTTF)}{\partial\lambda_0}, \frac{\partial(MTTF)}{\partial\lambda_n}$.

Varying the failure rates one by one respectively as 0.1, 0.2, 0.3, 0.4, 0.5, 0.6, 0.7, 0.8, 0.9 in the partial derivatives of MTTF with respect to different failure rates, one can obtain the Table 4 and Fig. 5 respectively.

Table 4

Sensitivity of MTTF as function of failure rates

Variation in λ_c, λ_0, λ_n	$\frac{\partial(MTTF)}{\partial\lambda_c}$	$\frac{\partial(MTTF)}{\partial\lambda_0}$	$\frac{\partial(MTTF)}{\partial\lambda_n}$
0.1	-113.94557	-15.27777	-2.59151
0.2	-35.21005	11.57407	-1.56770
0.3	-16.90906	-7.62500	-1.04945
0.4	-9.90189	-5.24444	-0.75138
0.5	-6.49548	-3.78873	-0.56437
0.6	-4.58659	-2.85167	-0.43939
0.7	-3.41050	-2.21836	-0.35175
0.8	-2.63499	-1.77229	-0.28794
0.9	-2.09680	-1.44710	-0.24004

6.4.2 Sensitivity of Reliability

Here, authors perform a sensitivity analysis for changes in reliability resulting from changes in the system parameters λ_c, λ_0 and λ_n by taking all repair rates equal to zero and then taking the inverse Laplace transform in Eq. (25) and then differentiating it with respect to failure rates λ_c, λ_0 and λ_n respectively and by putting λ_c=0.02, λ_0=0.2, λ_n=0.15, get the values of $\frac{\partial R(t)}{\partial \lambda_c}, \frac{\partial R(t)}{\partial \lambda_0}, \frac{\partial R(t)}{\partial \lambda_n}$.

Now, taking t=0 to 10 units of time in the partial derivatives of reliability with respect to different failure rates, one can obtain the Table 5 and Fig. 6 respectively.

Table 5
Sensitivity of Reliability as function of time

Time (t)	$\frac{\partial R(t)}{\partial \lambda_c}$	$\frac{\partial R(t)}{\partial \lambda_0}$	$\frac{\partial R(t)}{\partial \lambda_n}$
0	0	0	0
1	-0.80600	-0.28036	-0.00094
2	-1.30893	-0.82969	-0.00546
3	-1.60326	-1.38480	-0.01324
4	-1.75275	-1.83099	-0.02253
5	-1.80150	-2.13324	-0.031638
6	-1.78071	-2.29624	-0.039342
7	-1.71294	-2.34196	-0.045008
8	-1.61467	-2.29749	-0.048458
9	-1.49808	-2.18897	-0.049821
10	-1.37209	-2.03889	-0.049407

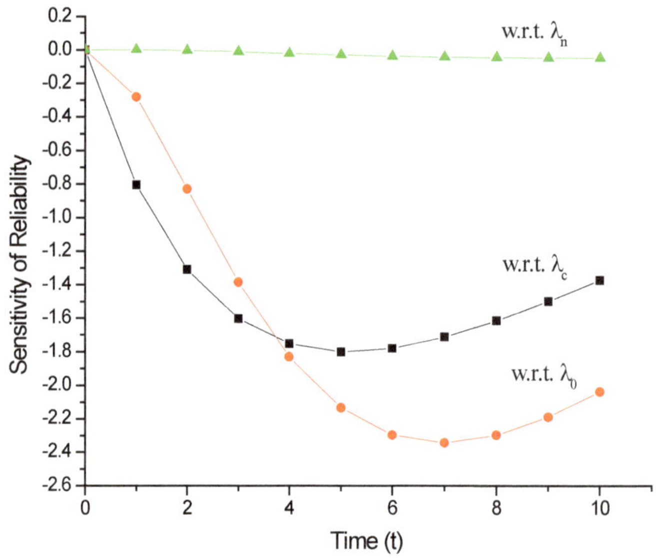

Fig. 6. Sensitivity of Reliability as function of time

6.5 Expected Profit

The expected profit during the interval [0, t) is given as

$$E_p(t) = K_1 \int_0^t P_{up}(t)dt - tK_2 \tag{30}$$

Using Eq. (25), expected profit for the same set of parameters, we have

$$E_p(t) = \begin{pmatrix} K_1[0.820668693 + 0.1793313070e^{-1.275t}\cos(0.1391194109t) \\ +0.205891151e^{-1.275t}\sin(0.1391941091t)] - tK_2 \end{pmatrix} \tag{31}$$

Setting K_1= 1 and K_2= 0.1, 0.2, 0.3, 0.4, 0.5, respectively in Eq. (31), one can get the Table 6 and correspondingly Fig.7.

Table 6
Expected profit as function of failure rates

Time (t)	Expected Profits				
	$K_2 = 0.1$	$K_2 = 0.2$	$K_2 = 0.3$	$K_2 = 0.4$	$K_2 = 0.5$
0	0	0	0	0	0
1	0.82819	0.72819	0.62819	0.52819	0.42819
2	1.58290	1.38290	1.18290	0.98290	0.78290
3	2.31401	2.01401	1.71401	1.41401	1.11401
4	3.03781	2.63781	2.23781	1.83781	1.43781
5	3.75939	3.25939	2.75939	2.25939	1.75939
6	4.48032	3.88032	3.28032	2.68032	2.08032
7	5.20106	4.50106	3.80106	3.10106	2.40106
8	5.92175	5.12175	4.32175	3.52175	2.72175
9	6.64242	5.74242	4.84242	3.94242	3.04242
10	7.36309	6.36309	5.36309	4.36309	3.36309

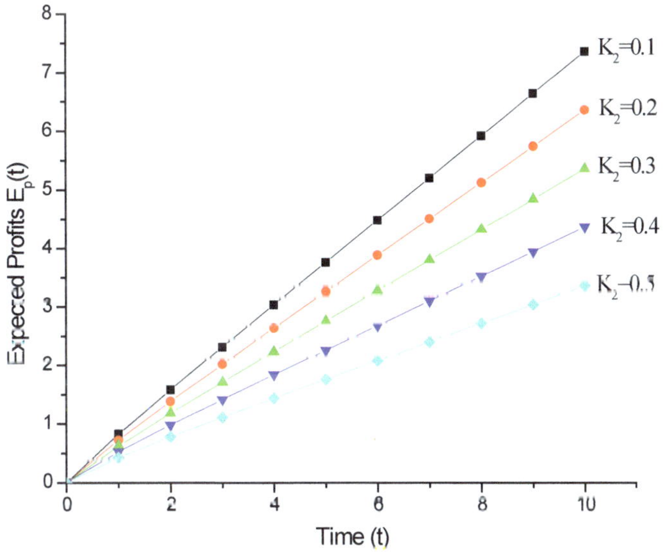

Fig.7. Expected profit as function of failure rates

7. Result Discussion

A casting model in foundry work is studied in this work. The authors have analyzed the availability, reliability, MTTF, sensitivity analysis and cost effectiveness. They numerically examined the behavior and sensitivity analysis of the system. On the basis of the above calculation and from Fig. 2, one can conclude that the availability of the system decreases swiftly when the time increases then attains a uniform value. Fig. 3 represents the variation of reliability of the system. It shows that the reliability of the system decreases precisely with the increment in time. By critically examining the Fig. 4, one can conclude that MTTF of the system decreases with respect to variation in failure rate of mold shift, Shrinkage and Blowholes and with respect to the failure rate of cold shut, first it increases then decreases. So the MTTF is the highest with respect to the failure rate of shrinkage and blowholes and the lowest with respect to the failure rate of Cold shut.

Fig. 5 shows the sensitivities of MTTF with respect to the failure rate of mold shift, shrinkage and blowholes and cold shut, which shows that it increases with the increment in failure rates. Critical observation of the graph point out that MTTF of the system is more sensitive again with respect to Failure rate of mold shift. Furthermore, the sensitivities of the system reliability with respect to the failure rate of mold shift, shrinkage and blowholes and cold shut are shown in Fig. 6. It reveals that sensitivity initially decreases with time passes. It is clear from the graph that system reliability is more sensitive with respect to failure rates of mold shift, shrinkage and blowholes. Keeping the revenue per unit time at one and varying service cost as 0.1, 0.2, 0.3, 0.4, and 0.5, one can obtain Fig. 7. It is very clear from the graph that the profit decreases as the service cost increases.

8. Conclusions

Most of the previous works were focused on finding process-related causes of individual defects, and optimized the parameter values to reduce the defects. In this work, the main focus was to predict that up to what extent our system could get affected if one of the above taken defects exists that is finally, explaining its dependency on parameter like mold shift, shrinkage, cold shut and blowholes. This will be helpful to the quality control department of casting industries to improve their productivity by minimizing the rejection of the cast parts. This work concludes the importance of the application of reliability in foundry work. Castings unfortunately can contain defects, which may render them unsuitable for service, resulting in higher costs and/or lower profits for the production foundry and delivery delays to the customer. It is also clear that the sensitivity of the system depends much more on system failure rates that is, the system can be made less sensitive by controlling its failures. It asserts that the result of this research will be useful in casting problems.

References

Akhil, K. T., Arul, S., & Sellamuthu, R. (2014). The Effect of Section Size on Cooling Rate, Microstructure and Mechanical Properties of A356 Aluminium Alloy in Casting. *Procedia Materials Science*, *5*, 362-368.

Barabady, J., & Kumar, U. (2007). Availability allocation through importance measures. *International Journal of Quality & Reliability Management*, *24*(6), 643-657.

Cavalca, K. L. (2003). Availability optimization with genetic algorithm. *International Journal of Quality & Reliability Management*, *20*(7), 847-863.

Choudhari, C. M., Narkhede, B. E., & Mahajan, S. K. (2014). Casting Design and Simulation of Cover Plate Using AutoCAST-X Software for Defect Minimization with Experimental Validation. *Procedia Materials Science*, *6*, 786-797.

Cleary, P. W. (2010). Extension of SPH to predict feeding, freezing and defect creation in low pressure die casting. *Applied Mathematical Modelling*, *34*(11), 3189-3201.

Filieri, A., Ghezzi, C., Grassi, V., & Mirandola, R. (2010). Reliability analysis of component-based systems with multiple failure modes. In *Component-Based Software Engineering* (pp. 1-20). Springer Berlin Heidelberg.

Gupta, P. P., & Sharma, M. K. (1993). Reliability and MTTF evaluation of a two duplex-unit standby system with two types of repair. *Microelectronics Reliability*, *33*(3), 291-295.

Haghayeghi, R., Zoqui, E. J., Green, N. R., & Bahai, H. (2010). An investigation on DC casting of a wrought aluminium alloy at below liquidus temperature by using melt conditioner. *Journal of Alloys and Compounds*, *502*(2), 382-386.

Hamasaiid, A., Dour, G., Loulou, T., & Dargusch, M. S. (2010). A predictive model for the evolution of the thermal conductance at the casting–die interfaces in high pressure die casting. *International Journal of Thermal Sciences*, *49*(2), 365-372.

Hojjati-Emami, K., Dhillon, B., & Jenab, K. (2012). Reliability prediction for the vehicles equipped with advanced driver assistance systems (ADAS) and passive safety systems (PSS). *International Journal of Industrial Engineering Computations*, *3*(5), 731-742.

Joshi, D., & Ravi, B. (2010). Quantifying the Shape Complexity of Cast Parts. *Computer-Aided Design and Applications*, *7*(5), 685-700.

Kumar, A., & Ram, M. (2013). Reliability measures improvement and sensitivity analysis of a coal handling unit for thermal power plant. *International Journal of Engineering-Transactions C: Aspects*, *26*(9), 1059.

Li, Q., Rottmair, C. A., & Singer, R. F. (2010). CNT reinforced light metal composites produced by melt stirring and by high pressure die casting. *Composites Science and Technology*, *70*(16), 2242-2247.

Mares, E., & Sokolowski, J. H. (2010). Artificial intelligence-based control system for the analysis of metal casting properties. *Journal of Achievements in Materials and Manufacturing Engineering*, *40*(2), 149-154

Moses, J. J., Dinaharan, I., & Sekhar, S. J. (2014). Characterization of Silicon Carbide Particulate Reinforced AA6061 Aluminum Alloy Composites Produced via Stir Casting. *Procedia Materials Science*, *5*, 106-112.

Onat, A. (2010). Mechanical and dry sliding wear properties of silicon carbide particulate reinforced aluminium–copper alloy matrix composites produced by direct squeeze casting method. *Journal of Alloys and Compounds*, *489*(1), 119-124.

Pan, J. N. (1997). Reliability prediction of imperfect switching systems subject to multiple stresses. *Microelectronics Reliability*, *37*(3), 439-445.

Park, Y. K., & Yang, J. M. (2011). Maximizing average efficiency of process time for pressure die casting in real foundries. *The International Journal of Advanced Manufacturing Technology*, *53*(9-12), 889-897.

Qi, H., & Li, Y. (2012). Metadynamic recrystallization of the as-cast 42CrMo steel after normalizing and tempering during hot compression. *Chinese Journal of Mechanical Engineering*, *25*(5), 853-859.

Ram, M. (2010). Reliability measures of a three-state complex system: a copula approach. *Applications and Applied Mathematics: An International Journal*, *5*(10), 1483-1492.

Ram, M., & Kumar, A. (2014). Performance of a Structure Consisting a 2-out-of-3: F Substructure Under Human Failure. *Arabian Journal for Science and Engineering*,*39*(11), 8383-8394.

Ram, M., & Singh, S. B. (2008). Availability and cost analysis of a parallel redundant complex system with two types of failure under preemptive-resume repair discipline using Gumbel-Hougaard family copula in repair. *International Journal of Reliability, Quality and Safety Engineering*, *15*(04), 341-365.

Ram, M., & Singh, S. B. (2010). Analysis of a complex system with common cause failure and two types of repair facilities with different distributions in failure. *International Journal of Reliability and Safety*, *4*(4), 381-392.

Ram, M., Singh, S. B., & Singh, V. V. (2013). Stochastic analysis of a standby system with waiting repair strategy. *Systems, Man, and Cybernetics: Systems, IEEE Transactions on*, *43*(3), 698-707.

Sakallı, Ü. S., Baykoç, Ö. F., & Birgören, B. (2011). Stochastic optimization for blending problem in brass casting industry. *Annals of Operations Research*, *186*(1), 141-157

Soltani, R. (2014). Reliability optimization of binary state non-repairable systems: A state of the art survey. *International Journal of Industrial Engineering Computations*, *5*(3), 339-364.

Sutaria, M., Gada, V. H., Sharma, A., & Ravi, B. (2012). Computation of feed-paths for casting solidification using level-set-method. *Journal of Materials Processing Technology*, *212*(6), 1236-1249.

Tabibian, S., Charkaluk, E., Constantinescu, A., Oudin, A., & Szmytka, F. (2010). Behavior, damage and fatigue life assessment of lost foam casting aluminum alloys under thermo-mechanical fatigue conditions. *Procedia Engineering*, *2*(1), 1145-1154.

Thomas, A. T., Parameshwaran, R., Muthukrishnan, A., & Kumaran, M. A. (2014). Development of Feeding & Stirring Mechanisms for Stir Casting of Aluminium Matrix Composites. *Procedia Materials Science*, *5*, 1182-1191.

Tzong, R. Y., & Lee, S. L. (1992). Solidification of arbitrarily shaped casting in mold-casting system. *International Journal of Heat and Mass Transfer*, *35*(11), 2795-2803.

Venkatesan, A., Gopinath, V. M., & Rajadurai, A. (2005). Simulation of casting solidification and its grain structure prediction using FEM. *Journal of Materials Processing Technology*, *168*(1), 10-15.

Wang, B., Zhang, J. Y., Li, X. M., & Qi, W. H. (2010). Simulation of solidification microstructure in twin-roll casting strip. *Computational Materials Science*, *49*(1), S135-S139

Wang, Y., Gong, C., Zhang, S., & Guo, H. (2010). Experimental study and numerical analysis on heavy-duty cast steel universal hinged supports for large span structures. *International Journal of Steel Structures*, *10*(1), 99-114.

Wu, H., Li, D., Chen, X., Sun, B., & Xu, D. (2010). Rapid casting of turbine blades with abnormal film cooling holes using integral ceramic casting molds. *The International Journal of Advanced Manufacturing Technology*, *50*(1-4), 13-19

Yang, Y., & Li, J. F. (2010). Study on mechanism of chip formation during high-speed milling of alloy cast iron. *The International Journal of Advanced Manufacturing Technology*, *46*(1-4), 43-50.

Yourui, T., Shuyong, D., & Xujing, Y. (2014). Reliability modeling and optimization of die-casting existing epistemic uncertainty. *International Journal on Interactive Design and Manufacturing (IJIDeM)*, 1-7, DOI:10.1007/s12008-014-0239-y.

Zhang, L., & Li, L. (2013). Determination of heat transfer coefficients at metal/chill interface in the casting solidification process. *Heat and Mass Transfer*, *49*(8), 1071-1080.

13

Analysis of three level supply chain of inventory with deterioration for multi-items

Narayan Singh*, **Bindu Vaish and S.R. Singh**

Department of Mathematics D.N. (P.G) College, Meerut (U.P), India

CHRONICLE

Keywords:
Multi-item inventory
Deteriorating items
Three level supply chains

ABSTRACT

The objective of this work is to generalize the three echelon supply chain model proposed by Jaber and Goyal (2008) [Jaber, M. Y., & Goyal, S. K. (2008). Coordinating a three-level supply chain with multiple suppliers, a vendor and multiple buyers. International Journal Production Economics, 116, 95-103.] for multi-items where single item was considered in production and distribution. This paper develops the coordination amongst different parties in a three-echelon supply chain with a centralized decision process. Producer, suppliers and retailers are the parties of the supply chain where multiple suppliers deliver various types of raw materials to a producer; producer produces different types of items, multi-items, in different units of the factory and supplies the items to multiple retailers. Different deterioration rates for finished items and raw materials are also considered. The model developed of this paper guarantees that the local costs for the members either remain the same as before coordination, or decrease as a result of coordination. A numerical example along with graphical illustrations is considered and the sensitivity analysis is provided to test the feasibility of the proposed model.

1. Introduction

A supply chain normally consists of various facilities, where raw materials, intermediate products, or finished goods, which are purchased, produced, processed, stored or sold and they are inter-connected through transportation links, networks, along which the products flow. These facilities can be managed by one company and can be operated by vendors, customers, third-party providers, as divisions of other firms in which the company has business arrangements. To manage the effective and efficient flow of raw materials and products, coordination of activities is necessary among different players of the supply chain. Coordination schemes in supply chains are either centralized or decentralized decision-making processes. A centralized decision-making process assumes a unique decision-maker (a team) managing the whole supply chain with an objective to minimize (maximize) the total supply chain cost (profit); whereas in a decentralized decision-making process, multiple decision-makers with conflicting objectives are involved. This paper assumes a centralized decision-making process as a coordination mechanism in the supply chain model discussed herein (e.g., Munson & Rosenblatt, 2001; Jaber et al., 2006).

* Corresponding author.

Clark and Scarf (1960) were the first to study the two-echelon inventory model. They proved the optimality of a base stock policy for the pure serial inventory system and developed an efficient decomposing method to compute the optimal base stock ordering policy. Integrating inventory decision models of parties in a supply chain is a natural way of achieving coordination (e.g., Goyal & Gupta, 1989). Investigations reporting coordination in a three-level supply chain are few and far between in the literature. Coordinating orders in a two-level (vendor–buyer(s)) supply chain has been addressed by Hill (1997). Goyal and Gunasekaran (1995) observed an integrated production– inventory–marketing model to determine economic production quantity and economic order quantity for raw materials in a multi-echelon production system. Thomas and Grifin (1996) remarked that an efficient supply chain requires planning and coordination among the various channels. Goyal (2000) discussed the single-vendor single-buyer integrated production inventory model with a generalized policy.

The literature on multi-item dynamic inventory models is really sparse, since most of the classical studies are concerned with a single-item inventory model. We cite some of the most well-known works in order to give an idea on the wide range of optimal control applications in the multi-item inventory-production system. Ben-Daya and Raouf (1993) developed an approach for a more realistic and general Single Period Inventory Problem (SPIP), they considered a multi-item with budgetary and floor- or shelf- space constraints and assumed that, the demand of the items follows uniform probability distribution. In addition, they discussed a multi-item inventory model with stochastic demand subject to the restrictions on available space and budget. Lenard and Roy (1995) defined another approach to determine inventory policies based on the notion of efficient policy surface and extend this notion to multi-item inventory control by defining the concepts of family and aggregate item. Rosenblatt (1981) discussed multi-item inventory system with budgetary constraint comparison between the Lagrangian and the fixed cycle approach.

The area of supply chain management has gained significant amount of interest from researchers as well as practitioners in the industry. For a vertically integrated supply chain owned partially or jointly by the same company, such coordinated production– shipment policy provides valuable insights and optimal decisions, which lead to global optimization. On the other hand, when individual entities are owned separately, such policy may not benefit all parties equally as some may encounter an increase in their costs and hence become less eager to depart from their locally optimized policies. In such circumstances, sharing those benefits resulting from the coordinated approach becomes a major issue. By using effective incentive systems such as accounting methods, transfer pricing schemes, quantity discount, etc., the objective of each partner can be aligned to that of the supply chain as a whole (Ganeshan, 1999). Munson and Rosenblatt (2001) considered a single-product centralized three-level supply chain consisting of a single supplier, a single manufacturer, and a single retailer. In their model, Munson and Rosenblatt (2001) assumed that the manufacturer is the most influential channel player who would be able to obtain a quantity discount from the supplier without worsening the supplier's financial performance. The manufacturer may pass some, or all, of the monetary discount obtained from the supplier to the retailer to entice the retailer to order in larger lots than its economic order quantity (EOQ). They also suggested that the compensation paid to the retailer is the difference in holding and ordering costs between the retailer's old (no coordination) and new ordering (with coordination) policies. Viswanathan and Wang (2003) discussed a discount pricing decisions in distribution channels with price-sensitive demand. Jain and Singh (2011) developed an inflation implication on an inventory with expiration date, capital constraint and uncertain lead time in a multi-echelon supply chain. Jaber and Goyal (2008) discussed coordination a three-level supply chain with multiple suppliers, a vendor and multiple buyers. Sadjadi et al (2012) considered a profit maximizing firm who wants to jointly determine the optimal lot-sizing, pricing, and marketing decisions along with manufacturing requirements in terms of flexibility and reliability of the process. Singh et al. (2012) studied a three echelon supply chain inventory model for deteriorating items with storage facility and lead time under inflation. Pal et al (2012) discussed a production inventory model for different types of items where multiple suppliers, a manufacturer and the multiple non-competing retailers were the members of the supply chain. In this model, each supplier supplies only one type of raw material to the manufacturer. The manufacturer produces a finished item by the combination of certain percentage of the various types of raw materials. The manufacturer produces also multi-items and delivers them according to the demand of the different retailers. Tsao and Sheen (2012) considered a multi-item supply chain with a credit period and weight freight cost discounts. Aliabadi et al. (2013) investigated an integrated multi-item supplier selection model. The mathematical model, which is a nonlinear binary programming was derived. Hanbali and Heijden (2013) analyzed the interval availability of a two-echelon, multi-item spare part inventory system. They considered a scenario inspired by a situation that they encountered at Thales Netherlands, a manufacturer of naval sensors and naval command and control systems. Chui et al. (2013) addressed the joint determination of a rotation cycle time and number of shipments for a multi-item EPQ model with random defective rate.

Jaber and Goyal (2008) in a novel work discussed the supply chain with multiple suppliers by investigating a problem where a manufacturer and multiple buyers for the production of single item are involved. We extend the paper this work for multi-items, production and supply, and consider the number of suppliers equal to the number of items required by the manufacture of the product to assemble one unit of the finished product. We consider a three-layer supply chain model involving multiple suppliers, a producer and multiple retailers as members of the chain. The multiple suppliers supply raw materials to a producer who produces multiple finished products, which are delivered to the multiple retailers and the retailer sale the items to the customers. This model have been accomplished with the different rate of deterioration i.e. a deterioration rate for raw material and another deterioration rate for finished items of retailers. The setup has been explored numerically as well, an optimal solution has been reached at and the sensitivity of that solution has also been checked with respect to various system parameters. The result shows that the model is not only economically feasible but also it provides stable results. A cost minimization model is derived along with an efficient solution algorithm that is based on the calculus approach.

2. Assumptions and Notations

In this study, we assume

2.1 Assumptions

1. Demand rate and production rate are deterministic and constant.
2. Production rate is highly greater than any demand d, i.e. $P > d$.
3. One product requires m items.
4. Shortage is not allowed.
5. Lead time is zero at each level of the supply chain.
6. Time horizon is infinite.
7. Multi-items are considered.
8. A constant fraction of the on hand inventory deteriorates and no replacement of Deteriorated items are allowed.
9. Multiple suppliers, single producer and multiple retailers are considered.
10. Single producer produces multi-items of different kinds.
11. The study considered supplier producer and retailer co-operation.

2.2 Notations

The input parameters and decision variables for retailers, producer and suppliers are denoted by the subscripts *r, p* and *s*, respectively.

n	Number of items, where $i = 1, 2, 3, \ldots\ldots n$
m	Number of supplier and each supplier supply n different kind of items to the producer for producing n different items or number of units required in one unit of the finished product.

k	Number of retailers
l	Number of deliveries from producer to the retailer during total cycle time
d_i	Annual demand rate of ith item (units/year)
P_i	Production rate of ith item, where $i = 1, 2, 3, \ldots\ldots n$
$I_s(t)$	Inventory level of supplier
$I_p(t)$	Inventory level of producer
$I_r(t)$	Inventory level of retailer
θ_{1i}	Inventory deterioration rate for supplier
θ_{2i}	Inventory deterioration rate for producer
θ_{3i}	Inventory deterioration rate for retailer
$A_{r\alpha}$	Ordering cost per cycle for α^{th} retailer where $\alpha = 1, 2, 3, \ldots\ldots k$
$h_{r\alpha}$	Holding cost of αth retailer per unit per year
A_{sj}	Order cost for supplier j where $j = 1, 2, 3, \ldots\ldots m$
A_p	Fixed order/setup cost per cycle for producer
h_p	Holding cost per unit of a finished product per year
h_{sj}	Holding cost per unit per unit time for j^{th} supplier
c_0	Fixed cost per unit of the product
c_{pi}	Producer's finished goods per unit cost
$c_{r\alpha}$	Retailer's finished goods per unit cost
c_{sj}	Supplier's raw material per unit cost
Q_s	One kind of raw material's order quantity for one supplier
Q_p	Producer's finished goods production quantity per production
Q_r	One retailer's received quantity of one kind per delivery from producer
MI_p	The maximum inventory level of producer
MI_r	Inventory lot size of all k retailers in one delivery of ith item
T_1	The production period
T_2	The non-production period
T_3	The period that a retailer is not out of stock
T	Cycle time
TCS	Supplier's total cost per unit time
TCP	Producer's total cost per unit time
TCR	Retailer's total cost per unit time
TC	The total system cost

3. Mathematical Model

The following scope applies to the study. Suppliers procure raw materials from outside suppliers and deliver the fixed quantities to the producer's warehouse at a fixed time interval. The producer withdraws raw materials from the warehouse and produces finished goods. The fixed quantities finished goods is delivered to retailers at a fixed time interval. This study develops an integrated inventory model for deteriorating multi-items under a multi-echelon supply chain system and is shown in Fig. 1. A mathematical model with integrating multiple suppliers, single producer and multiple retailers is derived to obtain the optimal number of deliveries, production time/non-production time and order lot size, when the joint total cost of the supplier, the producer and the retailer under centralization is minimized.

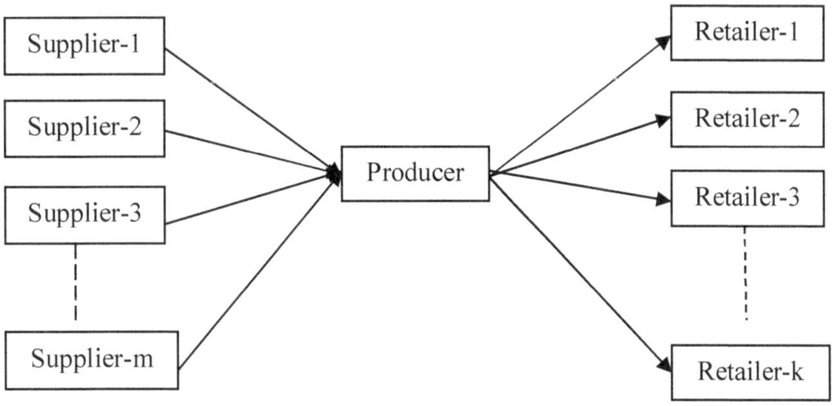

Fig.1. A three-echelon supply chain system

3.1 Supplier's Inventory Model

The raw materials Inventory System is shown in Fig 2(a). A supplier procures the raw materials and delivers the fixed quantities Q_s to the producer's warehouse at a fixed-time interval. The producer withdraws raw materials from the warehouse. During the time period T_1, the inventory level decreases due to both producers demand and deterioration. The supplier's inventory system can be represented by the following first order linear differential equation;

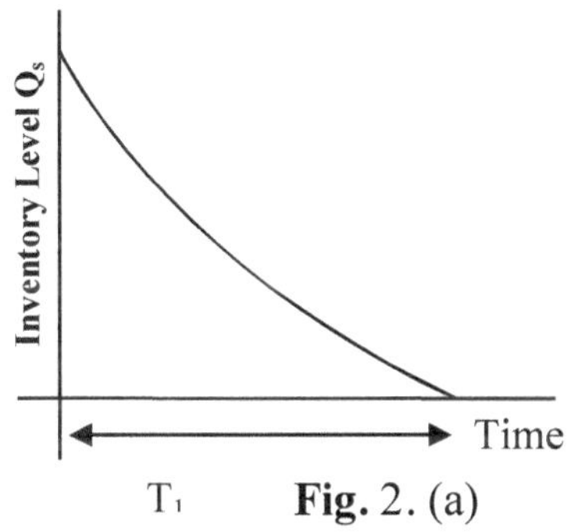

Fig. 2. (a)

$$\frac{dI_{si}(t_1)}{dt_1} = -\sum_{j=1}^{m} P_{ij} - \theta_{1i} I_{si}(t_1) \quad 0 \le t_1 \le T_1 \text{ and } i = 1,2,3,\ldots n \tag{1}$$

Using the boundary condition, $I_{si}(T_1) = 0$, the differential equation can be solved as follows,

$$I_{si}(t_1) = \sum_{j=1}^{m} P_{ij} \frac{\left\{e^{\theta_{1i}(T_1 - t_1)} - 1\right\}}{\theta_{1i}} \quad \text{where } 0 \le t_1 \le T_1 \tag{2}$$

Based on Fig. 2 (a) and $I_{si}(0) = Q_s$, the maximum inventory level of raw material, i.e., the order quantity per order from outside suppliers is as follows,

$$Q_s = \sum_{j=1}^{m} P_{ij} \frac{\left\{e^{\theta_{1i} T_1} - 1\right\}}{\theta_{1i}} \approx \sum_{j=1}^{m} P_{ij}\left(T_1 + \frac{\theta_{1i} T_1^2}{2}\right) \tag{3}$$

For one supplier inventory level at any time t_1 is

$$I_{si}(t_1) = P_{i1} \frac{\left\{e^{\theta_{1i}(T_1 - t_1)} - 1\right\}}{\theta_{1i}}, \; Q_s = I_{si}(0) = P_{i1}\left(T_1 + \frac{\theta_{1i} T_1^2}{2}\right) \tag{4}$$

1. There is an initial replenishment ordering cost at the start of the cycle is

$$OC_s = \sum_{j=1}^{m} A_{sij} \tag{5}$$

2. Inventory is carried during the time period T_1. The holding cost for supplier is

$$HC_S = \sum_{j=1}^{m} h_{sij} \int_0^{T_1} I_{si}(t_1)\,dt_1 = \sum_{j=1}^{m} \frac{h_{sij} P_{ij}}{\theta_{1i}} \int_0^{T_1} \left\{ e^{\theta_{1i}(T_1 - t_1)} - 1 \right\} dt_1$$

$$HC_S \approx \sum_{j=1}^{m} h_{sij} P_{ij} \left(\frac{T_1^2}{2} + \frac{\theta_{1i} T_1^3}{6} \right) \tag{6}$$

3. The item cost includes the loss due to deterioration as well as the cost of the item sold.

$$IT_s = c_{sij} Q_s \approx \sum_{j=1}^{m} c_{sij} P_{i1} \left(T_1 + \frac{\theta_{1i} T_1^2}{2} \right) \tag{7}$$

The total cost during the cycle is the sum of the ordering cost (OC_s), the holding cost (HC_S) and the item cost (IT_s) for all m suppliers per unit time is as follows,

$$TCS = \frac{OC_s + HC_S + IT_s}{T}$$

$$TCS \approx \frac{1}{T} \sum_{i=1}^{n} \sum_{j=1}^{m} \left[A_{sij} + h_{sij} P_{ij} \left(\frac{T_1^2}{2} + \frac{\theta_{1i} T_1^3}{6} \right) + c_{sij} P_{ij} \left(T_1 + \frac{\theta_{1i} T_1^2}{2} \right) \right] \tag{8}$$

3.2 Producer's Inventory Model

The manufactures inventory system in Fig. 2(b) can be divided into two independent phases depicted by T_1 and T_2. This methodology reduces the complexity of our problems derivation on and analysis. Each phase has its own time unit, t_i which starts from the beginning of the phase T_i. During time period T_1 there is an inventory buildup and hence deterioration becomes effective. At $t_1 = T_1$, the production stops and the inventory level increase to its maximum level MI_p. There is no production during period T_2, the inventory level decrease due to demand and deterioration. The Inventory level becomes zero at $t_2 = T_2$.

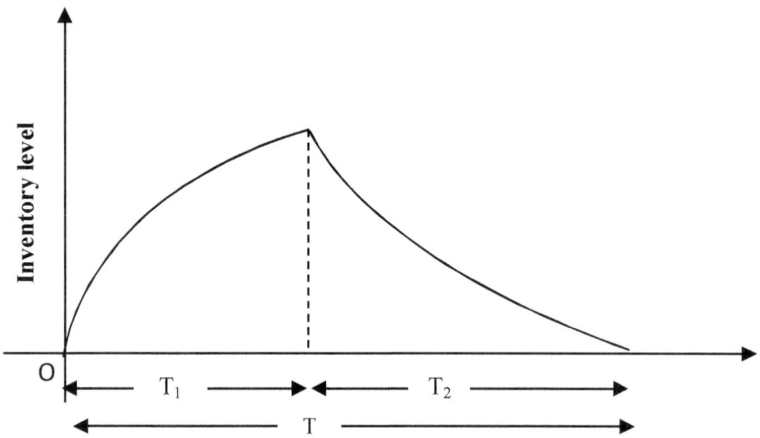

Fig. 2 (b)

The instantaneous state of inventory for the ith item $(1 \le i \le n)$ over the cycle time T_i is given by the following first order linear differential equation;

$$\frac{dI_{p_1i}(t_1)}{dt_1} = P_i - \sum_{\alpha=1}^{k} d_{i\alpha} - \theta_{2i} I_{p_1i}(t_1) \; 0 \le t_1 \le T_1 \;\; i = 1,2,3,\ldots n \tag{9}$$

$$\frac{dI_{p_2i}(t_2)}{dt_2} = -\sum_{\alpha=1}^{k} d_{i\alpha} - \theta_{2i} I_{p_2i}(t_2) \quad 0 \le t_2 \le T_2 \tag{10}$$

The above differential equations are solved by using the boundary conditions,

$I_{p_1i}(0) = 0$, $I_{p_2i}(T_2) = 0$, One has;

$$I_{p_1i}(t_1) = \left(P_i - \sum_{\alpha=1}^{k} d_{i\alpha}\right) \cdot \left(\frac{1 - e^{-\theta_{2i} t_1}}{\theta_{2i}}\right) \qquad 0 \le t_1 \le T_1 \tag{11}$$

$$I_{p_2i}(t_2) = \sum_{\alpha=1}^{k} d_{i\alpha} \cdot \left(\frac{e^{\theta_{2i}(T_2 - t_2)} - 1}{\theta_{2i}}\right) \qquad 0 \le t_2 \le T_2 \tag{12}$$

Since $I_{p_{2i}}(0) = MI_p$ the producer's maximum inventory level is

$$MI_p = \sum_{\alpha=1}^{k} d_{i\alpha} \cdot \left(\frac{e^{\theta_{2i} T_2} - 1}{\theta_{2i}}\right) \approx \sum_{\alpha=1}^{k} d_{i\alpha}\left(T_2 + \frac{\theta_{2i} T_2^2}{2}\right) \tag{13}$$

The production quantity of the item is

$Q_{pi} = P_i . T_1$

1. At the of the cycle, the has an initial production setup cost and it is

$$S_p = A_{pi} \tag{14}$$

2. Inventory is carried during T_1 and T_2 periods. If this system does not consider the retailer, all of holding cost belongs to producer. They are the first two terms of Eq. (15). If this system considers the retailer, the holding costs of the items delivered to the retailer belong to the retailer and it should be subtracted from producer, which is the last term in Eq. (15).

The holding cost for producer is

$$HC_p = h_{pi}\left[\int_0^{T_1} I_{p_1i}(t_1)dt_1 + \int_0^{T_2} I_{p_2i}(t_2)dt_2 - l\int_0^{T_3} I_{ri}(t_3)dt_3\right] \tag{15}$$

$$HC_p = h_{pi}\left[\int_0^{T_1}\left(P_i - \sum_{\alpha=1}^{k} d_{i\alpha}\right)\cdot\left(\frac{1 - e^{-\theta_{2i}t_1}}{\theta_{2i}}\right)dt_1 + \int_0^{T_2}\sum_{\alpha=1}^{k} d_{i\alpha}\cdot\left(\frac{e^{\theta_{2i}(T_2 - t_2)} - 1}{\theta_{2i}}\right)dt_2 - l\int_0^{T_3}\sum_{\alpha=1}^{k} d_{i\alpha}\cdot\left(\frac{e^{\theta_{3i}(T_3 - t_3)} - 1}{\theta_{3i}}\right)dt_3\right]$$

$$HC_p \approx h_{pi}\left[\left(P_i - \sum_{\alpha=1}^{k} d_{i\alpha}\right)\cdot\left(\frac{T_1^2}{2} - \frac{\theta_{2i}T_1^3}{6}\right) + \sum_{\alpha=1}^{k} d_{i\alpha}\cdot\left(\frac{T_2^2}{2} + \frac{\theta_{2i}T_2^3}{6}\right) - l\sum_{\alpha=1}^{k} d_{i\alpha}\cdot\left(\frac{T_3^2}{2} + \frac{\theta_{3i}T_3^3}{6}\right)\right]$$

$$HC_p \approx h_{pi}\left[P_i\cdot\left(\frac{T_1^2}{2} - \frac{\theta_{2i}T_1^3}{6}\right) - \sum_{\alpha=1}^{k} d_{i\alpha}\cdot\left\{\frac{1}{2}\left(T_1^2 - T_2^2 + lT_3^2\right) - \frac{1}{6}\left(\theta_{2i}T_1^3 + \theta_{2i}T_2^3 - l\theta_{3i}T_3^3\right)\right\}\right] \tag{16}$$

3. Annual deterioration cost for producer is as follows,

$$DC_p = c_{pi}\left(P_i T_1 - l.MI_{ri}\right) \approx c_{pi}\left[P_i.T - l\sum_{\alpha=1}^{k} d_{i\alpha}\left(T_3 + \frac{\theta_{3i}T_3^2}{2}\right)\right] \tag{17}$$

The total cost during the cycle is the sum of the setup cost (S_p), the holding cost (HC_p) and the deterioration cost (DC_p) for producer per unit time is

$$TCP = \frac{S_p + HC_p + DC_p}{T}$$

$$TCP \approx \frac{1}{T}\left[A_{pi} + h_{pi}\left\{P_i.\left(\frac{T_1^2}{2} - \frac{\theta_{2i}T_1^3}{6}\right) - \sum_{\alpha=1}^{k} d_{i\alpha}.\left\{\frac{1}{2}\left(T_1^2 - T_2^2 + lT_3^2\right) - \frac{1}{6}\left(\theta_{2i}T_1^3 + \theta_{2i}T_2^3 - l\theta_{3i}T_3^3\right)\right\}\right\}\right.$$

$$\left. + c_{pi}.\left\{P_i T - l\sum_{\alpha=1}^{k} d_{i\alpha}\left(T_3 + \frac{\theta_{3i}T_3^2}{2}\right)\right\}\right]$$

For the production of n different kind of items

$$TCP \approx \frac{1}{T}\sum_{i=1}^{n}\left[A_{pi} + c_{pi}.\left\{P_i T - l\sum_{\alpha=1}^{k} d_{i\alpha}\left(T_3 + \frac{\theta_{3i}T_3^2}{2}\right)\right\}\right.$$

$$\left. + h_{pi}\left\{P_i.\left(\frac{T_1^2}{2} - \frac{\theta_{2i}T_1^3}{6}\right) - \sum_{\alpha=1}^{k} d_{i\alpha}.\left\{\frac{1}{2}\left(T_1^2 - T_2^2 + lT_3^2\right) - \frac{1}{6}\left(\theta_{2i}T_1^3 + \theta_{2i}T_2^3 - l\theta_{3i}T_3^3\right)\right\}\right\}\right] \quad (18)$$

3.3 Retailer's Inventory Model

A realization of the inventory level in the system is given in Fig. 2 (c). The depletion of the inventory level during $[0, T_3]$ is due to the joint effect of demand and deterioration. MI_r is the lot size of one delivery for all k retailers of one kind of finished goods. Hence the differential equation, which describes the variation of inventory level $I_{ri}(t)$ with respect to time t is as follows,

$$\frac{dI_{ri}(t_3)}{dt_3} = -\sum_{\alpha=1}^{k} d_{ij} - \theta_{3i} I_{ri}(t_3) \qquad 0 \le t_3 \le T_3 \quad (19)$$

with boundary condition $I_{ri}(0) = MI_{ri}$ or $I_{ri}(T_3) = 0$

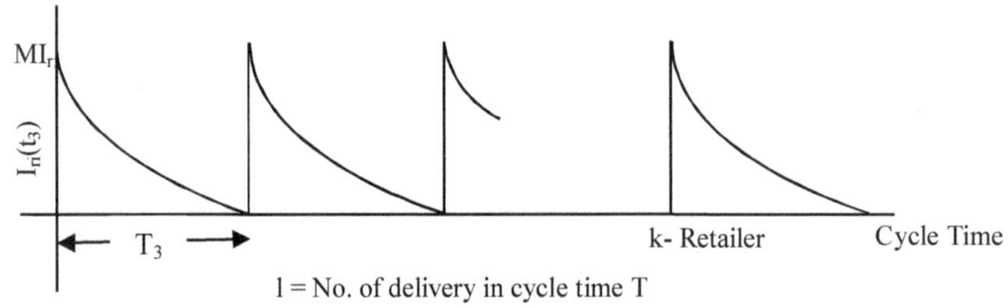

Fig. 2 (c)

The solution of the equation is as follows,

$$I_{ri}(t_3) = \sum_{\alpha=1}^{k} d_{i\alpha}.\left(\frac{e^{\theta_{3i}(T_3 - t_3)} - 1}{\theta_{3i}}\right) \qquad 0 \le t_3 \le T_3 \quad (20)$$

From the Fig. 2 (c) and $I_{ri}(0) = MI_{ri}$, the retailer's maximum inventory level is

$$MI_{ri} \approx \sum_{\alpha=1}^{k} d_{i\alpha}\left(T_3 + \frac{\theta_{3i}T_3^2}{2}\right), \; Q_r \approx d\left(T_3 + \frac{\theta_3 T_3^2}{2}\right) \quad (21)$$

1. The ordering cost is

$$OC_r = \sum_{\alpha=1}^{k} A_{ri\alpha} \quad (22)$$

2. Inventory carried during the period T_3. The holding cost for retailers is

$$HC_r = \sum_{\alpha=1}^{k} h_{ri\alpha} \cdot \int_0^{T_3} I_{ri}(t_3) dt_3 \qquad 0 \le t_3 \le T_3$$

$$HC_r = \sum_{\alpha=1}^{k} h_{ri\alpha} \cdot \int_0^{T_3} \sum_{\alpha=1}^{k} d_{i\alpha} \cdot \left(\frac{e^{\theta_{3i}(T_3 - t_3)} - 1}{\theta_{3i}} \right) dt_3 \approx \sum_{\alpha=1}^{k} h_{ri\alpha} d_{i\alpha} \left(\frac{T_3^2}{2} + \frac{\theta_{3i} T_3^3}{6} \right) \tag{23}$$

3. The item cost includes loss due to deterioration as well as the cost of item is

$$IT_r \approx \sum_{\alpha=1}^{k} c_{ri\alpha} . d_{i\alpha} \left(T_3 + \frac{\theta_{3i} T_3^2}{2} \right) \tag{24}$$

The total cost during the cycle is the sum of the ordering cost (OC_r), the holding cost (HC_r) and the item cost (IT_r) for producer per unit time is

$$TCR = l . \frac{OC_r + HD_r + IT_r}{T}$$

$$TCR \approx \frac{l}{T} \left[\sum_{\alpha=1}^{k} A_{ri\alpha} + \sum_{\alpha=1}^{k} h_{ri\alpha} d_{i\alpha} \left(\frac{T_3^2}{2} + \frac{\theta_{3i} T_3^3}{6} \right) + \sum_{\alpha=1}^{k} c_{ri\alpha} . d_{i\alpha} \left(T_3 + \frac{\theta_{3i} T_3^2}{2} \right) \right]$$

$$\approx \frac{l}{T} \sum_{\alpha=1}^{k} \left[A_{ri\alpha} + h_{ri\alpha} d_{i\alpha} \left(\frac{T_3^2}{2} + \frac{\theta_{3i} T_3^3}{6} \right) + c_{ri\alpha} . d_{i\alpha} \left(T_3 + \frac{\theta_{3i} T_3^2}{2} \right) \right] \qquad \text{Where } T_3 = \frac{T}{l}$$

For n different items

$$TCR \approx \frac{l}{T} \sum_{i=1}^{n} \sum_{\alpha=1}^{k} \left[A_{ri\alpha} + h_{ri\alpha} d_{i\alpha} \left(\frac{T_3^2}{2} + \frac{\theta_{3i} T_3^3}{6} \right) + c_{ri\alpha} . d_{i\alpha} \left(T_3 + \frac{\theta_{3i} T_3^2}{2} \right) \right] \tag{25}$$

The relation between the period T_1 and T_2 can be computed by the Eq. (11) and Eq. (12). In order to solve the objective function, represent T_1 by T_2. From $I_{P_{1i}}(T_1) = I_{P_{2i}}(0)$, one has

$$\left(P_i - \sum_{\alpha=1}^{k} d_{i\alpha} \right) \cdot \left(\frac{1 - e^{-\theta_{2i} T_1}}{\theta_{2i}} \right) = \sum_{\alpha=1}^{k} d_{i\alpha} \cdot \left(\frac{e^{\theta_{2i} T_2} - 1}{\theta_{2i}} \right) \tag{26}$$

Neglecting second and higher degree term, from Eq. (26) and $T_1 + T_2 = T$ we get

$$T_1 \approx \frac{\sum_{\alpha=1}^{k} d_{i\alpha}}{P_i} . T, \quad T_2 \approx \frac{\left(P_i - \sum_{\alpha=1}^{k} d_{i\alpha} \right)}{P_i} . T \tag{27}$$

The study develops an integrated three echelon supply for multi items under different rates of deterioration separately. For small rates θ_{1i}, θ_{2i} and θ_{3i} ($\theta_{1i}, \theta_{2i}, \theta_{3i} \le 1$), an approximate model with multiple supplier, single producer and multiple retailers with centralized decision policy is developed to derive the optimal production policy and lot size. The annual supply chain cost is determined by summing TCS, TCP and TCR. Since $T_3 = T / l$ and $T_1 + T_2 = T$, the problem can be stated as an optimization problem and it can be formulated as

Minimize $TC\ (l,\ T) = TCS + TCP + TCR$ (28)

Subject to; $l \ge 1,\ 0 \le T$ (29)

4. Analysis and solution procedure

The objective of this study is to minimize the annual integrated system cost TC defined in Eq. (28). The following results are obtained.

4.1 The convexity of the functions TC (T)

For convenience, we treat the convexity property of function TC (T) defined on T> 0. At a particular value of *l*, Eq. (28) yields

$$TC = \Delta_1 T^2 + \Delta_2 T + \frac{1}{T}\Delta_3 + \Delta_4$$

$$TC' = 2\Delta_1 T + \Delta_2 - \frac{1}{T^2}\Delta_3 \qquad (30)$$

$$TC'' = 2\Delta_1 + \frac{2}{T^3}\Delta_3 > 0 \qquad (31)$$

where

$$\Delta_1 = \sum_{i=1}^{n}\sum_{j=1}^{m}\sum_{\alpha=1}^{k}\left[\left\{h_{sij}P_{ij}\theta_{1i} + h_{pi}\left(P_i - d_{i\alpha}\right)\theta_{2i}\right\}\frac{d_{i\alpha}^3}{6P_i^3} + h_{pi}d_{i\alpha}\theta_{2i}\frac{\left(P_i - d_{i\alpha}\right)^3}{6P_i^3} + \frac{1}{6l^2}\left(h_{ri\alpha} - h_{pi}\right)d_{i\alpha}\theta_{3i}\right]$$

$$\Delta_2 = \sum_{i=1}^{n}\sum_{j=1}^{m}\sum_{\alpha=1}^{k}\left[\begin{array}{l}\left\{\left(h_{sij} + c_{sij}\theta_{1i}\right)P_{ij} + h_{pi}\left(P_i - d_{i\alpha}\right)\right\}\dfrac{d_{i\alpha}^2}{2P_i^2} + h_{pi}d_{i\alpha}\dfrac{\left(P_i - d_{i\alpha}\right)^2}{2P_i^2} \\ + \dfrac{1}{2l}\left(h_{ri\alpha} - h_{pi}\right)d_{i\alpha} + \left(c_{ri\alpha} - P_i\right)d_{i\alpha}\theta_{3i}\end{array}\right]$$

$$\Delta_3 = \sum_{i=1}^{n}\sum_{j=1}^{m}\sum_{\alpha=1}^{k}\left[A_{sij} + A_{pi} + lA_{ri\alpha}\right]$$

and

$$\Delta_4 = \sum_{i=1}^{n}\sum_{j=1}^{m}\sum_{\alpha=1}^{k}\left[\left(\frac{c_{sij}P_{ij}}{P_i} - c_{pi} + c_{ri\alpha}\right)d_{i\alpha} + c_{pi}P_i\right]$$

Eq. (30) and Eq. (31) show that the following results hold true

Lemma 1. The function TC(T) is convex on T > 0 if $\Delta_1, \Delta_3 > 0$
$P_i > d_{i\alpha}$ and $h_{ri\alpha} > h_{pi}$ this implies $P_i - d_{i\alpha} > 0$ and $h_{ri\alpha} - h_{pi} > 0$ (because of $h_{ri\alpha} > h_{pi}$)Therefore $\Delta_1 > 0$, Δ_3 is the sum of all positive terms, that is, $\Delta_3 > 0$
By letting $TC' = 0$ and solving the eq. (30), we obtain

$$T^* = \frac{\Delta_2^2}{6\Delta_1\left(-\Delta_2^3 + 54\Delta_1^2\Delta_3 + 6\sqrt{3}\sqrt{-\Delta_1^2\Delta_2^3\Delta_3 + 27\Delta_1^4\Delta_3^2}\right)^{1/3}} + \frac{\left(-\Delta_2^3 + 54\Delta_1^2\Delta_3 + 6\sqrt{3}\sqrt{-\Delta_1^2\Delta_2^3\Delta_3 + 27\Delta_1^4\Delta_3^2}\right)^{1/3}}{6G_1} - \frac{\Delta_2}{6\Delta_1}$$

as the solution of Eq. (30)

Also if T^* exists then we find

$$TC = \begin{cases} < 0 & 0 < T < T^* \\ = 0 & T = T^* \\ > 0 & T > T^* \end{cases} \qquad (32)$$

Therefore it follows that the function TC is decreasing on (0 T^*] and increasing on [T^* ∞).

4.2 Solution procedure

Require: Delivery per order l where $l \in I^+$.
Ensure: minimum value $TC(l^*,T^*)$ of $TC(l,T)$ given in Eq. (28).

begin
Choose l such that $l \geq 1$;
$TC(l^*,T^*) = 100^{100}$; // initially we have taken a very large quantity

Repeat
find $\frac{\partial}{\partial T} TC(l,T)$;
put $\frac{\partial}{\partial T} TC(l,T) = 0$ and find all the values of T; // let $T_1, T_2 .... T_n$ are all such values of T
for *(i = 1 to n)* do
if $\left(\frac{\partial^2}{\partial T^2}(TC(l,T_i)) \geq 0\right)$ then
calculate $TC(l,T_i)$;
if $\left(TC(l,T_i) \leq TC(l^*,T_i^*)\right)$
$TC(l^*,T_i^*) - TC(l,T_i)$
end if
end if
end for
until (minimum value $TC(l^*,T^*)$ of $TC(l,T)$ is found for all possible values of l)
derive the T_1^*, T_2^* .... and ....;
end

5. Numerical Example

Consider a three-echelon supply chain with three retailers $(\alpha = 1,2,3)$, a producer and two suppliers $(j = 1,2)$ and the numbers of items $(i = 1,2)$, the value of parameters adopted in this study are A_{pi} =90, A_{si}=40, A_{ri}=80, h_{pi}=0.8, h_{si}=0.5, h_{ri}=1, θ_{1i}=0.3, θ_{2i}=0.2, θ_{3i}=0.5, c_{pi}=6, c_{sij}=2, c_{ri}=10, P_i=800, d_i =200, k=3, l=2 and m=2.

The computational results are shown in Table 1 (For n=1) and Table 2 (For n=2). The raw material, producer and retailer's costs are presented in Table 3.
The major conclusions and the special condition are drawn from numerical are as follow;

- When producer's different units produce the two type of items i.e. for n=2, the optimal values of The Total Cost is \$ 26380 and other optimal values of $l, T_1^*, T_2^*, T_3^*, T, Q_s^*, Q_p^*, Q_r^*, TCS^*, TCP^*$ and TCR^* are 2, 0.039, 0.013, 0.026, 0.052, 125 units, 124 units, 31 units, \$ 19972, \$17874, and \$91117.
- Since TC is the function of T, an optimization technique as shown on section 4(solution procedure) is used to find the optimal solution. A graphical representation and numerical analysis are also presented to show the convexity of the TC. Based on above analysis and graphical representation

of Fig. 3(a) and Fig. 3(b), one can say that TC is a convex function. When $l^*=2$, the sufficient condition is $TC^{!!} = 2.29654 \times 10^6$

Table 1

The numerical results for illustrated example when n=1

l	T_1	T_2	T_3	T	Q_s	Q_p	Q_r	TCS	TCP	TCR	TC
1	0.068	0.022	0.091	0.091	109.9	108.8	56.0	5751	4581	21212	6868
2	0.048	0.016	0.032	0.063	77.3	76.8	19.3	5743	5010	4666	7845
3	0.043	0.014	0.018	0.054	69.2	68.8	10.8	6180	5113	19518	8516

Table 2

The numerical results for illustrated example when n=2

l	T_1	T_2	T_3	T	Q_s	Q_p	Q_r	TCS	TCP	TCR	*TC*
1	0.043	0.014	0.058	0.058	138	137	70	20157	17351	81739	29793
2	0.039	0.013	0.026	0.052	125	124	31	19972	17874	91117	26380
3	0.034	0.011	0.015	0.045	109	108	18	23078	18517	85003	27334

- This whole discussion is made for n=2 i.e. the producer produces and supplies to the all retailers the two types of items (Table 2 and Table 3).
- When l increases T_1, T_2, and T_3 will decrease. The reason is multiple deliveries will avoid the excess inventory.
- If $l > 3$, all costs consistently increase, i.e. l=2 is the optimal value.
- When the deterioration is not considered (i.e.θ_1, θ_2, $\theta_3 = 0$), l=2 and TC^* is 16111.7. The holding cost and item cost will increase.

Table 3

The Raw material, Producer and Retailer's cost (For n=2)

Cost Item	*l=1*	*l=2*	*L=3*
S_p	180	180	180
HC_p	0.776	0.646	0.484
DC_p	1296	1497	1305
TCP	17351	17874	18517
OC_s	80	80	80
HC_s	5.95	4.89	3.715
IT_s	874	1010	879
TCS	20157	19972	23078
OC_r	160	160	160
HC_r	12.25	2.44	0.0812
IT_r	3283	1886	1084
TCR	81739	91117	85003
TC	29790	26380	27334

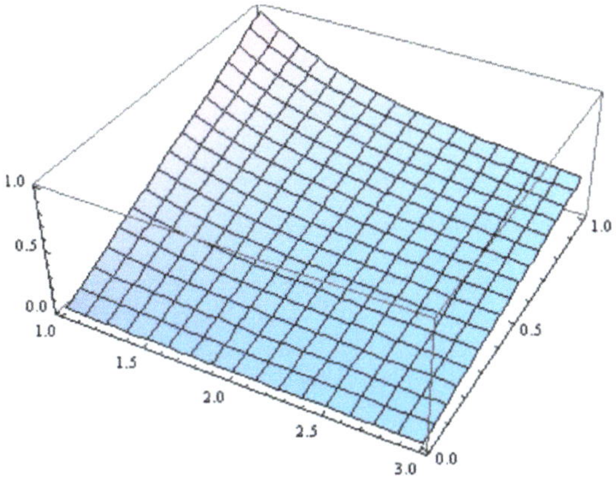

Fig. 3(a)

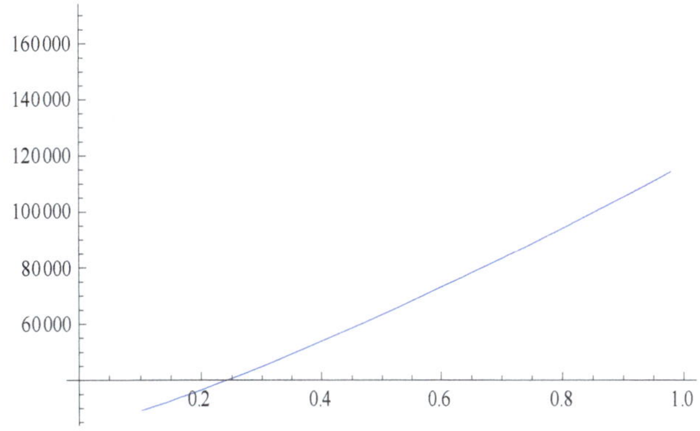

Fig. 3(b)

- Fig. 3 (a) shows the variation of total system cost with respect to the no. of delivery (*l from 1 to 3*) and cycle time (*T from 0 to 1*).
- Fig. 3 (b) shows the variation of total system cost with respect to cycle time (*T*).

6. Conclusions

This paper has presented a coordination policy among the suppliers, the producer and the retailers. To best of our knowledge, this is the first work in this field. The paper is considered the problem in which multiple suppliers, single producer and multiple retailers are involved and producer produces various kinds of multi-items and supplies all types of items to the retailers. A mathematical model has been developed with numerical examples provided. This model achieves coordination amongst the members in a supply chain assuming common cycle time for all non-identical retailers. This facilitates the consolidation of orders by producer and subsequently by the suppliers. Consolidation of orders in a supply chain results in reducing the order processing costs of chain members, while fulfilling the annual demand. Separate rate for deterioration have been taken for suppliers, producer and retailers, which is completely practical (raw material, finished goods in factory and finished goods in shop always deteriorate with different rate of deterioration).

Multiple deliveries are the most important policies to reduce inventory. The integrated decision also results in a lower optimal joint cost when compared with an independent decision by the producer or the retailers. To make it acceptable to all parties, the integrated policy should offer some kind of profit sharing. The study is particularly useful for the inventory systems where producer, their suppliers and their retailers form a strategic alliance with a mutually benefit objective. Future research can be performed for multi-producer-retailer chain.

Acknowledgement

The first author is very much thankful to the council of scientific and industrial research (CSIR) New Delhi, India for the financial assistance in the form of Junior Research Fellowship (JRF).

References

Aliabadi, D. E., Kaazemi, A. & Pourghannad, B. (2013). A two-level GA to solve an integrated multi-item supplier selection model. *Applied Mathematics and Computation*, 219(14), 7600–7615.

Clark, A. J., & Scarf, H. (1960). Optimal policies for a multi echelon inventory problem. *Management Science,* 6, 475–490.

Chui, Y. S., Huang, C. C., Wu, M. F. & Chang, H. H. (2013). Joint determination of rotation cycle time and number of shipments for a multi-item EPQ model with random defective rate. *Economic Modelling*, 35, 112–117.

Goyal, S. K., & Gupta, Y.P. (1989). Integrated inventory models: The buyer–vendor coordination. *European Journal of Operational Research*, 41(3), 261–269.

Goyal, S. K., & Gunasekaran, A. (1995). An integrated production–inventory–marketing model for deteriorating items. *Computers and Industrial Engineering,* 28, 755–762.

Ganeshan, R. (1999). Managing supply chain inventories: a multiple retailer, one warehouse, multiple supplier models. *International Journal of Production Economics*, 59, 341–354.

Goyal, S. K. (2000). On improving the single-vendor single-buyer integrated production inventory model with a generalized policy. *European Journal of Operational Research*, 125 (2), 429–430.

Hill, R. M. (1997). The single-vendor single-buyer integrated production–inventory model with a generalized policy. *European Journal of Operational Research*, 97 (3), 493–499.

Hanbali, A. A. & Heijden, M. V. (2013). Interval availability analysis of a two-echelon, multi-item system. *European Journal of Operational Research*, 228 (1), 494-503.

Jaber, M. Y., Osman, I. H., & Guiffrida, A.L. (2006). Coordinating a three-level supply chain with price discounts, price dependent demand and profit sharing. *International Journal of Integrated Supply Management*, 2 (1–2), 28–48.

Jaber, M. Y., & Goyal, S. K. (2008). Coordinating a three-level supply chain with multiple suppliers, a vendor and multiple buyers. *International Journal of Production Economics,* 116, 95-103.

Jain, R. & Singh, S. R. (2011). Inflation implication on an inventory with expiration date, capital constraint and uncertain lead time in a multi-echelon supply chain. *International Journal of Procurement Management*, 4 (4), 419-432.

Singh, S. R., Kumar, N. & Kumari, R. (2012). Three echelon supply chain inventory model for deteriorating items with storage facility and lead time under inflation. *International Journal of Services and Operations Management,* 13 (1), 98-118.

Lenard, J. D. & Roy, B. (1995). Multi-item inventory control: A multi criteria view, *European Journal of Operational Research,* 87, 685-692.

Ben-Daya, M. & Raouf, A. (1993). On the constrained multi-item single-period inventory problem. *International journal of Production Management*, 13, 104-112.

Munson, C. L. & Rosenblatt, M. J. (2001). Coordinating a three-level supply chain with quantity discounts. *IIE Transactions,* 33 (5), 371–384.

Pal, B., Sana, S. S. & Chaudhari, K. S. (2012). A three layer multi-item production–inventory model for multiple suppliers and retailers. *Economic Modelling*, 29(6), 2704–2710.

Rosenblatt, M. J. (1981). Multi-item inventory system with budgetary constraint: A comparison between the Lagrangian and the fixed cycle approach. *International Journal of Production Research*, 19(4), 331-339.

Sadjadi, S. J., Yazdian, S. A. & Shahanaghi, K. (2012). Optimal pricing, lot-sizing and marketing planning in a capacitated and imperfect production system. *Computers & Industrial Engineering,* 62(1), 349–358.

Thomas, D. J. & Grifin, P. J. (1996). Coordinated supply chain management. *European Journal of Operational Research*, 94, 1–15.

Viswanathan, S. & Wang, Q. (2003). Discount pricing decisions in distribution channels with price-sensitive demand. *European Journal of Operational Research*, 149 (3), 571–587.

Tsao, Y. C. & Sheen, G. J. (2012). A multi-item supply chain with credit periods and weight freight cost discounts. *International Journal of Production Economics*, 135(1), 106–115.

14

Intermodal network expansion in a competitive environment with uncertain demands

Fateme Fotuhi and Nathan Huynh*

Department of Civil & Environmental Engineering, University of South Carolina, Columbia, SC USA

C H R O N I C L E

Keywords:
Intermodal terminal location
Competition
Robust optimization
Simulated annealing

A B S T R A C T

This paper formulates robust optimization models for the problem of finding near-optimal locations for new intermodal terminals and their capacities for a railroad company, which operates an intermodal network in a competitive environment with uncertain demands. To solve the robust models, a Simulated Annealing (SA) algorithm is developed. Experimental results indicate that the SA solutions (i.e. objective function values) were comparable to those obtained using GAMS, but the SA algorithm could obtain solutions faster and could solve much larger problems. In addition, the results verify that solutions obtained from the robust models were more effective in dealing with uncertain demand scenarios.

1. Introduction

Intermodal freight transport is the movement of goods in one and the same loading unit or road vehicle, which uses successively two or more modes of transport without handling the goods themselves in changing modes (United Nations, 2001). This research deals with the locations of rail-highway intermodal terminals where the modal shift occurs. A significant portion of the total cost and time in intermodal services is attributed to the drayage movements and intermodal terminal operations. Thus, the location of an intermodal terminal plays an important role in improving efficiency and attractiveness of intermodal services (Sorensen et al., 2012).

Most of the intermodal terminal location studies in the literature solve for the optimal locations without considering existing terminals in the network. This assumption is not realistic in practice as pointed out by Gelarch et al. (2010). In today's competitive environment, railroad companies are constantly looking to expand their intermodal networks to meet customers' demands and to increase market share. This is often accomplished by incrementally adding a few new terminals at a time. Solving the location problem that takes into account a company's existing terminals as well as those of competitors is more challenging. This study seeks to fill this gap in existing literature by developing a mathematical model that addresses competition in intermodal terminal location decisions. Competition involves new incoming terminals competing against existing terminals in the network for market share.

* Corresponding author.

There are a few additional challenges involved in developing the proposed model. The first is uncertainty in demand. Demand for an intermodal terminal is the result of the commodity flow originated or terminated in the region where the terminal is located (Chiranjivi, 2008). Accurate long-range prediction of commodity flow is difficult because of uncertainty in economic situations and changes in supply chain decisions, infrastructure, and regulations. For example, most freight-related forecasts failed to predict the global recession that started in 2009. Thus, it is crucial for a strategic model to explicitly account for uncertainty in demand. The second challenge is determining the appropriate throughput capacity for the new terminal to avoid the situation of under-equipping the terminal which would lead to delays at the terminal (Nocera, 2009) or over-equipping the terminal which would lead to underutilized staff and resources. Throughput capacity is the total number of containers that can be processed by a terminal in a year and is usually expressed in TEUs (Twenty-foot Equivalent Units) (Bassan, 2007).

The objective of this work is to develop a mathematical optimization model which addresses all of the challenges and issues mentioned above. Specifically, the model seeks to determine the locations for the new intermodal terminals and their throughput capacities while considering competition and uncertainty in freight demands. The developed model contributes to the existing body of work on intermodal terminal location by explicitly incorporating competition and uncertainty in freight demand in the formulation. The proposed model is applicable for intermodal networks where private rail carriers are responsible for their own maintenance and improvement projects; the U.S. intermodal networks operate under this model.

The rest of the paper is organized as follows. Section 2 provides a summary of related studies; three topics are addressed: (1) rail-highway intermodal terminal location problem, (2) terminal throughput capacity, and (3) competitive location. Section 2 also provides a brief review of the robust optimization concept. Section 3 presents the developed mathematical model. Section 4 discusses the developed simulated annealing algorithm. Section 5 discusses the results from numerical experiments and the case studies. Section 6 discusses the practice implications of various managerial decisions. Lastly, Section 7 provides concluding remarks and directions for future work.

2. Literature review and background

2.1 Literature review

2.1.1 Rail-highway intermodal terminal location problem

Studies of terminal locations are performed at strategic planning level (Crainic, 1998) which involves different stakeholders with different objectives (Sirikijpanichkul & Ferreira, 2005). Over the years, the hub-based network structure has emerged as the preferred method for moving intermodal shipments (Ishfaq & Sox, 2011). A hub is a location where flow are aggregated/disaggregated, collected and redistributed (Arnold, Dominique & Isabelle, 2004). Similar to hubs, intermodal terminals are the transfer points at which containers are sorted and transferred between different modes (Meng & Wang, 2011). The emergence of hub based intermodal networks indicates that economies of scale are the principle force behind their preferred design (Slack, 1990). Also, because intermodal networks are combinations of their respective modal networks, it is natural that the hub network has emerged as the most suitable network design for intermodal logistics (Bookbinder & Fox, 1998).

In an intermodal hub network, smaller shipments are gathered and consolidated at distribution centers. At the next step, all consolidated containers are collected from these distribution centers and shipped to the terminals via drayage and then between a set of transfer terminals (i.e. rail-highway intermodal terminals). Finally, trucks transport loaded containers to their final destinations (Ishfaq & Sox, 2011).

Rutten (1995) was the first to find terminal locations which will attract enough freight volume to schedule daily trains to and from the terminal. Arnold et al. (2004) developed a rail-highway intermodal terminal location problem with each mode as a sub-graph and considered transfer links to connect these sub-graphs to each other. Racunica and Wynter (2005) developed a model to find terminals in a rail-highway intermodal network. They considered a nonlinear concave-cost function to find these optimal hubs. Groothedde et al. (2005) developed a hub-based network for the consumer goods market. They compared the single highway mode with a highway-water intermodal. They showed that the intermodal approach is more effective than the unimodal approach (with just highway). Limbourg and Jourquin (2009) proposed a model to find hub locations in a rail-highway intermodal network. They developed a heuristic to find hub locations for a road network and found rail links which passes through these hubs. Meng and Wang (2011) proposed a mathematical program for a hub-and-spoke intermodal network. The main difference between their model and earlier works is that it considered more than one pair of hubs for moving containers from an origin to a destination. Their work considered a chain of terminals to move shipments with different types of containers.

Mode choice has been incorporated into the hub location models. Ishfaq and Sox (2010) developed an integrated model for an intermodal network dealing with air, highway and rail modes. Their model allowed for direct shipment between origin and destination pairs using highway. It found the optimal locations for intermodal terminals and distribution of shipments among pairs of intermodal terminals by minimizing the total transportation cost, transfer cost at the terminal and fixed cost of opening a hub. In their later work, they proposed a rail-highway hub intermodal location-allocation problem (Ishfaq & Sox, 2011). Their model found the optimal location of hubs as well as optimal allocation of shipments for an Origin-Destination (OD) pair to selected hubs. Their model considered the fixed cost of opening a terminal, transportation cost, and the cost of delay at terminals. Sorensen et al. (2012) modeled a hub-based rail-highway intermodal network with the option of direct shipment. Different fraction of shipments for an OD pair can use highway only or a combination of highway and rail (i.e. intermodal). Fotuhi and Huynh (2013) proposed a model, which jointly selected terminal location, shipping modes and optimal routes for shipping different types of commodities. Their model allowed decision makers to evaluate scenarios with more than two modes.

2.1.2 Terminal throughput capacity

The traditional capacitated facility location problem in which facilities have limited capacities has been studied extensively. Drezner (1995) provided a survey of facility location studies with limited capacity. Some researchers have investigated the location planning problems with variable capacities. Verter and Dincer (1995) were the first to integrate location decision and variable capacity planning for a new facility. They developed a model to minimize the fixed cost of opening a new facility, variable cost for capacity acquisition, and total transportation cost. In the transportation domain, Taniguchi, Noritake and Izumitani (1999) were the first to integrate location decision and capacity planning (number of berths) for public logistic terminals in urban areas that serve only the truck mode. Their proposed model selected logistic terminals from a set of predefined candidate locations and found the optimal number of berths for each terminal. Tang, Tang and Wang (2013) developed a model to find the best location for a logistics park, size of park and allocation of customers to it. They considered different layouts for the park and their model selected a lay out which can serve all demands. There has been limited work in capacity planning of intermodal terminals (Ballis & Golias, 2004; Nocera, 2009). To date, no study has examined intermodal terminal location and terminal size jointly.

2.1.3 Competitive location

All of the aforementioned studies addressed the problem of designing a new network without consideration of existing road networks and rail terminals. Marianov et al. (1999) developed a competitive hub location model that considered existing terminals in the network. They assigned the demand for each OD pair to a pair of potential hubs to maximize this newcomer's market share. Transportation cost was the main factor for these assignments. In 2009, Eiselt and Marianov proposed a model of competitive hub location problem by incorporating a gravity model based on the work of Huff (1964). They allocated the demand to pairs of new hubs based on their attractions to maximize market share for the new hubs. Huff's gravity model is a popular approach for estimating the captured market share by a facility. Based on this model, the probability that a customer chooses a facility is proportional to the attractiveness of the facility and is inversely proportional to the distance to the facility. Eiselt and Marianov (2009) mentioned that their model is suitable for a new incoming airline that has to compete with existing airlines. Chiranjivi (2008) studied the environmental impact of adding a new terminal to an existing rail-highway network. They introduced factors that made a terminal attractive and investigated the effects of the new terminal on accessibility and mobility of the intermodal network. Gelareh et al. (2010) studied the competitive hub location for a liner shipping network. They considered a newcomer liner service provider which has to compete with existing liner service companies. They introduced an attraction function to estimate the total captured market share by a new terminal by considering the travel time from the origin to the destination using that specific terminal and transportation rate. Lüer-Villagra and Marianov (2013) formulated a new competitive hub location problem to find optimal locations for a new airline company and optimal pricing to maximize their profits. They modeled consumers' behaviors using the Logit discrete choice model.

Table 1 provides a summary of capabilities of previous models and this study's proposed model, which extends the work of Eiselt and Marianov (2009) by considering more than one mode for a competitive p-hub network as well as uncertainty in demand. It enhances previous models in the area of intermodal terminal location problem by considering competition. As explained previously, competition involves new incoming terminals competing against existing terminals in the network for market share. Although Limbourg and Jourquin (2009) considered existing intermodal terminals in their model, they did not consider competition between the new terminals and existing ones. To our knowledge, competition has not been addressed in any intermodal network design studies. As indicated in Table 1, this paper advances the modeling of intermodal network design by considering competition and the joint location and terminal throughput capacity decisions. Additionally, it is the first intermodal network design study to use robust optimization to address uncertainty in demand. A brief overview of robust optimization as well as relevant literature is presented in the next subsection.

2.2 Background (robust optimization)

In developing models for real world systems, researchers often face incomplete and noisy data (Mulvey et al., 1995). To address uncertainty in data, researchers have developed a technique called robust optimization. It deals with uncertainty by considering a set of finite discrete scenarios for the parameter with noisy data and finds a solution that is near-optimal for any realization of scenarios (Snyder & Daskin, 2005).

Min-max regret and minimum expected regret are the two common robust optimization approaches (Kouvelis & Gu, 1997). To understand these approaches, consider a situation where S denote a set of s finite scenarios for the uncertain parameter and x represents a feasible solution for the robust problem. Let $Z_s(x)$ represents the solution of the feasible point x in scenario s and Z_s^* represents the optimal solution for scenario s (over all x). The min-max regret finds a solution which minimizes the maximum "regret" value for all scenarios and is formulated as follows.

$$\min_{x \in X}(\max_{s \in S}(Z_s(x) - Z_s^*)) \tag{1}$$

The "regret" represents the difference between $Z_s(x)$ and Z_s^*. For maximization problems, the regret is negative for each scenario; thus, for these problems, the objective of the robust model is to maximize the minimum regret. For situations where there is information about the probability of each scenario occurring, the minimum expected regret approach is preferred, which will find the near-optimal solution by minimizing the expected regrets over all scenarios (Daskin et al., 1997).

There are a few studies in the literature that have utilized robust optimization to address uncertainty for hub location problems. Huang and Wang (2009) were the first to use robust optimization to find the near-optimal hub-and-spoke network design for an airline given uncertain demands and costs. They developed a multi-objective model and minimized total cost for all scenarios. Makui et al. (2012) developed a robust optimization model for the multi-objective capacitated p-hub location problem to deal with uncertainty in the demands for each OD pair and the processing time for each commodity at a hub. In the area of competitive location problem, Ashtiani et al. (2013) were the first to develop a robust optimization model for the leader-follower competitive facility location problem. This class of problems deals with the situation where the leader and follower have existing facilities, and the follower wants to open some new facilities, but the number of new facilities for the follower to open is uncertain. The objective of the leader-follower model is to maximize the market share for the leader after the follower has opened its new facilities.

Table 1 Comparison of current paper's and related studies' capabilities

Reference	Model Features					Variables				Goals	
	Parameter		Competitive	Mode							
	certain	uncertain		single	intermodal	Location	capacity	allocation	responsiveness	profit	cost
Marianov et al. (1999)	✓		✓	✓		✓		✓		✓	
Taniguchi et al. (1999)	✓			✓		✓	✓				✓
Arnold et al. (2004)	✓				✓	✓		✓			✓
Groothedde et al., (2005)	✓				✓	✓					✓
Racunica & Wynter (2005)	✓				✓	✓		✓			✓
Eiselt & Marianov (2009)	✓		✓	✓		✓		✓		✓	
Huang & Wang (2009)		✓		✓		✓		✓	✓		
Limbourg & Jourquin (2009)	✓				✓	✓					✓
Gelareh et al. (2010)	✓		✓	✓		✓		✓		✓	
Ishfaq & Sox (2011)	✓				✓	✓		✓			✓
Meng & Wang (2011)	✓				✓	✓					✓
Makui et al. (2012)		✓		✓		✓		✓	✓		
Sorensen et al. (2012)	✓				✓	✓		✓			✓
Lüer-Villagra & Marianov (2013)	✓		✓	✓		✓		✓		✓	
Current paper		✓	✓		✓	✓	✓	✓	✓		

3 Modeling framework

Consider a railroad company's rail-highway intermodal network that has competing railroad companies' infrastructure. Let $G(N_1, A_1)$ and $G(N_2, A_2)$ represent road and rail networks, respectively. Thus, N_1 represent cities, and N_2 represent intermodal terminals in the rail network. Similarly, A_1 represent the highway links in the highway network, and A_2 represent the railway links in the rail network. A shipment from origin *i to* destination *j* can be transported either directly by truck only via links on A_1 or by a combination of truck and rail (i.e. intermodal). The intermodal option involves trucks transporting cargo from origin *i* to terminal *k* via links on A_1, then trains transporting cargo from terminal *k* to terminal *m* via links on A_2, and finally trucks transporting cargo from terminal *k* to destination *j* via links on A_1. Let *W* represent the set of selected OD pairs with demands between them from N_1 cities.

Suppose a railroad company decided to expand its network by opening *q* new terminals from N_{new} candidate locations. It wants the new terminals to attract as much demand as possible (i.e. increase its market share). However, the railroad company already has N_{eo} terminals in the proximity of the market area for candidate locations and its competitors have N_{ec} terminals in the same area. Although there are more terminals operating in the network, the new incoming terminals only have to compete against those in the sets N_{eo} and N_{ec}; it is assumed that only those terminals located in the proximity of the candidate locations will have a direct impact on the market share of new incoming terminals. Thus, N_2, as defined previously, includes the railroad company's and competitors' existing terminals around candidate locations, the new terminals at candidate locations, and all other terminals in the network. Logically, the company should locate the new terminals at some distance, *M,* away from its existing ones to avoid serving the same market. Note that *M* may have different values based on the demographics of different parts of the network. According to Cunningham (2012) *M* has a value of 100 miles for the Eastern parts of the U.S. and 250 miles for the Western parts. Thus, the decision that the railroad company has to make is where to open the new terminal(s). Let this decision be defined by the binary decision variable y_k, which is equal to 1 if the candidate terminal $k \in N_{new}$ is selected. In a prescreening process, candidate terminals with a distance of less than *M* from the company's existing terminals are excluded from the list of eligible candidate terminals. If location *k* is selected, then the binary decision variable x_{km} indicates whether there is a connection between terminals *k* and *m*. If neither *k* nor *m* is open, then x_{km} cannot be 1. For existing terminals (k,m), x_{km} is 1.

Shipments going from origin *i* to destination *j* can be transported via multiple routes if there are several intermodal terminals available. The utility (i.e. attractiveness) of the intermodal option via the pair of terminals (k,m) for shipments going from origin *i* to destination *j* can be defined as follows.

$$u_{ijkm} = \frac{1}{(d_{ik} + d_{km} + d_{mj})^{\alpha}} \tag{2}$$

where d_{ik} and d_{mj} denote the delivery and pickup drayage distances, respectively, and d_{km} is the line-haul distance. The term α in Equation 2 can be used to give less significance to those facilities that are far from the origin and/or destination (Huff, 1964). In this study, a simple inversely proportional relationship is assumed; thus α is set to 1. Similarly, the utility of the truck-only option for shipments going from origin *i* and destination *j* is defined as follows.

$$v_{ij} = \frac{1}{d_{ij}} \tag{3}$$

The Huff gravity functions, Eq. (2) and Eq. (3), can be used to compute the utilities of the two competing modes, intermodal and truck-only. Using these utilities, the probability that a shipper chooses a particular mode can be calculated using the Logit choice model. The probability that a shipper uses the intermodal option via terminals (k,m) to transport cargo from origin *i* to destination *j* is:

$$p_{ijkm} = \frac{u_{ijkm}x_{km}}{\sum_{(k \text{ or } m) \in \{N_{new}\}} u_{ijkm}x_{km} + \sum_{(k,m) \in \{N_2 - N_{new}\}} u_{ijkm}x_{km} + v_{ij}} \tag{4}$$

Similarly, the probability that shippers choose the truck-only option to move their cargo is:

$$p_{ij} = \frac{v_{ij}}{\sum_{(k \text{ or } m) \in \{N_{new}\}} u_{ijkm}x_{km} + \sum_{(k,m) \in \{N_2 - N_{new}\}} u_{ijkm}x_{km} + v_{ij}} \tag{5}$$

It is assumed that all demands are met. That is, for a specific OD pair (i,j), the sum of all probabilities is equal to 1 ($\sum_{(k,m)} p_{ijkm} + p_{ij} = 1$).

In this study, we accounted for the fact that future freight demand is uncertain and that we have a finite set of demand scenarios. Let these scenarios be denoted as $S = \{1..s\}$. The demand for OD pair (i, j) under scenario s is denoted as h_{ij}^{s}. The probability that demand between nodes i and j is served by the intermodal option via terminals (k,m) is p_{ijkm}. It follows that the total demand (i.e. market share) captured by terminals (k,m) for OD pair (i, j) under scenario s is $h_{ij}^{s} p_{ijkm}$. The higher the probabilities for pairs of terminals (k,m) as computed by Equation (4), the more demand the company will attract and thus increase its market share when either k or m is a new terminal.

In addition to determining the locations for the new terminals, our model also seeks to determine the annual throughput capacity, z_k, for the new terminal k which depends on its total attracted demand. This capacity needs to be sufficiently large to accommodate all demand scenarios. The objective of this problem is to maximize the new terminals' profits for all scenarios by maximizing the minimum regret. The revenue generated by terminal k per container is denoted as r_k. It is a fee that a shipper pays to the terminal for handling the container. There is an annual fixed cost f_k to operate the terminal, in addition to an operating cost c_k for handling the container.

3.1 Mathematical formulation

The mathematical model for the max-min intermodal terminal location problem in a competitive environment can be formulated as follows (P1).

P1:

$$\max Z \tag{6}$$

subject to:

$$\sum_{(i,j)\in W,(k \text{ or } m)\in N_{new}} h_{ij}^{s} p_{ijkm} r_k - \sum_{k\in N_{new}} f_k y_k - \sum_{k\in N_{new}} c_k z_k - O_s^{*} \geq Z, \qquad \forall s \in S \tag{7}$$

$$p_{ijkm} = \frac{u_{ijkm} x_{km}}{\sum_{(k \text{ or } m)\in N_{new}} u_{ijkm} x_{km} + \sum_{(k,m)\in\{N_2 - N_{new}\}} u_{ijkm} x_{km} + v_{ij}}, \qquad \forall (i,j) \in W, (k \text{ or } m) \in N_{new} \tag{8}$$

$$\sum_{k\in N_{new}} y_k = q, \tag{9}$$

$$x_{km} \leq y_k, \qquad \forall k \in N_{new}, m \in N_2 \tag{10}$$

$$x_{km} \leq y_m, \qquad \forall m \in N_{new}, k \in N_2 \tag{11}$$

$$\sum_{(i,j)\in W, m\in N_2} (p_{ijkm} h_{ij}^{s} + p_{ijmk} h_{ij}^{s}) \leq z_k, \qquad \forall k \in N_{new}, \forall s \in S \tag{12}$$

$$y_k, x_{km} \in \{0,1\}, z_k \geq 0, \qquad k \in N_{new}, m \in N_2 \tag{13}$$

The objective function (6) maximizes the minimum regret. O_s^{*} in constraints (7) is the optimal objective function for scenario s that is obtained by considering scenario s alone. The regret associated with each scenario is the difference between the total profit of new terminals comprising all scenarios and O_s^{*}. Constraints (7) show that each scenario's regret is greater than a minimum regret. Constraints

(8) compute the probability that the intermodal option is used with the demand allocated to each pair of open terminals. Constraints (9) guarantee that q terminals will be selected. Constraints (10) and (11) ensure that the variable x_{km} is 0 if either terminal k or m is not selected. Constraints (12) define throughput capacities of selected terminals. Constraints (13) define the range of the decision variables. To obtain the regret of scenario s in constraints (7), O_s^* is determined by solving the following model (P2).

P2:

$$O_s : Max \sum_{(i,j)\in W,(k \text{ or } m)\in N_{new}} h_{ij}^s p_{ijkm} r_k - \sum_{k\in N_{new}} f_k y_k - \sum_{k\in N_{new}} c_k z_k \tag{14}$$

subject to: $Eqs. (8)-(13)$

The first term in objective function (14) is the total revenue generated by the new terminals. The second term is the annual fixed cost of operating the terminals, and the third term is the variable cost of operating the terminal. If the decision maker knows the probability of each scenario occurring, then the objective of the robust optimization model would be to minimize the expected regret. As mentioned previously, the regret for problems with maximization objective is negative so the robust model's objective function is to maximize the expected regret. If scenario s occurs with probability β_s and R_s shows its related regret, then the maximum expected regret model is defined as follows (P3).

P3:

$$O_{\exp} : \max \sum_s \beta_s R_s \tag{15}$$

subject to: (16)

$$R_s = \sum_{(i,j)\in W,(k \text{ or } m)\in N_{new}} h_{ij}^s p_{ijkm} r_k - \sum_{k\in N_{new}} f_k y_k - \sum_{k\in N_{new}} c_k z_k - O_s^*, \quad \forall s \in S$$

$Eqs.(8)-(13)$

$O_{\exp}$ in Eq. (15) maximizes the expected regret over all scenarios and R_s in Eq. (16) is the regret of each scenario.

4. Solution method

The aforementioned model is a nonlinear integer program, which is NP-hard (Krumke, 2004) and is not solvable by standard Mixed Integer Nonlinear Programing solvers (Eiselt & Marianov, 2009) while it may be possible to find the exact solutions for realistic-sized problems by exhaustive enumeration, such an approach will likely take days to solve, even with today's high performance desktops and workstations. For this reason, there is an increasing body of work that focuses on researching efficient algorithms using meta-heuristics such as tabu search and genetic algorithm to find the exact solutions for strategic problems (e.g., Ishfaq & Sox, 2011; Meng & Wang, 2011). In this research, a simulated annealing algorithm is proposed to find the optimal solutions for the three models discussed above: P1, P2 and P3.

4.1 Background on simulated annealing (SA) algorithm

Kirkpatrick et al. (1983) were the first to propose SA to solve combinatorial optimization problems. The SA algorithm begins with an initial feasible solution and then its neighborhood is randomly searched for improvement. If the objective function improves, the solution is accepted and it becomes the new solution from which the search continues. Otherwise, it will accept a non-improving solution with a probability determined by the Boltzmann function $\exp(-\Delta / T)$, where Δ is the difference between the objective functions of two consecutive iterations and T is the temperature at that iteration. This probability is high at the beginning of the algorithm. It increases the chance of accepting a worse solution to avoid getting trapped in a local solution, but it decreases as the algorithm proceeds (i.e. cools down to its frozen temperature). Readers are referred to Kirkpatrick et al. (1983) for a complete description of the SA algorithm.

For SA, the cooling schedule requires a starting temperature T_0, cooling rate γ, maximum number of iterations at each temperature $K_{\max}$ and the stopping number σ. T_0 is selected so that the probability of accepting non-improving solutions is P_0. A number of non-improving neighborhoods for the initial solution which is a fraction of the neighborhood size (5% to 10%) are evaluated and their average cost increase (for cost minimization problems) $\overline{\Delta C}$ is computed. Then T_0 is computed based on this formula $\exp(-\overline{\Delta C}/T_0) \approx P_0$ [39]. A simple decay function of the parameter γ updates the temperature at the end of each epoch r; i.e. $T(r+1) = \gamma T(r)$. The value of γ is typically between 0.85 and 0.95, with higher values generating more accurate results but with a lower convergence rate. The number of iterations $K_{\max}$ is determined by the neighborhood size. The algorithm terminates when no improvement is found in a specific number of temperatures σ.

SA has been applied to a number of facility location problems and hub location problems (Murray & Church, 1996, Ernst & Krishnamoorthy, 1999, Arostegui et al., 2006). Drezner et al. (2002) were the first to apply SA for solving Huff-like competitive facility location problems. They proposed five different algorithms and showed that SA has promising results. The next subsection discusses how the SA algorithm was applied to solve the developed models.

4.2 Proposed simulated annealing algorithm

In this subsection, how the SA was adapted to solve P2 is first discussed. Then, how it was modified to solve P1 and P3 is presented. A feasible solution for P2 is any configuration of q new terminals and their capacities. Thus, among the candidate locations, the ones that are furthest from the company's existing terminals are selected as the initial set of terminals. In this problem, constraints (10) and (11) may be replaced by the following equation:

$$x_{km} = \min\{y_k, y_m\} \qquad \forall (k \text{ or } m) \in N_{new} \tag{17}$$

Eq. (17) indicates that x_{km} values are determined based on the initial terminal set. The parameters u_{ijkm}, p_{ijkm} and z_k are computed based on y and x values. u_{ijkm} values are determined based on the distances to terminals regardless of the terminal being open or not; thus, they remain constant through the end of the algorithm. The complete neighborhood for a solution is the set of all solutions found by closing one terminal and opening a closed terminal from the set of unselected terminals. For this problem, the neighborhood size is $q^*(N_{new} - q)$. Given an incumbent solution, one of the neighboring solutions is selected by closing the terminal with the highest fixed and variable costs and opening a candidate terminal that is furthest from the set of unselected terminals. From this new terminal set (solution), the x_{km}, p_{ijkm} and z_k values are computed and objective function (14) is evaluated.

For this problem, 10% of a neighborhood is evaluated to compute T_0. Initial testing found that the SA algorithm obtained optimal solutions for small cases with $\gamma = 0.9$ and $\sigma = 3$. Thus, these values were used for larger problems as well, but with a small increase in σ based on the problem size. The overall algorithm for P2 is outlined in Fig. 1.

$T \leftarrow T_0$, $O^* \leftarrow O_{initial}$, $y \leftarrow y_{initial}$, $K \leftarrow 1$, $\sigma_0 \leftarrow 0$, $\sigma_{\max}$: Non improving temperatures
$O_{best} \leftarrow O_{initial}$, $T_{\min}$: Frozen Temperetaure

Repeat while $T > T_{\min}\ or\ \sigma_0 < \sigma_{\max}$
  Repeat while $K \le K_{\max}$
    $(y_{new}, z_{new}, O_{new})$ = Generate a neighborhood
    $\Delta = O_{new} - O^*$
    If $\Delta \ge 0$
      $y \leftarrow y_{new}, O^* \leftarrow O_{new}$
    Else if $e^{-\Delta/T} \le rand$
      $y \leftarrow y_{new}$
    End
  If $O_{best} = O^*$
    $\sigma_0 = \sigma_0 + 1$
  Else
    $O_{best} = O^*$
  End
  $K \leftarrow 1, T = \gamma T$

Fig. 1 Simulated annealing algorithm for solving P2

The SA algorithm discussed above can also be used to solve P1 and P3 with a minor change. The capacity constraints (12) in P1 and P3 determine the throughput capacity of open terminals under each scenario. It should be sufficiently large to accommodate any realization of demand values; thus, at each iteration of the SA algorithm the throughput capacity z_k for terminal k with $y_k = 1$ is computed as $\max_S\left(\sum_{(i,j)\in w, m\in N_2} (p_{ijkm}h_{ij}^s + p_{ijmk}h_{ij}^s)\right)$.

5. Computational experiments

The SA algorithm was coded in MATLAB R2012a, and the developed algorithm for P2 was tested on several randomly generated networks. Its performance was compared against GAMS/BARON solutions. The Branch-And-Reduce Optimization Navigator (BARON) is a GAMS commercial solver designed to find the global solution of Non-Linear Programs (NLP) and Mixed Integer Non-Linear Programs (MINLP) (Sahindis, 2013). All experiments were run on a desktop computer with an Intel Core 2 Duo 2.66 GHz processor and 8 GB of RAM and their computational times were reported.

In order to examine the performance of SA for P2, 20 experiments with different problem sizes were randomly generated. The parameters for these problems are given in Table 2. These values were selected to reflect real world scenarios. The size of the test networks range from 4 to 15 existing terminals, 2 to 15 candidate locations, and 1 to 4 new terminals to open. Theoretically, q can be changed from 1 to N_new. However, in reality, it is likely that the number of terminals that can be opened and be profitable based on the demand OD pair pattern, shipper's expenditures, existing terminals in the market area, and terminal costs will be fewer than N_new. Thus, for each test network, only a limited range of q is solved to find their optimal locations.

Table 2
Values of parameters used in numerical experiments

Parameter	Value
Highway miles	Normal(1,000, 100)
Line haul miles	Normal(700, 100)
Drayage miles	Normal(450, 100)
Fixed cost ($ per year)	Uniform(10,000, 30,000)
Variable cost ($ per container)	Uniform(10, 20)
Revenue ($ per container)	Uniform(20, 30)
Distance (miles) between competing terminals (existing and new)	Normal(400, 100)
Demand (containers)	Uniform(100, 300)

Table 3 summarizes the results of the test problems. Column 1 indicates the experiment number. Columns 2, 3, and 4 show number of existing terminals in the competition area, number of existing terminals far from the competition area, and number of candidate locations for the new terminals, respectively. q in column 5 indicates the number of new terminals to be opened. Columns 6 and 7 show the objective function values found by SA (Z_{SA}) and GAMS (Z_{GAMS}) respectively. Column 8 shows the gap between the ZSA and ZGAMS; gap is computed as $100*(\frac{z_{GAMS}-z_{SA}}{z_{GAMS}})$. The last two columns show the execution time in seconds of SA (t_{SA}) and GAMS (t_{GAMS}), respectively.

It can be seen in Table 3 that the developed SA obtained the same objective function values as GAMS for all experiments. The asterisk in column 6 indicates that the network with the corresponding q new terminals yield the optimal profit. For example, for a network with 5 existing terminals and 5 candidate locations (experiment number 6 to 9), 3 new terminals yield the maximum profit for the company. The execution times indicated that the SA algorithm can obtain solutions in much shorter time than GAMS for larger problems. The execution time for GAMS grows exponentially with the problem size. It takes more than 6 hours for GAMS to find the optimal solution for a problem with 50 OD pairs, 10 existing terminals and 15 candidate locations for the new terminals while SA obtains the same results in a few seconds. GAMS was not able to obtain a solution for problems with more than 10 existing terminals and 15 candidate locations due to out of memory error. To show the application of the developed model for larger problems, the two case studies discussed in the next subsections are solved using our developed SA method.

Table 3
Performance of SA compared against GAMS for test problems

Exp.#	$N_{existing-competitin}$	$N_{existing-other}$	N_{new}	q	Z_{SA}	Z_{GAMS}	Gap(%)	t_{SA} (s)	t_{GAMS} (s)
(1)	(2)	(3)	(4)	(5)	(6)	(7)	(8)	(9)	(10)
1	2	2	2	1	6,810*	6,810	0	1.6	1
2	2	2	2	2	1,425	1,425	0	1.2	0.55
3	3	2	3	1	17,715	17,715	0	2.6	14.18
4	3	2	3	2	25,205*	25,205	0	3.1	14.45
5	3	2	3	3	19,816	19,816	0	3.05	37
6	3	2	5	1	18,558	18,558	0	2.09	25.3
7	3	2	5	2	25,194	25,194	0	2.18	27.1
8	3	2	5	3	26,133*	26,133	0	2.15	28.2
9	3	2	5	4	18,859	18,859	0	2.1	32
10	4	5	6	1	21,548	21,548	0	2.33	367
11	4	5	6	2	32,354*	32,354	0	2.19	440
12	4	5	6	3	31,097	31,097	0	2.44	520
13	5	7	8	1	24,494	24,494	0	3.7	3663
14	5	7	8	2	39,303*	39,303	0	2.97	3605
15	5	7	8	3	31,850	31,850	0	2.6	3720
16	7	8	10	1	14,214	14,214	0	3.4	15121
17	7	8	10	2	20,343*	20,343	0	3.25	14700
18	7	8	10	3	19,384	19,384	0	3.29	16850
19	7	3	15	1	4,802*	4,802	0	3.2	18050
20	7	3	15	2	1,272.6	1,272.6	0	5.6	25265

*Optimal for specified network

5.1 Larger-sized instances

The robust models P1 and P3 were applied to two larger-sized case studies. The first case study involves an actual intermodal network in the U.S. and a set of freight demand scenarios derived from the Freight Analysis Framework (FAF3) (Battelle, 2011). The FAF3 database is provided by the U.S. Department of Transportation and it provides estimates of freight tonnage, value, and domestic ton-miles by region of origin and destination, commodity type, and mode, as well as state-to-state flows. To demonstrate the usability and generality of the developed model and solution approach, the second case study uses a larger random network configuration, as well as random demand volume and OD patterns.

5.1.1 Case study 1

This case study involves an actual intermodal network in the U.S., east of the Mississippi River. In the study area, there are two Class 1 railroad companies, A and B. Company A is considering expanding its network by adding a new terminal in South Carolina (SC). The candidate locations are Greenville, North Augusta, Lexington, and Florence. According to FAF3, these cities have the highest freight flow in South Carolina. They also have a good accessibility to interstates. Currently, both railroad companies have 4 to 5 terminals in South Carolina and neighboring states and a total of 18 in the study network. The goal of this analysis is to identify the optimal location for the new terminal and its throughput capacity. Fig. 2 depicts the study area.

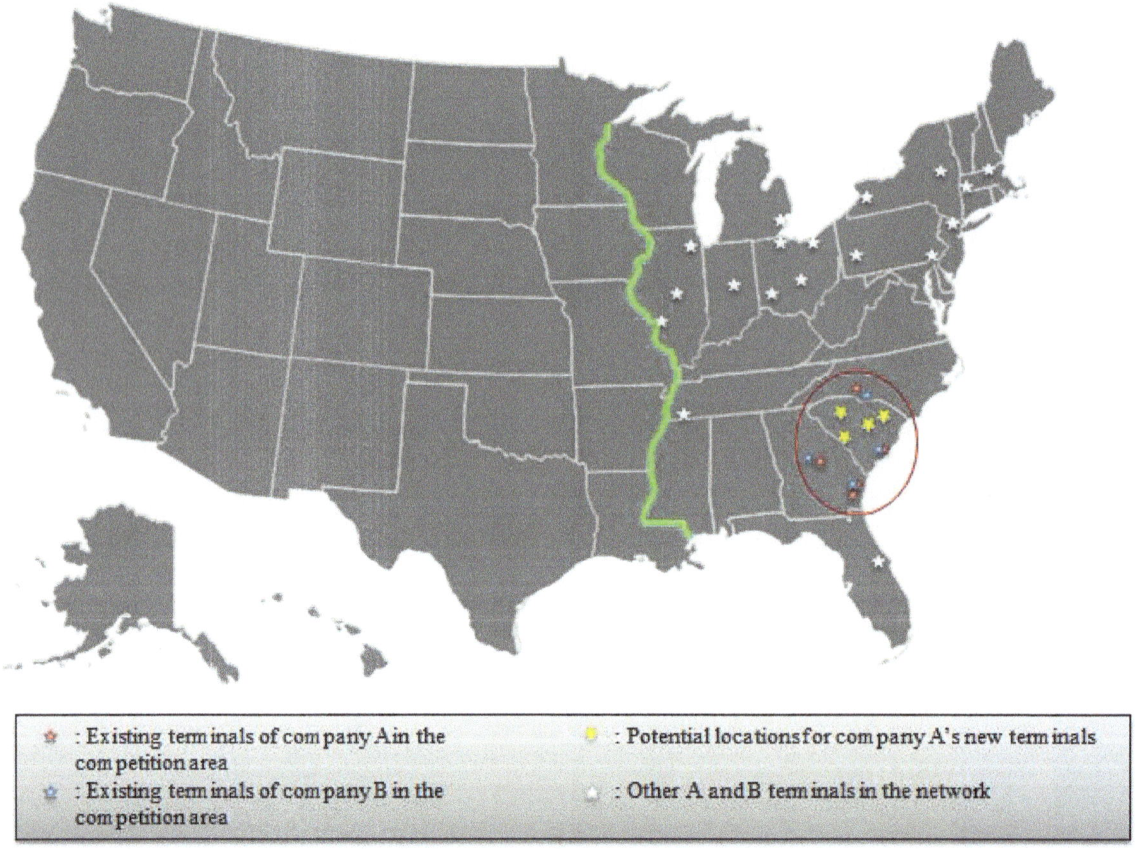

Fig. 2 Map of study area for case study 1

The analysis considered only domestic shipments that would use the intermodal option, which are those that need to be transported more than 750 miles and has an annual tonnage of more than 125 tons (ITIC manual, 2005). Live animals/fish, specific agricultural products, meat/seafood, alcoholic beverages, pharmaceuticals, plastics/rubber, wood products, newsprint/paper, paper articles, printed products, base metals, machinery, and furniture are the non-eligible commodities for intermodal transportation, and thus, were excluded from the analysis. After disaggregating the FAF3 data for 2040 using the proportional weighting method and using population as the surrogate variable, 482 eligible OD pairs were identified from/to SC counties to/from 16 states outside SC. Considering an average of 80,000 lbs as the maximum allowable weight for a 40-foot container, FAF3 commodity flows were converted to their equivalent container units. Fig. 3 shows the quantity of 2040 demand in number of containers for SC counties. As shown, Greenville, Charleston and their neighboring counties have the highest forecasted freight movement. Lexington and Richland counties are also forecasted to have high freight movement. Cost-of-living index was used to determine the relative relationship between the fixed costs and operating costs between the four candidate locations. Based on this index, Lexington is the most expensive county and parameters for the other three locations were computed based on the index. Google Maps was used to determine the drayage and line-haul distances.

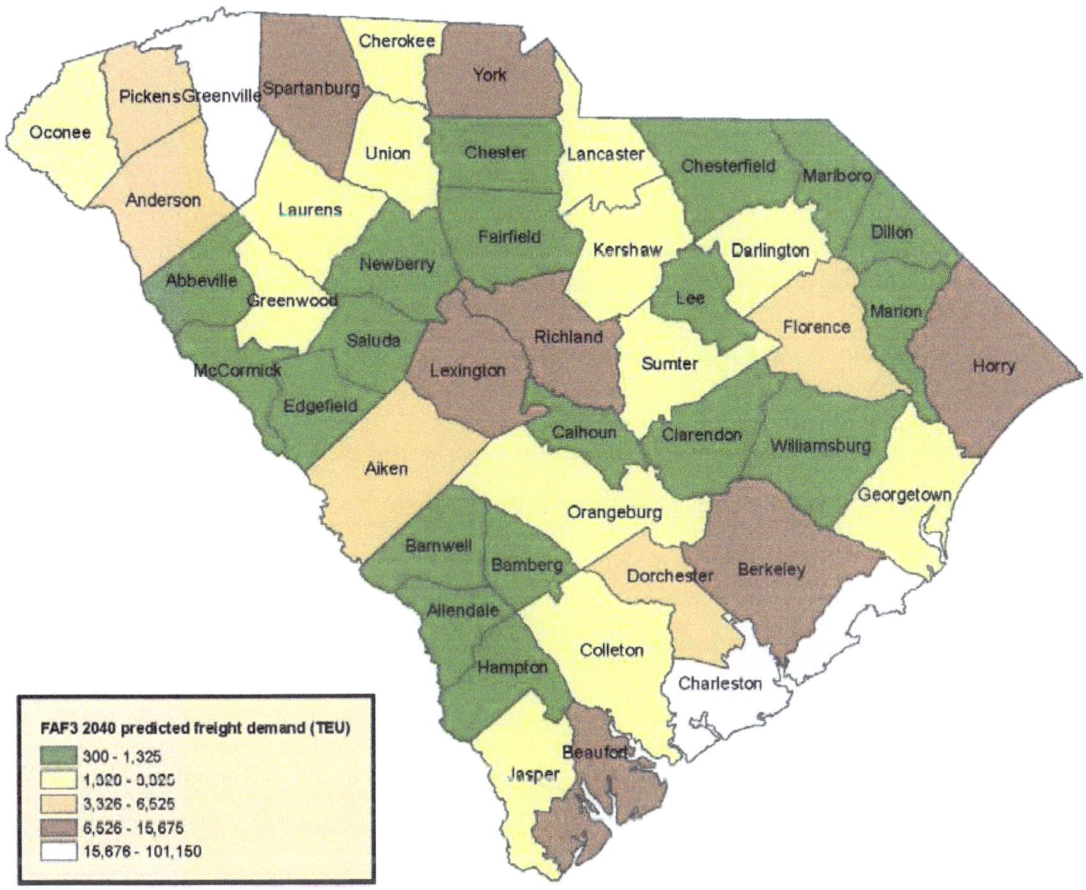

Fig. 3. FAF3 2040 predicted freight demand for SC counties.

Ten demand scenarios were considered, based on the FAF3 predicted values for 2040. Scenario 1 is the FAF3 2040 demand estimate. Scenarios 2 to 4 are those with demands 5, 10 and 20% over the 2040 estimate. Scenarios 5 to 7 are those with demands 5, 10, and 20% under the 2040 estimate. Scenarios 8 to 10 considered the possibility of new developments that may take place in the industrial counties. Table 4 shows the best location and its associated capacity for each scenario. If investment decisions are made using only the 2040 forecasted demand, then Greenville with a throughput capacity of 41,176 TEUs is the optimal location and size. However, that is not the case when other demand scenarios are considered, as illustrated in Table 4. If a terminal with a capacity of 41,176 TEU is built (based on the 2040 demand estimate) and scenario 2 occurred, then the terminal will not have enough capacity to meet the demand, 43,235 TEUs. This result shows that decision makers need to explicitly account for the different demand scenarios. The analysis showed that even if company A had the budget to build more than one new terminal, building just one new terminal is optimal because the profit decreases with each additional terminal.

Table 4
Results for individual scenarios

Row	Scenario	Selected terminal	Capacity (TEU)
1	FAF3 predicted demand for 2040	Greenville	41,176
2	5% increase in the demand for 2040	Greenville	43,235
3	10% increase in the demand for 2040	Lexington	44,850
4	20% increase in the demand for 2040	Lexington	48,927
5	5% decrease in the demand for 2040	Greenville	39,118
6	10% decrease in the demand for 2040	Greenville	37,059
7	20% decrease in the demand for 2040	Greenville	32,941
8	50% increase in the demand in Charleston, Horry, Beaufort and Berkeley counties	Lexington	46,595
9	50% increase in the demand in Lexington, Richland and Aiken counties	Greenville	42,960
10	30% increase in the demand in Greenville, Spartanburg, York, Richland, Lexington, Charleston, Berkeley, Beaufort and Horry counties	Lexington	50,215

Table 5 presents the results for the robust models P1 and P3. Column 1 shows how many scenarios are considered for each experiment. Column 2 shows which scenarios are considered, i.e. 1-3 refers to scenarios 1 to 3. Columns 3 and 4 indicate the optimal objective functions for P1 and P3, respectively. The selected site by P1 and P3 are presented in columns 5 and 6 and their associated capacities are shown in columns 7 and 8, respectively. The last two columns show the execution times of P1 and P3, respectively. Greenville is the optimal location, but its capacity changes with inclusion of different scenarios in the decision for both models. These results indicated that the demand scenarios play a key role in determining the throughput capacity of the terminal for both robust models. It is noted that in scenario 1 (row 1 of Table 4), almost half of the freight demands reside in the northern counties (i.e. Greenville, Spartanburg, York, Pickens and Anderson). Thus, Greenville was a suitable location to meet the demand for scenario 1 since it is located furthest north among the candidate locations.

Table 5
Solutions of the robust models: Z for P1 and O for P3

# of scenarios (1)	scenarios (2)	Z^* (3)	$O^*_{\exp}$ (4)	$y(Z)$ (5)	$y(O_{\exp})$ (6)	$z(Z)$ (7)	$z(O_{\exp})$ (8)	t_Z (9)	$t_{O_{\exp}}$ (10)
2	1-2	-146690	-110020	Greenville	Greenville	43235	43235	8.62	7.26
3	1-3	-293380	-212850	Greenville	Greenville	45294	45294	9.71	9.04
4	1-4	-586760	-491980	Greenville	Greenville	49412	49412	10.14	10.31
5	1-5	-733460	-505480	Greenville	Greenville	49412	49412	11.36	11.83
6	1-6	-880150	-552190	Greenville	Greenville	49412	49412	12.76	13.83
7	1-7	-1173500	-587500	Greenville	Greenville	49412	49412	15.18	14.55
8	1-8	-1173500	-508380	Greenville	Greenville	49412	49412	48.78	16.35
9	1-9	-1173500	-476940	Greenville	Greenville	49412	49412	50	17
10	1-10	-1267200	-432180	Greenville	Greenville	50726	50726	87	20

To illustrate the impact of probabilities on site selection using P3, a set of four scenarios (1, 8, 9 and 10) with various probabilities was considered and the results were compared to those obtained by P1. Recall that Greenville was the optimal site for P1 regardless of probability values. It can be observed in Table 6 that Greenville is the optimal location with higher probabilities for scenarios 1 and 9, but Lexington became the optimal site when scenarios 8 and 10 have higher probabilities (highlighted in

Table 6). This is because of the higher freight demands in central and southern counties (Richland, Lexington, Charleston, Berkeley, Beaufort and Horry) in scenarios 8 and 10. These results verified that demand scenarios and their probability values are significant factors in site selection.

Table 6
Impact of scenario probabilities on terminal selection

Experiment	Scenario probabilities				Selected Terminal
	Scenario 1	Scenario 8	Scenario 9	Scenario 10	
1	0.5	0.1	0.1	0.3	Greenville
2	0.4	0.1	0.1	0.4	Greenville
3	0.3	0.1	0.1	0.5	Greenville
4	0.2	0.1	0.1	0.6	Greenville
5	0.1	**0.1**	0.1	**0.7**	Lexington
6	0.1	**0.3**	0.2	**0.4**	Lexington
7	0.2	**0.15**	0.05	**0.6**	Lexington

5.1.2 Case study 2

While case study 1 involves an actual intermodal network, its characteristics led to predictable results. To gain additional insights, case study 2 used a random network with various scenarios of OD pair patterns and demand volumes. The random network, generated on a 1,000 by 1,000 miles grid, has 15 existing terminals and 15 candidate locations. The objective was to find the optimal locations for up to 5 new terminals and their corresponding throughput capacities. Fig. 4 depicts the intermodal network utilized in case study 2, with the 15 candidate locations (with their IDs labeled) and 15 existing terminals. It was assumed that there exists 20 cities, located randomly within a radius of 100 miles around each existing and candidate terminal. Given a combined total of 30 existing and candidate terminals, there is a total 600 cities in the intermodal network. The locations of the cities, represented by (x, y) coordinates, were generated as follows.

$x = x_t + \beta \cos\theta, \qquad y = y_t + \beta \sin\theta$

where β is a random number between 0 and 100 which defines the distance (in miles) between the city and the terminal t, and θ is a random number between 0 and 360 degree. (x_t, y_t) denotes the coordinates of the terminal t. 1000 OD pairs were randomly generated from the 600 cities with a Euclidean distance of more than 500 miles because the intermodal option is not applicable for shorter distances. Note that although there are 15 existing terminals in the network, each candidate terminal only has to compete with those located within a 300 miles radius from it.

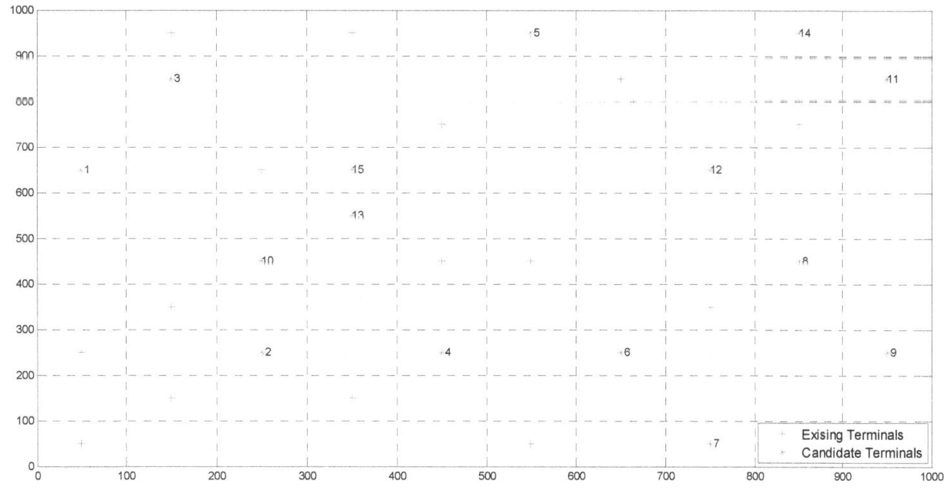

Fig. 4. Network layout for case study 2

Monte Carlo simulation was used to generate up to 45 scenarios for the OD patterns and their demand volumes. Each scenario involves a different set of OD demand patterns and demand volume. The OD pairs were randomly selected from the set of 600 cities, and the demand volume was randomly generated from the distribution U[1,000, 30,000]. The case study consists of 9 experiments, with experiment 1 having 5 scenarios and each subsequent experiment has an additional 5 scenarios. It was assumed that shippers will not select the intermodal option if it has a drayage distance (either pickup or delivery) of more than 250 miles.

Table 7 presents the results of the case study. Column 1 shows the experiment number. Column 2 presents how many scenarios were considered for the robust problem. Columns 3 and 4 present the optimal terminals and their sizes, respectively. The results show that locations 9 and 11 were never selected because they are located in isolated areas of the network. Since they both have a much smaller market, it would not be profitable to open new terminals at these locations. On the other hand, locations 4, 7, 8, 10 and 15 were included in the optimal set in more than 50% of the experiments. Due to the randomness in OD patterns, the decision of where to locate new terminals is more complicated than when the OD patterns do not change. The results indicate that as the number of scenarios increases, the results of the robust model becomes more consistent. It be can be seen in Table 7 that as the number of scenarios gets higher, the solutions converge to a set of similar candidate locations. Specifically, it indicates that regardless of the scenario, candidate terminals 4, 7, 10 and 15 should be selected. An interesting observation from this case study is that the optimal locations could be identified using a smaller set of scenarios, but the optimal throughput capacities will need to use a much larger set of scenarios. In reality, it is unlikely to have scenarios where the OD demand patterns and demand volume differ drastically. Thus, it is expected that the developed robust model will be able to identify both optimal locations and terminal sizes using a relatively small number of scenarios.

Table 7
Solution of the robust model P1 for case study 2

Experiment #	# of scenarios	Selected terminals	Throughput capacity (TEU)
1	5	7, 10, 14	8,408,300;4,445,800;7,434,700
2	10	1, 4, 7, 10, 15	4,872,100; 2,817,200; 7,779,800; 5,130,000; 441,300
3	15	1, 6, 10, 14, 15	625,199; 7,735,600; 3,596,500; 6,790,600; 3,813,900
4	20	3, 4, 7, 8, 12	6,898,000; 4,335,000; 7,472,000; 15,674,000; 799,400
5	25	5, 8, 10, 12, 15	15,008,000; 73,300,000; 4,576,000; 7,224,000; 5,156,000
6	30	2, 7, 8, 10, 15	3,482,000; 8,353,000; 15,369,000; 4,119,000; 5,344,000
7	35	3, 4, 7, 8, 12	7,430,000; 4,469,000; 15,616,000; 7,961,000; 7,812,000
8	40	4, 7, 8, 10, 15	5,759,000; 15,224,000; 8,557,000; 5,436,000; 4,985,000
9	45	4, 7, 10, 13, 15	15,325,000; 15,623,000; 4,225,000; 3,481,000; 3,276,000

6. Managerial implications

To gain insights on the implications of different managerial actions, two additional situations were analyzed. The first involves investigating the sensitivity of drayage distance on a terminal's ability to capture market share, and the second involves investigating the managerial option of closing an existing terminal and opening 1 or 2 new terminals at the candidate locations. The analysis was applied using the same network used for case study 1 and the 2040 FAF3 predicted freight flow for South Carolina. In the proposed model, shipments going from i to j are allocated to terminals (k, m) based on their utility. The longer the drayage distances, from origin i to terminal k and from terminal m to destination k, the less attractive the terminal pair (k, m) is to shippers. To test the sensitivity of drayage distance on a terminal's ability to capture market share, we analyzed scenarios where shippers have a threshold on the maximum drayage distance they are willing to consider. In other words, we considered scenarios where shippers will only consider a terminal pair if their resulting drayage distances is less than their desired threshold. From the modeling standpoint, we effectively set the utility of terminals (k, m) to 0 if its drayage distances exceed the threshold. Table 8 presents the results of this analysis. Column 1 shows the different drayage distance thresholds considered. Column 2 shows how many new terminals will be opened. Columns 3 and 4 present the company's intermodal share and the competitor's intermodal share, respectively. Column 5 shows the remaining percentage of shipments using the truck-only option. The last column shows the obtained best locations for new terminals.

Table 8

Effect of drayage distance thresholds on intermodal market shares and locations

Drayage Distance threshold (miles)	# of new terminals	Own company's intermodal share	Competitor's intermodal share	Truck only modal share	Selected terminals
100	1	27%	19%	54%	Greenville
	2	33%	18%	49%	Greenville, Florence
	3	35%	18%	47%	Greenville, Florence, Augusta
	4	37%	17%	46%	All
250	1	50%	30%	20%	Lexington
	2	53%	27%	20%	Lexington, Augusta
	3	56%	24%	20%	Lexington, Augusta, Greenville
	4	59%	22%	19%	All
350	1	50%	31%	19%	Lexington
	2	53%	28%	19%	Augusta, Lexington
	3	56%	26%	18%	Lexington, Augusta, Greenville
	4	58%	24%	18%	All
500	1	51%	31%	18%	Augusta
	2	54%	29%	17%	Augusta, Lexington
	3	56%	27%	17%	Florence, Augusta, Lexington
	4	58%	25%	17%	All

It can be seen in Table 8 that when the drayage threshold is low (i.e. 100 miles), the truck uni-mode is generally preferred over intermodal. This is because the lower the threshold, the fewer opportunities there are for the intermodal option. In scenarios which have a higher number of new terminals, the railroad company has a better chance to increase its market share. The results indicate that when the drayage distance threshold ranges from 250 to 500, there is little difference in market share for intermodal and truck uni-mode. However, increasing the number of new terminals will increase the market share for the railroad company. It is also worth mentioning that different drayage distance thresholds affect the optimal location selection. As shown in Table 8, Greenville is the optimal terminal location when there is 1 new terminal and the drayage distance threshold is 100 miles, but Lexington becomes the optimal location when the drayage distance threshold is 250 and 350 miles. Thus, an important design consideration in determining the optimal locations is the shippers' drayage distance threshold. Such information could be easily obtained via survey and be incorporated into the model.

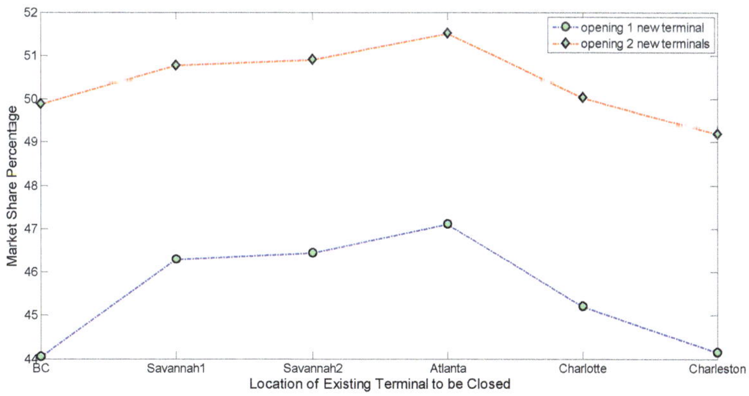

Fig. 5. Change in market share by closing one existing terminal and opening new terminals.

Typically, a railroad company would expand its network by opening new terminals. Another option the manager may want to consider is closing an existing terminal which is not attracting enough demand and opening new terminals in more attractive locations. Such a situation was investigated. Two sets of experiments were conducted. The first involves closing one existing terminal and opening one new terminal, and the second one involves closing one existing terminal and opening two new terminals. The base case (BC) scenario for the first set of experiments involves closing no existing terminal and opening no new terminal, and the BC for the second set of experiments involves closing no existing terminal and opening one new terminal. The results shown in Fig. 5 indicate that by closing any of the existing terminals at the indicated locations (see x-axis labels) and opening 1 or 2 new terminals, the railroad company will gain market share compared to the base case. The only exception is Charleston. Note that the market share when closing the Charleston terminal is 49.2 % compared to 49.9% of the BC. Closing the terminal located in Atlanta has the highest impact on market share for both cases (opening 1 or 2 new terminals). This result suggests that Atlanta terminal is the least attractive terminal among the existing terminals. It should be noted that the greatest increase in the total market share is about 3% (scenario involving closing the Atlanta terminal and opening one new terminal). Thus, the manager will need to conduct a benefit-cost analysis to determine whether it is beneficial to close an existing terminal and open a new one.

7. Conclusions

This paper developed a mixed integer nonlinear programming model to find the best locations for new intermodal terminals and their capacities in a competitive environment with uncertain demand. Robust optimization models with min-max regret and minimum expected regret criteria were used to find solutions which are near optimal for any realization of demand scenarios. A simulated annealing algorithm was developed to solve the developed models. Computational experiments showed that the developed SA algorithm was able to find solutions with 0% gap compared to GAMS solutions, but in much shorter time for midsize problems. Moreover, the developed SA algorithm was able to solve larger-sized problems that GAMS could not (on a computer with 8 GB of RAM). The results verified that location and capacity decision is more robust when considering different scenarios of freight demands.

This work contributed to the literature of intermodal terminal location problem by considering competition between existing terminals and new terminals, terminal capacity, and uncertainty in freight demands. In future work, there are several potential areas for improvement. In the area of competition, it could be enhanced by considering utility functions based on transportation rates and dynamic travel times. In the area of terminal capacity, it could be enhanced by considering capacity expansion for existing terminals based on predicted freight demands. Lastly, it could be enhanced by utilizing fuzzy or stochastic approaches to deal with uncertainty in freight demands.

While the proposed model and solution approach have been validated via case studies, key limitations should be considered when reviewing study results. These included: 1) choice of network topology and size, 2) accuracy of FAF3 predicted freight flows, 3) design of the scenarios and experiments, and 4) objective of the optimization model that considers only profit from the new terminals.

References

Arnold, P., Dominique, P., & Isabelle, T. (2004) .Modeling a rail/road intermodal transportation system. *Transportation Research Part E*, 40, 255–270.

Arostegui, M.A., Kadipasaoglu, S.N., & Khumawala, B.M. (2006). An empirical comparison of Tabu search simulated annealing, and genetic algorithms for facilities location problems. *International Journal of Production Economics*, 103(2), 742–754.

Ashtiani, M.G, Makui, A., & Ramezanian, R. (2013). A robust model for a leader–follower competitive facility location problem in a discrete space. *Applied Mathematical Modeling*, 37(1), 62-71.
Ballis, A., & Golias, J. (2004). Towards the improvement of a combined transport chain performance. *European Journal of Operational Research,*152, 420–436.
Bassan, S.H. (2007). Evaluating seaport operation and capacity analysis_ preliminary methodology. *Maritime Policy & Management: The flagship journal of international shipping and port research*, 34(1), 3-19.
Battelle. FAF3 Freight Traffic Analysis. Freight Analysis Framework Version 3 (FAF3). Oak Ridge National Laboratory. FHWA, U.S. Department of Transportation, 2011.
Bookbinder, J.H., & Fox N.S. (1998). Intermodal routing of Canada–Mexico shipments under NAFTA. *Transportation Research Part E: Logistics and Transportation Review*, 34(4), 289–303.
Chiranjivi, S.B. (2008). Framework for Evaluation of System Impacts of Intermodal Terminals using Commodity Flow Data. Center for Virginia Transportation Studies at the University of Virginia.
Crainic, T.G. (1998). A Survey of Optimization Models for Long-Haul Freight Transportation', Publication CRT-98-67. Centre for Research on Transportation.
Cunningham V (2012) ' Siting of Freight Facilities',
http://www.fhwa.dot.gov/planning/freight_planning/talking_freight/july182012transcript.cfm.
Daskin, M.S, Hesse, M.S, & Revelle, CH.S. (1997). α-reliable P-Minimax regret: A new model for strategic facility location planning. *Location science,* 5(4), 227-246.
Drezner, Z. (1995). Facility location-a survey of applications and methods. Berlin: Springer.
Drezner, T., Drezner, Z., & Salhi, S. (2002). Solving the multiple competitive facilities location problem. *European Journal of Operational Research,* 142, 138–151.
Eiselt, H.A, & Marianov, V. (2009). A conditional *p*-hub location problem with attraction functions. *Journal of Computers & Operations Research*, 6, 3128 – 3135.
Ernst, A.T., & Krishnamoorthy, M. (1999). Solution algorithms for the capacitated single allocation hub location problem. *Annals of Operations Research,* 86, 141-159.
Fotuhi, F., & Huynh, N. (2013). A new planning model to support logistics service providers in selecting mode, route, and terminal location. *Polish Maritime Research*, 20, 67-73.
Gelareh, S., Nickel, S., & Pisinger, D. (2010). Liner shipping hub network design in a competitive environment. *Transportation Research Part E*, 46, 991–1004.
Groothedde, B., Ruijgrok, C., & Tavasszy, L. (2005). Towards collaborative, intermodal hub networks, A case study in the fast moving consumer goods market. *Transportation Research Part E*, 41(6), 567-583.
Huang, J., & Wang, Q. (2009). Robust optimization of hub and spoke airline network design based on multi-objective genetic algorithm. *Journal of Transportation Systems Engineering & IT*, 9(3), 86-92.
Huff, D.L. (1964). Defining and estimating a trading area. *Journal of Marketing,* 8, 28-34.
Ishfaq, R., & Sox, C.R. (2010). Intermodal logistics: The interplay of financial, operational and service issues. *Transportation Research Part E*, 46(6), 926-949.
Ishfaq, R., & Sox, C.R. (2011). Hub location–allocation in intermodal logistic networks. *European Journal of Operational Research*, 210(2), 213–230.
Johnson, D.S, Aragon, C.R, Mcgeoch, L.A., & Schevon, C. (1989). Optimization by Simulated Annealing: an experimental evaluation; Part 1, Graph Partitioning. *Operations Research*, 37(6), 865-892.
Kirkpatrick, S., Gelatt, C.D., & Vecchi, M.P (1983). Optimization By simulated annealing. *Science,* 220, 671–680.
Kouvelis, P., & Yu, G. (1997). *Robust discrete optimization and its applications*. Kluwer, Dordrecht.
Krumke, S.O. (2004). Nonlinear optimization. Technische Universität Kaiserslautern.
Limbourg, S., & Jourquin, B. (2009). Optimal rail–road container terminal locations on the European network. *Transportation Research Part E*, 45(4), 551–563.
Lüer-Villagra, A., & Marianov, V. (2013). A competitive hub location and pricing problem. *European Journal of Operational Research*, 231(3), 734-744.

Makui, A., Rostami, M., Jahani, E.,& Nikui, A. (2012). A multi-objective robust optimization model for the capacitated P-hub location problem under uncertainty. *Management Science Letters*, 2, 525–534.

Marianov,V., Serra, D., & Revelle, C. (1999). Location of hubs in a competitive environment. *European Journal of Operational Research*, 114(2), 363-371.

Meng, Q., & Wang, X. (2011). Intermodal hub-and-spoke network design: Incorporating multiple stakeholders and multi-type containers. *Journal of Transportation Research Part B*, 45, 724–742.

Mulvey, J.M., Vanderbei, R.J., & Zenios, S.A. (1995). Robust optimization of large-scale systems. *Journal of Operations Research,* 43(2), 264-281.

Murray, A.T., & Church, R.L. (1996). Applying simulated annealing to location-planning models. *Journal of Heuristics*, 2, 31-53.

Nocera, S. (2009). A heuristic solution for the yearly capacity of an intermodal terminal. *Journal of Interdisciplinary Mathematics,* 12(3), 367–393.

Racunica, I., & Wynter, L. (2005). Optimal location of intermodal freight hubs. *Transportation Research Part B*, 39, 453–477.

Rutten, B.J.C.M. (1995). On medium distance intermodal rail transport. Ph.D. thesis, Delft University of Technology, Delft.

Sahindis, N. (2013). Baron. Carnegie Mellon University, Department of Chemical Engineering. http://www.gams.com/dd/docs/solvers/baron.pdf.

Sirikijpanichkul, A., & Ferreira, L. (2005). Multi-objective evaluation of intermodal freight terminal location decisions. In Proceedings of 27th Conference: Australian Institute of Transport Research.

Slack, B. (1990). Intermodal transportation in North America and the development of inland load centers. *Professional Geographer*, 42(1), 72–83.

Snyder, V.L., & Daskin, M. (2005). Stochastic p-Robust Location Problems. *IIE Transactions*, 38 (11), 971-985.

Sorensen, K., Vanovermeire, CH., & Busschaert, S. (2012). Efficient Meta heuristics to solve the intermodal terminal location problem. *Computers & Operations Research*, 39(9), 2079-2090.

Tang, J., Tang, L., & Wang, X. (2013). Solution method for the location planning problem of Logistics Park with variable capacity. *Computers & Operations Research*, 40, 406–417.

Taniguchi, E., Noritake, M., & Izumitani, T. (1999). Optimal size and location planning of public logistics terminals. *Transportation Research Part E*, 35, 207_222.

United Nations (Economic Commission for Europe), European Conference of Ministers of Transport (ECMT), and the European Commission (EC). Terminology on combined transport, New York and Geneva, 2001.

U.S. Department of Transportation Federal Railroad Administration. 2005. "Intermodal Transportation and Inventory Cost Model: Highway-to-Rail Intermodal (ITIC) User's Manual (computer software)".

Verter, V., & Dincer, M.C. (1995). Facility Location and Capacity Acquisition: An Integrated Approach. *Naval Research Logistics*, 42, 1141-1 160.

Permissions

All chapters in this book were first published in IJIEC, by Growing Science; hereby published with permission under the Creative Commons Attribution License or equivalent. Every chapter published in this book has been scrutinized by our experts. Their significance has been extensively debated. The topics covered herein carry significant findings which will fuel the growth of the discipline. They may even be implemented as practical applications or may be referred to as a beginning point for another development.

The contributors of this book come from diverse backgrounds, making this book a truly international effort. This book will bring forth new frontiers with its revolutionizing research information and detailed analysis of the nascent developments around the world.

We would like to thank all the contributing authors for lending their expertise to make the book truly unique. They have played a crucial role in the development of this book. Without their invaluable contributions this book wouldn't have been possible. They have made vital efforts to compile up to date information on the varied aspects of this subject to make this book a valuable addition to the collection of many professionals and students.

This book was conceptualized with the vision of imparting up-to-date information and advanced data in this field. To ensure the same, a matchless editorial board was set up. Every individual on the board went through rigorous rounds of assessment to prove their worth. After which they invested a large part of their time researching and compiling the most relevant data for our readers.

The editorial board has been involved in producing this book since its inception. They have spent rigorous hours researching and exploring the diverse topics which have resulted in the successful publishing of this book. They have passed on their knowledge of decades through this book. To expedite this challenging task, the publisher supported the team at every step. A small team of assistant editors was also appointed to further simplify the editing procedure and attain best results for the readers.

Apart from the editorial board, the designing team has also invested a significant amount of their time in understanding the subject and creating the most relevant covers. They scrutinized every image to scout for the most suitable representation of the subject and create an appropriate cover for the book.

The publishing team has been an ardent support to the editorial, designing and production team. Their endless efforts to recruit the best for this project, has resulted in the accomplishment of this book. They are a veteran in the field of academics and their pool of knowledge is as vast as their experience in printing. Their expertise and guidance has proved useful at every step. Their uncompromising quality standards have made this book an exceptional effort. Their encouragement from time to time has been an inspiration for everyone.

The publisher and the editorial board hope that this book will prove to be a valuable piece of knowledge for researchers, students, practitioners and scholars across the globe.

List of Contributors

Ashok Kumar Sahoo
School of Mechanical Engineering, KIIT University, Bhubaneswar-24, Odisha, India

Arun Kumar Rout
School of Mechanical Engineering, KIIT University, Bhubaneswar-24, Odisha, India

Dipti Kanta Das
School of Mechanical Engineering, KIIT University, Bhubaneswar-24, Odisha, India

Vadhana Jayathavaja
Department of Mathematics, King Mongkut's University of Techology Thonburi, 126 Pracha-utid Road, Bangmod, Bangkok 10140 Thailand

Adisak Pongpullponsaka
Department of Mathematics, King Mongkut's University of Techology Thonburi, 126 Pracha-utid Road, Bangmod, Bangkok 10140 Thailand

Zulqurnain Sabira
Department of Mathematics, Unique Science College (for girls) Dina, Pakistan

Muhammad Asif Zahoor Raja
Department of Electrical Engineering, COMSATS Institute of Information Technology, Attock Campus, Attock Pakistan

Ezzatallah Baloui Jamkhaneh
Department of Statistics, Qaemshahr Branch, Islamic Azad University, Qaemshahr, Iran

Asoke Kumar Bhuniaa
Department of Mathematics, The University of Burdwan, Burdwan - 713104, West Bengal, India

Ali Akbar Shaikh
Department of Mathematics, Krishnagar Govt. College, Krishnagar-741101, West Bengal, India

S.R. Singh
Mathematics, D. N. College, Meerut, 250103,India

Leena Prasher
Centre for Mathematical Sciences, Banasthali University, Banasthali, Rajasthan 304022, India

Masoud Rabbani
School of Industrial Engineering, College of Engineering, University of Tehran, Tehran, Iran

Seyed Mahmood Kazemi
School of Industrial Engineering, College of Engineering, University of Tehran, Tehran, Iran

Jorge Alberto Achcara
Departamento de Matemática, Estatística e Computac¸aõ, UNESP, Universidade Estadual Paulista, Presidente Prudente, SP, Brazil
Departamento de Medicina Social, FMRP, Universidade de Saõ Paulo, Avenida Bandeirantes, 3900, CEP: 14048-900, Ribeirão Preto, SP, Brasil

Fernando Antônio Moala
Departamento de Matemática, Estatística e Computac¸aõ, UNESP, Universidade Estadual Paulista, Presidente Prudente, SP, Brazil

Juliana Boleta
Departamento de Medicina Social, FMRP, Universidade de Saõ Paulo, Avenida Bandeirantes, 3900, CEP: 14048-900, Ribeirão Preto, SP, Brasil

Vinod Kumar
Research Scholar, Department of Mechanical Engineering, YMCA University of Science and Technology, Faridabad, India

Vikas Kumar
Department of Mechanical Engineering, YMCA University of Science and Technology, Faridabad, India

Kamal Kumar Jangra
Department of Mechanical Engineering, PEC University of Technology, Chandigarh, India

R. P. Tripathi
Department of Mathematics, Graphic Era University, Dehradun (U.K.) India

Manoj Kumar
Department of Mathematics, Shivalik College of Engineering, Dehradun (U.K.) India

Ehram Safari
Department of Industrial Engineering, Iran University of Science and Technology, Tehran, Iran

Masoud Babakhani
Department of Industrial Engineering, Iran University of Science and Technology, Tehran, Iran

Amit Kumar
Department of Mathematics, Graphic Era University Dehradun-248002, Uttarakhand, India

Aman Kumar Varshney
Department of Mechanical Engineering, Graphic Era University Dehradun-248002, Uttarakhand, India

Mangey Rama
Department of Mathematics, Graphic Era University Dehradun-248002, Uttarakhand, India

Narayan Singh
Department of Mathematics D.N. (P.G) College, Meerut (U.P), India

Bindu Vaish
Department of Mathematics D.N. (P.G) College, Meerut (U.P), India

S. R. Singh
Department of Mathematics D.N. (P.G) College, Meerut (U.P), India

Fateme Fotuhi
Department of Civil & Environmental Engineering, University of South Carolina, Columbia, SC USA

Nathan Huynh
Department of Civil & Environmental Engineering, University of South Carolina, Columbia, SC USA